The Sacrament of Desire

The Sacrament of Desire

The Poetics of Fyodor Dostoevsky and Friedrich
Nietzsche in Critical Dialogue with Henri de Lubac

ALEX D. SUDERMAN

⁌PICKWICK *Publications* • Eugene, Oregon

THE SACRAMENT OF DESIRE
The Poetics of Fyodor Dostoevsky and Friedrich Nietzsche in Critical Dialogue with Henri de Lubac

Copyright © 2022 Alex D. Suderman. All rights reserved. Except for brief quotations in critical publications or reviews, no part of this book may be reproduced in any manner without prior written permission from the publisher. Write: Permissions, Wipf and Stock Publishers, 199 W. 8th Ave., Suite 3, Eugene, OR 97401.

Pickwick Publications
An Imprint of Wipf and Stock Publishers
199 W. 8th Ave., Suite 3
Eugene, OR 97401

www.wipfandstock.com

PAPERBACK ISBN: 978-1-6667-3122-4
HARDCOVER ISBN: 978-1-6667-2348-9
EBOOK ISBN: 978-1-6667-2349-6

Cataloguing-in-Publication data:

Names: Suderman, Alex D., author.

Title: The sacrament of desire : the poetics of Fyodor Dostoevsky and Friedrich Nietzsche in critical dialogue with Henri de Lubac / Alex D. Suderman.

Description: Eugene, OR : Pickwick Publications, 2022 | Includes bibliographical references and index.

Identifiers: ISBN 978-1-6667-3122-4 (paperback) | ISBN 978-1-6667-2348-9 (hardcover) | ISBN 978-1-6667-2349-6 (ebook)

Subjects: LCSH: Desire—Religious aspects—Christianity. | Dostoyevsky, Fyodor,—1821–1881—Criticism and interpretation. | Nietzsche, Friedrich Wilhelm,—1844–1900—Criticism and interpretation. | Lubac, Henri de, 1896–1991—Criticism and interpretation.

Classification: PG3328 Z6 S876 2022 (print) | PG3328 Z6 S876 (ebook)

09/14/22

This book is dedicated to my best friend and wife, Carla Mae

Contents

Preface | ix
Acknowledgments | xi
Note on Translation of Primary Texts | xiii

Introduction | 1
    Dostoevsky and Nietzsche as "Hostile Brothers" | 4
    Thesis and Procedural Overview | 6

1. The Politics of the Sacrament in the Theology of Henri de Lubac | 13
    Introduction | 13
    The Desire for the Divine and the Image of God | 14
    The Death of God and the Politics of Modernity | 44

2. Karamazovian Desire and the Politics of the
Inquisitor in *The Brothers Karamazov* | 61
    Introduction | 61
    Karamazovian Desire | 63
    The Politics of the Grand Inquisitor | 80

3. Dionysian Desire and the Church and the
Modern State in *Zarathustra* | 114
    Introduction | 114
    The Desire for a New Image | 115
    The Politics of the Church and State | 135
    Interlude | 149

4. Eternal Return and the Politic of Friendship in *Zarathustra* | 152
    Introduction | 152
    The Dramatic Embodiment of the Eternal Return | 153
    Beyond Resentment: The Way of the Warrior and Friend | 185

5. The Mysticism of Resurrection and the Sacrament of
   Friendship in *The Brothers Karamazov* | 199
    Introduction | 199
    Out of the Darkness into the Light of Love | 204
    Beyond Retribution—The Kiss of Christ and
       the Eucharistic Community | 233
    The Way of the Friend: Nietzsche and
       Dostoevsky Compared | 259

Conclusion | 263
    The Desire for a Higher Unity | 265
    The Sacrament of the Eternal | 269
    Political Embodiment | 273

Bibliography | 281

Preface

THE GENERAL ARGUMENT OF this book contends that the poetics of Dostoevsky and Nietzsche, in particular a comparison between *The Brothers Karamazov* and *Thus Spoke Zarathustra*, remain profitable for political theological ethics. I conduct this analysis in critical comparison with the political theology of Henri de Lubac, with a focus on the question of desire and the sacramental mediation of the divine as it is embodied politically. Following de Lubac, especially in *The Drama of Atheist Humanism*, I demonstrate that both Dostoesvky and Nietzsche were both deeply attuned to the fundamental human desire for the transcendent in modernity, a desire which engenders the creation of new images of the divine to unify society, mediating new forms of political identity. More specifically, I examine the problem of retributive desire in the poetics of *The Brothers Karamazov* and *Thus Spoke Zarathustra* as it connects with the historical development of Western Christianity and modernism. I explicate how their poetic formulations of retribution relates to suffering and the desire for the transcendent. In particular, I compare the characters of Dostoevsky's novel, especially Ivan Karamazov and the Grand Inquisitor with the antagonists in the narrative of *Thus Spoke Zarathustra*, the "dragon" of Christian valuation and the "cold monster" of the modernist state.

Furthermore, I demonstrate that Dostoesvky, Nietzsche, and de Lubac espouse conceptions of sacramental mediation that reflect a desire for a higher social unity that circumvents imperialistic intention, stimulating new possibilities for posthumanist political community. I maintain that *Zarathustra* can be interpreted as the poetic embodiment of immanent Dionysian desire, mediating a conception of transcendence, expressed through the thought of eternal recurrence, which transvaluates retributively rooted Western Christianity and modernist morality. In *Zarathustra*, Nietzsche reimagines a politic of friendship, whereby adversarial oriented relationships spur healthier life-affirming forms of living, courageously confronting the sick, unhealthy values of Christianity and modernism. In *The Brothers Karamazov*, as reflected in the story of Alyosha Karamazov, Dostoevsky imagines the divine as a mystery that envelops the immanent, mediated through the Incarnation of Christ, freely embraced through the sacrifice of the self. Dionysian desire is transfigured through the power of Resurrection, generating a cruciform way of living, embodied in the active, commitment of neighbour-love and a forgiveness-oriented spirit. For de Lubac, what remains decisive is the recovery of the social meaning of the Eucharist, the sacramental self-offering of Christ mediated through the church. Like Dostoevsky, de Lubac argues for the necessity of an inner, transformative reception of the divine Word embodied socially, yet this possibility is mediated through the liturgical practice of Roman Catholicism. For the Russian Dostoevsky, the ecclesial form of community is less defined institutionally. His poetics accentuate the reality of an innate eucharistically oriented "social structure," expressed as a prophetic hope for the possibility of a healthier, life-affirming politic in Western culture if incarnationally embraced by the peoples of the West.

Acknowledgments

THIS BOOK IS A revised version of the dissertation I conducted under the supervision of Dr. Travis Kroeker in Religious Studies program at McMaster University. I am grateful for Dr. Kroeker's encouragement and critical engagement as the project developed. I would not have reached the finish line without Dr. Kroeker, whose own political theological work was a constant inspiration. I would also like to thank Dr. Peter Widdicombe, Professor Emeritus of McMaster University and Dr. Bruce Ward, Professor Emeritus at Laurentian University, who were a part of the committee. I greatly appreciated both their critical feedback and thoughtful questions, which improved the final draft, as well as made for a very interesting Defence. Moreover, I also want to thank Dr. Joseph Mangina, Professor of Systemic Theology at Wycliffe College, for his external review and stimulating participation during the Defence of the dissertation.

I am also grateful to the Social Sciences and Humanities Research Council of Canada, the Ontario Graduate Scholarship, and McMaster University for the financial support necessary for completing this project. I wish to thank family, friends, and faith community in Kitchener, Ontario, for the encouragement to complete this thesis. I would like to thank Ann McInnis for the initial editing of the manuscript. I especially want to thank my wife, Carla, for her support and patience as I completed the work.

Note on Translation of Primary Texts

THIS BOOK CONTAINS EXTENDED exegetical treatment of Fyodor Dostoevsky's *The Brothers Karamazov* and Friedrich Nietzsche's *Thus Spoke Zarathustra*. I will be using the translation of Richard Pevear and Larissa Volokhonsky, *The Brothers Karamazov* (New York: Farrar, Straus, and Girouz, 2012). For the Russian edition I will be using *Polnoye sobranie sochinenii v tridsati tomakh*. See the website lib2.pushkinskijdom.ru. For Nietzsche's *Thus Spoke Zarathustra*, I will be using Walter Kaufmann's translation in *The Portable Nietzsche* (New York: Penguin Books, 1976). But for the German text I will use the German critical edition of the complete works of Nietzsche edited by Giorgio Colli and Mazzina Montinari. See the website nietzschesource.org.

The definitive Russian-language edition of Fyodor Dostoevsky's complete works is *Polnoye sobranie sochinenii v tridsati tomakh*. Leningrad: Nauka, 1966–77.

The Critical German Edition for Nietzsche is *Nietzsche's Werke in Zwei Bänden*. Salzburg/Stuttgart: Bergland-Buch.

Introduction

AT THE OUTSET OF his celebrated work, *A Secular Age*, Charles Taylor poses the question, "what does it mean to say that we live in a secular age?"[1] The emphasis on the term "live" is significant, as it centers his work on the meaning of ethical living in the secular age as much as the question of the modern reality of (un)belief in God. Another way that Taylor poses the question pertains to the meaning of "human flourishing" in relation to transcendence, "does the highest, the best life involve our seeking, or acknowledging, or serving a good which is beyond, in the sense of independent of human flourishing?"[2] While it is beyond the scope of this thesis to examine Taylor's response, the question itself is relevant to the work I have undertaken, a consideration of the theological meaning of ethics in light of the secularity of Western, modern culture.[3] This work compares the poetics of Friedrich Nietzsche's *Thus*

---

1. Taylor, *Secular Age*, 1.
2. Taylor, *Secular Age*, 16.
3. Taylor's distinction between "transcendence" and "immanence" is useful for our purposes, "the great invention of the West was that of an immanent order in Nature, whose working could be systematically understood and explained on its own terms, leaving open the question whether this whole order had a deeper significance, and whether, it did, we should infer a transcendent Creator beyond it." Taylor, *Secular Age*, 15.

Spoke Zarathustra[4] with Fyodor Dostoevsky's *The Brothers Karamazov*[5] through the political theology of the Catholic scholar Henri de Lubac. In placing de Lubac into critical dialogue with Nietzsche and Dostoevsky, I build on de Lubac's *The Drama of Atheist Humanism*.[6] The underlying research question of this project simply begins with why Nietzsche and Dostoevsky were important for de Lubac in addressing theologically the spiritual meaning of "humanity" in light of atheistic humanism. In *The Drama of Atheist Humanism*, de Lubac explores the emergence of atheist humanism in Western political culture.[7] For de Lubac, despite the variety of ideological and political expressions of atheism in the West, from the communism of Karl Marx to the progressivism of Auguste Comte, there is a deeper undercurrent of the "death of God," which de Lubac describes as an "immense *drift*; through the action of a large proportion of its foremost thinkers, the peoples of the West are denying their Christian past and turning away from God."[8] As a Roman Catholic theologian, de Lubac is interested in the theological meaning of Western peoples—and European cultures in particular—spiritually migrating from faith in the Christian God and by implication as well, the sacramental realism of the Eucharist mediated through the church.[9] What is pertinent for de Lubac is the repercussions of the "drama of the atheist humanism" for the significance of "humanity as a whole," for "contemporary atheism is increasingly positive, organic, and constructive."[10] For de Lubac, it is not just that the language of the divine is abandoned or redefined, but that

---

4. I will be using Walter Kaufmann's translation in *The Portable Nietzsche* (New York: Penguin, 1976). But for the German text I will use the German critical edition of the complete works of Nietzsche edited by Giorgio Colli and Mazzina Montinari. See the website nietzschesource.org.

5. I will be using the translation of Richard Pevear and Larissa Volokhonsky, *The Brothers Karamazov* (New York: Farrar, Straus, and Girouz, 2012). For the Russian edition I will be using *Polnoye sobranie sochinenii v tridsati tomakh*. See the website lib2.pushkinskijdom.ru.

6. De Lubac, *Drama of Atheist Humanism*.

7. For specific comparison between Dostoevsky and Nietzsche: De Lubac, *Drama*, 277–346.

8. De Lubac, *Drama of Atheist Humanism*, 11.

9. For instance, in addressing progressive "eschatology" of Marxism, de Lubac states, "Let us suppose, nevertheless, that in creating the economy of an 'end of the world'—bypassing Christ who forms the real unity of his Mystical Body and through whom God will be 'all in all'—man can attain this blessed end that Marx has dreamed for him." De Lubac, *Drama of Atheist Humanism*, 440.

10. De Lubac, *Drama of Atheist Humanism*, 11.

the conception of humanity itself is transformed. Atheistic humanism, asserts de Lubac, is not only interested in the critique of faith in God, but still reflects a desire for a higher transcendence in which to form political unity. Therefore, the crisis of modernism is, argues de Lubac, a profoundly spiritual problem, expressing a new desire for transcendence freed from the assumptions of Western Christendom:

> It is a spiritual problem. It is the human problem as a whole. Today it is not one of the bases or one of the consequences of Christianity that is exposed to attack: the stroke is aimed directly at its heart. The Christian conception of life, Christian spirituality, the inward attitude which, more than any particular act or outward gesture, bespeaks the Christian—that is what is at stake.[11]

What interests us here is the underlying critique of the spiritual and moral ideal that is embodied in Christianity and the church. De Lubac does not ignore the political criticism aimed at the church, "against what is termed her thirst for earthly domination," nor most ambitiously, the modernist intent to "go so far as to reject, in the State's favour, the distinction between temporal and spiritual that the world owes to the Gospel."[12] That is, de Lubac is referring to particular theories of the state that also presume a deeper "spiritual" or historical meaning than simply an external managerial body.[13] For de Lubac, the political question is symptomatic of the spiritual problem: "Those of the new generation do not intend to be satisfied with the 'shadow of the shadow.' They have no desire to live upon the perfume of an empty vase. They are pouring quite a different fluid into it."[14] According to de Lubac, it is the moral and spiritual ideal of the church that is being removed: "To the Christian ideal they oppose a pagan ideal. Against the God worshipped by Christians they proudly set up new deities."[15] That is, it is the spiritual problem of the creation of new gods, new constructed images of sovereignty that venture to mediate

---

11. De Lubac, *Drama of Atheist Humanism*, 113.

12. De Lubac, *Drama of Atheist Humanism*, 112.

13. Again, for de Lubac, the communism of Marx is an example. We could also include Nationalist Socialism and perhaps even more current expressions of social democracy.

14. De Lubac, *Drama of Atheist Humanism*, 113.

15. De Lubac quotes Schopenhauer that "it is the spirit and moral tendency that constitute the essence of religion, and not the myths with which they are clothed." De Lubac, *Drama of Atheist Humanism*, 114.

a new transcendent reality in the immanent, embodied politically. In other words, according to de Lubac, as people created in the image of God, even moderns cannot escape the *desire* for the transcendent and therefore create new images of the divine to unify society, mediating new forms of political identity.

Dostoevsky and Nietzsche as "Hostile Brothers"

In attending to the question of the desire for transcendence in relation to political formation, de Lubac devotes most of *The Drama of Atheist Humanism* to interpreting the work of Nietzsche and Dostoevsky, whom he describes as "hostile brothers."[16] Because I am using de Lubac as an interlocutor between Dostoevsky and Nietzsche, it is appropriate to briefly summarize a portion of his analysis and conclusions. This will assist us in situating our interpretation. First, de Lubac notes the affinity that Nietzsche perceived in Dostoevsky, when he discovered *Notes from Underground*, declaring, "Immediately I heard the call of the blood (how else can I describe it?) and my heart rejoiced."[17] Moreover, according to de Lubac, Nietzsche and Dostoevsky were prophetic thinkers who, despite their differing responses to it, perceived the apocalyptic dissolution of humanity as a result of atheist humanism:

> The comparison is inevitable. Everything suggests it, especially the grim contest that is now in progress in the human mind under their combined and contrasted constellations. What is at stake in the drama we are watching, and in which we are all actors, is the victory of Nietzsche or of Dostoevsky, and the outcome of the struggle will decide which of them was, in the fullest sense of the word, a prophet.[18]

De Lubac asserts that both Nietzsche and Dostoevsky understood what was at stake in the emergence of atheistic humanism: "There is the same criticism of Western rationalism and humanism; the same condemnation of the ideology of progress; the same impatience with scientism and the foolishly idyllic prospects it opened up for so many; the same disdain of a wholly superficial civilization, from which they both remove

---

16. De Lubac, *Drama of Atheist Humanism*, 277.

17. Quoted from the French *Lettres choisies*, edited by Walz, 455. De Lubac, *Drama of Atheist Humanism*, 277.

18. De Lubac, *Drama of Atheist Humanism*, 277.

the gloss; the same foreboding that should soon engulf it."[19] Moreover, both "predicated the vengeance of the 'irrational elements' that the modern world tramples underfoot but does not succeed in rooting out."[20] That is, Nietzsche and Dostoevsky perceived underlying "desires" that challenge modernity's rationalist and idealist endeavours to limit and control the body and its passional desire.[21] In comparing their work, de Lubac argues that they are prophets who reintroduced the tragic in life: "They will not agree to avoid contradiction by mutilating man: smashing down the artificial but comfortable universe in which man has let himself be parked, they give him back the sense of his tragic destiny."[22] Like Nietzsche's dionysianism, de Lubac observes in Dostoevsky's literary work the trace of a "mysticism of life, or, more precisely, a telluric mysticism not unlike the cult of Dionysus. The whole Karamazov family, upon whom he so strongly set his stamp, is possessed by a 'thirst for living,' by a raging appetite for life,' that no despair can quell."[23] In other words, they are prophets of "desire," profoundly attuned to a dimension of human experience that goes beyond "logic," a desire that immanently strives toward the transcendent.

However, despite the similarities, de Lubac observes a deeper confrontation between Dostoevsky and Nietzsche. As Balthasar asserts with respect to de Lubac's comparative study, "the duel between Nietzsche and Dostoevsky is more dramatic—approaching the exchange of rapiers as in Hamlet."[24] When warned about the "wholly Christian sentiment" in the thought of Dostoevsky and that he was an adherent of "slave morality," Nietzsche replied, "I have vowed a queer kind of gratitude to him, although he goes against my deepest instincts."[25] The deeper instinctual discrepancy pertains to faith in the crucified Christ, to which Dostoevsky was a follower. As de Lubac states, "Nietzsche, in cursing our age, sees in it the heritage of the Gospel, while Dostoevsky, cursing it just as vigorously, sees in it the

19. De Lubac, *Drama of Atheist Humanism*, 279.
20. De Lubac, *Drama of Atheist Humanism*, 279.
21. As Berdyaev, Camus, and others have shown, they were apocalypticists, who prophesied the catastrophe of modernity, anticipating the impending political chaos and violence that did occur. Camus, *Rebel*, 55.
22. De Lubac, *Drama of Atheist Humanism*, 280.
23. De Lubac, *Drama of Atheist Humanism*, 280–81.
24. Balthasar, *Henri de Lubac*, 51.
25. This was a response to Georg Brandes. See *Lettres choisies*, 455 and 512. See also De Lubac, *Drama of Atheist Humanism*, 279.

result of a denial of the Gospel."[26] As we will see, Nietzsche created a new image, Zarathustra, who dramatically embodies Dionysian desire. I interpret *Thus Spoke Zarathustra* as a theopoetic narrative that functions as an expression of a sacramental mediation, intending to provoke Westerners to create new values beyond those inherited within Western Christendom and the politics of atheist humanism. Certainly, there are Dostoevskian characters, as we will see, such as Ivan Karamazov, who also strive "to reach a region situated 'beyond good and evil,'"[27] but the stated hero of *The Brothers Karamazov* is Alyosha, the "lover of humankind," who patterns his life on the humility of Christ, embodied in the elder Zosima. Alyosha is the one whom we must compare Zarathustra with. I will demonstrate that between them is a divergence with respect to the *reality* of the ideal of Christian messianism as embodied in the church. For Dostoevsky, faith in the crucified Christ is not simply an ideal, but an eternal presence that envelops an embodied soul that is inherently immortal. In the last analysis, argues de Lubac, "disagreeing as to man and as to God, they disagree just as completely on the meaning of the world and on our human history, since between them is planted the sign of contradiction."[28] That is, what is the attitude toward the Crucified One? As Nietzsche clearly stated:

> Dionysus verses the 'Crucified': there you have the antithesis. It is not a difference in regard to their martyrdom—it is the difference in the meaning of it. Life itself, its eternal fruitfulness and recurrence, creates torment, destruction, the will to annihilation. In the other case—the 'Crucified as the innocent one'—counts as an objection to this life, as a formula to its condemnation.[29]

Thesis and Procedural Overview

The general argument of this thesis contends that the poetics of Dostoevsky and Nietzsche, in particular a comparison between *The Brothers Karamazov* and *Thus Spoke Zarathustra*, remain profitable for theological reflection on political ethics. This thesis intends to contribute to the theopolitical meaning of Dostoevsky and Nietzsche.[30] De Lubac is an

26. De Lubac, *Drama of Atheist Humanism*, 285.
27. De Lubac, *Drama of Atheist Humanism*, 283.
28. De Lubac, *Drama of Atheist Humanism*, 285.
29. Nietzsche, *Will to Power*, 542–43.
30. In particular, I am attentive to the work of P. Travis Kroeker and Bruce K. Ward

interesting interlocutor for the reasons stated above, that is, focusing our attention on the question of desire and the mediation of the divine as it is embodied politically. For de Lubac, the desire for transcendence is also a desire for higher unity that reconciles humanity as a "whole." His interest in Nietzsche and Dostoesvky pertains to how their poetics address a fundamental desire for a higher image that unites people spiritually, but also politically. I am also interested in de Lubac as a Roman Catholic theologian, whose larger theological aim, as I show in chapter 1, is to recover the social implications of the *corpus mysticum*, the mystical body of Christ in light of the challenge of atheist humanism and modern secular culture.[31] De Lubac, Dostoevsky, and Nietzsche are interested in the question of what comes *after* modernism. Or perhaps better formulated, what are the new possibilities for political identity that emerge *out of* the decline of Christendom and atheistic humanism? To frame the question this way is to interpret their poetics apocalyptically.[32] With respect to Dostoevsky and Nietzsche, we are not attempting to determine or evaluate who was the more exact "prophet," as de Lubac poses the comparison.[33] Rather we aim to consider, using de Lubac as a theological interlocutor, the kinds of

in *Remembering the End*, where they examine the nature of the meaning of the prophetic in a modern/postmodern era. They draw our attention to Martin Heidegger's argument that the poet is the prophet in our modern age because he/she "stands attentively in the realm of the Between—between the gods and human beings." That is, the poet plays a mediational role between the immanent and transcendent, which we could even describe as "sacramental." Moreover, the poet is prophetic in the sense of the power of creation and novelty. For Heidegger, the prophet is "the visionary poet who names the 'new god.'" While this designation could be applied to Nietzsche, with respect to Dostoevsky, Kroeker and Ward argue that spiritual novelty is an incomplete appreciation of Dostoevsky's prophetic art, "the power of Dostoevsky's word is not primarily a matter of novelty. The word in Dostoevsky that still can burn the hearts of his readers is a *remembered* word." See Kroeker and Ward, *Remembering the End*, 2–3.

31. Perhaps it should be stated at this point that I am not a part of the Roman Catholic Tradition, but work from the Mennonite, Anabaptist tradition, which has a different understanding of the sacraments. However, I read de Lubac as objectively and with as much sympathy as possible.

32. I have David Barr's definition of the apocalyptic in mind, "At the broadest level we are talking about a very widespread anticipation that the end of an era was approaching, that the old ways were passing, that somehow the divine word was impinging on this world to bring about basic changes, including final judgement. . . . Apocalypticism is used to designate a social movement based on this sense of anticipation and change. Such an anticipation involves a critique of the present system, often viewed as evil." See Barr, *Tales of the End*, 154.

33. I critique de Lubac's interpretation of Nietzsche's "mysticism of the eternal return" in chapter 4.

prophetic community they imagined emerging in the wake of modernism and the political revolutions that the modern enlightenment engendered. This will be studied in more depth in chapters 4 and 5, when we examine the poetic "heroes" of their respective narratives, Zarathustra and Alyosha Karamazov.[34] However, before we can properly consider the political implications of Zarathustra and Alyosha, we must situate our interpretation theologically. I argue that the Catholic thought of de Lubac resources us with a rich theological, comparative partner to assist us in drawing out the apocalyptic movement embedded in their poetics. As we see in *The Drama of Atheist Humanism*, as well as in *Catholicism*, de Lubac is keen to respond to the development of the politics of atheistic humanism in Western modern culture. More specifically, de Lubac is interested in the question of the inescapable desire for the transcendent and how this desire is mediated politically. As I develop in chapter 1, for de Lubac, it is the sacramental agency of the eucharistic body that unites humanity as a new creation, fulfilling the transcendent desire of humanity, created in the *Imago Dei* (the image of God). It is from this perspective that we must consider his interpretation of atheistic humanism, since it expresses the consequences of a particular theological interpretation of the "natural" or the "pure" will. De Lubac is critical of interpretations of Thomas Aquinas that did not recognize the intrinsic desire for God implanted within the "natural" human will. This assists us in understanding why a recovery of a proper conception of the desire for God within humanity is so critical

---

34. Zarathustra and Alyosha are the poetic creations that form the heart and centre of their respective narratives. This is important because the basic dramatic plot and movement of narrative is the basic nucleus of the thought and intention of the author. As literary characters, they are protagonists of a narrative within a specific plot structure which includes a particular crisis or conflict that demands some form of resolution. There is, of course, the surface plot of their narratives, Alyosha as the third brother in a broken family, who after the death of his biological father (Fyodor) and his spiritual father (Zosima), returns from the monastery to care for his brothers, one who is prison (Mitya) and the other (Ivan) who goes insane. That is, it tells the story of a strained and complicated Russian family that leads to patricide, the murder of the father. Zarathustra is not a straightforward "story," nor is it a novel. However, it has a narrative structure. It tells the story of a monkish figure, who communes with strange creatures, such as a serpent and an eagle on a mountain, but who returns to human society after ten years of solitude to offer his teaching of the Übermensch. In the process, he is rejected by the masses and therefore resolves to search out companions who will join him on the journey of becoming a creator of new values, teaching those who seek him out. The climax of the story is arguably at the end of book III, whereby Zarathustra, after much resistance, accepts the thought of the eternal return and his role as the prophet of such a message.

for de Lubac. Humanity is created for the gracious reception of the Incarnation and destined for an eternal future in the trinitarian God. This eternal future is already concretely mediated on earth through the church and its sacraments. As indicated above, however, for de Lubac, the politics of atheistic humanism is symptomatic of the radical inversion of the image of God in humankind. Nonetheless, the human yearning toward transcendent unity remains, conveyed in the uplifting and deification of the material and the "natural." Humanity cannot escape its desire for the eternal and therefore creates new images of the divine.

In chapters 2 and 3, I examine the critique of Christendom and modernism in the poetics of Dostoevsky and Nietzsche. I demonstrate that both Dostoevsky and Nietzsche were deeply attuned to the political desire at work in Western history to unite the spiritual and the temporal, the transcendent and the immanent. I attend to what they perceive as the deceptive, idolatrous illusions that both the church and state are tempted to create to coercively enforce unity and form political identity. Like de Lubac, Nietzsche and Dostoevsky perceive in Western Christendom and the emergence of modernism the result of a spiritual crisis. In my exegesis, however, I go beyond what de Lubac addresses with respect to desire, that is, the desire for retribution.[35] The narratives of *The Brothers Karamazov* and *Thus Spoke Zarathustra* are stories that address the problem of retribution. In *The Brothers Karamazov*, Dostoevsky depicts the desire for retribution against the powerful Karamazovian force, the latent thirst for life, that has been demonically twisted. However, retribution is not disconnected from the desire for transcendence, since it reflects a particular moral valuation assumed to be universal. Through the character, Ivan Karamazov, retribution is expressed against the created freedom of humanity, a freedom which in the Christian tradition derives from God. However, Dostoevsky's thought on retribution is much more politically concrete. It is in this retributive soil that the legend of the Grand Inquisitor is created, the promotion of the necessity of religious myth and political coercion to quell the violent erotic impulses of freedom. I elucidate how the legend of the Grand Inquisitor expresses an underlying retributive desire against the concept of humanity as created in the *Imago*

---

35. While I acknowledge the distinction between "revenge," as a more "personalist" desire to inflict suffering for harm done, and "retribution," as a more "impersonalist," even legal, aim for justice, I show how the personalist desire for revenge and the political and institutional desire of justice are related and overlap in complex ways in the thought of Dostoevsky and Nietzsche. See also Kaufman, *Honor and Revenge*.

Dei, which for Dostoevsky is a radical freedom, but also a desire for a higher spiritual beauty, as revealed in the image of Christ. In congruity with de Lubac, this is the essence of Dostoevsky's critique of atheistic humanism as well, the conjecture of a new image of humanity disconnected from the *Imago Dei*, which mediates a political authority, endeavouring to limit erotic, passional desire and moral chaos through the pretensions of "miracle, mystery, and authority."

Nietzsche's poetics also addresses what he describes as the "spirit of revenge." The spirit of revenge is the spirit of "heaviness," which derives from the twisted, unhealthy expression of the fundamental "will to power." However, as I demonstrate in chapter 3, this desire for retribution is rooted in a latent "despairing body" which, despairing of suffering, seeks to create the image of a higher transcendence. It is this despair that engenders the spirit of revenge, which is a spiritual, psychological attitude that is ultimately against life itself, a revenge that creates conceptions of the eternal, including the notion of "eternal punishment." For Nietzsche, the history of Western Christendom is the history of the spirit of retribution embodied in the church and state, which attempted to reconcile immanent existence with a deceptive, twisted, retributively driven conception of transcendence. For Nietzsche, the church and the modern state are rivals, both claiming to express the "belly of being," mediating the divine in the immanent. For Nietzsche, this spirit of retribution is also reflected in atheistic humanism, which still assumes the ascetic idealism and moralism of Christianity as embodied in the neighbour-love ethic as well as the doctrine of equality. Therefore, Nietzsche espouses the creation of a new image, which could transcend and overcome the cultural valuations of Christendom, as well as the "cold monster" of the modernist, nationalist state. The way of the Übermensch (overman) is the necessary teaching of Zarathustra which endeavours to overcome the spirit of retribution, but this brings us to chapter 4.

As stated above, the interest in this thesis is to consider how the poetics of Nietzsche and Dostoevsky depict desire, and how the desire for the transcendent is embodied sacramentally. For de Lubac, the transcendence of the divine is mediated through the Eucharist, through the self-offering of the flesh and blood of the Crucified. The church is, therefore, a priestly community, which stands in a prophetic tension with the world and its political institutions precisely because it represents a higher divine sovereignty. The church is fully embedded within the world, but also transcends it, as it is enveloped by the eternity of God through Christ.

Introduction

The church mediates the mystery of the Incarnation apocalyptically, the inbreaking movement of the eternal love of God which transfigures and transforms the world. However, what may come "after" modernism, for Dostoevsky and Nietzsche? I argue that *The Brothers Karamazov* and *Thus Spoke Zarathustra*, via their respective heroes, Alyosha and Zarathustra, poetically embody a political ethic that de Lubac does not sufficiently address, that is, the possibility of overcoming retributive desire. In chapter 4, I examine Nietzsche's conception of the thought of eternal return dramatically embodied in the narrative of Zarathustra. I consider de Lubac's assessment of Nietzsche's mysticism of the eternal return as the attempt to unite the paradoxical concepts of fate and freedom. Nietzsche designs the myth of Zarathustra to portray the possibility of the natural, healthy, desiring body rising to a "thinkable" transcendence to affirm life in the body. This entails a profound transvaluation of the Christian conception of life, time, and being, and ultimately, a transvaluation of the concept of the eternal. In this way, Nietzsche conceives of Zarathustra as overcoming the spirit of retribution through the affirmation of an eternal struggle with the spirit of retribution, including the ways in which that spirit is embodied politically. This means the free, life-affirming politic of contention against the spirit of retribution, a "war" that occurs in solitude precisely because it is a "self-overcoming." Nietzsche imagines a new community of "warriors," who stimulate one another in a spirit of friendship to overcome the spirit of retribution through the affirmation of eternal recurrence. Zarathustra's community of friendship, therefore, stands too in a kind of prophetic tension with the world, spurring the Western world ensnared by the "dragon" and its values to transcend itself in a higher form of "becoming." Concretely, this means overcoming the sick Christendom values latent within Western culture, including those of the modern state.

In *The Brothers Karamazov*, I focus my attention on the character Alyosha, who is portrayed as one whose soul is "struggling from the darkness of worldly wickedness towards the light of the love." I interpret the narrative arc of Alyosha as Dostoevsky's reimaging of the vocation of the church in relation to the "flooding wind" of atheistic humanism that is blowing into Russia. At the death of the elder Zosima, Alyosha, too, struggles with the desire for retribution and the temptation of the Inquisitor. Following de Lubac, I consider the mystical experience of the resurrection embedded in the story, signalling Dostoevsky's prophetic vision of the eucharistic wedding of the feast of Christ. That is,

Dostoevsky's literary art has an iconic function, unveiling a sacramental reality rooted in the mediation of the Incarnate Word. The literary style in the chapter "Cana of Galilee" itself reflects the mystical element in the mediation of the divine Word. Dostoevsky portrays Alyosha's experience in the form of a fragmented reflection, his consciousness waving between waking reality and a dreamlike state, whereby he receives a vision of the elder Zosima, inviting him to participate in an eschatological messianic banquet. The effect of this mystical experience for Alyosha is enormous, expressed in an ecstasy of the soul embracing all creation. Moreover, the temptation of retributive desire is transfigured into a desire for forgiveness and a desire to forgive "all in all." From within the narrative of Alyosha, which climaxes in "Cana of Galilee," I argue we are in a better position to interpret the teachings of the elder Zosima and the monastic path as a response and alternative to Ivan and the Grand Inquisitor. I conclude chapter 5 with an examination of the kind of political ethic engendered through the story of Alyosha and the teachings of Zosima, which is comparable to the community of friendship in Zarathustra, but structured on the sacrificial, *kenotic* love of the Messiah. Chapter 5 concludes with a comparative analysis between *Thus Spoke Zarathustra* and *The Brothers Karamazov* on the meaning of friendship in their poetics. In the concluding chapter, I situate the findings of my research on Dostoevsky and Nietzsche more comparatively with that of de Lubac, organized under the themes: the desire for a higher unity, the sacrament of the eternal, and political embodiment.

1

The Politics of the Sacrament in the Theology of Henri de Lubac

Introduction

IN THIS CHAPTER, I explore the political theology of Henri de Lubac. The function of this chapter is to position my interpretation of Dostoevsky and Nietzsche's poetics in critical dialogue with de Lubac. Section I situates de Lubac's theology of the *corpus mysticum* in relation to Carl Schmitt's concept of sovereignty, especially the underlying conceptual relationship between transcendence and immanence. I demonstrate how the concept of the sacrament of the *corpus mysticum* provides a particular vision of how the mystery of the divine is mediated and embodied in the immanent. For de Lubac, the critical concept is the redemption and renewal of the image of God, culminating in the *mysterium crucis*. For de Lubac, humanity is created with the desire for the divine that requires the Incarnation as the necessary mediation to God, not just for the redemption of the individual soul, but for the reunion and redemption of humanity and its means to its eternal destiny. Moreover, using selections from *The Splendor of the Church*, I explore the political implications of de Lubac's conception of the sacrament. For de Lubac, the *corpus mysticum* is the nexus of divine sovereignty in the immanent, an apocalyptic community, neither escapist nor imperialistic, that embodies and mediates the mystery of the cross.

In Section II, I consider de Lubac's understanding of atheist humanism as the inversion of the image of God, including its political implications. Furthermore, drawing on de Lubac's *The Drama of Atheist Humanism*, I examine the significance of Dostoevsky and Nietzsche, especially in relation to the problem of how the sacred is mediated in the context of modernism.

The Desire for the Divine and the Image of God

Carl Schmitt argued that the concept of sovereignty is the most critical concept pertaining to political theology. Schmitt famously defines sovereignty as the power that "decides on the exception."[1] Sovereignty is thus understood as a decisive, intervening political *will*, a particular personal authority that decides if and when the systemic legal structure may be suspended in the face of its perception of the "exception." Sovereignty is therefore, in effect, "beyond good and evil." It determines moral estimation both in and beyond the law. In this regard sovereignty reflects divine agency. According to Schmitt, "the exception in jurisprudence is analogous to the miracle in theology"; that is, "an exception brought about by direct intervention, as is found in the idea of a miracle, but also the sovereign's direct intervention in a valid legal order."[2] The "miracle" of sovereignty, at least from a Western perspective, is rooted in the biblical narrative, whereby YHWH creates the world of time and space *ex nihilo* and bestows on humanity his divine image (Gen. 1:26–28). This biblical text has deep roots in political theological thought, from Augustine's *The City of God* to Aquinas' *Summa Theologica*, but in early modern thought as well. For instance, a close examination of the political thought of Thomas Hobbes and John Locke reveals a deep engagement with this biblical conception as they sought to reinterpret it against monarchist renderings of the text.[3] The concept of the image of God in humankind

---

1. Schmitt, *Political Theology*, 5.
2. Schmitt, *Political Theology*, 36.
3. Locke's treatise begins with a critical examination of a particular interpretation of Gen 1–3 that sought to legitimize the divine sovereignty of monarchical rights. Hobbes, anticipating Rousseau, begins with "natural man," an examination that begins with empirical observation. The conclusion of the necessity of sovereignty is rooted in a particular observation about "man" in relation to human desires which place society in a perpetual state of war: "Hereby it is manifest, that during the time men live without a common Power to keep them all in awe, they are in the condition, which is called Warre, as is every man, against every man." See Hobbes, *Leviathan*, 185.

in relation to the question of political sovereignty is also critical for de Lubac, Dostoevsky, and Nietzsche. What does it mean to be the divine representative on earth? What does it mean to exercise authority, determining the ethical formation of political society? Ultimately, who determines what is *moral*, that is, what is "good and evil?" In Schmitt's formulation, earthly political sovereignty is a mediation of the "miracle," through a "decision" that *transcends* the law of a particular society. As alluded to above, political sovereignty mirrors the concept of a divine intervention, whereby even "natural law" is suspended in the case of the "exception," however that exception is determined.

Furthermore, the concept of sovereignty is critical because, argues Schmitt, all modern political language of sovereignty derives from the theological. For instance, he asserts that

> all significant concepts of the modern theory of the state are secularized theological concepts not only because of their historical development—in which they were transferred from theology to the theory of the state, whereby, for example, the omnipotent God became the omnipotent lawgiver—but also because of the systematic structure, the recognition of which is necessary for sociological consideration of these concepts.[4]

Ultimately, suggests Schmitt, sovereignty pertains to the question of how *transcendence* is mediated in the *immanent*. With the modernist shift away from God, the concept of transcendent sovereignty is transferred to a conception of immanent sovereignty. For instance, Schmitt observes in the shift from early to late modernity that

> the conception of God in the seventeenth and eighteenth centuries belongs to the idea of his transcendence vis-à-vis the world, just as to that period's philosophy of the state belongs the notion of the transcendence of the sovereign vis-à-vis the state. Everything in the nineteenth century was increasingly governed by conceptions of immanence.[5]

The result of this shift is that modern political identities rest on conceptions of immanence. In more concrete terms, immanence pertains to

---

4. The clearest example of this transference of language, asserts Schmitt, is the thought of Leibniz. Schmitt, *Political Theology*, 36–37.

5. As a result of this shift, "conceptions of transcendence will no longer be credible to most educated people, who settle for either a more or less clear immanence-pantheism or a positivist indifference toward any metaphysics." Schmitt, *Political Theology*, 49–50.

"the democratic thesis of identity of the ruler and the ruled, the organic theory of the state with the identity of the state and sovereignty," as well as stricter constitutional and legal theories of the state.[6] According to Schmitt, when transcendence is fully lost, politics also loses the personalistic and decisionistic elements of sovereignty. It is beyond the scope of this project to examine Schmitt's political theology in depth, but we consider it here to raise the question of sovereignty as a problem of the relationship between the transcendent and the immanent as it is mediated politically. The language of "transcendence" and "immanence," as well as "mediation" in relation to Western political theological thought, has a long tradition that stems back, not only to the Hebrew scriptures, but also to Plato, as in *The Symposium* and the *Republic*.[7] As I will articulate further below, de Lubac

---

6. Schmitt cites the constitutional and legal theories of Krabbe and Kelsen. Schmitt, *Political Theology*, 49–50.

7. I have already briefly discussed "transcendence" and "immanence" in an above footnote. However, more explanation is necessary. By "transcendence" we mean what is "eternal" and "divine." We can also use the language of "being." This contrasts with "immanence," which is the "material," "mortal," the world of "becoming." In many ways, these are plastic concepts that are meaningless unless filled with content. Nonetheless, according to Plato, the transcendent and the immanent do not coexist or commingle. Therefore, "mediation" is necessary. Briefly addressing Plato's thought in *The Symposium* will assist us in using the language of transcendence and immanence. Diotima teaches Socrates that *eros* (love or desire) is a "*daemon*," a mediational power, that "unites" transcendence and the immanent. There is no confusion of the two spheres and mediational power—the demonic (*daemon*)—is necessary to "unite the whole." For Plato, the demonic power of *eros* functions to "interpret and to ferry across to the gods, things given by men, and to men things from the gods . . . and being in the middle it completes them and binds them all into a whole." What *eros* signifies is the fundamental human *desire* for the transcendent, a transcendence which Plato describes as an absolute "beauty" and "eternal wisdom." It is an idealism of "what is" (being) that transcends the immanent, material world. For Plato, the desire of *eros* is not only the basis of religion, but it also strives to unite the "whole" politically. That is, as we will see in de Lubac, humanity perpetually seeks a transcendent meaning for its earthly immanent existence. Even modernist political programs such as Marxism cannot escape this desire. Indeed, Marxism is an expression of a materially rooted transcendent desire. For de Lubac, Nietzsche does not escape this desire either. Desire or *eros* pertains also to the desire for *sovereignty*, the mediational power and "knowledge" that seeks to "unite" the immanent with the transcendent. According to Plato, through these "demons"—mediators—moves all "the art of divination, and the art of priests, and all concerned with sacrifice and the mysteries and incantations, and all sorcery and witchcraft." And for Plato, *eros*, as the desire for eternal wisdom, justice, and beauty, is a great mediational power that engenders a sovereignty that orders the *polis*, the "earthly city." The political conceptions of sovereignty were conceived in the realm of the demonic as a transcendent desire to unite with the gods and it gave birth to nations and imperial machinations. See Plato, *Symposium*, 201A–204C.

maintains that the revelation of messianic sovereignty in Christ has introduced a tension and dualism in the world. With respect to the confession that "Jesus is Lord," the intrinsic link in the ancient world between priest and king with that of the divine world has been disrupted.[8] Therefore, the pre-Christian notion of "sovereignty" has been disrupted. Paul describes this as the mystery (*mystérion*) of the Gospel, unveiled in the crucifixion of Christ.[9] If we follow Schmitt and conclude that political sovereignty addresses the deeper question of the relation between transcendence and immanence, then, following de Lubac (and Paul), political sovereignty pertains to the *mystical*, or the mystery of how the divine impinges in the sphere of the human and its historical experience. The mystical, that is, relates to *mediation*, that which unites the transcendent and the immanent. In the biblical conception, the divine is not, as in Plato, an ideal of "justice" or "beauty" that transcends the gods, but it is revealed in a divine *person* (YHWH—I am who I am—Exod. 3:14) who has agency and intervenes historically in the world, personally interacting with humanity.

The Embodiment of Desire

In the thought of de Lubac, the apocalyptic unveils a mystical unification of the transcendent and the immanent mediated by the incarnational embodiment of Christ on earth, the political body of which is the church.[10] For de Lubac, the church is the political embodiment of the mystery of the

8. This will be further elaborated on below, but de Lubac refers to a "dualism" introduced by the Gospel that was "unknown to the ancient world; there, even when the priest was distinct from the head of the family, the military leader, or the magistrate, each man's religion was that of his polity. When new cults arose, civil society granted them recognized status only by absorbing them, and they lent themselves to this reasonable solution." See de Lubac, *Splendor of the Church*, 162–63.

9. In 1 Cor. 2:6–8, "We do, however, speak a message of wisdom among the mature, but not the wisdom of this age or the rulers of this age, who are coming to nothing. No, we declare God's wisdom, a mystery [mystériō] that has been hidden and that God destined for our glory before time began."

10. The mystery of the revelation of this sovereignty is the root of all Christian thought that follows. As the Protestant theologian Karl Barth argues, without the "root" of this revelation of divine sovereignty in the person of Christ, there would be no conception of God as Trinity. Moreover, the mediation of this divine sovereignty is embodied in a very particular and historical way. It is the *church*, the followers of the lamb, that now exists to give faithful witness to this rightful transcendent sovereignty, personally striving to live in proper unification with the Mystery of Christ. The tension that now exists between the sovereignty of Christ embodied in the church in relation to political formulations of sovereignty in "the world" is a theme we will return to in the course of this work.

"slain lamb." Travis Kroeker has recently suggested that de Lubac's "sacramental ecclesiocentrism," which is "rooted in the Pauline and Augustinian vision of the messianic body as fully divine and fully human, both mystically hidden and fully public, offers a . . . compelling critique of Carl Schmitt's secularized Christendom political theology."[11] While Schmitt seeks to recover the concept of the transcendent, his study concludes on the question of the legitimization of dictatorship.[12] While it recovers the personalist, decisionistic element in the political, it forgoes the "freedom" of the immanent, so as to decide on the "exception." In de Lubac, however, transcendence and immanence are mystically reunited. The mystery of this unity is sacramental, embodied in the *corpus mysticum*.[13]

De Lubac's political theology resists the strict distinction between "private *oikos* and the public *polis*," between "governmentality or pastoral household management."[14] His theology of the *corpus mysticum* is an attempt to express the unification of "all things" as reflected in the thought of the apostle Paul. We may also add, it reflects the political vision of the "heavenly city" in the Apocalypse, yet it acknowledges the realities of the "earthly city" in which we still live. As I will show, de Lubac acknowledges the tension between ecclesial *oikos* and the earthly *polis*. The exposure of tension is crucial for an ecclesial, political realism. What is important, for de Lubac, is the recognition that the apocalyptic Gospel reveals a *mystery* that sovereignly unites the transcendent and the immanent. The mystery of the Incarnation, mediated by the *corpus mysticum*, is the personalist unveiling of an embodied sovereignty in the world. We must learn to live in the tension.

11. Kroeker, *Messianic Political Theology*, 4.

12. See Tracy B. Strong's foreword to Schmitt's *Political Theology*.

13. Kroeker is also critical of a particular interpretation of Augustinian political theology whereby the "eschatologizing" of the Apocalypse is domesticated, restricting "messianic sovereignty" to the private liturgical sphere of the church. The transcendence of God is not relegated to some idealized future state, where the present politics are left to immanent "realism." The Anabaptist theological ethicist John Howard Yoder perceived with great theological clarity the political tension the Gospel of Christ introduced into the world, a tension that de Lubac also acknowledges, as we will explore further below. There is a clear distinction between "the church" and "the world," yet also an underlying link which keeps them yoked together inseparably. As we see in the next chapter, that link is the fact that both church and world are of an intrinsic, connected "whole" that we may articulate as a common *humanity*. See Kroeker, *Messianic Political Theology*, 4. See also Yoder's *Politics of Jesus* and Hauerwas, *Peaceable Kingdom*.

14. Kroeker, *Messianic Political Theology*, 4.

The Politics of the Sacrament in the Theology of Henri de Lubac

My aim in this work is not to delve into the intricacies of Augustinian thought, but an engagement with de Lubac means it cannot be ignored either.[15] While we will not directly engage with Augustine's political theology as expressed in *The City of God*, via de Lubac, we will interact with his interpretation of Augustine. As I will demonstrate, de Lubac's "Augustinian" theology stresses the catholic universalism of the mystery of the Incarnation, as mediated in the Eucharist. De Lubac's theological project is more than a revisionist reading of Augustine. It is also an attempt to reshape the witness of the (Roman Catholic) church. De Lubac's political theological vision is certainly "universal," but not imperialistic. It encompasses all humanity, but along with Dostoevsky, affirms human freedom, resisting coercive decisionism in ensuring the unity of the religious and the political order. Indeed, de Lubac's theology of the church is a corrective to particular "Roman Catholic" interpretations for which Dostoevsky was critical. We address this in chapter 2.

However, our interest in de Lubac is not to defend Roman Catholicism, but to situate our interpretation of Dostoevsky and Nietzsche theologically. De Lubac's thought is rich and useful in comparing the apocalyptic and political elements of Dostoevsky and Nietzsche's thought as it pertains to the political in modern Western thought. As Kroeker argues, de Lubac's "eucharistic realism and ecclesial realism are united in the sacramental realism of the messianic body, which has implications for political theology."[16] This pertains to a dynamic relation between the "outer" and "visible" reality of Christ embodied in the church and the "inner" and "invisible" inner mystery. The two cannot be separated, reduced to either private mystical experience nor its external practices and piety.[17] As I suggested above, de Lubac's theology affirms the tension

---

15. According to de Lubac, a regrettable theory was propounded on two conceptions of the "nature and relationship of the 'two powers' that governed Christendom: the 'spiritual' and the 'temporal'—or what are commonly, but quite improperly, called Church and the State." Augustine is then characterized as promoting a "theocratic" conception that prioritizes the sovereignty of the church, while Aquinas, influenced by Aristotle, was "more refined and balanced, more respectful of the temporal order's autonomy in political matters." The chapter essentially debunks this conception. See de Lubac, "Political Augustinism?," in *Theological Fragments*, 235.

16. Kroeker, *Messianic Political Theology*, 6.

17. Kroeker critiques John Howard Yoder's political theology which "is too lacking in *mysterion* (the Greek word that *sacramentum* translates), about which Paul has much to say, precisely with reference to the crucified Christ." Kroeker, *Messianic Political Theology*, 11.

that this introduces between the church and the world—"church and state,"—which will be explored below. It is, as Kroeker suggests, a question of the mediation of the mystery of Christ in the visible world that gives adequate witness to the reality of the divine.[18] This concerns more than the sociological practices of the church in alternative witness in the world, and must attend to the proper embodiment of *desire*: "The embodied, intimate 'desire' question touches more nearly the mysterious heart of this theological-political nexus than do sociological markers, inductively derived and straightforwardly translated into the social ethical 'sacramental practices' of the church."[19] The question of desire penetrates the heart and soul of humanity at its deepest core. It attends to our loves and our worship, which reveals dispositions that have consequences for political judgement and its ordering in the world. The question of the embodiment of desire deeply pertains to the question of *peace* and how it is related to *justice*.

First, however, more elaboration is necessary to grasp de Lubac's vision of political sovereignty as he develops it with reference to the *corpus mysticum* in the Pauline and early Christian tradition. As I have already stated, a guiding question for this project is why Nietzsche and Dostoevsky are important for de Lubac in relation to the question of a theological conception of sovereignty that mystically reunites the transcendent and the immanent. De Lubac was interested in the thought of Nietzsche and Dostoevsky because it connected deeply with his interest in the relation between the natural and the supernatural as it developed in Western thought. For de Lubac, the drama of atheist humanism is the consequence of a conception of nature that was dislodged from the "supernatural," the transcendent conception of the sovereignty of Christ. Therefore, a better understanding of de Lubac's greater theological work will help us understand why Nietzsche and Dostoevsky were significant for him as thinkers who envisioned forms of sovereignty that go beyond modernist humanism.

De Lubac was a Jesuit scholar and deeply influential French Catholic theologian in the twentieth century.[20] His corpus of work is extensive and incredibly diverse.[21] In particular, the most significant thesis of de

---

18. Kroeker, *Messianic Political Theology*, 3.

19. In this section is Kroeker's critique of Yoder, who did not attend to the "heart" and the question of desire, or the "mystery." Kroeker, *Messianic Political Theology*, 11.

20. For a good overview of his work, see Balthasar, *Theology of Henri de Lubac*.

21. A representation of his writings, which are relevant for our examination,

The Politics of the Sacrament in the Theology of Henri de Lubac 21

Lubac was the critique of "pure nature" doctrine, which radically separated the natural from the supernatural. According to John Milbank, de Lubac is most famously known for his work *Surnaturel*, which reconceptualized the scholastic understandings of "reason and grace, as well as . . . neo-scholastic conceptions of philosophy and theology and the relation between them."[22] Indeed, as Han Urs von Balthasar perceived, the "dynamism" of de Lubac's thought moves him into a "suspended middle in which he could not practice philosophy without its transcendence into theology, but also no theology without its essential inner substructure of philosophy."[23] De Lubac sought to reconceive a theological understanding of "nature," which presupposed the necessity of "grace." He challenged the concept of "pure nature," as conceived by late medieval scholastic interpretations of Thomas Aquinas.[24] He wanted to recover the paradoxical nature of humanity as created in the image of God, as fully human within the historical limits of time and space, yet created for a transcendent, eternal destiny. That is, there is a mysterious, indestructible connection between human nature and the grace of God. Above all, de Lubac engaged with the meaning of the *mystery* of the supernatural in relation to the natural, as distinct from but not in opposition to nature, demanded by the requirements of *incarnation*: "By revealing the Father and by being revealed by him, Christ completes the revelation of [humanity] to himself."[25]

With this reconsideration of the relationship of nature and grace, reinterpreting Thomas Aquinas in a greater "Augustinian" way, de Lubac influenced contemporary Roman Catholic thought on the nature of humanity as created in the image of God.[26] De Lubac's position on nature

---

include *Catholicism: Christ and the Common Destiny of Man*; *Corpus Mysticum: The Eucharist and the Church in the Middle Ages*; *The Drama of Atheist Humanism*; *The Mystery of the Supernatural*; *The Splendor of the Church*; and *Theological Fragments*.

22. Milbank, *Suspended Middle*, 3.

23. Balthasar, *Theology of Henri de Lubac*, 15.

24. See de Lubac's *The Mystery of the Supernatural*.

25. De Lubac, *Mystery of the Supernatural*, 19.

26. Much of de Lubac's theological work is the attempt to recover more faithful readings, not only of Aquinas, but also Augustine. See de Lubac, *Augustinianism and Modern Theology*. Of course, there was much controversy and criticism surrounding de Lubac's *Surnaturel* thesis when it was first published, even by a theologian such as Karl Rahner. According to David L. Schindler, Rahner agreed with de Lubac, "insofar as it rejected the older 'extrinicism' that made grace into a kind of 'accidental' appendage to an already constituted nature." Rahner was concerned that de Lubac risked

and supernatural has become normative, at least within contemporary Catholic thought. As David L. Schindler notes in his introduction to *The Mystery of the Supernatural*, "who holds a 'pure nature' hypothesis any longer?"[27] Yet despite having persuaded many Catholic theologians and leaders, such as Pope John Paul II, and deeply impacting the results of Vatican II, de Lubac perceived that the result of the dualism between "nature" and "grace," espoused for so many centuries, "may be only just beginning to bear it bitterest fruit."[28] That is, the "pure nature" doctrine is a contributing source of Western secularization, whereby "God" is perceived as an unnecessary appendage to the "natural" evolution of humankind. What is crucial for de Lubac is affirming the paradox of humanity as a creature of immanence, yet created for the transcendent, which is a mystery. The human being, the early church fathers tell us, "is in the 'image of God,' not merely because of his intellect, his free will, his immortality, not even because of the power he has received to rule over nations: beyond and above all this, he is so ultimately because there is something incomprehensible in his depths."[29] There is a hidden depth of an "unknown desire" within the human soul, created there by God, which can only be fulfilled by Godself. And for de Lubac, this depth of desire for God is awakened and fulfilled through the Incarnation of Christ. De Lubac quotes St. Robert Bellarmine, "The vision of God, in which eternal life properly consists, is not only a supernatural thing, but exceeds even every created nature, so that it can be neither known, nor grasped, nor understood unless God himself reveals it: The eye hath not seen, etc."[30] For de Lubac, it is the grace of God that takes nature beyond itself into the transcendent divine through the mystery of Christ, the paradox of the human and divine as distinct, yet one. This is the sovereign mystery of the God of love, a creative love that brought human existence into being and has given Godself to humanity:

"fusing the gratuity of creation with the gratuity of God's self-revelation, thereby leveling the order of nature and grace." In response, Rahner proposed the concept of a "supernatural existential" that had been planted by God in human nature. As Schindler asserts, the difference between Rahner and de Lubac "takes the form of a difference regarding the priority of a 'supernatural existential,' as distinct from 'paradox,' as the best way to conceive human persons in their concrete-constitutive relation to God" (see the introduction to *Mystery of the Supernatural*, xxiii).

27. Schindler, "Introduction," in *Mystery of the Supernatural*, xxviii.

28. Schindler, "Introduction," in *Mystery of the Supernatural*, xxviii.

29. De Lubac, *Mystery of the Supernatural*, 210.

30. De Lubac, *Mystery of the Supernatural*, 221. See also Bellarmine, *De Justificatione*, bk. 5, c. 12 (*Opera*, vol. 6, 1873), 368.

"God could have refused to give himself to his creatures, just as he could have, and has, given himself. The gratuitousness of the supernatural order is truly individual and total. It is gratuitous itself."[31] Divine love is as mysterious as it is sovereign. And for de Lubac, this love is the fulfillment of the deepest of human desire and longing.

The Sacrament of the *Corpus Mysticum*

De Lubac is also known for his contribution to a theological conception of *corpus mysticum*, the Mystical Body.[32] This is not disconnected to the question of "nature" in relation to the "supernatural." In fact, it is central to it, for the *corpus mysticum* is where the supernatural and the natural intersect and connect. It is the embodiment of the mystery of divine love. The *corpus mysticum* is the fulfillment of human nature and its destiny. De Lubac's conception of the *corpus mysticum* is deeply sacramental. It is the mystery of the Eucharist in relation to the living members of the church. It is the nexus by which humanity is *united* through the grace of God. Indeed, as Jennifer Rust has shown, de Lubac's theology of the *corpus mysticum* is "political" in the deepest sense: the "long story of the 'degeneration of the *mystical body*' is a major concern" for de Lubac. In light of the "pure nature" doctrine, the "dynamic, social, and also deeply symbolic traditional logic behind the original sense of the *corpus mysticum* was gradually effaced by a growing rationalism and politicization of the church in the late Middle Ages."[33] The "degeneration" or "rationalization" of the mystical body led to the Reformation, and subsequently to modern humanism.[34] The *corpus mysticum* attends to the "whole" of humanity, humanity as both body and soul, individual and collective. It is *universal*. It is *catholic* in the fullest sense of encompassing heaven and earth. It is where God's incarnational sovereignty is mediated on earth. However, this statement is, of course, prone to misinterpretation, especially if its paradoxical nature is not appreciated. Therefore, the recovery of a proper, dynamic, "performative" conception of the mystical body, as fully human

---

31. De Lubac, *Mystery of the Supernatural*, 236.
32. See Henri de Lubac's *Corpus Mysticum*.
33. See Rust, "Political Theologies," 105.
34. Rust, "Political Theologies," 106.

and divine reality, becomes important to grasp the "paradoxical union of transcendence and immanence."[35]

De Lubac uncovers the patristic and medieval conception of the *corpus mysticum* through a complex historical and theological approach. His work may be formally characterized as historical theology, yet it is so much more than this. De Lubac's historical and theological research intended to bring to the modern foreground the authentic voice of the "Tradition."[36] In fact, de Lubac's theological approach is less about his own "voice" than a constructive attempt for modern readers to "hear" the voice of the "Tradition."[37] I believe that he wanted his own voice to be nothing more, nor less, than a vehicle of the living voice of the great Tradition of the church that stems from the Apostles. If we discern any underlying emphasis in the work of de Lubac, anything we may call "de Lubacian," I suggest that in his work we see the *universal* intention of the Incarnation of Christ. That is, the divine intention is to restore unity to all humankind, mediated through the Eucharist, the "heart of the church."[38] De Lubac is *catholic* in the broadest sense of the term. It is, therefore, also *political*, in the deepest sense of the term. Humanity, created in the image of God, was created for the divine. We were created to be mystically united in the personal transcendent reality of God. The church as the mystical body of Christ reflects the Incarnation, revealed as both fully divine and human, mediated through the sacrament of the Eucharist in a visible, dynamic way. The invisible and visible aspects of the body must not be separated as its unity is signified in the Eucharist with all this entails. Above all, this does not give an imperialistic licence to the church to function as a "Grand Inquisitor." Yet it does, as we will see, introduce a *tension*, a dualism between church and world that will not be made "whole" until the eschatological fulfillment of Christ. Meanwhile the mystical body of Christ which mediates grace in the world gives an immanent witness to this transcendent destiny. Therefore, it is possible to describe de Lubac's political theology as "apocalyptic," for as the church

---

35. Rust, "Political Theologies," 119.

36. As de Lubac states, explaining his tendency to use extended footnotes in work citing patristic texts, "There are, I know, plenty of texts cited at the foot of each page—sometimes haphazardly, I am afraid—but that is only with the idea of giving the reader a direct line of the essential text of the Tradition; for my ambition is simply to be its echo—that is all." See de Lubac, *Splendor*, 9.

37. De Lubac, *Splendor*, 9.

38. De Lubac, *Splendor*, 161.

awaits the fulfillment of time and history, it gives witness to the present reality of God through its participation in the Sacrament of the Eucharist.

Foundational to an understanding of de Lubac's conception of the *corpus mysticum* is the assumption that humanity is in the unique image of God. It is the image of God in humankind that is foundational for a Christian conception of humanity and the Christian moral "ideal."[39] For de Lubac, this biblical concept is the basis for genuine "social unity."[40] This theme of social unity was fundamental in de Lubac's earliest and programmatic work, *Catholicism: Christ and the Common Destiny of Man* (1938), which Balthasar describes as a break-through work and the other "major works that followed grew from its individual chapters much like branches from a trunk."[41] In the first section of *Catholicism*, de Lubac outlines the "heart of the mystery" as the drama of the "unique image" of humankind, resourced by the early church theologians.[42] Following the church fathers, de Lubac asserts, "the supernatural dignity of one who has been baptized rests, we know, on the natural dignity of man, though it surpasses it in infinite manner: *agnosce, Christiane, dignitatem tuam— Deus, qui humanae substantiae dignitatem mirabiliter condidisti*.[43] This unique image encompasses humanity as a "whole." In fact, according to de Lubac, "the unity of the Mystical Body of Christ, a supernatural unity, supposes a previous natural unity of the human race."[44] Here we detect the theme of the natural and supernatural in which the supernatural and the natural are not in opposition. The inner orientation of humanity toward the supernatural is a *mystery*. That is, the unity of humanity is rooted in the biblical revelation of creation, whereby God created humanity in his unique image (Gen 1:26–28). De Lubac argues that, in the patristic treatment of grace and redemption, the early Christian theologians and philosophers "delighted to contemplate God creating humanity as a whole."[45]

Moreover, it is necessary to stress that the redemption of the Word-made-flesh pertains not to the salvation of singular individuation only, but to humanity as a *whole*: "The lost sheep of the Gospel that the Good

39. See de Lubac, *Catholicism*, 25.
40. De Lubac, *Catholicism*, 16–17.
41. Balthasar, *Theology of Henri de Lubac*, 35.
42. De Lubac, *Catholicism*, 25–47.
43. "Recognize, O Christian, your dignity—God, who in a wonderful manner created and ennobled human nature." De Lubac, *Catholicism*, 25.
44. De Lubac, *Catholicism*, 25.
45. De Lubac, *Catholicism*, 25.

Shepherd brings back to the fold is no other than the whole of human nature."⁴⁶ De Lubac asserts that, for the early church fathers, "all [people] were made in the one image of the one God. It was a sort of divine monogenism, forging the link between the doctrine of divine unity and that of human unity, the foundation in practice of monotheism and its full significance."⁴⁷ In fact, in the language of the first centuries, "Adam was not generally called the 'father of the human race'"; he was only the "'first made,' 'the first begotten by God.'"⁴⁸ To believe in the one God was to believe at the same time "in a common Father of all: *unus Deus et Pater omnium.*"⁴⁹ The monotheistic prayer of Jesus assumes this divine origination of the unity of all humankind. This common humanity, rooted in the natural, but oriented toward the supernatural, or the transcendent, is fundamental to understanding the meaning of de Lubac's conception of the *corpus mysticum*.

However, according to de Lubac, the concept of the mystery of humanity as the unique image of God introduces us to a paradox between the relationship of universality of humanity and personal distinction: person and society. The paradox is this: "That the distinction between the different parts of a being stands out the more clearly as the union of these parts is closer."⁵⁰ In fact, argues de Lubac, unification is necessary to distinguish and clarify each individual part. The doctrine of the Trinity, the unity, yet distinction between, the divine Persons is crucial for understanding this paradox. The doctrine of the Trinity enables us to free ourselves from "those habits of thought that contemplation of material things develops."⁵¹ That is, reflection on the Three in One, whose image humankind reflects, enables us to imagine this "distinctive logic."⁵² Unity in diversity and diversity in unity. Does not, probes de Lubac, this "distinction imply a certain connection, and by one of the most living bonds, that of a mutual attraction? True union does not tend to dissolve into one another the beings that it brings together, but to bring them to

---

46. De Lubac, *Catholicism*, 25.
47. De Lubac, *Catholicism*, 31.
48. De Lubac, *Catholicism*, 31.
49. De Lubac, *Catholicism*, 31.
50. De Lubac, *Catholicism*, 328.
51. De Lubac, *Catholicism*, 329.
52. De Lubac, *Catholicism*, 329.

completion by means of one another."[53] The "Whole," asserts de Lubac, "is not the antipodes, but the very pole of Personality."[54] That is, the mystery of the image of God in humanity is also the mystery of the person. No soul is created in isolation. Indeed, the human "other" is necessary in order to discover oneself: "We must be *looked* at in order to be *enlightened*, and the eyes that are 'bringers of light' are not only those of the divinity."[55]

Furthermore, according to de Lubac, the personal destiny of each person is wrapped up into the "whole" of humanity as created in the image of God, which is, as we saw above, the mystery of divine love. For de Lubac, the summons to personal life is a *vocation*; that is, a summons to play an eternal role.[56] The historic character of Christianity helps us to understand the significance of the social aspect: "Since the flow of time is irreversible nothing occurs in it more than once, so that every action takes on a special dignity and an awful gravity; and it is because the world is a history, a single history, that each individual life is a drama."[57] The role that the personal plays in the universal, rooted in the divine, is characterized as "gift": "In the all-sufficient Being there is no selfishness but the exchange of a perfect Gift . . . there is no solitary person: each one in his very being receives of all, of his very being must give back to all."[58] The *perichoresis* of the Trinity is reflected in humanity.[59] It is in the "whole" of humanity that the individual discovers her personal distinct vocation. This "whole" of humanity is undergirded in a transcendent relation to the unity of God in three persons: "If there is not admitted beyond all visible mortal societies a mystical and eternal community, beings are left in their solitary state or are crushed into annihilation; in any case they are destroyed, for suffocation too can cause death."[60] In this important statement, de Lubac provides a hint toward the political implications of this theological anthropology. The supernatural is necessary to complete and fulfill the divine intention of humanity created in the image of God. "Pure nature" cannot be left to its own devices.

---

53. De Lubac, *Catholicism*, 330.
54. De Lubac, *Catholicism*, 330.
55. De Lubac, *Catholicism*, 331.
56. De Lubac, *Catholicism*, 331.
57. De Lubac, *Catholicism*, 332.
58. De Lubac, *Catholicism*, 332.
59. De Lubac, *Catholicism*, 333.
60. De Lubac, *Catholicism*, 333.

The Redemptive Drama and the *Mysterium Crucis*

Redemption of the image of God, the reunification of humanity, is necessary because it has been broken to pieces and fragmented because of sin: "All infidelity to the divine image that man bears in him, every breach with God, is at the same time a disruption of the human unity."[61] According to de Lubac, a consideration of the brokenness of humanity as a whole is a "way of considering evil in its inmost essence."[62] Rather than trying to "find within each individual nature what is the hidden blemish and, so to speak, of looking for the mechanical source of the trouble . . . these Fathers preferred to envisage the very constitution of the individuals considered as so many cores of natural opposition."[63] That is, the secondary social disruption is intricately linked with the prior severance of humanity with God. Although the image of God that establishes the unity of humanity is indestructible, by sin it is tarnished. De Lubac draws on Maximus the Confessor to articulate the breaking of the unity of humanity: "The one nature was shattered into a thousand pieces."[64] The humanity, which "ought to constitute a harmonious whole, in which 'mine' and 'thine' would be no contradiction, is turned into a multitude of individuals, as numerous as the sands of the seashore, all of whom show violently discordant inclinations."[65] And now, argues Maximus, "We rend each other like the wild beasts."[66] In this world, "the devil, . . . man's tempter from the beginning, had separated him in his will from God, had separated men from each other."[67] As Cyril of Alexandria asserted, "Satan has broken us up."[68]

Augustine's discussion on the broken image in *De Trinitate* provides a rich complement to de Lubac's analysis on the broken unity of humanity.[69] Interpreting Genesis 3, where the first humans, tempted by demonic desire, grasped for the fruit of the knowledge of good and evil, Augustine

---

61. De Lubac, *Catholicism*, 33.
62. De Lubac, *Catholicism*, 33.
63. De Lubac, *Catholicism*, 24.
64. De Lubac, *Catholicism*, 33. See Maximus the Confessor, *Quaestiones ad Thalassium*, q. 2.
65. De Lubac, *Catholicism*, 34. And Maximus, *Quaestiones ad Thalassium*, q. 2.
66. De Lubac, *Catholicism*, 34.
67. De Lubac, *Catholicism*, 35.
68. De Lubac, *Catholicism*, 34.
69. See Augustine, *De Trinitate*, 333.

asserts, "What happens is that the soul, loving its own power, slides away from the *whole* which is common to all into the part which is its own private property" [italics mine].[70] Augustine, like de Lubac, assumes the common unity of humanity which sin seeks to destroy through individualist grasping: "By following God's directions and being perfectly governed by his laws it could enjoy the whole universe of creation; but by the apostasy of pride which is called the beginning of sin, it strives to grab something more than the whole and to govern it by its own laws; and because there is nothing more than the whole it is thrust back into anxiety over a part, and so by being greedy it gets less."[71] This dense text articulates the ironic nature of grasping for more than the "whole" of which each person is an integral member. There is nothing more than the "whole" of humanity created in the image of God that entails the shared ontological reality of all its members. Greed is the root of evil because it discloses a corrupted possessive desire that inadequately reflects the divine image, the eternal self-giving nature of God. The desire for more than the "whole" is also the disordered possessive grasping for divine sovereignty.

According to de Lubac, the redemption of the Incarnation is the "recovery of lost unity—the recovery of the supernatural unity of man with God, but equally the unity of men among themselves."[72] De Lubac roots this concept in Augustine: "Divine mercy gathered up the fragments from every side, forged them in the fire of love, and welded into one what had been broken . . . He who remade was himself the Maker, and he who refashioned was himself the Fashioner."[73] The means by which God accomplishes the reunion of humanity is through the Incarnation, the Word-become-flesh (Jn. 1:14): "Christ from the very first moment of his existence virtually bears all men within himself—*erat in Christo Jesu omnis homo*. The Word did not merely assume a human body, but God incorporated himself into humanity: *Universitatis nostrae caro est factus*."[74] All of humanity and human nature, whole and entire, is assumed in the Incarnation. All humanity, therefore, is incorporated in the divine. In the flesh of the Word lies the reuniting of the severed fabric of humankind.

70. Augustine, *De Trinitate*, 333.

71. Augustine, *De Trinitate*, 333.

72. De Lubac, *Catholicism*, 35.

73. De Lubac, *Catholicism*, 35–36. See also Augustine, *In Psalm*, 195, n. 12 (PL 37:1236).

74. Quoting Hilary, "He became the flesh of our universal humanity." De Lubac, *Catholicism*, 37–38.

The entire life of Jesus, from incarnational birth to resurrection, reincorporates humanity in the divine: "Whole and entire he will bear it then to Calvary, whole and entire he will raise it from the dead, whole and entire he will save."[75] According to de Lubac, "Christ the Redeemer does not offer salvation merely to each one; he effects it, he himself is the salvation of the whole, and for each one salvation consists in a personal ratification of his original 'belonging' to Christ, so that he be not cast out, cut off from this Whole."[76] Quoting Cyril of Alexandria, the redemption of the Incarnation is the basis of the *corpus mysticum*: "The Word dwells in us, in that one temple he took through us and of us, so that we should possess all things in him and he should bring us all back to the Father in one Body."[77]

It is important to underscore the apocalyptic character of de Lubac's conception of the incarnational basis of the *corpus mysticum*. With respect to the "church in the world," de Lubac asserts in *Splendor*, "Again, the paradox; the mystical Bride, the Church with the hidden heart, is also a being very much visible among the beings of this world."[78] The Incarnation not only redeems, but also creates a new humanity: "Christ's resurrection created a new world; it marked the beginning of a fresh age and set up on earth a new type of existence that is absolutely novel—'Behold all things are made new.' It inaugurated 'the eighth day.'"[79] The church is the socially visible—even institutional—embodied witness to the new creation. In *Catholicism*, de Lubac argues that the "unity of humanity" mediated in the *corpus mysticum* represents the eschatological fulfillment of history: "Amid this universal chorus Christianity alone continues to

---

75. De Lubac, *Catholicism*, 39.

76. De Lubac, *Catholicism*, 25–26. While acknowledging the Platonic connection to the doctrine of the humanity espoused by the early fathers, de Lubac argues that it is better to go to St. Paul and St. John to account for them. In other words, Catholic social doctrine is oriented within prophetic drama of scripture. De Lubac emphasizes the ironic prophecy of Caiaphas: "He prophesied that Jesus should die for the nation. And not only for the nation, but to gather together in one the children of God that were dispersed." The sacrifice of the Incarnation becomes the structure of a new unification for humanity as embodied and represented in the people of God. De Lubac argues that this heart of Johannine vision, as symbolized in the Good Shepherd who "must gather his sheep, all the peoples of the earth, that is to say, into one flock." This is an echo—and fulfillment—of the prophecy of Isaiah: "I will bring forth thy seed from the east and gather thee from the west: I will say to the north: Give up; and to the south: Keep not back; bring my sons from afar, and my daughters from the ends of earth."

77. De Lubac, *Catholicism*, 40. See Cyril of Alexandria, *In Joannem*, lib. I.

78. De Lubac, *Splendor*, 161.

79. De Lubac, *Splendor*, 167.

assert the transcendent destiny of [humans] and the common destiny of [humankind]. The whole history of the world is a preparation for this destiny."[80] Eternity itself is experienced mystically in the present through the sacramental life of the body of Christ, the church. Grace touches and transforms human nature, a "nature" created in the image of God to be fulfilled and completed by "grace." The future "destiny" of humanity and its unity is conditioned by its inner structure, oriented by the desire for the eternal. This conviction is sustained by the biblical revelation that humanity is created in the image of God. The importance of the mystery of the "unity of humanity" is critical for de Lubac because it is central to the biblical revelation itself: "Fundamentally the Gospel is obsessed with the idea of the unity of human society."[81] The purpose for which God-becomes-flesh is to reunite the whole of human nature, a restoration and fulfillment of its divinely created nature as made in the divine image.

According to de Lubac, the church is the reunified humanity created in the image of God, mystically united with the supernatural through the mediation of the Incarnation in the Eucharist. This the true meaning of *catholicism*. De Lubac quotes E. Masure: "We must bring back to the foreground the dogma of the Mystical Body in which the Church consists, where there are jointed limbs, a single nervous system, a single circulation of the blood and a single head, for the mystery of the Word incarnate is first and foremost the mystery of the New Adam and the Head of Humanity."[82] This is an apocalyptic vision rooted in the biblical drama of redemption. It accents the uplifting of humanity itself, through the *corpus mysticum*, engendering a renewed life in God. It constitutes the apocalyptic "awaiting vision" incarnationally lived in the present moment, embedded "naturally" within time and space.

This sacramental life itself constitutes a political "ethic" that is neither imperialistic nor schismatic: "Our treatise *De Ecclesia* in its regular form has been built up in two main stages: one in opposition to the imperial and royal jurists, the other in opposition to Gallican and Protestant doctrines."[83] De Lubac's work may be interpreted as an attempt to recover the *spiritual* unity of the *corpus mysticum*. He does so by going back to the basic "dogma" as resourced by the early church's theological

80. De Lubac, *Catholicism*, 140–41.

81. De Lubac, *Catholicism*, 15.

82. De Lubac, *Catholicism*, 320. See E. Masure, *Semaine sociale de Nice* (1934), 230–31.

83. De Lubac, *Catholicism*, 314.

interpretation of scripture. Indeed, in *Catholicism*, de Lubac attempts a penetrating and comprehensive engagement with the earlier tradition to recast a new social vision for not just the church, but in and through the church also for all humanity. The strategy is not to retreat from the "traditional" historic dogma and teaching of the church, but to undertake a deeper engagement with it and fidelity to it, so as to recover for the contemporary church and world the transfigural transformative power of the "mystery."

According to de Lubac, since the sacraments are "the means of salvation they should be understood as instruments of unity. As they make real, renew, or strengthen man's union with Christ, by the very fact they make real, renew, or strengthen his union with the Christian community."[84] Again, de Lubac stresses the social dimension of Catholic sacramentalism. Baptism, for instance, is "essentially a social event, even in the primary, extrinsic meaning of the word."[85] Baptism incorporates persons into the visible church, but its consequences are not solely juridical; they are also spiritual, mystical, because the Church is not a purely human society."[86] Indeed, supernatural grace is mediated to the church sacramentally, constituting, through the visibility of the sacrament, the inner unity of the *corpus mysticum*. De Lubac's primary focus, however, will concentrate on the significance of the Eucharist. For him, "the sacrament in the highest sense of the word—*sacramentum sacramentorum, quasi consummatio spiritualis vitae et omnium sacramentorum finis*[87]— the sacrament 'which contains the whole mystery of our salvation,' the Eucharist, is also especially the sacrament of unity: *sacramentum unitatis ecclesiasticae.*"[88] De Lubac's interpretation of the mystical union that the sacrament of the Eucharist puts into effect is rooted in St. Paul's teaching: "For we being many are one bread, one body, all that partake of the one bread."[89] This teaching derives from Jesus himself who broke bread and drank the cup with his disciples prior to his suffering sacrifice. According to de Lubac, the grace of God is mediated in the symbolic action of the

---

84. De Lubac, *Catholicism*, 82.

85. De Lubac, *Catholicism*, 83.

86. De Lubac, *Catholicism*, 83.

87. "Sacrament of sacraments, the consummation, as it were, of the spiritual life and the goal of all the sacraments." De Lubac, *Catholicism*, 89.

88. "The sacrament of church unity." De Lubac, *Catholicism*, 88–89

89. 1 Cor. 10:17.

institution, engendering a mystical community that unites the transcendent and the immanent.

Characteristically, de Lubac marshals a host of patristic texts to substantiate the mystical tradition. We reproduce the mystical articulation of St. Cyril of Alexandria as a sample:

> To merge us with God among ourselves, although we have each a distinct personality, the only Son devised a wonderful means: through one only body, his own, he sanctifies his faithful in mystic communion, making them one body with him and among themselves. Within Christ no division can arise. All united to the single Christ through his own body, all receiving him, the one and indivisible, into our own bodies, we are the members of this one body, and he is thus, for us, the bond of unity.[90]

The Eucharist is the apocalyptic heart of the church, where God divests his divine presence through the flesh and blood of Jesus into his very "immanent" body. The sovereignty of Christ is embodied in the sacramental "action," experienced in real space and time. The result of the Eucharist, argues de Lubac, is an authentic communion: "*In (hoc) sacramento fideles quique communicantes pactum societatis et pacis ineunt.*"[91] That is, we might say, it engenders a new, mystical body politic, united by the sovereignty of Christ mediated through the bread and the wine, the sacrificial incarnate body offered to the entire world. In the Eucharist, the inner and outer, the invisible and the visible, the transcendent and the immanent, the eternal and the temporal are united, dynamically reuniting a fragmented humanity torn apart by the sinful, possessive grasping after this perfect "whole." The Eucharist faithfully unveils the mystery of Christ to the body and in turn, the body participates in the mystery of Christ in its embodied life offered to the world.

This sacrament of the Eucharist gives witness to the apocalyptic "mystery." For de Lubac, "dogma" is not simply a rational or juridical teaching

---

90. Moreover, Cyril of Alexandria says, "We are all of us, by nature, separately confined in our own individualities, but in another way, all of us are united together. Divided as it were into distinct personalities by which one is Peter or John or Thomas or Matthew, we are, so to say, molded into one solely in Christ, feeding on one flesh alone. One Spirit singles us out for unity, and as Christ is one and indivisible, we are all no more but one in him. So did he say to his heavenly Father, 'That they may be one, as we are one.'" De Lubac, *Catholicism*, 91. See Cyril of Alexandria, *In Joannem*, 11, 11.

91. "In [this] sacrament the faithful who communicate enter a covenant of brotherhood and peace." De Lubac, *Catholicism*, 93.

but the "heart of its mystery," the revealed truth of the Christian faith.[92] The *corpus mysticum* unveils the meaning of humanity and its history in space and time. It is the mystery of the Incarnation, God in the flesh. It is witnessed in the scripture, but also clarified and confirmed in the great councils of the early church.[93] It is the mystery of the relation between the "supernatural" with the "natural," the redemptive drama of God in the history of humankind. It entails a mystical communion of those incorporated into the body of Christ. Above all, the apocalyptic mystery consists in a return to a participatory consideration of the body of *Christ* that the bread and wine embody—"Christ and Him crucified" (1 Cor. 2:2). According to de Lubac, *the corpus mysticum* is the *mysterium crucis*: "The whole mystery of Christ is a mystery of resurrection, but it is also a mystery of death . . . Through Christ dying on the Cross, the humanity which he bore whole and entire in his own Person renounces itself and dies. But the mystery is deeper still . . . The universal Man died alone. This is the consummation of the *Kenosis* and the perfection of sacrifice."[94] This is the mystery that unites humankind in a "common destiny" through the sacramental body. It is the paradox of solitude and severance as the "only efficacious sign of a gathering together and of unity: the sacred blade piercing indeed so deep as to separate soul from spirit, but only that universal life might enter."[95] The *mysterium crucis* unveils the inner meaning of the "natural" history of humankind: its purpose and fulfillment. This can be understood as an apocalyptic mystery which unveils the historic "destiny" of humanity and embodied in the living presence of the *corpus mysticum*. How de Lubac envisions this will be elaborated in the next section on the meaning of the priesthood. Yet, as we saw above, it pertains to the living embodiment of the mystery of divine love in the "natural world," the self-giving nature of God lived out and expressed through the Eucharist in communion with the saints as a priesthood.[96]

92. As de Lubac asserts, "Revealed truth is therefore primarily dogma, in the sense that the mind receives it without argument on the authority of the Church of Christ, which here below is the very voice of God, in the same way that the will receives the commandments: but this dogma is always a *mystery*." De Lubac, *Corpus Mysticum*, 231.

93. We refer to the councils of Nicaea and Chalcedon.

94. De Lubac, *Catholicism*, 368.

95. De Lubac, *Catholicism*, 368.

96. It is this question of the embodiment of divine love that is at the heart of Dostoevsky's poetics, but also of Nietzsche's critique. The following chapters will address this.

To reiterate, de Lubac's theological vision of the church is both social and cosmic. Rooted in Paul and Augustine, de Lubac anticipates a cosmic unification of humanity within all creation: "St. Paul could see the course of human history as it progressed toward its end: the liberation of all creation, the consummation of all things in the unity of the Body of Christ now fully perfected."[97] This describes the "awaiting vision" of the perfection of the city of God, the *corpus mysticum*. Established in the mystery of the cross of the Christ, the sacramental body on earth—the church—is a heavenly city still incomplete until the last day: "Jesus Christ will not be whole until the number of saints is complete. Our gaze must ever be fixed on this consummation of God's work."[98] In this apocalyptic beatific vision of the city of God, de Lubac sets out to explore the social and political implications of the *corpus mysticum*. To be sure, as de Lubac states, "I have no intention of drawing up for this century a plan of social reform inspired by Christianity. Confining myself to the implications of dogma I shall be concerned first and foremost with the society of believers—that on earth and that of the world to come, that which is visible and especially that which is invisible."[99] Yet *Catholicism* does conclude with a section entitled "Social Action and Catholicism."[100] De Lubac is not simply concerned with "afterworldly hopes." As we will develop below, de Lubac's "political theology" pertains to a call to return to the Mystery, the incarnate embodiment of the eternal Christ in the presence of the church: "That, then, is first and foremost the social role of the Church; she brings us back to that communion which all her dogma teaches us and all her activity makes ready for us."[101] It is a universal call to all people throughout the world to surrender themselves to the Apocalypse of the Incarnation, mediated through the *corpus mysticum*, in order to be reunited as a new humanity.

As seen in *The Splendor of the Church*, an analysis of de Lubac's conception of the *corpus mysticum* is incomplete without reference to the meaning of priesthood and the hierarchical structure of the church. We must remember that de Lubac's conception is extremely concrete and particular. The mystical body is the inner reality of Christ that unites the

97. De Lubac, *Catholicism*, 120.
98. De Lubac, *Catholicism*, 133.
99. De Lubac, *Catholicism*, 16.
100. De Lubac, *Catholicism*, 361.
101. De Lubac, *Catholicism*, 362.

eternal and the temporal, but this is mediated in a profoundly corporal institution: "The church produces the Eucharist, and it was principally to that end that her priesthood was instituted—'Do this for a commemoration of me.'"[102] De Lubac stresses that "every Christian is of course a priest . . . every Christian participates in the one and only sacrifice of Jesus Christ."[103] The church entire shares in the royal dignity of the kingly priest: "All dignity is communal in the unity of the faith and of baptism . . . the sign of the cross makes kings of all those who have been regenerated in Christ, and the unction of the Holy Spirit consecrates them all as priests."[104] This is the vision of Moses, as well as the Apostle Peter, that the people of God are a "kingdom of priests and a sacred nation."[105] De Lubac asserts that this is not mere metaphor. We may describe it as an ecclesial "realism." It is a "mystical reality that cannot be surpassed or further deepened—in its own order—by any additional institution or consecration, any other priesthood. For this is what makes a Christ of a Christian, who is a member of the eternal King and Priest."[106] Thus, asserts de Lubac, it is not the priesthood of the faithful "merely," it is "priesthood of the whole church."[107] This is the spiritual reality of the church affected by the eucharistic mediation of grace that unites persons to the new humanity revealed in the image of Christ. The Christian community is a priestly city, a living temple, a representation of humanity before Christ, but also the embodiment of Christ to the world.[108]

102. De Lubac, *Splendor*, 133.

103. De Lubac, *Splendor*, 133.

104. De Lubac quotes St. Leo the Great, *Sermo* 4, chap. 1. De Lubac, *Splendor*, 133–34.

105. De Lubac, *Splendor*, 134.

106. De Lubac, *Splendor*, 134.

107. De Lubac, *Splendor*, 135.

108. De Lubac asserts that the redemptive work of Christ and the founding of the church are in truth one work: "All that we have said so far applies equally to the visible Church and the invisible body of Christ, and any attempt at separation will in this case run counter to the facts of history." It pertains to proper theological understanding of *ekkleisia* in continuity with the Hebrew concept of "Qahal." According to de Lubac, "Qahal" does not mean "a restricted group of a purely empirical gathering, but the whole people of God, a concrete reality which, however small it may seem outwardly, is yet always far greater than it appears." The Greek work, *ekkleisia*, was suitable because it implies the divine call to be the people of God. The *ekkleisia* that neither "Paul nor any other of the first disciples ever imagined as an entirely invisible reality, but which they always understand as a mystery surpassing its outward manifestations, this *ekkleisia* is in logical sequence to the *kleitoi*." The church as those who are "called"

The Politics of the Sacrament in the Theology of Henri de Lubac 37

Establishing this perspective of the priesthood, de Lubac then turns to the priesthood of the bishop and the clergy. This office of bishop is "not properly speaking, a higher dignity in the order of the Christian's participation in the grace of Christ."[109] De Lubac critiques a conception of the church with discriminatory membership of a type "postulated by the gnostic or Manichean sects; for us there is no question of 'psychics' and 'spirituals' divided into two classes."[110] De Lubac underscores the letter of Hebrews in this regard:

> Similarly, there are no more distinctions like those which held good under the old dispensation. Then the priests alone had their sacred vestments that had to be worn for the ceremonial; but all the baptized have put on Christ and, more than that, have reconceived the anointing formerly kept for the High Priest alone. Then, it was he alone who could go into the Holy of Holies, and that once a year only; now, faith gives us all free entry through the blood of our Lord.[111]

It is the inner, spiritual priesthood is united to the Christ as the *corpus mysticum*. How might this relate to the "exterior" priesthood? According to de Lubac, "we are concerned here not with a superior rank of the 'interior priesthood'—for that is common to all and cannot

---

are also those who "call"—"She is a *convocatio* before being a *congregatio*." The church is more than simply a "mere federation of local assemblies. Still less is she the simple gathering together of those who as individuals have accepted the Gospel and henceforward have shared their religious life." The church is the very embodiment of a reunified humanity through the mystery of the Incarnation. This is expressed in the flesh and blood gathering of the people of God: "She is properly called the Church because she calls all to herself and gathers all into unity." The church "summons all men so that as their mother she may bring them forth into divine life and eternal light." Now this part of a mother is indeed allotted to the visible Church. This Jerusalem, our "mother," "is not envisaged by Paul as being merely in some far-off heavenly future; he sees it rather on the earth, in every city that has received the Gospel, already beginning its work of liberation; she it is who speaks by the mount of the Apostles and of the heads of the churches." De Lubac recites a well-known principle by Cyprian: "He cannot have God the Father who has not the Church for Mother." That is, the unity of Christ is not abstracted from the material gathering of the church in its flesh and blood manifestation. The church is a visible reality, embodied in local cultures, ethnic groups, and languages. De Lubac even quotes the Protestant theologian, Karl Barth: "If we seek to solve the question of unity of the Church by appealing to an invisible church, we speculate as Platonists instead of listening to Christ." De Lubac, *Catholicism*, 62–77.

109. De Lubac, *Splendor*, 139.
110. De Lubac, *Splendor*, 139.
111. De Lubac, *Splendor*, 139.

be surpassed in rank—but an 'exterior priesthood' that is reserved for some only, a charge entrusted to some only with a view to the 'exterior sacrifice'—'*Onus Diaconii, Onus Presbyterii, Onus Episcopatus*.'[112] It is the "particular priesthood" within the "general priesthood."[113] However, the particular priesthood is not, argues de Lubac, a "sort of emanation from the community of the faithful," for "the faithful cannot confer or delegate a power that is not theirs."[114] Certainly, there is a representational aspect of the office of the priest.[115] However, at the essential moment, argues de Lubac, the priest "acts by the power of Christ, or rather—to use the compact formulas of St. Thomas—he prays and offers *in persona omnium* but consecrates *in persona Christi*."[116] That is, there is an authoritative vocation entrusted to the "particular" priesthood by the sovereignty of Christ. Despite the fact that "all are called, as from this present world, to the same divine life."[117] Despite the "'Christian dignity' that is a wonderful renewal of the dignity of [humanity], there is an indissoluble difference of situation and power between priests and laity, pastors and faithful."[118] In other words, there is a particular vocation for certain *men*.[119] For those who "are invested with it, whatever the human circumstances of their appointing, participate in the Church's mission to engender and maintain the divine life in us, and this by a delegation from God himself. Christ, the true and only Priest, has chosen them as the instruments through which he is to act upon us, and to this end has passed on to them something of what he received from His Father."[120] This is the theological rationale for the Catholic hierarchy, which serves a "sacred function" for the "perfecting" of the "new creature." The divinely instituted hierarchy is a service for the church's sanctification through the unifying mystery of the Christ mediated through the sacraments: "To hold in their own hands the

---

112. De Lubac, *Splendor*, 140.

113. De Lubac, *Splendor*, 140.

114. De Lubac, *Splendor*, 141.

115. As de Lubac asserts, in relation to the Mass, "The Collect at the beginning of the Mass is the priest's summing up of the people's prayer—a fact that is also witnessed to by the plural *quaesumus* and expressions such as *Ecclesia tua* and *populus tuus* and *familia tua*, as also by the final 'Amen' said by the server." De Lubac, *Splendor*, 141

116. De Lubac, *Splendor*, 142. St. Thomas Aquinas, ST III, q. 80.

117. De Lubac, *Splendor*, 143.

118. De Lubac, *Splendor*, 143.

119. De Lubac does not justify the gender-specific requirements of the priesthood.

120. De Lubac, *Splendor*, 143.

Eucharist—that is the supreme prerogative of those who form the hierarchy in the Church ... The supreme exercise of its power, lies in consecrating Christ's body and thus perpetuating the work of the Redemption—in offering the 'sacrifice of praise' which is the only one pleasing to God."[121]

This is the sacred function of those called by God to authoritatively extend the mystical unity of the divine and the human, incarnated in the *corpus mysticum*, lived in the flesh and blood of the church: "Each bishop constitutes the unity of his flock, 'the people adhering to its priests, cohering with the heavenly sacraments.'"[122] The bishops of the church form "one episcopate only and are all alike 'at peace and in communion' with the Bishop of Rome, who is Peter's successor and the visible bond of unity; and through them, all the faithful are united."[123] For de Lubac, the Roman Catholic hierarchy exists in a dynamic relation to the body of Christ, the church, and forms the means by which the transcendence of the divine is mystically united in the immanent experience of earthly life. This communion, spread across the world, is the visible expression of an inner divine reality, united in Christ, mediated through the Eucharist, administered by this specific priesthood. Liturgy, therefore, the worship of God in Christ in and through the sacrament, is the basis of the new humanity revealed in Christ: "What happens in that solemn gathering at the heart of each diocese happens also, with the same fullness and the same effects, in the humblest village Mass or the quiet Mass of the monk in his 'desert.'"[124] There is a mystical consecrating power that extends to each priest from the bishop: "He has received a communication of the same 'spirit', and wherever he officiates he always forms part of its 'precious spiritual crown.'"[125] Everything else then follows. The unity of the mystical body is upheld through this apocalyptic mediational embodiment of the sovereignty of Christ.

The Political Significance of the *Corpus Mysticum*

From this analysis, we are in a better position to consider the political implications of de Lubac's conception of the *corpus mysticum*. De Lubac

121. De Lubac, *Splendor*, 148.
122. De Lubac, *Splendor*, 148.
123. De Lubac, *Splendor*, 149.
124. De Lubac, *Splendor*, 150.
125. De Lubac, *Splendor*, 150.

clarifies for us the rationale for this "catholic" emphasis. On the one hand, de Lubac seeks to recover the social dimension of the *corpus mysticum* because of the modernist drift toward individualism. The "degeneration" of the mystical body has contributed to the individualist drift, but so did the counter-Reformation Catholic reaction. Responding to the critique of the individualism of the church, as expressed in a counter-reformative sacramental theology of the "objective presence," the basic argument in *Catholicism* (and the general thrust of his entire theology) is that Catholicism is essentially social: "It is social in the deepest sense of the word: not merely in its applications in the field of natural institutions but first and foremost in itself, in *the heart of its mystery*, in the essence of its *dogma*."[126] Moreover, in connecting the church's individualism in relation to the political movements of late modernity de Lubac references an interesting remark by Père Philippe de Régis, who suggested that "perhaps Marxism and Leninism would not have arisen and been propagated with such terrible results if the place that belongs to collectivity in the natural as well as in the supernatural order had always been given to it."[127] Indeed, for de Lubac, the political hopes of Marxism, among other modernist ideologies, reflect the inescapable human desire for transcendence: "The unity of this human family as a whole is the subject, we have said, of some of the deepest yearnings of our age. It longs to organize it, to bring it to complete awareness of itself, in fine to humanize it by making it fully one."[128] We shall further explore de Lubac's investigation into the antitheistic roots of the "drama of atheist humanism" in subsequent chapters.

On a deeper level, however, the Gospel itself introduced a political tension in the world. The "visible" expression of the church, mediated by a "particular" priesthood, *disturbs* the world, for it proclaims the "universal" sovereignty of Christ: "The fact that the [church] is a mystery lived by faith does not make her any less a reality in this world; she walks in broad daylight, making her presence known to all and claiming her own rights."[129] The *corpus mysticum* is woven into the fabric of society. The church is an incarnational expression of the sovereignty of Christ, the "lamb who was slain." As a human institution it is embedded within all human life, but simultaneously divine, pointing to the eternal destiny of

---

126. De Lubac, *Catholicism*, 15.
127. De Lubac, *Catholicism*, 309.
128. De Lubac, *Catholicism*, 353.
129. De Lubac, *Splendor*, 161.

humankind. Yet, argues de Lubac, with the claims to political sovereignty in the world, "there is—disastrously—a rivalry between the two and a more or less unceasing struggle."[130] De Lubac observes that "twenty centuries of history bear witness to the fact that balance between the two is almost impossible to come by. Sometimes the State becomes the persecutor, and sometimes churchmen usurp the rights of the church."[131] It seems an enduring cycle from one "head" of the eagle to the next:[132] "Every form of separation and union of the two has its own dangers, and the symbioses of the greatest perfection are by that very fact the more dangerous, for here the best runs easily into the worst, and when it does it is not always clear which power has become the slave of the other—whether it is the Church that is domineering over "the world," or the world that is taking possession of the Church."[133]

According to de Lubac, in the pagan mind there was still a firm and direct correlation between religion and the political: "Such a dualism was unknown to the ancient world; there, even when the priest was distinct from the head of the family, the military leader, or the magistrate, each man's religion was that of his polity."[134] In fact, I suggest that within de Lubac's formulation of the broken image of God, pagan religion represents the "natural" attempt to restore a shattered unity of humankind, a mystical unification between the natural and the supernatural, the immanent and the transcendent. As I argued above, out of this emerges political expressions of human sovereignty that claim divine status, such as the "beastly empires" that opposed the people of God in the history of Israel (Babylon, for example). De Lubac asserts that even the Greeks and the Jews "knew nothing of this running sore which the institution of the Catholic Church has set up in states and consciences; the trouble dates from the proclaiming of the Gospel."[135] While the prophets of Israel anticipated a messiah that would truly unite heaven and earth, the Hebrew monarchs were perpetually tempted to imitate the nations that

---

130. De Lubac, *Splendor*, 161.

131. De Lubac, *Splendor*, 162.

132. The double-headed eagle is an ancient symbol of empire, but in the medieval period in Europe it came to symbolize the two powers of the church and state as the sovereign "heads" of the Holy Roman Empire. This is how de Lubac is interpreting it here in relation to Rousseau's reflection of the church and state in a Western context.

133. De Lubac, *Splendor*, 162.

134. De Lubac, *Splendor*, 163.

135. De Lubac, *Splendor*, 163.

surrounded them. However, argues de Lubac, it was the Gospel that distinguished what we call today "the temporal and the spiritual."[136] It was "the Gospel that made two things of Church and State."[137] De Lubac's reflection on this political implication of the *corpus mysticum* is in conversation with Jean-Jacques Rousseau. As Rousseau asserted, "Separating the theological system from the political system, [the Gospel] made the State no longer one and caused the internal divisions that have continually disturbed the Christian peoples."[138] The result is "a perpetual conflict of jurisdiction that has made any kind of good polity impossible."[139] As de Lubac interprets Rousseau's solution, "Only one remedy alone will prove effective; a return to the ancient system—'reunion of the two heads of the eagle' and 'a reduction of all political unity, without which neither the State nor government will ever be well constituted.'"[140]

According to de Lubac, Rousseau is a sounding board, summarizing a long tradition, that asserts the necessity of the sovereignty of the state over the church, to unite society in a form of political justice. Rousseau, in the tradition of Hobbes, seeks to find a way to eliminate the "disturbance" of the church that limits, indeed precludes the possibility of such unity. But the problem is only so construed on the side of the conceptions of "immanent sovereignty." On the other hand, de Lubac acknowledges that "theologians and canonists, going beyond the great Augustinian dream of spiritual unity and peace in justice . . . have been irritated by the same complications and carried away by the same ideal of oversimplification."[141] In the late medieval period, theologians used Augustine to theologically substantiate the temporal sovereignty of the bishop of Rome. Papal authority was conceived as regal authority that governed both the spiritual and the temporal, the Eucharist and the Sword. It is a political vision that sought to rejoin the transcendent and the immanent in pagan terms. The simplicity of the ideal of political unity between the temporal and spiritual spheres, argues de Lubac, the state and the church, is not possible nor even desirable: "The coming of human dominion has already made things extremely complicated on this planet. From the moment of the first glimmer

---

136. De Lubac, *Splendor*, 163.
137. De Lubac, *Splendor*, 163.
138. De Lubac, *Splendor*, 163. See Rousseau, *Social Contract*, bk. 4, chap. 8.
139. De Lubac, *Splendor*, 163.
140. De Lubac, *Splendor*, 162.
141. De Lubac, *Splendor*, 164.

of intelligence and the first prick of the moral law there have been problems, conflicts, scruples, and inhibitions without number, complication and disorder without end."[142] This stands in opposition to Rousseau, who was "tempted by the idea of a return to a paradise conceived as existing before all the dissociative process discussed above."[143] The nostalgic desire to return to a more "simplistic" and ideal past is delusive temptation: "The condition of simplicity, which pulls at us so irresistibly, is to be found in our end, not in our beginning."[144]

We will return to de Lubac's political theology in comparison with Dostoevsky and Nietzsche. For now, it is enough to recognize that the political problem of unity pertains deeply to the question of the mystical reunion of the transcendent and the immanent. It is an apocalyptic problem that seeks to resolve the problem of "humanity" and the broken, fragmented image of God because of spiritual rebellion. This stems from de Lubac's theological anthropology; that is, humanity's "nature is twofold—he is animal and spirit. He lives on this earth and is committed to a temporal destiny; yet there is in him something that goes beyond any terrestrial horizon and seeks the atmosphere of eternity as its natural climate."[145] For de Lubac, it is the grace of the Gospel, the Incarnation, mediated by the church that fulfills this transcendent destiny:

> The duality set up by the Gospel will obtain to an even greater degree if it is true that God has intervened in history, our own history, if he wished to provide not only secretly for the good of each individual but publicly—socially, as it were—for the good of the whole human race; if the Christian mystery is founded on real facts, and the whole divine revelation has taken a historical form, so that we cannot recognize it save through the succession of an authentic witness, and so that it reaches us through a Tradition.[146]

Moreover, "Christ's resurrection created a new world; it marked the beginning of a fresh age and set up on earth a type of existence that is absolutely novel—'Behold all things are new.'" It inaugurated the 'eighth

---

142. De Lubac, *Splendor*, 165.
143. De Lubac, *Splendor*, 165.
144. De Lubac, *Splendor*, 165.
145. De Lubac, *Splendor*, 166.
146. De Lubac, *Splendor*, 167.

day.'"[147] This is the apocalyptic intervention of the Gospel which mystically unites humanity through Christ.

Despite this "good news," however, de Lubac is not triumphalist. Following Augustine, de Lubac asserts that we still live in two cities; the eighth day "neither transformed the social nature of man nor cancelled out the temporal conditions of existence . . . For the time being, the new world fits into the old one; the eighth day exists in the seven others, and from now onward man will, in this life, form part of two cities, whose content will be these two worlds respectively."[148] This is the Augustinian heart of de Lubac's ecclesial "realism," the tension that the *corpus mysticum* experiences as it faithfully and patiently anticipates the eschatological fulfillment of Christ in history. To reiterate a New Testament slogan, the body of Christ is in the world but not of it. Its experience in time and space is deeply oriented within and toward the eternal. It is both immanent and transcendent in a way that does not delimit nor demean either sphere. It is possible only though the gracious mediation of Christ through the sanctifying power of the Holy Spirit.

Nonetheless, the allure of Rousseau, the *desire* for a politics based on "pure nature," has continued to run its course in modernity. While Hobbes and Rousseau still thought deeply in the environment of Christendom, they paved the way for new forms of humanistic politics to emerge. As we saw above, for de Lubac the antecedents to this shift began earlier in the post-Thomist preconceptions of "grace" in relation to "nature," where the sufficiency and autonomy of "nature" apart from "grace" began to take precedence. The transcendent presupposition of the Gospel was gradually rejected for more "immanent" conceptions of humanity and their resulting political expressions. Humanity was no longer conceived as existing for a transcendent destiny, but the desire for that transcendence remained all the same. This is for de Lubac, as we will see, the spiritual meaning of atheist humanism and its desire for political unity.

The Death of God and the Politics of Modernity

In the previous section, I provided a theological outline of de Lubac's political theology as rooted in the *corpus mysticum*, the reunification of humanity, created in the image of God, through the Incarnation. In

147. De Lubac, *Splendor*, 167.
148. De Lubac, *Splendor*, 167.

this section of the introductory chapter, we will consider the crisis of modernity as an inversion of the image of God. If the medieval period represented the church's attempt to maintain a Catholic unity mediated through the Eucharist, the scholastic doctrine of "pure nature" began the slow degenerative erosion of this theological and political unity. Of course, I am not suggesting that this unity was attained in medieval Catholicism, or that de Lubac so represents it.[149] The medieval presupposition of humanity as created in the image of God began to erode in western modernity—that is, the vision of humanity as a spiritual being created for a transcendent destiny. The previous theological outline accentuates what precisely atheist humanism attempts to leave behind, and de Lubac intends to recover for modernity a robust social and political meaning of *corpus mysticum* that fully appreciates the mystery of the Incarnation. The consequence of the "pure nature" doctrine has degenerated, despite its complex history and the variety of its expressions, into a modernist movement whereby humanity attempts to recreate itself and its destiny apart from "God." This means that not only the mystery of the Incarnation is lost, but also the mystery of humanity as uniquely created for a higher destiny, rooted in the divine calling has degenerated. This presupposition is largely nonexistent today in the modern West.

To be sure, de Lubac's theological approach welcomes an open, yet critical engagement with modernist thought. In *Catholicism*, de Lubac asserts that the "progress in the physical and natural sciences combined with the increasing use of the genetic method in all branches of science has enabled us to discover not only the immensity but also the fecundity of the historical process."[150] According to de Lubac, the modern social sciences have helped us to see more clearly that "every individual [is] rooted in humanity as humanity itself is rooted in nature, and the scientific enrichment of this perception provides a natural basis of great value for a better understanding of our Catholicism."[151] De Lubac, therefore, is not strictly "antimodern." For instance, de Lubac was sympathetic to the work of his friend Pierre Teilhard de Chardin, who articulated a theology

---

149. As we will see, Dostoevsky, as a Russian within the Orthodox tradition, was deeply critical of Roman Catholicism as an expression of division rather than unity. We will address this in the next chapter. We see a critical stance toward Roman Catholicism in *The Idiot*, *The Brothers Karamazov*, and *A Writer's Diary*.

150. De Lubac, *Catholicism*, 351.

151. De Lubac, *Catholicism*, 351.

of natural evolution.[152] For de Lubac, the development of culture, science, and technology is not fundamentally averse to humanity as created in the *imago Dei*. The supernatural is not opposed to the natural: "In the image of God, is this to say according, first of all, to the image of the Creator? He should then imitate him in his manner of dominating nature."[153] Of course, this is intended to be provocative and de Lubac qualifies the meaning of such a statement. Nonetheless, I emphasize it here to assert that de Lubac's critical analysis of modernism has a redemptive intention rather than strictly negative one. The apocalyptic sovereignty of Christ is not inherently opposed to *scientia*, the rationalistic and scientific knowledge of the material world.

This redemptive intent explains de Lubac's critical engagement in developing a genealogy of atheism in *Drama*. The Catholic desire for the unity of humanity as mediated through the *corpus mysticum* necessitates this redemptive engagement. Balthasar describes de Lubac's engagement with atheistic humanism as an outworking of "the two essential front lines of missionary dialogue" that concerned de Lubac.[154] The first is the dialogue with modern atheism, the second with Buddhism.[155] This missionary impulse of de Lubac can already be strongly detected in *Catholicism*. It is the logical outcome of the concept of "catholicism." As Balthasar asserts, quoting de Lubac's *The Theological Foundation of the Missions*, "the Church is Catholic because, understanding herself to be universal *de jure*, she desires also to become so *de facto*."[156] For Milbank, however, the significance of *The Drama of Atheist Humanism* lies in the fact that it precedes the publication of *Surnaturel*.[157] It is significant in that it connects to de Lubac's underlying theme of demonstrating "the loss of the true doctrine of the supernatural for the false idea of a 'purely natural' human domain which becomes the space of the secular and of

---

152. De Lubac devoted numerous works to Pierre Teilhard de Chardin. According to Hans Urs von Balthasar, the most important are *La Pensée religieuse de Père Teilhard de Chardin* (1962), *La Prière de Père Teilhard de Chardin* (1964), *Blondel et Teilhard de Chardin* (1965). Balthasar asserts that de Lubac's interest in Teilhard was more than just obviating misunderstandings of his thought, but "Teilhard's work ... provides an occasion to develop more intensively a whole dimension—the cosmic dimension of Catholicism—in de Lubac's thought." See Balthasar, *Henri de Lubac*, 82.

153. De Lubac, *Drama of Atheist Humanism*, 414.

154. Balthasar, *Henri de Lubac*, 45.

155. Balthasar, *Henri de Lubac*, 46.

156. Balthasar, *Henri de Lubac*, 45–46.

157. Milbank, *Suspended Middle*, 11.

The Politics of the Sacrament in the Theology of Henri de Lubac 47

modern philosophy."[158] In *Drama*, de Lubac wanted to engage with and demonstrate the "logical" end of a humanism conceived of as intrinsically independent from the supernatural. Indeed, in combining Balthasar's interpretation with Milbank's, I suggest that this demonstration, which ends in an interpretation of the mystical despair of Nietzsche, comprises an aspect of de Lubac's missionary task to call Western humanity back to the "supernatural," or at least to recognize its deeper "natural" *desire* for the transcendent.

Modern Atheism as the Renovation of the Image of God

In *Drama*, de Lubac investigates what he describes as the "immense *drift*; through the action of a large proportion of its foremost thinkers, the peoples of the West are denying their Christian past and turning away from God."[159] That is, what is at stake in the Western drama pertains to the decline of faith in "God." As de Lubac makes clear throughout the work, the particular "God" is not simply an abstract deity, but the Christian God, the God of the church. It is a "drift" from the faith in the Incarnation mediated through the *corpus mysticum*. Despite the "numerous surface-currents" that drive contemporary thought, this "drama" is the deeper "undercurrent," which is moving Western culture along.[160] In thinkers such as Ludwig Feuerbach, Karl Marx, Auguste Comte, and Friedrich Nietzsche, de Lubac detects an atheism that is not purely critical, but an antitheism that is "increasingly positive, organic, constructive."[161] This atheism is "modern"—new—in the history of humanity in that it pursues a deeper *renovation* of thought that will engender new forms of political embodiment. In a fascinating chapter in *Drama*, "The Search for a New Man," de Lubac asserts, "We have been witnessing for some time, not only extraordinary events that are drastically changing the face of the world, but *one* even in depth, which is changing something in [humanity] itself."[162] There is a transformation occurring in the deeper societal consciousness of humanity, at least in the Western world, a "shedding of skins" as de Lubac describes it. The medieval Christian conception

158. Millbank, *Suspended Middle*, 11.
159. De Lubac, *Drama of Atheist Humanism*, 11.
160. De Lubac, *Drama of Atheist Humanism*, 11.
161. De Lubac, *Drama of Atheist Humanism*, 11.
162. De Lubac, *Drama of Atheist Humanism*, 402.

of humanity as created in God's image is like a skin being shed: "Now here in our own age a new ambition is born. An idée-force has emerged. [Humanity] has, little by little, raised [its] head against the destiny that was weighing [it] down."[163] While acknowledging their intermediaries and interpreters with various additions and admixtures, de Lubac acknowledges the powerful attraction of these particular thinkers, especially Marx, Comte, and Nietzsche in his own context.[164] That is, de Lubac uncovers the main contours of atheistic expression in these thinkers with their social and political implications.[165] In other words, de Lubac explores the creative attempts to construct a *unifying* philosophy of humanity—at least in the Western world—on antitheistic, antichristian materialist foundations.[166]

Moreover, the modernist "drift" away from God is directly antitheist and, in Nietzsche's case, explicitly antichristian: "The same Christian idea of man that had been welcomed as a deliverance was now beginning to be felt as a yoke. And the same God in whom man had learned to see the seal of his own greatness began to seem to him like an antagonist, the enemy of his dignity."[167] The meaning of humanity's dignity revealed in scripture, created in the image of God, which liberated the ancients from the "ontological slavery with which Fate burdened us," is now perceived as a threat to human freedom and the development and maturity of the human race.[168] Nietzsche, too, recognized the radical transformation that was occurring, as is evident in the famous "mad man" frantically declaring that "God is dead."[169] For de Lubac, the death of God in the West-

---

163. De Lubac describes three forms of "consciousness," among others: faith in science, experiential research and the precision of mathematics, which then oriented moderns toward an "operating science" or an orientation "toward the possession of the world," and third, a movement toward "the transformation of society." He cites the field of eugenics and political propaganda as examples of this modernist movement. We will address the politics of this briefly in the following section. De Lubac, *Drama of Atheist Humanism*, 402.

164. In turn, we might consider the influence of Nietzsche and Marx, for instance, on more recent thinkers such as Michel Foucault, Jacques Derrida, and even more recently, Peter Sloterdijk and Slavoj Žižek.

165. For instance, de Lubac will address the positivist movement espoused by Auguste Comte at length in *Drama*, 131–263.

166. De Lubac, *Drama of Atheist Humanism*, 12.

167. De Lubac, *Drama of Atheist Humanism*, 23.

168. De Lubac, *Drama of Atheist Humanism*, 24–25.

169. Nietzsche, *Gay Science*, 181.

ern world marks a tragic watershed, which reveals a particular spiritual disposition. It is not only a transformation of collective and individual consciousness, but also a spiritual condition. What is essential for de Lubac, as a Christian, is to "take cognizance of the spiritual situation of the world" in which we are involved.[170] The crisis of modernism is spiritual, for it pertains to a disruption of a particular conception of humanity in relation to God. A new "mystical immanentism" has been introduced that, for de Lubac, essentially means the "annihilation of the human person."[171] To be sure, Christian thought can benefit from readings of these thinkers, especially Nietzsche, since "even at their most blasphemous, they advance criticisms whose justice [we] are bound to admit."[172] Nonetheless, the question of the "new atheism"[173] is fundamentally a spiritual problem—it is the "human problem as a whole."[174]

De Lubac describes this deliberate antitheistic-antichristian thought as a "tragic misunderstanding."[175] A tragic inversion of our understanding of humanity in relation to the divine has occurred. As we have seen, de Lubac's theological anthropology is rooted in the mystery of Genesis: "God made humankind in his own image and likeness" (Gen 1:26). This revelation was intended to reveal the dignity of humanity as created in the image of God, not to rob humanity of its dignity: "From its earliest beginnings Christian tradition has not ceased to annotate this verse, recognizing in it our first title of nobility and the foundation of our greatness."[176] This was the assumption of the early church fathers and continued as such into the medieval period. The mystery of the human person as a "natural" receptacle of the divine Word was upheld through the church, mediated through the sacrament. Humanity was redeemed to reflect the divine nature through the mediation of the Incarnation. However,

170. De Lubac, *Drama of Atheist Humanism*, 11.

171. De Lubac, *Drama of Atheist Humanism*, 11–12.

172. Hans Urs von Balthasar detects de Lubac's sympathy with Nietzsche. Balthasar, *Henri de Lubac*, 49.

173. Not to be confused with the so-called "new atheists," Richard Dawkins, Sam Harris, etc.

174. De Lubac, *Drama of Atheist Humanism*, 113.

175. De Lubac, *Drama of Atheist Humanism*, 19.

176. De Lubac goes on to say that "reason, liberty, immorality and dominion over nature are so many prerogatives of divine origin that God has imparted to his creatures. Establishing humankind from the outset in God's likeness, each of these prerogatives is meant to grow and unfold until the divine resemblance is brought to perfection." De Lubac, *Drama of Atheist Humanism*, 19.

with Feuerbach this symbolism is reversed, and God is perceived as the projection of human attributes.[177] The mystery of the image of God in humankind is inverted. God is created in the image of humankind. God is a human creation, a duplicate human, a mirror, and reflection of human aspiration. Indeed, the idea of God comes to be seen as a grievous crime against humanity. In traditional theology, humankind "defrauds his own self."[178] The human creation of God is an unwitting "*kenosis*" in service to a phantom. The human "impoverishes himself by enriching his God, in filling whom he empties himself. He affirms in God what he denies in himself."[179] Faith in God is a form of self-alienation: "Religion is thus transformed into a vampire that feeds upon the substance of humankind, its flesh and blood."[180] For Karl Marx, however, Feuerbach does not go far enough. In *Catholicism*, de Lubac quotes Marx: "Feuerbach dissolves the religious being into the human being. But the human being is not an abstraction that inheres in isolated individuals. It is found only in the whole body of social relationships."[181] As de Lubac interprets Marx, communist socialism completes the process begun by Feuerbach, by dissolving the "human" being into the "social" being: "What was to exalt man ended in his ruin."[182] The "eternal element" in humanity, created in God's image, the intrinsic—natural—link with the transcendent, was completely exorcised by modernist socialism.

The Politics of Atheist Humanism

As we have seen, according to de Lubac, atheist humanism, especially as expressed in socialism, means the renovation of the meaning of humanity. In other words, the modernist atheistic philosophies are attempts to reunify humanity modelled after traditional Christianity even as they revolt against it. Humanism is political in the sense that it attempts to offer a new vision for humankind to appropriate a deeper social-psychological transformation of human nature, engaged in a process of self-becoming and self-actualization. Politically, this means building society upon an

---

177. De Lubac, *Drama of Atheist Humanism*, 19.
178. De Lubac, *Drama of Atheist Humanism*, 27.
179. De Lubac, *Drama of Atheist Humanism*, 28.
180. De Lubac, *Drama of Atheist Humanism*, 29.
181. De Lubac, *Catholicism*, 358. See also Karl Marx, *Thesis on Feuerbach*, thesis 6.
182. De Lubac, *Catholicism*, 358.

antitheistic ontological foundation—humanity itself. Humanity itself becomes both the goal, but also the instrument, of such a self-transcendent destiny. Humanity becomes the supreme being in a trajectory of "becoming" that has no absolute or eternal point of reference, aim, or goal other than itself. In the chapter "The Search for a New Man," de Lubac explores this renovation in greater depth. Modernist humanity, through its technical rationality, is fundamentally "oriented toward the possession of the world."[183] In a rationalist, scientific modality, technique "thus no longer appeared to be an inferior genre, like a utilization more or less refused by a science fearing to be degraded: it was recognized as its necessary extension."[184] For de Lubac, the "mission" of modern humanity, at least in the Western context, means the transformation of nature, society itself, with the ultimate aim to "grasp" itself, so as to "forge its own destiny."[185] It is humanity that functions as creator, a divine sovereign on the earth. In other words, divorced from the supernatural, the natural limits of (human) nature are stretched and contorted beyond its capacity.

As I interpret de Lubac, here lies the underlying spiritual crisis. It means the yearning for transcendence in the immanent, for the eternal in the temporal, for the invisible in the visible, has been distorted into a completely immanent human project. For de Lubac this represents a form of the idolatrous exchange expressed in Romans 1:18ff, whereby the worship and devotion to God is replaced with the worship of the human ideal: "Without God, even truth is an idol, even justice is an idol. Idols too pure and pale in face of the flesh-and-blood idols that are regaining their pedestals; ideals too abstract in the face of the great collective myths that are reawakening the strongest instincts—'de-germed wheat,' as they have been called."[186] For de Lubac, this means, however, the annihilation of humankind.[187] For humanity itself cuts off the high branch on

---

183. This compares with Schmitt's argument that in the modernist state "there must no longer be political problems, only organizational-technical and economic-sociological tasks. The kind of economic-technical thinking that prevails today is no longer capable of perceiving a political idea. The modern state seems to have actually become what Max Weber envisioned: a huge industrial plant." Schmitt, *Political Theology*, 65. See also de Lubac, *Drama*, 405.

184. De Lubac, *Drama of Atheist Humanism*, 405.

185. De Lubac provides examples of the reign of scientism in which both biological and political engineering are exercised: eugenics and political propaganda. De Lubac, *Drama of Atheist Humanism*, 408.

186. De Lubac, *Drama of Atheist Humanism*, 71.

187. De Lubac, *Drama of Atheist Humanism*, 12.

which it was perched, and leads to existential despair as a result of this "metaphysical rebellion."[188] Moreover, de Lubac alludes to the political consequences of atheistic humanism as one of radical crisis: "The story is a dramatic one. At its maximum point of concentration, it is the great crisis of modern times, that same crisis in which we are involved today, and which takes its outward course in disorder, begets tyrannies and collective crimes, and finds its expression in blood, fire and ruin."[189] Furthermore, "the enormous success of the philosophies of "becoming" as well as the distressing results which have lately imperiled their authority have had in this respect the same effect. Empty dreams and fears, exacerbated by the violence of their contrast, hope in the future and anxiety in the morrow, have laid hold of our consciousness."[190] De Lubac, as Milbank points out, lived and wrote as blood was spilled over old European Christendom, as human life was sacrificed on behalf of grandiose political visions constructed on new modernist conceptions of humanity.[191] Of course, this is also what Nietzsche and Dostoevsky foresaw and this preceding analysis assists us in our interpretive orientation of these authors.

Myth and Mystery: The Importance of Dostoevsky and Nietzsche for de Lubac

Reading de Lubac's Augustinian theological approach in relation to Nietzsche and Dostoevsky provides an account of the apocalyptic; that is, the divine sovereign impingement on human experience, the mystical relation between transcendence and immanence. To reiterate, the underlying research question of this project may be articulated as follows: Why were Nietzsche and Dostoevsky important for de Lubac in addressing the question of a theological conception of sovereignty that mystically reunites the transcendent and the immanent? As indicated above, this question is not disconnected from the meaning of the church, the *ekklesia*, the *corpus mysticum*, which is divinely called to mediate the sovereign image of Christ in the world. The church is a collective priesthood. What I seek to accomplish in this work is to connect de Lubac's analysis of Nietzsche and Dostoevsky more deeply within his own theological project,

---

188. See Camus, *Rebel*.
189. De Lubac, *Drama of Atheist Humanism*, 25.
190. De Lubac, *Catholicism*, 357.
191. Millbank, *Suspended Middle*, 1.

but in doing so, draw out more clearly the forms of political embodiment that Nietzsche and Dostoevsky envisioned for the Western culture in the wake of modernist humanism.

However, as de Lubac demonstrates, at heart Nietzsche and Dostoevsky discerned the important underlying question of the meaning of humanity in relation to God. They were philosophers of the mystery of the transcendent meaning of immanence. We could also use the term "existential" to describe the question this way: What is the transcendent meaning (or lack thereof) of human existence? In the theological terms of de Lubac, both the atheist Nietzsche and the Christian Dostoevsky discerned that the nexus of the modern dilemma is the issue of the "natural" in relation to the "supernatural," "immanence" in relation to "transcendence," and "becoming" in relation to "being." Moreover, they were philosophers, who questioned the meaning of desire and its mysterious link between the body and the spirit. As I have shown, for de Lubac, the mysterious link between the natural and the supernatural is that humanity is created in the *imago Dei*, and the Incarnation of Christ reveals the mystical unification of the divine and human. It is this Judeo-Christian "God" in relation to "humanity" that is in question. And, therefore, it is this conception of "God" and "humanity" that is being renovated in modernity. Dostoevsky and Nietzsche both saw the transference of theological language of transcendence toward the immanent that implies the divinization of humanity as the sole sovereignty on earth. As Ivan's devil questions in *The Brothers Karamazov*, if "God" were eradicated from the image of humankind, what is then to become of the meaning of "humanity?"[192] This is one of the central questions that Dostoevsky explores in his poetic work. Or consider the "madman" in Nietzsche's *The Gay Science*, who questions the implications of the death of God, which no one else seems yet to notice: "What festivals of atonement, what sacred games shall we have to invent? Is not the greatness of this deed too great for us? Must we ourselves not become gods simply to appear worthy of it?"[193] In the death of the Christian God, modern Westerners are seeking to fill the void with new images and idols. For de Lubac, atheistic humanism is the creative force that engenders these new images of divine sovereignty.

192. Dostoevsky, *Brothers Karamazov*, 648.
193. Nietzsche, *Gay Science*, 181.

Moreover, for Dostoevsky, Nietzsche, and de Lubac, these religious questions have no less social and political importance: What ultimate values shape our conception of humanity and, therefore, structure the way we live? How does our conception of "good and evil"—moral valuations—shape our politics?[194] How does our conception of the "divine" and the "human" inform our practice of power?[195] This is the basic question of the meaning of theological sovereignty for political valuation and moral judgment. As Nietzsche asserted, if we have murdered "God," then what festivals must we invent? What myths of theological sovereignty must we create to ensure a healthy politic?[196]

For de Lubac, this means a consideration on the "myth-making" of these authors for the sake of attending to the mystery of the divine embodied in human existence. This mystery does not preclude the experience of suffering in human existence. As we will see in their poetics, desire and suffering are intimately connected. Moreover, according to de Lubac, especially in his examination of *The Birth of Tragedy*, there is a basic theme that undergirds Nietzsche's thought (this could be applied to Dostoevsky as well): "the relationship that art and culture as a whole (that is to say, everything that counts in humanity) bears to suffering."[197] The poetics of Nietzsche and Dostoevsky are attuned to the tragic element of life. How does theological poetics address the mystery of divine embodiment in the context of human suffering? As de Lubac interprets *The Birth of Tragedy*, Nietzsche attempts to go beyond the "Socratic" rationalism of modernism, which Nietzsche perceived as the dominant "Apollinism" of the West. Modern rationalism reflects a sick despair of life and longs for the "otherworldly hope."[198] It despises life and suffering in the body. Therefore, argues de Lubac, Nietzsche unearthed the sovereignty of the

---

194. These questions are not disconnected from the political theological problem posed by Carl Schmitt, whereby "sovereignty decides on the exception." They are also not disconnected from a biblical conception of sovereignty: political sovereignty too reflects the "image of God" in humankind, the desire to "have dominion over the earth" (Gen. 1:26–28). Schmitt, *Political Theology*, 5.

195. The question could also be inverted: What does our politics reveal about our conception of the divine?

196. Chapters 4 and 5 will address Nietzsche's and Dostoevsky's responses to the question of the death of God in Western culture and the mediational images they perceived as necessary for engendering a new politic for Western civilization.

197. De Lubac, *Drama of Atheist Humanism*, 76.

198. We will examine this in greater detail in chapter 2.

"subterranean kingdom of dark Dionysus."[199] According to de Lubac, for Nietzsche, "Dionysus" is the god most authentic to human existence, a paradoxical demonic substratum of earthly chaos that created human rationality.[200] Modern rationality has stripped away the mystical element in human existence, largely in denial of "Dionysus." As de Lubac interprets Nietzsche, the "Socratic man," is "'monstrously deficient in a sense of mysticism'—so much so that Socrates might serve as the type of nonmystical man, in whom 'the logical bent is developed to excess by superfetation, as instinctive wisdom is in the mystic.'"[201] This Socratic spirit is essentially a "myth destroying spirit." And a person or culture "starved of myths is a [person] without roots."[202] Within this formulation, modernism can be described as a problem of radical abstraction, the separation and strict distinction between the transcendent and the immanent, dissolving the mystery of the divine potential in the human. As de Lubac reads Nietzsche, the consequence of the Socratic rationalism of Western culture is a historicism that sucks the life out of culture and civilization. And, therefore, this modernist historicism lacks the ability to account for the meaning of suffering, domesticating our "knowledge" so that all mystery, the mystic element of existence, is lost. Losing the substratum of myth, argues de Lubac on Nietzsche, our civilization is now condemned to "exhaust all possibilities and to sustain its wretched existence at the cost of other civilizations . . . What accounts for the prodigious appetite of modern civilized man for historical knowledge, his way of gathering around him innumerable civilizations, his need to know everything? What can it be but that we have lost the bread that fed us, we have lost Myth?"[203]

In sympathy with Nietzsche's critique of the rational Socratic spirit of modernism, de Lubac asserts, "There is probably no thinking person today who does not feel the shallowness and impoverishment of a certain kind of intellectualism and the barrenness of a certain abuse of the historic discipline."[204] In the church itself, "reaching out beyond logical forms and methods of exposition that owed much to a Cartesian tradition of

---

199. De Lubac, *Drama of Atheist Humanism*, 75.
200. De Lubac, *Drama of Atheist Humanism*, 75–76.
201. De Lubac, *Drama of Atheist Humanism*, 80.
202. De Lubac, *Drama of Atheist Humanism*, 80.
203. De Lubac, *Drama of Atheist Humanism*, 80.
204. De Lubac, *Drama of Atheist Humanism*, 85.

scholarship, we have linked up again with a more substantial tradition."[205] That is, there has been a more "decided turn to the golden age of medieval thought, that of St. Thomas and Saint Bonaventure; and this movement of return, increasingly apparent, is gradually restoring the climate of 'mystery' that was eminently the climate of patristic thought."[206] For de Lubac, this means relearning the use and understanding of symbols: "We are feeling the need to go back to the deep springs, to investigate them with other instruments than clear ideas alone, to re-establish a life-giving and fruitful contact with the fostering soil."[207] Symbols are, of course, images that represent particular ideas and intellectual constructs. Symbols mediate reality indirectly as mediums of meaning. Symbols embody ideas and are the basis of poetics, the preferred mode of communication of thinkers such as Dostoevsky and Nietzsche. Symbols may become *icons*, images that mystically mediate between the transcendent and the immanent. Symbols as icons become mediations of forms of desire, bridges that draw the embodied soul upward into the divine. According to de Lubac, the use of symbols does not entail the elimination of "knowledge" or "reason," but rather that "we will no longer tolerate a divorce between knowledge and life."[208] This does not mean that we "set about creating a mythology in willful darkness, any mythology, no matter what."[209]

We turn our attention now briefly to Lubac's reading of Dostoevsky, he who also acknowledged the tragic suffering of life as well as the significance of myth that unveils the mystery. This is why Dostoevsky is more than a "psychologist" in the modernist sense of the term: "I am a realist in the highest sense of the term; that is to say, I show the depths of the human soul."[210] As I will show in greater detail in the next chapter, this is because Dostoevsky viewed the soul or the human psyche as the place where the divine image of God was reflected and embodied. For Dostoevsky, argues de Lubac, there is the deeper, God-created-image in humankind that is the "natural" receptacle of divine light and grace that comes through the mystery of divine revelation. Berdyaev describes well how the poetic for Dostoevsky expresses the mystery: "The truth is that

---

205. De Lubac, *Drama of Atheist Humanism*, 85.
206. De Lubac, *Drama of Atheist Humanism*, 85.
207. De Lubac, *Drama of Atheist Humanism*, 85.
208. De Lubac, *Drama of Atheist Humanism*, 86.
209. De Lubac, *Drama of Atheist Humanism*, 86.
210. De Lubac, *Drama of Atheist Humanism*, 274.

all essential art is symbolic: it is a bridge built between two worlds, a sign that expresses a deep, authentic reality; the end of art surpasses experimental reality and is to express hidden reality, not in a direct way, but by means of projected shadows."[211] In other words, Dostoevsky's novels are poetic expressions of the spirit intertwined with the flesh, the divine transcendence enmeshed in the immanence of human existence, which includes the experience of suffering. Dostoevsky's poetics reflect the struggle with God. De Lubac's quotation of Henri Troyat on the heroes of Dostoevsky's novels is poignant: "What torments these beings is not illness or fear of tomorrow: it is God. Their author obligingly relieves them of petty everyday worries to leave them, naked, face to face with Mystery. Their active life corresponds to our underlying life."[212] Our fifth chapter will examine this more thoroughly in a consideration of Dostoevsky's portrait of the "hero" of *The Brothers Karamazov*, Alyosha.

Returning to the problem of the "drama of atheist humanism" as the rationale for another comparative examination between Dostoevsky and Nietzsche, the question for Western civilization posed by de Lubac in light of the movement away from the mystery of Christ, is whether we are heading toward an age of "deliberate barbarism."[213] Is that the age in which we live? That is, "will it be possible, we ask ourselves, to rediscover some myth for our salvation, or shall we be engulfed by a catastrophe?"[214] This is a primordial question, and one that Nietzsche and Dostoevsky contended with. However, their responses profoundly differ. As de Lubac suggests, despite their convergence on a critique of modernism, Nietzsche and Dostoevsky are "hostile brothers."[215] While they agree regarding the impoverishment of modern secular rationalism as the embodiment of sovereignty in Western culture, they diverge on the question of "God." We must again return to those "accursed eternal questions," as Dostoevsky called them. The question of eternity and the desire for transcendence permeates the work of Nietzsche and Dostoevsky.

Nonetheless, at this point, argues de Lubac, a "second discernment becomes necessary, a spiritual discernment."[216] De Lubac asserts that

211. Berdyaev, *Dostoevsky*, 25.

212. De Lubac, *Drama of Atheist Humanism*, 275. The quotation is taken from Henri Troyat, *Fyodor Dostoevsky*, 567.

213. De Lubac, *Drama of Atheist Humanism*, 90.

214. De Lubac, *Drama of Atheist Humanism*, 90.

215. De Lubac, *Drama of Atheist Humanism*, 277.

216. De Lubac, *Drama of Atheist Humanism*, 91.

Nietzsche made no distinction between myth and mystery, "whereas a selective use could be made of these words to signify two opposite types of sacredness."[217] Although connected, for de Lubac there is a wide gulf between these two words:

> There is the sacredness of myth, which like a vapor rising from the earth, emanates from infrahuman regions; and there is the sacredness of mystery, which is like peace descending from the heavens. The one links us with Nature and attunes us to her rhythm but also enslaves us to her fatal powers; the other is the gift of the spirit that makes us free. One finds its embodiment in symbols that man molds as he pleases, and into which he projects his terrors and his desires; the symbols of the other are received from on high by man who, in contemplating them, discovers the secret of his nobility. In concrete terms, there is the pagan myth and the Christian mystery.[218]

Myth and mystery certainly can both engender a *mystique*, but these *mystiques* are "as opposite in character as in origin: one is the Dionysian state, with its 'heady, feverish, ambiguous' irrationality; the other is the chaste and sober rapture of the Spirit. If both shatter individuality . . . their ways of doing so are very different, for the first only succeeds in merging the human being in the life of the cosmos—or in that of a society itself wholly of this earth—while the second exalts the most personal element in each individual in order to create a fellowship among all [people]."[219] Mystery, of course, still makes use of myth, taking over "a part of it, filters it, purifies it—exorcises it, as it were. There is an authentic sacredness in the cosmos, for it is full of the 'vestiges' of divinity. There *is* a '*mystique* of the earth.'" But, argues de Lubac, myth needs to be christianized: "When it aspires to reign alone, it is no longer even terrestrial; the mark of the Spirit of Evil is upon it."[220] This difference, suggests de Lubac, the difference between myth and mystery, despite the overlapping thematic tendency, is the difference between the poetics of Nietzsche and Dostoevsky. Although they both write in the language of "myth," and even more so in the symbolic language of the apocalyptic, Nietzsche's apocalyptic is thoroughly envisioned as immanence rising to create an immanent-transcendence, whereas Dostoevsky's poetics reflect the mediation of the

---

217. De Lubac, *Drama of Atheist Humanism*, 91.
218. De Lubac, *Drama of Atheist Humanism*, 91.
219. De Lubac, *Drama of Atheist Humanism*, 91–92.
220. De Lubac, *Drama of Atheist Humanism*, 92.

transcendence as a divine sovereignty redeeming the immanent. This is how I will be interpreting their poetics.

These two thinkers differ on the question of the mystery revealed in the Incarnation. Nietzsche and Dostoevsky both lived and wrote within the Western context with its deep Christendom heritage. As de Lubac asserts, the "God" in question, for both Nietzsche and Dostoevsky, is always the Christian God.[221] More specifically, with Nikolai Berdyaev, de Lubac perceived in the difference of their thought the relentless questioning of the meaning of humanity *after* humanism, the dramatic apocalyptic struggle between Christ and antichrist. That is, their poetics are both oriented toward the *messianic*. As I will demonstrate, these are diametrically opposed mystical visions, which suggest two differing forms of political embodiment. Is it possible for Western culture to construct a political order apart from Christ? This question does not imply that the West was ever predominantly "Christian" in the de Lubacian sense. As I will show, both Dostoevsky and Nietzsche perceived that a spirit of revenge and retribution underlies Western thought. For Dostoevsky, the "spirit of revenge" also corrupted the church's mystical witness of apocalyptic "realism."

For Nietzsche, the "spirit of revenge" is the power that created the church and its mythology of a Christian apocalyptic. For Nietzsche, the systemic political structures of the church and modern state in the West are the crisis. These political structures must be overcome and negated. But this "overcoming" will not occur simply through a violent, political revolution, but rather through the creation of a new values. This pertains to Nietzsche's vision of the Übermensch, which we will explore in the following chapters. The overcoming of the Western church and the modern state is really the question of the possibility of a *unifying image* that mystically engenders—mediates—a redemptive, messianic politics. For Dostoevsky and Nietzsche, the future health and destiny of humanity pertains to the political choice between Christ and antichrist, to differing visions of human freedom and sovereignty. The "destiny" of Western civilization, for Nietzsche and Dostoevsky, relates to the stark contrast between a politics of the God-human or the Human-god, the sovereignty of the Judeo-Christian *Messiah* or the Dionysian Übermensch. For de Lubac, this is the modern apocalyptic drama in which "we are all actors."[222] De Lubac did not perceive himself as a mere spectator in this drama, nor did Nietzsche

---

221. De Lubac, *Drama of Atheist Humanism*, 114, 297.
222. De Lubac, *Drama of Atheist Humanism*, 277.

and Dostoevsky. They were personally invested in their pursuit of "God," for a "metaphysic," or a conception of the "supernatural" or the rejection of one for the redemption of the West's political culture. Along with de Lubac, I contend their poetics still provide fruitful soil in which to reflect on the questions of political theology in Western thought.

2

Karamazovian Desire and the Politics of the Inquisitor in *The Brothers Karamazov*

Introduction

IN *THE DRAMA OF Atheist Humanism*, de Lubac compares Nietzsche with the other "prophet" of the West, Fyodor Dostoevsky. He asserts that the work of Dostoevsky became more and more prophetic as he grew in stature.[1] De Lubac does not understand the prophetic nature of this work as merely predictive: "Dostoevsky drew in advance upon new forms of thought and of inward life which, through him, imposed themselves upon man and became a part of his heritage."[2] It is precisely his passionate questioning and exploration into the human spirit in relation to the mystery of God that unveils the particular prophetic quality of his literary art. It is not so much a question of doctrine (although not disconnected from doctrinal questions), as it is a question of the human spirit: "Dostoevsky was a prophet: because he not only revealed to man the depths that are in him, but opened up fresh ones for him, giving him, as it were, a new dimension; because in this way, he foreshadowed a new

---

1. De Lubac, *Drama of Atheist Humanism*, 275.
2. De Lubac, *Drama of Atheist Humanism*, 276.

state of humanity."³ We will explore this "new state" further in chapter 5, but it is prophetically expressed in the "new birth" of Alyosha. As we have seen in de Lubac, this entails the sacramental mediation of Christ in the *corpus mysticum*. In this chapter and the next, I explore the theme of "desire" in relation to the politics of the church and state in the poetics of Dostoevsky and Nietzsche. In fact, we could state that "desire" is the precise problem in their poetics, not only the passions of the body, but the embedded desire for transcendence and for "eternity." We will continue to focus on the theme of humanity as the image of God, especially as the natural relates to and is conjoined with the "supernatural" or, in the case of Nietzsche, the "suprasensual."⁴ As I mentioned in the introduction, de Lubac states with respect to Dostoevsky, "In analyzing his books, it would be possible to trace a mysticism of life, or, more precisely, a telluric mysticism not unlike the cult of Dionysus."⁵ However, at stake is the particular attitude and appropriation of desire. How does faith or intellectual disposition shape desire? If the intrinsic desire and love for life has been severed from God, what consequences follow?

It may be argued that Dostoevsky himself struggled with doubt and skepticism. As de Lubac said about the cry of Kirillov in *Demons*, "God has tormented me all my life," and this is also Dostoevsky's cry.⁶ For de Lubac, Dostoevsky "penetrated, in advance, into the lonely world where Nietzsche was soon to venture. He had a prophetic awareness of the crisis . . . of which Nietzsche was to make himself the herald and the artificer . . . He lived it. He was present at the 'death of God.'"⁷ However, rather than succumbing to the atheism he envisioned in the ideal of the overman he foresaw, "despite his complicities [Dostoevsky] was aware of harboring, he very deliberately, though not without repeated struggles, decided against them."⁸ In this way, argues de Lubac, Dostoevsky did more than foreshadow Nietzsche: "To put the matter succinctly, he forestalled Nietzsche. He overcame the temptation to which Nietzsche was to succumb."⁹ Yet the characters in Dostoevsky's novels still give witness

---

3. De Lubac, *Drama of Atheist Humanism*, 276.
4. This is a term I borrow from Stefan Zweig in *Struggle with the Daemon*, 11.
5. De Lubac, *Drama of Atheist Humanism*, 280.
6. De Lubac, *Drama of Atheist Humanism*, 285. See Dostoevsky, *Demons*, 116.
7. De Lubac, *Drama of Atheist Humanism*, 284.
8. De Lubac, *Drama of Atheist Humanism*, 284.
9. De Lubac, *Drama of Atheist Humanism*, 285.

to a variety of forms of expression of atheism, which the novelist not only observed in others, but also in himself, revealing the complexity and depth of his mind. Dostoevsky began his writing career in the literary circles where atheistic socialism was taking hold of the imagination of the Russian intelligentsia. He was influenced by atheistic socialists such as the influential Russian literary critic Belinsky.[10] Nonetheless, a great turn was taken in his life when he was sent to imprisonment in Siberia, accused of revolutionary insurrectionism. There he grappled deeply with the Gospel as he lived among Russian criminals. We address his spiritual transformation further in the next chapter.

With respect to the development of *The Brothers Karamazov*, initially Dostoevsky planned to write a five-volume work called "The Life of a Great Sinner," containing "everything for which (he himself had lived)."[11] The chief problem would be, stated Dostoevsky, "the one that has consciously and unconsciously tortured me all my life: the problem of the existence of God. In the course of his life the hero will be now an atheist, now a believer, now a fanatic, now a heresiarch, and then an atheist once more."[12] *The Brothers Karamazov* was the last novel that Dostoevsky published. Before his death, Dostoevsky reflected on the criticism he received on this work: "The dolts have ridiculed my obscurantism and the reactionary character of my faith. These fools could not even conceive so strong a denial of God as the one to which I gave expression . . . The whole book is an answer to *that*. You might search Europe in vain for so powerful an expression of atheism. Thus, it is not like a child that I believe in Christ and confess him. My hosanna has come forth from the crucible of doubt."[13] It is this "doubt," and, the skepticism of Ivan Karamazov that I explore in this chapter. However, this is set up by addressing the underlying problem of the Karamazovian desire as it is expressed through the father of the novel, Fyodor, and his first son, Mitya.

Karamazovian Desire

This section is structured in three movements. First, I examine Fyodor Karamazov in relation to sensual desire. I interpret the character of

10. Ward, *Dostoyevsky's Critique of the West*, 9–34.
11. De Lubac, *Drama of Atheist Humanism*, 286.
12. De Lubac, *Drama of Atheist Humanism*, 286.
13. De Lubac, *Drama of Atheist Humanism*, 296.

Fyodor as representing the most basic crisis in the novel, the question of "sensuality" and the inordinate obsession with what Zosima describes as the "lower" aspect of human nature, at the expense of the higher spiritual aspect, "but the spiritual world, the higher half of man's being, is altogether rejected, banished with a sort of triumph, even with hatred."[14] I suggest that Fyodor is also a cultural representation of the decadence of an increasingly modernist Russia. Dostoevsky attempts to link the perversity of Fyodor's Karamazovian desire as the underlying cause to the increasing atheism of the age, even if Fyodor signifies a crude form of this secularization. Second, I then consider his first son, Mitya, and demonstrate the complexity of desire. Humans are embodied souls and the nexus of a spiritual warfare between God and the devil, which revolves around the desire for higher beauty. In Mitya's case, his desire for Grushenka puts him in a twisted rivalry with his own father, who cheats him out of his inheritance, to swindle Grushenka from under his son. This provides what I would argue is the surface conflict of the plot of the novel. Mitya is a tormented soul who desires the divine, but cannot master passional, bodily desire, thus plaguing and torturing his conscience. Third, I then argue that "earthly" Karamazovian desire can expresses itself metaphysically in the desire for the transcendent. However, within Dostoevsky's theological framework, disconnected from the Incarnation and understanding humanity as created in the image of God, the desire to create a "higher image" of humanity only results in demonic "monstrosities." This analysis of Karamazovian desire situates us in a better position to consider the retribution of Ivan and his creation of the Grand Inquisitor. The demonic "monstrosities" in the novel are precisely the deceptive, false mediational attempts to unite the transcendent and the immanent, with the intent of bringing control over Karamazovian desire. This pertains to the idolatrous creation of darkened images of the divine, which then mediate a coercive politics of retribution.

Fyodor Karamazov and Sensual Desire

Part I of the novel introduces us to the characters in the family, as well as the primary conflict between father and son, Fyodor and Mitya respectively.[15] They are in conflict over the beautiful Grushenka, and the

---

14. Dostoevsky, *Brothers Karamazov*, 313.
15. Dostoevsky, *Brothers Karamazov*, 23.

scandal upsurges to the point where Fyodor Pavlovich in a fit of passion threatens Mitya: "Suddenly [Fyodor] screamed in a voice not his own, 'If only you weren't my son, I would challenge you to a duel this very moment . . . with pistols, at three paces . . . across a handkerchief! across a handkerchief!'"[16] Already at the very outset of the novel, the reader is forewarned about his "dark and tragic death."[17] He is also described as a landowner, who was a greedy "sponger," and an "evil buffoon and nothing more," despite his first wife initially perceiving him as "one of the boldest and sarcastic spirits of the transitional epoch—transitional to everything better."[18] However, the emerging picture in the novel is that he is primarily a "sensualist," who simply lived for the immediate desires of the flesh.[19] As one who pursues his own selfish pleasure, what we observe in the first few chapters is, whereby the narrator also describes Fyodor's three sons, his noted absence from their lives. However, in the chapter "The Third Son, Alyosha," there is an interesting description of Fyodor's "physiognomy," which the narrator asserts, "testified to the characteristic and essence of his whole life."[20] The picture is one of sagging skin and decay,[21] but with a few peculiar features that he himself was aware of: "He pointed especially to his nose, which was not very big but was very thin and noticeably, hooked. 'A real Roman one,' he used to say. 'Along with my Adam's apple, it gives me the real physiognomy of an ancient Roman patrician of the decadent period.'"[22] This detail is not insignificant and suggests that Fyodor also represents a kind of political decadence of the "landowner" class of Russian society of which he was a member. As representative of the "transitional epoch," we also see he

16. Dostovesky, *Brothers Karamazov*, 73.
17. Dostoevsky, *Brothers Karamazov*, 8.
18. Dostoevsky, *Brothers Karamazov*, 8.
19. Dostoevsky, *Brothers Karamazov*, 8.
20. Dostoevsky, *Brothers Karamazov*, 23.
21. He is described as having "long, fleshy bags under his eternally insolent, suspicious, and leering little eyes, besides multiple of deep wrinkles on his fat little face, a big Adam's apple, fleshy and oblong like a purse, hung below his sharp chin, giving him a sort of repulsively sensual appearance." Dostoevsky, *Brothers Karamazov*, 23.
22. Dostoevsky, *Brothers Karamazov*, 23. In the Russian, "Впрочем, и сам он любил шутить над своим лицом, хотя, кажется, оставался им доволен. Особенно указывал он на свой нос, не очень большой, но очень тонкий, с сильно выдающеюся горбиной: «Настоящий римский,—говорил он,—вместе с кадыком настоящая физи ономия древнего римского патриция времен упадка». Этим он, кажется, гордился."

is a "muddleheaded" atheist, whose intellectual views are more sarcastic than substantial. We observe this in the same chapter in his conversation with Alyosha, where Fyodor makes light of the nearby monastery, quick to point out the moral hypocrisy of the monastic community.[23] This is because, ultimately, Fyodor, as a "sensualist," who only understands the "realism" of the flesh and its immanent desires.

Furthermore, as we see in the elder's cell in the chapter "The Old Buffoon," more is unveiled about the character of Fyodor: "I am a natural-born buffoon, I am, reverend father, just like a holy fool, I won't deny that there's maybe an unclean spirit living in me, too, not a very high caliber one, by the way."[24] He is characterized as one who is lost in self-deception, enslaved to desires that are seemingly beyond his control and concern for the responsibility of others. He is a buffoon, and a kind of sarcastic trickster, whom no one can trust. However, although Fyodor acts shamelessly in social situations, the elder Zosima suggests that the root problem is precisely shame: "Be at ease and feel completely at home. And above all do not be so ashamed of yourself, for that is the cause of everything."[25] Fyodor plays the fool because he already perceives that his social standing is that of the buffoon. Therefore, his buffoonery derives from resentment that is rooted in shame. Fyodor lacks all self-respect and has no sense of the dignity of the self. Fyodor is created in the image of God, but he has denied the "higher" aspect of himself, although he cannot escape it either. This requires some brief explanation.

Theologically speaking, sensuality for Dostoevsky is only one aspect of the nature of humanity, the higher spiritual aspect being the other. The concept of the image of God is crucial for understanding Dostoevsky's conception of humanity, a conception deeply connected to the Orthodox tradition in which the image of God in humankind represents the "whole"

---

23. Fyodor accuses them of sexual immorality. Dostoevsky, *Brothers Karamazov*, 24.

24. Dostoevsky, *Brothers Karamazov*, 41. In the Russian, "Я шут коренной, с рождения, всё равно, ваше преподобие, что юродивый; не спорю, что и дух нечистый, может, во мне заключается, небольшого, впрочем, калибра, по важнее-то другую бы квартиру выбрал, только не вашу, Петр Александрович, и вы ведь квартира неважная."

25. Dostoevsky, *Brothers Karamazov*, 43. In the Russian, "Убедительной вас прошу не беспокоиться и не стесняться,—внушительно проговорил ему старец...—Не стесняйтесь, будьте совершенно как дома. А главное, не стыдитесь столь самого себя, ибо от сего лишь всё и выходит."

of humanity. The link between the transcendent and the immanent is a mystical reality. We cite the important words of the elder Zosima:

> Much on earth is concealed [скрыто] from us, but in place of it we have been granted a secret, mysterious [сокровенное] sense of our living bond with the other world, with the higher heavenly world, and the roots of our thoughts and feelings are not here but in other worlds. . . . God took the seeds from other worlds and sowed them on this earth, and raised up his garden; and everything that could sprout sprouted, but it lives and grows only through its sense of being in touch with other mysterious worlds [таинственным мирам]; if the sense is weakened or destroyed in you, that which has grown up in you dies.[26]

For Zosima, there is an intrinsic connection between our human "nature" and the higher transcendent world. Dostoevsky understands this mystically. The connection between the two worlds is concealed from us, but they form the basis of our understanding of humanity. This is the basis for Dostoevsky's emphasis on the immortality of the soul. It is the embodied soul of humanity that forms the nexus of that bond between the two worlds. As we saw above in de Lubac as well, this is the dignity of humanity created in the image of God. However, Dostoevsky goes further than de Lubac in exploring the "immanent" reality of bodily desire in relation to the spirit and the psyche. For Dostoevsky, this mystical link between the body and the spirit constitutes the essence of human freedom. Moreover, like de Lubac, it is also what links all persons together into an integrated, embodied, spiritual "whole" of a humanity created in the image of God. Considering the text quoted above, we also note the organic poetic language used to express the connection, the "seeds from other worlds," which are sown in this one, generating, creating, growing—living. The higher transcendent world is what sustains the lower immanent one. Humanity was not meant to remain the same,

---

26. *The Brothers Karamazov*, 320. In the Russian, "Многое на земле от нас скрыто, но взамен того даровано нам тайное сокровенное ощущение живой связи нашей с миром иным, с миром горним и высшим, да и корни наших мыслей и чувств не здесь, а в мирах иных. Вот почему и говорят философы, что сущности вещей нельзя постичь на земле. Бог взял семена из миров иных и посеял на сей земле и взрастил сад свой, и взошло всё, что могло взойти, но взращенное живет и живо лишь чувством соприкосно вения своего таинственным мирам иным; если ослабевает или уничтожается в тебе сие чувство, то умирает и взращенное в тебе. Тогда станешь к жизни равнодушен и даже возненавидишь ее. Мыслю так."

but to "naturally" grow into its transcendent destiny. This presupposition is comparable, I suggest, with de Lubac's conception of nature oriented toward the supernatural. Indeed, for Dostoevsky, it is precisely human nature in its "natural" freedom to choose between good and evil that reflects the divine image.

Returning to the elder's interaction with Fyodor, Fyodor has completely denied the higher aspect of himself and has become a faded ghost of his true self, covering his shame through the pretension of being shameless. As a result, argues Zosima, disregarding the thoughts of others, Fyodor shamelessly pursues sensual desire, blinded by erotic passion:

> Above all, do not lie to yourself. A man who lies to himself and listens to his own lie comes to a point where he does not discern any truth either in himself or anywhere around him, and thus falls into disrespect towards himself and others. Not respecting anyone, he ceases to love, he gives himself up to passions and coarse pleasures, in order to occupy and amuse himself, and in his vices reaches complete bestiality, and it all comes from lying to others and to himself.[27]

Following the logic of Zosima's diagnosis of Fyodor, if shame is the cause, it engenders the lie, the deception of the denial of one's fundamental dignity as created in the image of God. The self turns away from the "whole" of humanity in which it was intricately created, essentially in denial of its most authentic self in egotistical desire. Moreover, this self-deception has elevated the sensual aspect of its being, resulting in a perpetual existence of offence and resentment: "A man who lies to himself is often the first to take offense."[28] In fact, one comes to love and find beauty in the offence, in the resentment, even so, the desire for revenge: "It sometimes feels very good to take offense, doesn't it? And surely, he knows that none has offended him, and that he himself has invented the offense and told lies just for the beauty of it."[29] The love of resentment

---

27. Dostoevsky, *Brothers Karamazov*, 44. In the Russian, "Главное, самому себе не лгите. Лгущий самому себе и собственную ложь свою слушающий до того доходит, что уж никакой правды ни в себе, ни кругом не различает, а стало быть, входит в неуважение и к себе и к другим. Не уважая же никого, перестает любить, а чтобы, не имея любви, занять себя и развлечь, предается страстям и грубым сладостям и доходит совсем до скотства в пороках своих, а всё от беспрерывной лжи и людям и себе самому. Лгущий себе самому прежде всех и обидеться может."

28. Dostoevsky, *Brothers Karamazov*, 44.

29. Dostoevsky, *Brothers Karamazov*, 44. In the Russian, "Ведь обидеться иногда

is the result of a lie that has twisted the "higher" spiritual aspect of the self, a lie that denies and suppresses the higher desire for God. However, Fyodor mockingly acknowledges Zosima's diagnosis of the love of and the finding of, beauty in resentment and offence: "Beautiful! I'll make a note of that! And I've lied, I've lied decidedly all my life, every day and every hour. Verily I am a lie and the father of a lie (Воистину ложь есмь и отец лжи!)!"[30] Dostoevsky raises to the fore the deceptive, demonic nature of making the immanent sovereign with an allusion to John 8, where Jesus challenges his opponents with the nature of their true demonic origin, whereby the devil was "a murderer from the beginning" (John 8:44). That is, the devil is the twisted desire that tempted Cain to murder his brother in passion and envy for his brother (Gen 4). In *The Brothers Karamazov*, it is not the brother who is the object of envy and hatred, but the father is envious of the son and vice versa. For Fyodor is a shameless man who has lost all self-respect in relation to the "whole of humanity." Sensuality has become sovereign. This sovereign debauchery drives the plot of the narrative, as when we are informed by the narrator of the circumstances that gave birth to the fourth, bastard, son Smyerdyakov, who is arguably the most tragic figure in the novel. It is worth noting that the chapter "Stinking Lizaveta" directly precedes the chapters on Mitya's "confessions" of the love of sensuality.[31] This love for the sensual is the Karamazovian force that, although created to reflect the image of God, is also the source of violence, oppression, chaos, and death in the world. In Augustinian (and de Lubacian) terms, it is the source and power of the "earthly city" as *libido dominandi*.[32] That is, the sensual desire represented in Fyodor, the brute force of the Karamazov, is the desire of life that, left to its own devices, leads to moral, social, and political chaos. Fyodor represents the basic, crudest form, but its expression can imitate higher forms as well, as we see

---

очень приятно, не так зо ли? И ведь знает человек, что никто не обидел его, а что он сам себе обиду навыдумал и налгал для красы, сам преувеличил, чтобы картины создать, к слову привязался и из горошинки сделал гору,—знает сам это, а все-таки самый первый оби жается, обижается до приятности, до ощущения большого удо вольствия, а тем самым доходит и до вражды истинной..."

30. Dostoevsky, *Brothers Karamazov*, 44.
31. Dostoevsky, *Brothers Karamazov*, 97.
32. This is taken from Augustine in *The City of God*, meaning "the desire to dominate." In the English translation he describes "that city which, when it seeks mastery, is itself by the lust for mastery [*libido dominandi*] even though all the nations serve it." Augustine, *City of God*, 3.

in Mitya, and then Ivan, the intellectual who will devise a political scheme in which to limit Karamazovian desire, yet still cannot escape it either.

Mitya and the Desire for Beauty

However, Karamazovian desire is more complex. What, however, precisely is, "sensuality," as understood within the novel? After the "scandal" in the elder's cell, where the conflict ensued between father and son, Fyodor and Mitya, Rakitin and Alyosha "debrief" the drama.[33] Speaking of Mitya, Rakitin too defines the essential conflict of the drama between the brothers as rooted in their father, Fyodor, as "sensualist": "I'll tell you one thing: granted he's an honest man, Mitenka, I mean (he's stupid but honest), still he's a sensualist. That is his definition, and his true inner essence. It's his father who gave him his base sensuality."[34] In the novel, Mitya gives expression to the meaning of sensuality. It is the bedrock of humanity, where earthly and heavenly desire mysteriously coincide and commingle. Sensuality is expressed as bodily passion and desire, but it is a desire that points to beauty beyond itself. The power of this sensuality, the "Karamazovian force" is akin, as we will see, to Nietzsche's "will to power" (*der Wille zur Macht*). It is the immanent world of desire for power and sovereignty. It is the power that leads, as Hobbes states, to perpetual war and human violence: "They are in that condition which is called Warre; and such a warre, as is of every man, against every man."[35] This is the "realism" that Dostoevsky wants to acknowledge and express, for it is this "realism" that justifies political forms of sovereignty represented in the "Grand Inquisitor."[36] For Dostoevsky, "sensuality," the Karamazovian desire for power, is essentially a spiritual problem. The hinge in which this desire turns is on the perception of *beauty*. Beauty is a form of power. If the higher spiritual aspect of humankind, created in the image of God, is ignored, the desire for beauty is fulfilled in alternative ways. It will create a "higher" beauty for itself that can only be a descent into hell—spiritual ugliness falsely perceived as beauty. That is,

---

33. The chapter "A Seminarist-Careerist" follows the chapter "Why Is Such a Man Alive?"

34. Dostoevsky, *Brothers Karamazov*, 79.

35. Hobbes, *Leviathan*, 185.

36. It is the "realism" that produces political manuals such as Machiavelli's *The Prince*.

it descends into the love of the *grotesque*. That is why for Mitya beauty is experienced as a spiritual riddle:

> And all of us Karamazovs are like that, and in you, an angel, the same insect lives and stirs up storms in your blood. Storms, because of sensuality [сладострастье] is a storm, more than a storm! Beauty [Красота] is a fearful and terrible thing! Fearful because it's undefinable, and it cannot be defined, because here God gave us only riddles [загадки]. Here the shores converge, here all contradictions live together . . . Beauty! Besides, I can't bear it that some man, even with a lofty heart and the highest mind, should start from the ideal of the Madonna and end with the ideal of Sodom . . . can beauty be Sodom? Believe me, for the vast majority of people, that's just where beauty lies—did you know that secret? The terrible thing is that beauty is not only fearful but also mysterious [таинственная]. Here the devil is struggling with God [дьявол с богом борется], and the battlefield is the human heart [сердца людей]. But, anyway, why kick against the pricks? Listen, now to real business.[37]

In this text, Dostoevsky suggests that the mystery of humanity is not only the problem of sensual depravity, but the *love of depravity*. That is, the human heart finds earthly sensual baseness, "depravity," beautiful. To be sure, this desire is perverted, but the desire for "Madonna" exists commingled with the desire for "Sodom." Of course, "Madonna" signifies the virgin Mary who gave birth to the Incarnate Messiah, a representation of

---

37. Dostoevsky, *Brothers Karamazov*, 108. In the Russian, "брат, это самое насекомое и есть, и это обо мне специально и сказано. И мы все, Карамазовы, такие же, и в тебе, ангеле, это насекомое живет и в крови твоей бури родит. Это—бури, потому что сладострастье буря, больше бури! Красота—это страшная и ужасная вещь! Страшная, потому что неопределимая, а опреде лить нельзя потому, что бог задал одни загадки. Тут берега сходятся, тут все противоречия вместе живут. Я, брат, очень необра зован, но я много об этом думал. Страшно много тайн! Слишком много загадок угнетают на земле человека. Разгадывай как знаешь э и вылезай сух из воды. Красота! Перенести я притом не могу, что иной, высший даже сердцем человек и с умом высоким, начинает с идеала Мадонны, а кончает идеалом содомским. Еще страшнее, кто уже с идеалом содомским в душе не отрицает и идеала Мадонны, и горит от него сердце его и воистину, воистину горит, как и в юные беспорочные годы. Нет, широк человек, слишком даже широк, я бы сузил. Черт знает что такое даже, вот что! Что уму представляется позором, то сердцу сплошь красотой. В содоме ли красота? Верь, что в содоме-то она и сидит для огромного большинства людей,—знал ты эту тайну иль нет? Ужасно то, что красота есть не только страшная, но и таинственная вещь. Тут дьявол с богом борется, а поле битвы—сердца людей. А впрочем, что у кого болит, тот о том и говорит. Слушай, теперь к самому делу."

the iconic mediational agency of Mary who is the *Theotokos*, the bearer of God, a symbol of humble servant before God.[38] As we will see in chapter 5, Alyosha is the embodiment of the beauty of Madonna, the humble, sacrificial servant love that mediates the love of the divine in the immanent.[39] The image of "Sodom" derives from the famous story in Genesis 19, whereby desire is perverted into violence: the men of the city seek to assault the visiting angels of God in the home of Abraham's nephew, Lot. Within the symbolic matrix of the Bible, culminating in the Apocalypse of John, Sodom represents all that is distorted and perverted within the creation of God, a mediation of demonic bestial desire.[40] For Mitya, the fundamental riddle is that the desire for the beauty of the "Madonna" and the desire for "Sodom" are mysteriously connected within the heart of humanity. The desire for the beauty of the higher transcendent cannot be separated from the desire for the immanent. Dostoevsky embeds Mitya's confession with Schiller's *An die Freude*, a poetic vision of an immanent "compact" with the earth: "That men again may soar, let man and Earth with one another Make a compact evermore—Man the son, and Earth the mother."[41] However, for Mitya, this earthly embodied existence, this "compact" with the immanence of the earth, results in the deep confusion of what is "stench and shame" or "light and joy." When he follows the desire of the heart, he falls into the abyss: "Because when I fall into the abyss, I go straight into it, head down and heels up, and I'm even pleased that I'm falling in just such a humiliating position, for me I find it beautiful."[42] Mitya loves the baseness, loves the unrestrained sexual passion, finds sensual pleasure in the power of force, loves the feeling of domination. We see this concentrated in the passion of Mitya, who publicly beats and humiliates an officer.[43] We see it in his humiliating

---

38. We will develop this further in chapter 3, when we examine Alyosha and the memory of his mother. See Ware, *Orthodox Church*, 250

39. This is already signaled when we are first introduced to Alyosha and the memory of his mother, before the icon, "sobbing as if in hysterics, with shrieks and cries, seizing him in her arms, hugging him so tightly that it hurt, and pleading for him to the Mother of God, holding him out from her embrace with both arms toward the icon, as if under the protection of the Mother of God." Dostoevsky, *Brothers Karamazov*, 19.

40. Other biblical reference to Sodom includes Isa. 13:19–22; Ezek. 16:48–50; 2 Pet 2:4–10; Jude 1:7; and Rev 11:7–8.

41. Dostoevsky, *Brothers Karamazov*, 107.

42. Dostoevsky, *Brothers Karamazov*, 107.

43. The whole episode with Ilyusha occurs because of the disgrace his father experiences due to Mitya's shaming and dishonouring him in a public humiliation.

rejection of Katya for Grushenka. And we see it in the intended murder of his own father, Fyodor. Mitya is a brute force of nature, an erotic lover, and the embodiment of the "will to power."

Furthermore, for Dostoevsky, this "riddle" of beauty is spiritual because human passional desire for what it conceives as beauty is the battleground between God and the devil. Through this poetic expression, Dostoevsky rediscovered the spiritual realm where God and Satan are a part of human experience. It is the spiritual meaning of embodied desire. What orients human desires is the particular conception of beauty. This also connects with the question between transcendence and immanence. There is, of course, sensual beauty, the desires of the body. But as Plato recognized in *The Symposium*, sensual erotic beauty is analogous to a higher, transcendent, spiritual and moral beauty.[44] For Plato, it was the demonic power of *eros* that mediated the soul from the mortal, immanent world in an ascent toward the immortal, transcendent world.[45] Dostoevsky, however, recognizes that there are varying conceptions of the "beauty" that draws desire, the contrasting ideals of the Madonna and of Sodom which are nevertheless related. *Eros*, the desire for the beautiful, is the Karamazovian force that is the reality of the immanence of human earthly existence. The image of God is embodied within *eros*, the Karamazovian force, intricately conjoined. For Dostoevsky, the sensual, erotic passion of the body is an integral aspect of what it means to be created in the image of God. This is what Zosima's teaching means: "God took the seeds from other worlds and sowed them on this earth."

This is the fundamental mystery of human nature, the freedom to choose between two ideals, two images of "beauty," as we have delineated between "Madonna" and "Sodom." We suggest that the Genesis narrative of the drama in the garden between God and humanity (Gen 1–3) is echoed in the context of Mitya's confession.[46] Mitya leads Alyosha through a lush, fruitful garden into a corner that is damp and in decay, a symbolic image of the corruption of Mitya's soul. We take note of the setting of Mitya's confession in a garden, fenced off and filled with "fruit bearing trees" (Gen 1:29), "The garden was about three acres or a little less, but there were trees planted only around it, along all four fences—apple trees, maples, lindens, birches . . . There were rows of raspberries,

---

44. Dostoevsky, *Brothers Karamazov*, 110.
45. Plato, *Symposium*, 2910A–204C.
46. Dostoevsky, *Brothers Karamazov*, 104.

gooseberries, currants . . . ; there was a vegetable garden up next to the house."[47] However, where Mitya takes Alyosha to a gazebo, "built God knows when . . . everything was decayed, the floor was rotted, all the planks were loose, the wood smelled of dampness.[48]

It is possible that Dostoevsky provides us with an allusion to the garden of Eden, but also the "decayed" state of Mitya's soul, which then gives us a theological poetic context in which to interpret Mitya's confessions. The conflict of the desire for beauty is reminiscent of the alternative desire awakened in the garden of Eden: "When the woman saw that the fruit of the tree was good for food and pleasing to the eye, and also desirable for wisdom, she took it and ate it (Gen. 3:60)."[49] We observe here that the material, the fruit good for food, leads also to a "transcendent" desire, the fruit desirable for wisdom. What Dostoevsky discovers is that the devil cannot eradicate the desire for beauty in the heart of humanity, but he can only create a distorted mediation of that desire for what is beautiful and desirable. In the novel, Mitya represents the conscience that suffers from the torment of desires he knows are perverted, moving in a spiritual trajectory that is opposite to that of the humble, servant love as represented in the Madonna and Alyosha. Whereas the father, Fyodor, seems to have severed himself from all desire for the beauty of Madonna and only relishes in desire for the grotesque, in Mitya, these two desires coexist, divine desire and demonic desire in conflict within him as mystery that goes beyond rational comprehension.

To reiterate, the entire plot of *The Brothers Karamazov* is structured on the passional rivalry of Mitya and his father for the same woman, Grushenka, which reveals the war of eternity for the heart. This spiritual battle is reflected in the "desire for beauty" and unleashes the passional desire of humanity. In Mitya we see the same "seed" of his shameless father who lives for his own earthly erotic desire. The structural centre of the novel is the chapter "In the Dark," where Mitya intends to murder his father for the "inheritance" that was withheld from him.[50] Instead, Fyodor preferred to give it to Grushenka, the "beauty" both he and Mitya desire. Mitya's story ends in tragedy after being accused of murdering his father. Of course, Fyodor was murdered by his (bastard) son, Smerdyakov,

---

47. Dostoevsky, *Brothers Karamazov*, 104.
48. Dostoevsky, *Brothers Karamazov*, 104.
49. Gen. 3:6.
50. Dostoevsky, *Brothers Karamazov*, 393.

whose mother was "Stinking" Lizaveta. However, during his trial, Mitya freely confesses that he is guilty of the *desire* to murder his father. Indeed, this is what all the brothers, especially Ivan, struggle with. Indeed, it was Ivan who inspired Smyerdyakov to murder Fyodor, believing this is what Ivan truly wanted and desired.

The question is whether this "Karamazov" force, the force of the "flesh," can be redeemed, as Alyosha puts it to Lisa: "My brothers are destroying themselves . . . my father too. And they're destroying others with them. This is the 'earthy force of the Karamazovs [земляная карамазовская сила],' as Father Paissy put it the other day—earthy, violent, raw . . . Whether the Spirit of God [дух божий] is moving over that force [силы]—even I do not know."[51] Books III and IV of *The Brothers Karamazov* follow the brothers in the aftermath of the murdered father. Mitya, the falsely accused, goes to trial and is imprisoned; Smyerdyakov, the murderer, commits suicide; and Ivan, the tormented brother whose theory "justifies" and seemed to encourage the murder, is now spiritually tortured. He becomes mentally ill. The brothers are caught between two transcendent trajectories, God and the devil. Each of them ends up in some form of isolation, either in prison, or mentally ill, or in suicide. The underlying connection, it seems, is that as beings created in the image of God, despite their grandiose aesthetic, intellectual, and sensual desires, they cannot escape their *conscience*. Their actions, which they attempt to justify on new ontological grounds, are still judged by a deeper reality of eternity within them. It is what de Lubac describes as the "ambiguous experience" of eternity in the poetics of Dostoevsky.[52] Dostoevsky recognizes that "eternity" is set in the heart of humanity as made in the divine image. If torn away from God, humans are embodied souls lost in the darkness of a corrupted image of the eternal. As they seek transcendence, they see a "myth" rising from nature, but it is in fact a spiritual descent in each case.

Berdyaev's reflections on Dostoevsky's conception of humanity and its experience with the spirit and desire is useful here, especially to

---

51. Dostoevsky, *Brothers Karamazov*, 220. In the Russian, "Братья губят себя,—продолжал он,—отец тоже. И дру гих губят вместе с собою. Тут «земляная карамазовская сила», как отец Паисий намедни выразился,—земляная и неистовая, необделанная . . . Даже носится ли дух божий вверху этой силы—и того не знаю. Знаю только, что и сам я Карамазов . . . Я монах, монах? Монах я, Lise? Вы как-то сказали сию минуту, что я монах?"

52. De Lubac, *Drama of Atheist Humanism*, 348.

appreciate Dostoevsky's metaphysical contribution in relation to Western thought. Dostoevsky helps moderns rediscover the spiritual realities of "God" and the "devil," not necessarily in the objective order, but in an honest consideration of the immanence of human experience. According to Berdyaev, "it is very instructive to compare the respective conceptions of man of Dante, Shakespeare, and Dostoevsky. For Dante (as for Thomas Aquinas) man is an organic part of the objective order of the world, the divine cosmos... God and Satan, Heaven and Hell are not revealed within the human spirit and by human experience: they are given to man from outside and they have reality equal to that of the objects in the material world."[53] However, when the "humanist era was established, with its self-affirmation and shutting-up of man within the walls of nature, Heaven and Hell were closed—but an infinity of worlds opened.... this is the humanistic period of modern times, during which man's creative forces have been played out. He is no longer bound by any objective world-order, given from above: he feels free."[54] However, Berdyaev asserts that:

> Dostoevsky appeared at another epoch and further stage in the history of humankind. For him too, man does not belong to the objective world-order of which Dante's man was a part. [But] during the course of the modern period man had tried to confine himself to the surface of the earth and the enclose himself within a purely human universe. God and Satan, Heaven and Hell were definitely relegated to the regions of the unknowable as having no communication in this world, until at length they were deprived of all reality.[55]

Nonetheless, as Berdyaev also states, "the time came when the creative and joyous energy that marked the Renaissance dried up, and man began to feel that the earth was not so solid under his feet as he had thought: sudden rumblings were heard and the volcanic nature of the underworld was manifested. In man himself an abyss opened and therein God and Heaven, the Devil and Hell are revealed anew."[56] Dostoevsky's literary art, therefore, is a "descent into Hell. But there, man will find not only Satan and his kingdom, but also God and Heaven.

---

53. Berdyaev, *Dostoevsky*, 46.
54. Berdyaev, *Dostoevsky*, 47.
55. Berdyeav, *Dostoevsky*, 48.
56. Berdyeav, *Dostoevsky*, 49.

Conceptions of "beauty" and the "ideal" are then twisted. "Doubles" are created to mock and torment. It ends in the suffering of isolation because it severs the soul apart from the intended "whole" of which it was created. In grasping for more, the self becomes less. Ultimately, there is "something" in humanity, suggests Dostoevsky, that is deeper than the "rational." There is an "irrational" element in humankind that is "subterranean," connected to the body, but also mysteriously transcendent. It is described well by de Lubac, "The human Eros, a ceaseless yearning for the infinite, pines at finding nothing on earth that is not alien to it."[57] It is similar to what de Lubac sought to establish as "the mystery of the supernatural"—the hidden, unconscious desire for the eternal that is intrinsically linked to our "naturally," earthly immanent existence. We cannot escape this desire for the eternal, where "beauty" is either completed in God or descends into the abyss. The human "desire" for beauty (and for power) is a riddle and the human heart is the battleground where the divine and the demonic contest for sovereignty. Humanity, created in the image of God, displays this mysterious drama as the power of the demonic lie disorders the heart, unleashing the chaos of violence.

The Demonic Desire to Create a "Higher Image"

While Fyodor is the basic, animalistic expression of Karamazovian desire, and Mitya, having a more sophisticated understanding, represents the fraught, spiritual desire for beauty of the heart, these examples prepare us for the greater metaphysical desire that seek to go beyond the image of God in which humanity is created. In fact, we see an example of an "ascetic sensuality" that seems to deny the significance of the body and the flesh altogether, as represented in Father Ferapont, who because of his strict monastic life of fasting and prayer created the mystique of representing an otherworldly existence, living only on mushrooms as a heroic ascetic, as he declares eccentrically to a visitor, "Right. I can do with without their bread, I don't need it at all, I can go to the forest and live on mushrooms and berries, but they can't do without their bread here, that's why they're in bondage to the devil. Nowadays these unclean ones say there's no need to fast so much. Arrogant and unclean is their reasoning."[58] Furthermore, Ferapont claims to have supernatural authority over demons as well as

---

57. De Lubac, *Drama of Atheist Humanism*, 341.
58. Dostoevsky, *Brothers Karamazov*, 168.

direct mystical communication with the Holy Spirit. Yet interestingly, he is terrified of Christ, even threatened by a nearby tree, "'It happens during the night. Do you see these two branches? In the night, behold, Christ stretches forth his arms to me, searching for me with these arms, I see it clearly and tremble. Fearsome, oh, fearsome!'"[59] As we will see in chapter 5, at the elder's death, Ferapont's envy and pride are more acutely exposed, revealing the "hell" in his own heart, the other side of spiritual pride, which denies completely the importance of the body and its desire.

Near the conclusion of the chapter, "Father Ferapont," Father Paissy instructs Alyosha that the modernist atheistic movement is essentially the attempt to create a higher image of humankind for itself. This conversation occurs after the "scandal" in the elder Zosima's cell, whereby at issue the relationship between the father, Fyodor, and his son, Mitya. In book I, we are introduced to Ivan as well, who wrote an article of the ecclesiastical, whose intellectual influence is pervasive in the narrative, especially his notion that, "if there is no immorality of the soul, then there is no virtue, and therefore everything is permitted." Book II addresses Ivan's atheism more closely and the moral and political implications of it. The next section will examine this in greater detail. However, what I want to emphasis here, is that according to Paissy, atheistic modernism is a rejection of the reunion of the "whole" as revealed in the sacred scriptures, especially as it culminates in the redemption of the Incarnation:

> The science of this world [мирская наука], having united itself into a great force, has especially in the past century, examined everything heavenly that has been bequeathed to us in the sacred books, and, after hard analysis, the learned ones of this world have absolutely nothing left of what was once holy. But they have examined parts and missed the whole [целое], and their blindness is even worthy of wonder. Meanwhile, the whole [целое] stands before their eyes as immovable as ever, and the gates of hell shall not prevail against it.[60]

---

59. Dostoevsky, *Brothers Karamazov*, 169.

60. Dostoevsky, *Brothers Karamazov*, 171. In the Russian, "Помни, юный, неустанно,—так прямо и безо всякого предисловия начал отец Паисий,—что мирская наука, соеди нившись в великую силу, разобрала, в последний век особенно, всё, что завещано в книгах святых нам небесного, и после жестокого анализа у ученых мира сего не осталось изо всей прежней святыни решительно ничего. Но разбирали они по частям, а целое просмотрели, и даже удивления достойно, до какой слепоты. Тогда как целое стоит пред их же глазами незыблемо2 как и преждеj и врата адовы не одолеют его."

In this text, Dostoevsky alludes to the scientific historicism of Western thought, which has read and dissected the scriptures to the point where the "whole" of which they give witness has been eradicated and destroyed. Scientific and historical analysis has excised all the mystery of the whole that links the scriptures with the living Tradition of the church. We see in *Brothers Karamazov* an attempt to poetically restore and express this "whole," the link between the Incarnation, the scriptures, the church in the teachings of Father Zosima at the end of book II. The essential issue here is not historical criticism per se, but the underlying spirit of it, "those who renounce Christianity and rebel against it are in their essence of the same image of the same Christ, and such they remain, for until now neither their wisdom nor the ardor of their hearts has been able to create another higher image of man [высшего образа человеку] and his dignity than the image [образ] shown of old by Christ. And whatever their attempts, the results have been only monstrosities [уродливости]."[61]

How Dostoevsky expresses these "monstrosities"—the desire to create a higher image than that of Christ—is the prophetic genius of his literary art.[62] The context of this statement by Paissy addressed to Alyosha at the outset of Part II is significant, for it anticipates Ivan and the monstrous creation of the Grand Inquisitor. The logic of Paissy's instruction implies that since the "whole" of humanity is represented in the messianic image of Christ, then the desire and the attempt to create a higher image beyond the "whole" of Christ can only become a deformity, a "monstrosity." It

---

61. Dostoevsky, *Brothers Karamazov*, 171. In the Russian, "Ибо и отрекшиеся от христианства и бунтующие против него в существе своем сами того же самого Христова облика суть, тако вымі же и остались, ибо до сих пор ни мудрость их, ни жар сердца их не в силах были создать иного высшего образа человеку и достоинству его, как образ, указанный древле Христом. А что было попыток, то выходили одни лишь уродливости."

62. De Lubac interprets atheistic humanism in Dostoevsky's poetics as a kind of "second self," a double which emerges from the inversion of the image of God in humankind. According to de Lubac, the idea of second self, a double, haunted Dostoevsky. It is the ambiguity about the mystical experience of eternity that creates the dualistic tension: "A double appears and materializes. A double which is himself and not himself. A double which is a hidden caricature of him, the distorting mirror in which his human face becomes blotched and bloated, loses its shape and takes on all the signs of an inward life that is under a curse." Ivan's "devil" is an extreme case of this. This "splitting of personality sometimes occurs in dreams, then forming a basis for actions to which nothing in one's thoughts—not even in one's involuntary reveries—corresponds; and yet 'everything has long been there in embryo' in the depths of one's heart." Thus, in every person "there is a mystery. Contraries coexist in him: he is two, and these two are one." De Lubac, *Drama of Atheist Humanism*, 252.

is a distorted reflection of the transcendent element and desire of the human soul. Why does this desire to create a higher image beyond the "whole" revealed in Christ exist? Why does the desire exist to *unite* the transcendent and the immanent in revolt against the incarnate "image," to go beyond the whole of which it was created? Certainly, it connects to the "mystery" and paradox of human nature itself as created in the image of God. As I will demonstrate below, it is connected to the mystery of human freedom. This, too, is rooted in Orthodox tradition, which Zosima and Paissy represent. As Timothy Ware asserts, "The image, or to use the Greek term *icon*, of God signifies our human free will, our reason, our sense of moral responsibility—everything, in short, which marks us out from the animal creation and makes each of us a *person*."[63] However, the "riddle" of the mystery of this desire is taken up with Mitya's "confessions," but then explored most fully in the Grand Inquisitor. Authentic "freedom," as Dostoevsky understands it redemptively, will be examined in chapter 5, through the portrait of Alyosha, who embodies the whole in becoming a servant to his brothers and a friend to the afflicted, such as Grushenka. Nonetheless, this interaction between Paissy and Alyosha is critical for it anticipates the dramatic encounter between Alyosha and Ivan later in Part II and the "temptation" that the Grand Inquisitor will pose for Alyosha: "Perhaps, remembering this great day, you will not forget my words either, given as cordial words of parting for you, because you are young and the temptations of the world are heavy and your strength will not endure them. Well, go now, my orphan."[64]

The Politics of the Grand Inquisitor

What, indeed, will transform the erotic Karamazovian earthy, brutal force? What will apprehend and bring order to the "mystery" that is humanity, created in the image of God, yet driven by the chaotic "freedom" of the desire? Is the Spirit of God completing the redeeming of the image of God or is the image of God in humankind being eradicated? Is it Christ or antichrist? The eradication of God in the West, as we see Dostoevsky's novel, is not only an abstract individual ordeal, but it also occurs in the rivalry between the church and the secular socialist state for the moral conscience of the people. It is a rivalry for the moral beauty that might

---

63. Ware, *Orthodox Church*, 213.
64. Dostoevsky, *Brothers Karamazov*, 171.

capture the conscience, the moral imagination at the heart of people in society. This political conflict is expressed throughout the novel, but we see it clearly in the chapter "So Be It! So Be It!" whereby an article of Ivan's on the question of the ecclesiastical courts is discussed, as well as in Ivan's infamous "poem," "The Grand Inquisitor." However, we must interpret Ivan's "writings" somewhat suspiciously. As we are introduced to Ivan at the outset of the novel, he is an intellectually superior, who earned a living as a student, "running around to newspaper publishers, plying them with ten-line articles on street incidents, signed 'Eyewitness.'"[65] That is, Ivan too is a "liar" of sorts. Moreover, with respect to the article on the ecclesiastical courts, of which "churchmen decidedly counted the author as one of their own," the narrator asserts, "some quick-witted people concluded that the whole article was just a brazen farce and mockery."[66] That is, the writing of the article was a joke, perhaps aimed to demonstrate his proud intellectual superiority; yet I suggest there is more to it. While it may be true that Ivan wrote the article as mockery, it also raises the kinds of questions that Dostoevsky seeks to address in the novel, the question of the sovereignty that can rightfully mediate the unity between the transcendent and the immanent, especially in relation to the church and the state.

So Be It! So Be It! The Question of the Church and State

With respect to the article, the thrust of Ivan's argument is that he disagrees with the premise that "the Church occupies a precise and definite place within the state. I objected that, on the contrary, the Church [церковь] should contain in itself the whole state [государство] and not merely occupy a certain corner of it."[67] In light of the previous chapter, we can see that Dostoevsky's novel is concerned with what de Lubac saw in the thought of Rousseau, that is, how the religious and the political might be brought together in a unified whole. For Rousseau, along with characters such as Miusov and Rakitin, the state must assume sovereignty, while the religious element becomes subordinate to and informs the

---

65. Dostoevsky, *Brothers Karamazov*, 16.
66. Dostoevsky, *Brothers Karamazov*, 16.
67. Dostoevsky, *Brothers Karamazov*, 61. Я же возразил ему, что, напротив, церковь должна заключать сама в себе всё государство, а не занимать в нем лишь некоторый угол, и что если теперь это почему-нибудь невозможно, то в сущности вещей несомненно должно быть поставлено прямою и главнейшею целью всего даль нейшего развития христианского общества.

moral aspect of the state.⁶⁸ As Ivan's article states, at stake is the question of the *aims* of both Church and the State: "The whole point of my article is that in ancient times, during its first three centuries, Christianity was revealed on earth only by the Church . . . But when the pagan Roman state desired to become Christian, it inevitably happened that, having become Christian, it merely included the Church in itself."⁶⁹ This text refers to the historical development of Christianity within the Roman Empire, whereby Emperor Constantine legitimized Christianity as the religion of Rome. Constantine used the sword to consolidate and unify the Roman Empire under the name of Christ.⁷⁰ However, the problem is that the fundamental aims of the church and state are in conflict:

> But Rome as a state retained too much of pagan civilization and wisdom, for example, the very aims and basic principles [цели и основы] of the state. Whereas Christ's Church, having entered the state, no doubt could give up none of its own basic principles of that rock on which it stood, and could pursue none but its own aims . . . among which was the transforming of the whole world [обратить весь мир], and therefore of the whole ancient pagan state, into the Church.⁷¹

According to Ivan, the church and the state are in conflict because they share a common aim—the *transformation* of the world. Ivan

68. See de Lubac's discussion of Rousseau, as also discussed in chapter 1. De Lubac, *Splendor*, 164.

69. Dostoevsky, *Brothers Karamazov*, 62.

70. It should be noted that this history is deeply connected to the creation and formation of the Russian Orthodox Church and Empire, which was modelled on Constantine's unification of the church and state. Indeed, Russians perceived in Moscow a "third Rome."

71. Dostoevsky, *Brothers Karamazov*, 62. In the Russian, "Вся мысль моей статьи в том, что в древние времена, пер вых трех веков христианства, христианство на земле являлось лишь церковью и было лишь церковь. Когда же римское языче ское государство возжелало стать христианским, то непременно 40 случилось так, что, став христианским, оно лишь включило в себя церковь, но само продолжало оставаться государством языческим по-прежнему, в чрезвычайно многих своих отправлениях. В сущ ности так несомненно и должно было произойти. Но в Риме, какв государстве, слишком многое осталось от цивилизации и мудрости языческой, как например самые даже цели и основы госу дарства. Христова же церковь, вступив в государство, без сом нения не могла уступить ничего из своих основ^ от того камня, на котором стояла она, и могла лишь преследовать не иначе как свои цели, раз твердо поставленные и указанные ей самим господом, между прочим: обратить весь мир, а стало быть, и всё древнее языческое государство в церковь."

himself, of course, does not support this view, but seeks to expose the political and world-transforming pretensions of the church and the state. As Dostoevsky would have been fully aware that, in the context of nineteenth-century Russia, the city of Moscow was perceived to be the "third Rome," after Constantinople, the holy Russian Orthodox empire. That is, according to the poetics of the novel, the church and state are world-transforming agencies, seeking to unite, often in a political rivalry, the transcendent and the immanent into a completed "whole." The aims of both church and state are *catholic* in that church and state attempt to completely unite the divine and the human. At stake is the question of sovereignty, the power necessary to "decide" on the exception. The church seeks the support of the sword of the state to enforce the sovereignty of its divine authority over humanity. The state seeks the church to morally justify its aim to assert sovereignty. What or who is sovereign? Who decides what is "good" and "evil?" What power can overcome the erotic force of the "Karamazov" in humanity? And what should dissolve into what, the church into the state or the state into the church? Perhaps the point of Ivan's article is that church and state are essentially indistinguishable, two sides to the same coin in a common quest for political sovereignty over humanity. Ivan, in writing the article, is subtly mocking the pretensions to sovereignty of both the state and church, cloaked in the supposed authority of divine transcendence. Dostoevsky wants his readers to connect his novel to the roots of Western civilization and the use of the Caesarean force to ensure the unity of the political order. It anticipates the temptation of the church to use the sword of Caesar to ensure the unity of humankind. That will be addressed below.

The monks in the elder's cell, of course, welcome Ivan's thesis, since it provides a critique of the transcendent, imperialist intentions of the modern state, especially the threat of the atheistic socialism, the "flooding wind," that was storming into the Russian intelligentsia, and capturing the political imagination of a younger generation. The aim of the atheistic political state is to transform the church into a higher moral form of the state, "from a lower [низшего] to a higher species [высший вид], as it were, so as to disappear into it eventually, making way for science, the spirit of the age, and civilization."[72] In concrete historical terms, it means

---

72. Dostoevsky, *Brothers Karamazov*, 63. In the Russian, "по иным теориям, слишком выяснив шимся в наш девятнадцатый век, церковь должна перерождаться в государство, так как бы из низшего в высший вид, чтобы затем в нем исчезнуть, уступив науке, духу времени и цивилизации."

that the modernist atheistic state, especially, for Dostoevsky, expressed in the emerging Russian revolutionary socialism, is the fulfillment of a process of transformation into a "higher type." What Ivan succeeds in demonstrating is the impossibility of a "coexistence" between the duality of the church and state, for the aims of both are universal. This is expressed in concrete terms in the novel with respect to the discipline of criminals. What political body has sovereignty to restore society, particularly, to restore the *consciences* of people in society? The state uses force and coercive violence to reform the criminal, and the church, such as during the Inquisition, used the same form coercive discipline. The elder Zosima recognizes that a deeper question of conscience is at stake, and to acknowledge a dualism between the pagan state and the church is necessary. For Zosima, it is the "law of Christ" that is necessary for the regeneration and transformation of the criminal, and therefore of society.[73] The elder also acknowledges that there is an eschatological expectation at work, a regenerative work awaiting fulfillment: "Now Christian society itself is not yet ready, and stands only on seven righteous men; but as they are never wanting, it abides firmly the same, awaiting its complete transfiguration [преображения] from society as still an almost pagan organization, into one universal, sovereign Church [дычествующую церковь]. And so be it, so be it, if only at the end of time, for this alone is destined [предназначено] to be fulfilled!"[74]

The character Miusov, a progressive liberal of the "1840s," is astounded by the claim of the elder, "'But, what, really are you talking about?' Miusov exclaimed, as if suddenly bursting out: "The state is abolished on earth, and the Church is raised to the level of the state! It's not even Ultramontanism, it's arch-Ultramontanism! Even Pope Gregory the Seventh never dreamed of such a thing!"[75] That is, Miusov perceives the elder's "desire" as an expression of the sovereign, centralized, hierarchical

---

73. Dostoevsky, *Brothers Karamazov*, 64.

74. Dostoevsky, *Brothers Karamazov*, 66. In the Russian, "лишь на семи праведниках; но так как они не оскудевают, то и пребывает всё же не зыблемо, в ожидании своего полного преображения из общества как союза почти еще языческого во единую вселенскую и вла дычествующую церковь. Сие и буди, буди, хотя бы и в конце веков, ибо лишь сему предназначено совершиться!"

75. Dostoevsky, *Brothers Karamazov*, 66. In the Russian, "Да что же это в самом деле такое?—воскликнул Миусов, как бы вдруг прорвавшись,—устраняется на земле государство, а церковь возводится на степень государства! Это не то что ультра монтанство, это архиультрамонтанство! Это папе Григорию Седь мому не мерещилось!"

conception of the church as both the spiritual and secular sovereign in society. Ultramontanism is a theory that derives from medieval Roman Catholic thought that emphasized papal authority. Paissy responds defensively, arguing that Miusov has misunderstood, "It is not the Church that turns into the state, you see. That is Rome and its dream. That is the third temptation of the devil. But on the contrary it is the state that turns into the church over all the earth, which is the complete opposite of Ultramontanism and of Rome, and of your interpretation, and is simply the great destiny of the Orthodoxy on earth."[76] This text anticipates the other writing of Ivan, the Grand Inquisitor, for it addresses the third temptation of the devil, the question of the use of coercion and violence to enforce peace and unity in human society. Nonetheless, with respect to Paissy's insistence, Miusov remains unconvinced, providing an anecdote of an experience he had earlier in Paris, whereby a French political agent was addressing the problem of "socialist revolutionaries." Citing this particular "important and official person," Miusov insinuates that the socialist Christian may be a greater threat than atheistic one, "We are not, in fact, afraid of all these socialists, anarchists, atheists, and revolutionaries . . . but there are some special people among them, although not many: these are believers in God and Christians, and at the same time socialists. They are the ones we are most afraid of: they are terrible people! A socialist Christian is more dangerous than a socialist atheist."[77]

While Miusov's interpretation of the elder's eschatological vision of the church may be misunderstood, there is also something that rings true, which Dostoevsky, I suggest, wants the reader to consider. That is, there is a fine line that exists between radical Christianity and atheistic

---

76. Dostoevsky, *Brothers Karamazov*, 66. In the Russian, "Совершенно обратно изволите понимать!—строго прого ворил отец Паисий,—не церковь обращается в государство, поймите это. То Рим и его мечта. То третье диаволово искушение! А, напротив, государство обращается в церковь, восходит до церкви и становится церковью на всей земле, что совершенно уже противоположно и ультрамонтанству, и Риму, и вашему тол кованию, и есть лишь великое предназначение православия на земле. От Востока звезда сия воссияет."

77. Dostoevsky, *Brothers Karamazov*, 67. In the Russian, "Опуская главную суть раз говора, приведу лишь одно любопытнейшее замечание, которое у этого господчика вдруг вырвалось: «Мы,—сказал он,—соб ственно этих всех социалистов—анархистов, безбожников и рево люционеров—не очень-то и опасаемся; мы за ними следим, и ходы их нам известны. Но есть из них, хотя и немного, несколько особенных людей: это в бога верующие и христиай'е, а в то же время и социалисты. Вот этих-то мы больше всех опасаемся, это страш ный народ! Социалист-христианин страшнее социалиста-безбож ника»."

socialism. As de Lubac suggests, Dostoevsky explores the "deeper renovation" of humanity to fulfill a desire for justice and equality. As we see in the section, "So Be It! So Be It," Dostoevsky perceives the growing rivalry between Christianity and socialism, beyond the modernist liberal politics that Miusov and Rakitin represent. Rakitin too still believes in the "virtue" of atheist humanism; he is a progressive who believes that modernism will transform the world into something higher. Rakitin criticizes Ivan's theory: "If there is no immortality of the soul [бессмертия души], then there is no virtue [добродетели], and therefore everything is permitted [всё позволено]."[78] For Rakitin's modern atheism, humankind "will find strength in itself to live for virtue, even without believing in the immortality of the soul! Find it in the love of liberty, equality, and fraternity."[79] It is the modernism of the early French revolutionists who overcame monarchism and ecclesiastical sovereignty to create a new society that is structured on science and reason. According to Rakitin, this form of liberalist modernism is the antidote to the Karamazovian "sensuality."

However, with respect to atheistic socialism, this is how the narrator describes the ultimate aim of the socialist state: "Socialism [социализм] is not only the labour question or the question of the so-called fourth estate, but first of all the question of atheism, the question of the modern embodiment of atheism [современного воплощения атеизма], the question of the Tower of Babel built precisely without God, not to go from earth to heaven [небес с земли], but bring heaven to earth [небес на землю]."[80] The question of political revolution is explored in Dos-

---

78. Dostoevsky, *Brothers Karamazov*, 82. In the Russian, "Нет бессмертия души, так пет и добродетели, значит, всё позволено."

79. Dostoevsky, *Brothers Karamazov*, 82. In the Russian, "Человечество само в себе силу найдет, чтобы жить для добродетели, даже и не веря в бессмертие души! В любви к свободе, к равен ству, братству найдет."

80. Of course, the imagery of the Tower of Babel represents humanity's attempt to "unite" heaven and earth through its newly developed technology. It is the attempt to create a higher image for itself affirming the image of God in humankind. The political embodiment of atheism as expressed in the emerging socialism of his own day is one of the major questions that Dostoevsky seeks to answer in *The Brothers Karamazov*. This vision is represented in the genius of the middle brother, Ivan, who outwardly appears confident, and proud, but by the end of the novel is psychologically and spiritually tortured by the "devil," whereby the moral and political implication of modernist atheism and its true intention is exposed: "In my opinion, there is no need to destroy anything, one need only destroy the idea of God [идею о боге] in mankind, that's where the business should start. . . . Once mankind has renounced God, one and all . . . then the entire worldview will fall itself, without anthropophagy, and, above all, the entire

toevsky's previous novels as well, in particular, *Demons*.[81] According to de Lubac, Dostoevsky offers us two formulas for an atheist socialism, "both diabolical: one is the subject of his novel [*Demons*]; the other set forth by the Grand Inquisitor."[82] For de Lubac, although *Demons* was first intended as a polemic, it became a profound "ascent into the darkest depths of the human soul and at the same time the great prophetic *geste* in which Europe was to read its destiny."[83] There we see the desire of "self-will"—the sovereignty of the self—conspires to murder for the sake of its utopian dreams. In *Demons*, Dostoevsky exposes the demonic revolutionary modernist spirit that ends in destruction. The novel is prefaced on the story of the drowning of the pigs in the Gospel of Luke.[84] Like the demons that are cast out into the pigs which rush headlong into the water to drown, so Western society is possessed by modern devils of modern atheistic socialism and is destined for a similar end. However, this does not mean that Dostoevsky is reactionary, anti-revolutionary. "He would be the last person," argues Berdyaev, "to defend the old bourgeois world; in spirit he is a revolutionary; but he wasn't a revolutionary without God and without Christ."[85] Moreover, as de Lubac attests, something in Dostoevsky's soul "conspires even with the demolishers whom he execrates, and the apocalyptic vision that rises before his eyes does not derive its

---

formal morality [прежняя нравствен ность], and everything will be new." It is the advent of the man-god, where humanity will be "exalted with the spirit of the divine, titanic pride, and the man-god will appear." Humanity will conquer nature with its science creating a happiness for itself and replacing "all his former hopes of heavenly delight." In this creation of humankind as a divine sovereign on earth, "everything is permitted" (всё дозволено). See *Brothers Karamazov*, 26, 649. In the Russian, "ибо социализм есть не только рабочий вопрос, или так называемого четвертого сословия, но по преимуществу есть атеистический вопрос, вопрос современного воплощения атеизма, вопрос Вавилонской башни, строящейся именно без бога, не для достижения небес с земли, а для сведения небес на землю."

81. The other translation of the Russian *Besy* is *Possessed*. However, according to Pevear and Volokhonsky, "*Besy* refers not to possessed but to possessors, we then apply this new term 'demons' to the same set of characters in an unexamined way." That is, to reflect on who the demons are in the novel is how best to interpret the novel. Dostoevsky called the novel "*Demons*, we suggest, precisely because the demons in it *do not appear*, and the reader might otherwise overlook them. The demons are visible only in their distortions of the human image, the human countenance, and their force is measurable only by the degree of the distortion." Dostoevsky, *Demons*, xiv.

82. De Lubac, *Drama of Atheist Humanism*, 321.

83. De Lubac, *Drama of Atheist Humanism*, 321.

84. Dostoevsky, *Demons*, 3.

85. Berdyaev, *Dostoevsky*, 133.

whole substance from horrors actually experienced; it is partly inspired by his own 'apocalyptic bent.'"[86] As I will show in chapter 5, it is not as if Dostoevsky is "anti-revolutionary"; he aims to demonstrate the necessity of a deeper revolution of the human heart.[87]

Ivan's Atheistic Mystical Immanentism: Desire for Retribution

It is not coincidental that the teaching of Father Paissy to Alyosha occurs at the outset of Part II of the novel, a section that will comprise another significant conversation, but between Ivan and Alyosha. In Part II, we are given the heart of Dostoevsky's struggle with the crucible of doubt, not only concerning the existence of God, but also about humanity created in the image of the Incarnation. What Ivan contests is "God's world," where humans are bestowed the gift of freedom, to eat from the "tree of the knowledge of good and evil."[88] That the beast of sensuality is given free rein is the problem. The best that "God's world" has offered humanity is the sensual, animalistic creature that is inherently unlovable, rooted in the unfortunate gift of human "freedom." The conversation between Ivan and Alyosha spans three famous chapters, "The Brothers Get Acquainted," "Rebellion," and "The Grand Inquisitor." In these texts, we are given a glimpse into Ivan's heart and mind, the reasons for his atheism, and his political solution to the problem of human freedom in a godless world.

Ivan, like Mitya, is an erotic Karamazov. In "The Brothers Get Acquainted," Ivan claims to be a lover of life: "I would want to live, and as

---

86. De Lubac, *Drama of Atheist Humanism*, 322.

87. As we see in *Demons*, as well as *Brothers*, the revolutionary socialists are the heirs of the liberals who embraced atheism. There is a genealogy of modernism, an evolution. The revolutionary socialists take the project of building up a humanity without God to its logical conclusion: "Not only is heaven emptied but man is secularized; henceforth nothing about him must recall a transcendent origin and a sacred destiny." The character Stepan Trophimovich articulates this atheistic movement in *Demons*: "In the last scene the Tower of Babel suddenly appears; the 'athletes,' singing the anthem of the new hope, are putting the finishing touches to it; and, when it is completed to the very top, the owner (let us call him the Master of Olympus) decamps (this bit should be made grotesque), and mankind, not knowing where it stands, takes his place and immediately inaugurates a new era, at the same time forming a new conception of the universe." In other words, humanity is sovereign and free. However, for Dostoevsky, the logical outcome of an unlimited human freedom and sovereignty without God is only tyranny and slavery. See de Lubac, *Drama*, 323. See also Dostoevsky, *Demons*, 10.

88. Dostoevsky, *Brothers Karamazov*, 237.

long as I have bent to this cup, I will not tear myself from it until I've drunk it all!"[89] Ivan has a "thirst for life" (жажду жизни). He is a lover of this material world, with an irrational love that is precedes human logic, a "Karamazov" force: "True, it's a feature of the Karamazovs, to some extent, this thirst for life despite all; it must be sitting in you too; but why is base? There is still an awful lot of centripetal force on our planet, Alyosha."[90] In this sense, Ivan too is an "immanent mystic" who seeks the immediacy of life and its enticing pleasures. Ivan is keenly aware of a deeper "will to power" that governs reason itself, but also the power that reason seeks to scientifically comprehend—and control. Ivan is in this regard a thoroughly "Western" man. It is the passion for the material, for the earth, and for scientific control that draws Ivan to Europe. In the West, "the precious dead lie there, each stone over them speaks of such ardent past life, of such passionate faith in their deeds, their truth, their struggle, and their science."[91] Ivan knows there is only "death" there, precious stones, but it is the memory and image of the struggle of the Westerner, who struggled to overcome God and the church in order to recover a proper love for life and the material world, that draws him. In the West, humans dared to remove God and turn their attention more fully on the material world so as to make it over in a more truly human image. As de Lubac argues, it is the sovereignty of humanity that will transform the world through its science and its reason. As we see in this section, Ivan brings again to the fore the theme of the world transforming intention of atheist socialism, not different from the church, but from a materialistic worldview, reflecting upon "none other than the universal questions: is there a God, is there immortality? And those who do not believe in God, well, they will talk about socialism [социализме] and

---

89. Dostoevsky, *Brothers Karamazov*, 230. In the Russian, "а я все-таки захочу жить и уж как припал к этому кубку, то не оторвусь от него, пока его весь не осилю!"

90. Dostoevsky, *Brothers Karamazov*, 230. In the Russian, "Черта-то она отчасти карамазов- ская, это правда, жажда-то эта жизни, несмотря ни на что, в тебе она тоже непременно сидит, но почему ж она подлая? Центро стремительной силы еще страшно много на нашей планете, Алеша."

91. Dostoevsky, *Brothers Karamazov*, 230. In the Russian, "Дорогие там лежат покойники, каждый ю камень над ними гласит о такой горячей минувшей жизни, о такой страстной вере в свой подвиг, в свою истину, в свою борьбу и в свою науку, что я, знаю заранее, паду на землю и буду целовать эти камни и плакать над ними,—в то же время убежденный всем сердцем моим, что всё это давно уже кладбище, и никак не более."

anarchism [анархизме], about transforming [переделке] the whole of mankind [человечества] according to a new order, but it's the same damned thing, the questions are all the same, only from the other end."[92]

Ivan argues that faith in God, or the notion of the "necessity of God" (мысль о необходимости бога) is beyond the intellectual capabilities of even the most intelligent, who doubt that "the whole of being was created purely with Euclidean geometry.... I humbly confess that I do not have any ability to resolve such questions, I have a Euclidean mind [ум эвклидовский], an earthly [земной] mind, and therefore it is not for us to resolve things that are not of this world."[93] That is, within Euclidean geometry, humanity is capable of only understanding three dimensions of space. To include a fourth goes beyond human comprehension. It is not as if Ivan excludes the transcendent, eternal realm, but he advises his younger brother "never to think about it . . . all such questions are completely unsuitable to a mind created with a concept of only three dimensions."[94] It would seem as though Ivan is truly agonistic. We cannot know God or the intentions and actions of God. Yet, this anticipates the next chapter, "rebellion" or revolt: "It's not God that I do not accept . . . it is this world of God's, created by God, that I do not accept and cannot agree to accept."[95] What Ivan pronounces is not a rational critique of theism or Christianity, but a morally superior judgment against an unrealistic, "otherworldly" Christian morality and redemption. It is a radical modernist critique of the injustice, the shed blood of the innocent of this world. It is also deeply antichristian. It is a rejection of Christian

---

92. Dostoevsky, *Brothers Karamazov*, 234. О мировых воп росах, не иначе: есть ли бог, есть ли бессмертие? А которые в бога не веруют, ну те о социализме и об анархизме заговорят, о пере делке всего человечества по новому штату, так ведь это один же черт выйдет, всё те же вопросы, только с другого конца. И множество, множество самых оригинальных русских мальчиков толь ко и делают, что о вековечных вопросах говорят у нас в наше время. Разве не так?

93. Dostoevsky, *Brothers Karamazov*, 235. Я, голубчик, решил так, что если я даже этого не могу понять, то где ж мне про бога понять. Я смиренно сознаюсь, со что у меня нет никаких способностей разрешать такие вопросы, у меня ум эвклидовский, земной, а потому где нам решать о том, что не от мира сего.

94. Всё это вопросы совершенно несвойственные уму, созданному с понятием лишь о трех измерениях.

95. Dostoevsky, *Brothers Karamazov*, 235. In the Russian, "Ну так представь же себе, что в окончательном результате я мира этого божьего—не принимаю и хоть и знаю, что он существует, да не допускаю его вовсе. Я не бога не принимаю, пойми ты это, я мира, им созданного, мира-то божьего не принимаю и не могу согласиться принять."

apocalyptic hope of universal redemption as witnessed to in the church, founded upon the "slain lamb": "I have a childlike conviction that the sufferings will be healed, smoothed over . . . and that ultimately . . . in the moment of eternal harmony [вечной гармонии], there will occur and be revealed something so precious that it will suffice for all hearts, to allay all indignation, to redeem all human villainy, all bloodshed: it will suffice not only to make forgiveness possible, but also to justify [оправдать] everything that has happened with men—let all this come true and be revealed, but I do not accept it and do not want to accept it!"[96] This forms the basis of Ivan's "rebellion." It is rooted in a "self-will" that seeks the sovereignty of moral judgment, one rooted in the self that will take its own Euclidean measure of justice.

Ivan's "rebellion" consists in the fact that it is impossible to accept the world as God created it. It needs transformation, but a transformation on a completely materialistic foundation. The Christian conception of an eternal, transcendent, eschatological redemption goes beyond the Euclidean mind. Moreover, as a result, it is impossible, argues Ivan, to truly love one's neighbour. Divine, incarnate love for the neighbour is impossible. One can only do so abstractly, but never "up close."[97] Zosima's teaching on "active love" is an outright impossibility to accomplish with any authenticity. Ivan is convinced that the attempt to love one's neighbour, such as the example of John the Merciful, is done with the "strain of lie, out of love enforced by duty, out of self-imposed penance."[98] It is, to

---

96. Dostoevsky, *Brothers Karamazov*, 236. In the Russian, "Оговорюсь: я убежден, как младенец, что страдания заживут и сгладятся, что весь обидный комизм человеческих противоречий исчезнет, как жалкий мираж, как гнусненькое измышление мало сильного и маленького, как атом, человеческого эвклидовского ума, что, наконец, в мировом финале, в момент вечной гармонии, случится и явится нечто до того драгоценное, что хватит его на все сердца, на утоление всех негодований, на искупление всех злодейств людей, всей пролитой ими их крови, хватит, чтобы не только было возможно простить, но и оправдать всё, что случи лось с людьми,—пусть, пусть это всё будет и явится, но я-то этого не принимаю и не хочу принять!"

97. Dostoevsky, *Brothers Karamazov*, 237.

98. Dostoevsky, *Brothers Karamazov*, 237. In the Russian, "Я читал вот как-то и где-то про «Иоанна Милостивого» (одного святого), что он, когда к нему пришел голодный и обмерз ший прохожий и попросил согреть его, лег с ним вместе в постель, w обнял его и начал дышать ему в гноящийся и зловонный от какой- то ужасной болезни рот его. Я убежден, что он это сделал с над рывом лжи, из-за заказанной долгом любви, из-за натащенной на себя эпитимии. Чтобы полюбить человека, надо, чтобы тот спрятался а чуть лишь покажет лицо свое—пропала любовь."

use Nietzsche's language, the asceticism of the "camel spirit."⁹⁹ According to Ivan, however, the facts of life show that humanity is truly animalistic, "sensual," a Karamazovian force. We cannot overcome this immanent "realism." It is only worth our scorn and contempt. Like Feuerbach and Marx, humanity is not created in the image of God. Yet contrary to these progressive modernists, reflected in Rakitin in the novel, there is no inherent virtue in humanity. In Ivan's ironic comment, if anything, it is not that humanity is created in the image of God; rather, "I think that if the devil does not exist, and man has therefore created him, he has created him in his own image and likeness [образу и подобию]."¹⁰⁰ In other words, in Ivan's cynical conception, there is nothing in humanity that reflects God's image; if anything, the devil is to be found there.

The greatest argument that Ivan produces to demonstrate the essentially animalistic nature of humanity is found in the suffering and oppression of innocent children. He marshals a host of examples of utter animalistic brutality against innocent children that force even the pure-hearted Alyosha to grimace with the spirit of retribution.¹⁰¹ Ivan makes a distinction between children and adults. Grownups, argues Ivan, "ate the apple, and knew good and evil, and became 'as gods' [яко бози]. And they still go on eating it. But little children have not eaten anything and are not yet guilty of anything."¹⁰² After producing the flood of examples, Ivan questions Alyosha, "Can you understand why this nonsense is needed and created? Without it, they say, man could not have lived on earth, for he would not have known good and evil. Who wants to know this damned good and evil at such a price? The whole world of knowledge is not worth the tears of that little child to 'Dear God.'"¹⁰³

99. We will look at this in our examination of Nietzsche's *Zarathustra* below.

100. Dostoevsky, *Brothers Karamazov*, 239. Я думаю, что если дьявол не существует и, стало быть, создал его человек, то создал он его по своему образу и подобию.

101. Dostoevsky, *Brothers Karamazov*, 241–43.

102. Dostoevsky, *Brothers Karamazov*, 238. In the Russian, "Во-вторых, о больших я и потому еще гово-рить не буду, что, кроме того, что они отвратительны и любви не заслуживают, у них есть и возмездие: они съели яблоко и познали добро и зло и стали «яко бози». Продолжают и теперь есть его. Но деточки ничего не съели и пока еще ни в чем не винов ны."

103. Dostoevsky, *Brothers Karamazov*, 242. In the Russian, "понимаешь ли ты эту ахинею, друг мой и брат мой, послушник ты мой божий и смиренный, пони маешь ли ты, для чего эта ахинея так нужна и создана! Без нее, говорят, и пробыть бы не мог человек на земле, ибо не познал бы добра и зла. Для чего познавать это чертово добро и зло, когда это столького стоит? Да ведь весь мир познания не стоит тогда этих слезок ребеночка к «боженьке»."

As result of the oppression of the innocent child, Ivan desires and seeks retribution: "I need retribution [возмездие], otherwise I will destroy myself. And retribution not somewhere and sometime in infinity, but here and now, on earth, so that I see it myself."[104] Ivan too yearns for the transformation of the world, but he demands its immediate fulfillment on his own terms: "I want to see with my own eyes the hind lie down with the lion, and the murdered man rise up and embrace the murderer. I want to be there when everyone suddenly finds out what it was all for. All religions in the world are based on this desire [желании], and I am a believer. But then there are the children, and what am I going to do with them?"[105] The Christian assertion of a higher redemption, rooted in forgiveness, does not overcome the suffering of innocent children: "You see, Alyosha, it may well be that if I live until that moment, or rise again in order to see it, I myself will perhaps cry out with all the rest, looking at the mother embracing her child's tormentor: 'Just art thou, O Lord!' but I do not want to cry out with them. While there's still time, I hasten to defend myself against it, and therefore I absolutely renounce all higher harmony."[106] And who would have the power to forgive such a crime? "Is there in the whole world a being who could and would have the right to forgive [право простить]?"[107] For the sake of "love of humankind" (любви к человечеству), Ivan rejects God and God's world: "I'd rather remain with my unrequited suffering and my unquenched indignation, *even if I am wrong*. Besides, they have put too high a price on harmony, we can't afford to pay so much for admission. And, therefore, I hasten to

---

104. Dostoevsky, *Brothers Karamazov*, 244. In the Russian, "мне надо возмездие, иначе ведь я истреблю себя. И возмездие не в бесконечности где-нибудь и когда-нибудь, а здесь, уже на земле, и чтоб я его сам увидал."

105. Dostoevsky, *Brothers Karamazov*, 244. In the Russian, "Я хочу видеть своими глазами, как лань ляжет подле льва и как зарезанный встанет и обнимется с убившим его. Я хочу быть тут, когда все вдруг узнают, для чего всё так было. На этом желании зиждутся все религии на земле, а я верую. Но вот, однако же, детки, и что я с ними стану тогда делать? Это вопрос, который я не могу решить."

106. Dostoevsky, *Brothers Karamazov*, 245. In the Russian, "Видишь ли, Алеша, ведь, может быть, и действительно так случится, ю что когда я сам доживу до того момента али воскресну, чтоб увидать его, то и сам я, пожалуй, воскликну со всеми, смотря на мать, обнявшуюся с мучителем ее дитяти: «Прав ты, господи!», но я не хочу тогда восклицать. Пока еще время, спешу оградить себя, а потому от высшей гармонии совершенно отказываюсь."

107. In the Russian, "Есть ли во всем мире существо, которое могло бы и имело право простить? Не хочу гармонии, из-за любви к человечеству не хочу."

return my ticket."[108] Ivan's atheism, therefore, is a moral protest against Christ and the Gospel. It is the creation of a "higher image" of justice that seeks to surpass and go beyond the "image of God" in humankind. It is rebellion because it expresses the demonic desire to claim the right to a higher "good and evil" than the one revealed in Christ. In doing so, Ivan claims a titanic, divine status as a human sovereign on earth. In other words, Ivan creates a political ideology of the *grotesque*. It is the same sensual Karamazovian force which turns in on itself through an attempt to limit human freedom. Everything is permitted in this political formulation—deception and violence. And so, out of this formulation of retribution, we have the creation of the Grand Inquisitor.

The Grand Inquisitor's Mediational Images of "Bread," "Mystery," and "Authority"

Ivan's rejection of the "ticket" represents a transition in his conversation with Alyosha. At root, Ivan's atheistic materialism is rebellion against Christ. In fact, Ivan's argument implies that his "love for humankind," by contrast to Christ's, is in the here and now, the immanent. The immediate demand for justice against the oppressor of the innocent is morally superior to the Christian hope of "otherworldly" redemption and transformation. The underlying question, therefore, pertains to what is necessary to bring order, peace, and justice to this worldly society. The entire discourse between Ivan and Alyosha is leading to a political solution that can adequately address the problem of the Karamazovian, earthly sensual force and the "insect" that resides in humanity. What will redeem the Fyodors and the Mityas of the world? Is the sacrifice of even one innocent child worth it? What will "unify" humankind as a whole? Ivan questions Alyosha:

> Tell me straight out, I call on you—answer me: imagine that you yourself are building the edifice of human destiny with the object of making people happy in the finale, of giving them peace and rest at last, but for that you must inevitably and unavoidably

---

108. Dostoevsky, *Brothers Karamazov*, 249. In the Russian, "Я хочу оставаться лучше со стра даниями неотомщенными. Лучше уж я останусь при неотомщен ном страдании моем и неутоленном негодовании моем, хотя бы. я был и неправ. Да и слишком дорого оценили гармонию, не по карману нашему вовсе столько платить за вход. А потому свой билет на вход спешу возвратить обратно. И если только я честный человек, то обязан возвратить его как можно заранее."

torture just one tiny creature, that same child who was beating her chest with her little fist, and raise your edifice on the foundation of her unrequited tears—would you agree to be the architect on such conditions?[109]

For Alyosha, as for Dostoevsky, the response to such a question revolves around whether one accepts the sacrifice of the Incarnation: "You asked just now if there is in the whole world a being who would have the right to forgive. But there is such a being, and he can forgive everything, forgive all *and for all*, because he himself gave his innocent blood for all and for everything. You've forgotten about him, but it is on him that the structure is building built, and it is to him that they will cry out: 'Just art thou, O LORD, for thy ways are revealed.'"[110] We will examine Dostoevsky's redemptive vision more fully in chapter 5, but here we note that what Ivan rejects from his standpoint of moral superiority is Christ. According to Alyosha, the sacrifice of the Incarnation, the Word become flesh, is the sufficient means to forgive all humanity for not only its unrestrained sensuality, but also creating a higher image for itself, a twisted "sensual" expression of the image of God that is responsible for such violence in the first place. For Alyosha, the Gospel is an apocalyptic hope upon which the new "structure" of humanity as a "whole" is being built.

However, it is in the mouth of the Grand Inquisitor that Ivan's argument against "God's world" is laid out to the full. It is also put into a greater historical context. In this text, Dostoevsky gives poetic vision to an alternative apocalyptic that is rooted in the demonic, as it relates to the "inner meaning" of European (and human) history. In this text, Ivan creates the portrait of a sixteenth-century Inquisitor, who questions a silent Jesus who has returned to earth. The Inquisitor is a representative

---

109. Dostoevsky, *Brothers Karamazov*, 245. In the Russian, "Скажи мне сам прямо, я зову тебя—отвечай: представь^ что это ты сам возводишь здание судьбы человеческой с целью в финале осчаст ливить людей, дать им наконец мир и покой, но для этого необ ходимо и неминуемо предстояло бы замучить всего лишь одно только крохотное созданьице, вот того самого ребеночка, бившего себя кулачонком в грудь, и на неотомщенных слезках его основать это здание, согласился ли бы ты быть архитектором на этих усло виях, скажи и не лги!"

110. Dostoevsky, *Brothers Karamazov*, 246. In the Russian, "ты сказал сейчас: есть ли во всем мире существо, которое могло бы и имело право простить? Но существо это есть, и оно может всё простить, всех и вся и за всё, потому что само отдало неповинную кровь свою за всех и за всё. Ты забыл о нем, а на нем-то и созиждется здание, и это ему вос кликнут: «Прав ты, господи, ибо открылись пути твои»."

of Roman Catholicism, or at least an extremist aspect of it.[111] According to Ivan, Roman Catholicism, as symbolized in the Inquisitor, does not represent the "freedom" of Christ, but an earthly power, namely, the church-become-state with the aim of bringing a unified, totalizing political order to the world, at the cost of transcendent freedom. The tension introduced in the Gospel and lived out in the church as an alternative community in the world has been dissolved. Humanity is conceived as in need of sovereign earthly power that will appease its conscience and fulfill its need for peaceful communality. This totalitarian religious state is necessary to overcome the intolerable "freedom" of the conscience, which humanity cannot bear, "for nothing has ever been more insufferable for man and for human society than freedom!"[112] According to de Lubac, the Grand Inquisitor "has never harbored the smallest atom of utopianism . . . Aiming, in his turn at the happiness of humankind, he knows from the outset on what conditions it can be had; he propounds a clear antithesis: freedom or happiness. The reproach he brings against Christ is precisely this: that he placed too much confidence in man."[113] What is interesting to note in this comment is that, if the Inquisitor is to bring "happiness" to humanity, he must reject the gift of freedom in Christ, a freedom that, as we will see below, is a torment to humanity. By implication, the suppression of freedom is, within the logic of the Inquisitor, the means to human happiness.

Furthermore, as de Lubac interprets this text, the Grand Inquisitor is "Shigalevism in its true and perfect form. It does not stop at outward constraint but enslaves souls as well."[114] As the character Shigalev in *Demons* concludes, "Having set out from unlimited freedom, I have ended up with unlimited despotism."[115] Indeed, "all the framers of social systems, from the remotest times up to the present year 187_, have been dreamers, tellers of fairy tales, simpletons who contradict themselves and knew nothing of natural science and that strange animal called man."[116] Therefore, humankind will be divided into two sections: one-tenth will exercise absolute sovereignty and authority over the other nine-tenths. Shigalev suggests

---

111. Dostoevsky, *Brothers Karamazov*, 260.
112. Dostoevsky, *Brothers Karamazov*, 252.
113. De Lubac, *Drama of Atheist Humanism*, 325.
114. De Lubac, *Drama of Atheist Humanism*, 325.
115. De Lubac, *Drama of Atheist Humanism*, 324.
116. De Lubac, *Drama of Atheist Humanism*, 324.

for ultimate happiness on earth, it would be necessary for the one-tenth to exterminate the nine-tenths. Then there would be "nothing left but a handful of educated men, who, organizing themselves according to scientific principles, would live happy ever after."[117] The only thing against this idea would be that it is too difficult to put into practice. However, the Grand Inquisitor provides a vision of how it may be practiced. The Tower of Babel may now be properly built. The Inquisitor has "dug down to the roots of being, and every disturbing seed has been extirpated."[118]

The Grand Inquisitor goes beyond the Shigalevs and the Verhovenskys who were "possessed" by devils. The sovereignty of the Inquisitor derives from a union with Satan. In this sense, the Inquisitor, too, is a "mystic," in a mysticism of the demonic. The Grand Inquisitor is portrayed as one who follows the devil, that "dread and intelligent spirit, the spirit of self-destruction and non-being," who tempted Jesus in the wilderness.[119] And as Kroeker and Ward suggest, "The Devil here, as elsewhere in the Bible, is identified as the accuser in the heavenly court, the chief prosecutor of legal demands for retributive justice."[120] The Grand Inquisitor is precisely characterized as such, one who questions the Christ as if on trial in a cosmic sovereign court. At this point, we may recall the apocalyptic grammar we developed in the introduction of this work. As Kroeker and Ward assert, "the larger symbolic context in which to understand these trials is the cosmic battle, depicted in the book of Revelation, between the power of light or divine rule and the rebellious powers of darkness headed by the great spirit of rebellion in the heavenly court, Satan or the Devil."[121]

According to the Inquisitor, Jesus' fatal error lay in rejecting the offer of the devil mediated through three "images." These "images" are the necessary forms of mediation that will create a false sense of unification between the transcendent and the immanent. The "realism" of the will to power demands the "realism" of such mediations to ensure "happiness." The Inquisitor is a "prophet of nothingness," for the sake of the "happiness" of humankind. Although this means that the one percent who rule over the ninety-nine percent must suffer knowing the truth of

---

117. De Lubac, *Drama of Atheist Humanism*, 324.
118. De Lubac, *Drama of Atheist Humanism*, 325.
119. Dostoevsky, *Brothers Karamazov*, 251–52.
120. Kroeker and Ward, *Remembering the End*, 107. See Rev 12:10; Job 1; Zech 3.
121. Kroeker and Ward, *Remembering the End*, 103.

the lies with which they construct society. Nonetheless, for the "love of humankind," the Inquisitor becomes a mediator of the devil, who has revealed the wisdom necessary to ensure the peace, order, and happiness of humanity. According to the Grand Inquisitor, in these three "demonic" questions, "all of subsequent human history is as if brought together into a single whole and foretold; three images are revealed that will take in all the insoluble historical contradictions of human nature over all the earth."[122] It is these three images that will maintain the power of the church over the new modernist "temple" that threatens the older religious order, the "Tower of Babel," the socialist state. These images are miracle (чудо), mystery (тайна), and authority (авторитет).

As Kroeker and Ward richly expound, the symbolic background of the Grand Inquisitor is the book of Revelation, especially chapters 12–18, where Rome is imaged as a woman riding the earthly beast which is an agent of the dragon/serpent, the devil. She holds a cup in her hand called "mystery." Revelation 12–18 depicts the cosmic victory of the lamb over the power of the seven-headed dragon, which after his fall, seeks earthly political dominion through the two beasts of the sea and the earth. The dragon's power through these beasts is the parodic deception of sovereignty mediated through the "miracle" and "mystery." As the dragon is a parody of the Creator, so the first beast is a parody of Christ: "this first beast, who rises out of the sea . . . and is given the healing of an apparently mortal wound."[123] The destructive authority of this beast is "rooted in the delusive power of idolatry."[124] This first beast corresponds to the second temptation of "mystery," an alternative, illusive mediation of redemption. The second beast, "who arises from the land . . . and who imitates both the false 'lamb' and the dragon, seeks to establish the worship of the first beast."[125] What is significant here is that the second beast does this through the working of "great signs"—the miracle that Christ refused to perform in the wilderness. The second beast, therefore, corresponds to the Inquisitor's first temptation, "where Christ is tempted to put an end to earthly suffering by satisfying his bodily hunger at the expense of the

---

122. Doestoevsky, *Brothers*, 252. In the Russian, "Ибо в этих трех вопросах как бы совокуплена в одно целое и пред сказана вся дальнейшая история человеческая и явлены три образа, в которых сойдутся все неразрешимые исторические противоречия человеческой природы на всей земле."

123. Kroeker and Ward, *Remembering the End*, 107.

124. Kroeker and Ward, *Remembering the End*, 107.

125. Kroeker and Ward, *Remembering the End*, 107.

spiritual freedom of human beings."[126] Therefore, what is established is a political religion that conjoins the material and the spiritual in mystical whole, but it is rooted in metaphysical rebellion against the sovereignty of Christ. This religious authority of the beasts is sustained by the third temptation, the "authority of the sword . . . that eliminates opposition through coercive punishment."[127]

First, the absolute sovereignty of the state, be it religious or secular, is necessary because of the necessity of earthly bread. The human being is an earthly creature. The heavenly bread of freedom in faith is an impossibility for most of humanity. The Grand Inquisitor prophesies that after a thousand years of socialist secular state, building its tower of Babel, the church will return to complete its work: "No science will give them bread as long as they remain free, but in the end, they will lay their freedom at our feet and say to us: 'Better that you enslave us, but feed us.' They will finally understand that freedom and earthly bread in plenty for everyone are inconceivable together, for never, never will they be able to share among themselves."[128] Moreover, the provision of earthly bread secures the political unity of humankind in their common worship of those who provide it. It is a materialist means toward a transcendent end. The socialist vision promises the assurance of earthly bread, for an "equality" in which each person's earthly immanent need is satisfied. This the modernist "religion" of socialist atheistic humanism, as Berdyaev asserts: "The socialist religion welcomes the three temptations of stones turned into bread, of kingdoms of the world, and of social miracle. It is not a religion for free sons of God, but for slaves to necessity, children of the dust whose spiritual primacy has been snatched away from them."[129] Since there is no absolute meaning, nor eternity, what is left for humanity is to seek its own "utopia," to "get together and organize world-happiness."[130]

126. Kroeker and Ward, *Remembering the End*, 108.
127. Kroeker and Ward, *Remembering the End*, 108.
128. Dostoevsky, *Brothers Karamazov*, 253. In the Russian, "Никакая наука не даст им хлеба, пока они будут оставаться сво бодными, но кончится тем, что они принесут свою свободу к ногам нашим и скажут нам: „Лучше поработите нас, но накормите нас". Поймут наконец сами, что свобода и хлеб земной вдоволь для вся кого вместе немыслимы, ибо никогда, никогда не сумеют они разделиться между собою!"
129. Berdyaev, *Dostoevsky*, 141.
130. Berdyeav, *Dostoevsky*, 141. In the Russian, "Вот эта потребность общности преклонения и есть главнейшее мучение каждого человека едино лично и как целого человечества с начала веков. Из-за всеоб щего преклонения они истребляли

However, as de Lubac argued, despite the fact of its rejection of the "higher world," socialist religion still seeks transcendence. Created in the image of God, which is indestructible, it cannot help but do so. Humanity argues the Grand Inquisitor, longs for communality of worship, "and this need for communality of worship [эта потребность общности преклонения] is the chief torment of each man individually, and of mankind as a whole, from the beginning of the ages. In the cause of universal worship [всеобщего преклонения], they have destroyed each other with the sword."[131] For even more than earthly bread, argues the Grand Inquisitor, is that humanity desires a transcendent destiny, "for the mystery of man's being is not only in living, but in what one lives for. Without a firm idea of what he lives for, man will not consent to live and will sooner destroy himself than remain on earth, even if there is bread all around him."[132] This need for unity is a fundamental aspect of humanity created in the image of God. Like de Lubac, Dostoevsky knew that this is a genuine desire of the human heart. However, the Inquisitor's solution for unity, the "image" of bread, bringing them into "one great anthill" is a deceptive and false unity that does not engender authentic freedom. In fact, freedom is the first thing that must be overcome: "The first object of the socialist religion is to overturn that freedom of the human spirit which introduces an irrational principle into life along with numberless sufferings."[133] Therefore, this justifies the sovereignty of Shigalev's "one percent," an aristocratic vision of governance that will organize the happiness of the other ninety-nine percent: "Man is unhappy and his history is tragic because he is endowed with spiritual liberty: force him to renounce that, win him over by an illusive offer of bread, and it will be possible to bring about happiness in the world."[134]

The elder Zosima also addresses the need for this "inner" universal unity in his teaching, in which "earthly bread" will not satisfy nor have

---

друг друга мечом. Они созидали богов и взывали друг к другу: „Бросьте ваших богов и придите поклониться нашим, не то смерть вам и богам вашим!"

131. Dostoevsky, *Brothers Karamazov*, 254.

132. Dostoevsky, *Brothers Karamazov*, 254.

133. Berdyaev, *Dostoevsky*, 143.

134. Berdyeav, *Dostoevsky*, 143. In the Russian, "Ибо тайна бытия человеческого не в том, чтобы только жить, а в том, для чего жить. Без твердого представления себе, для чего ему жить, человек не согласится жить и скорей истребит себя, чем останется на земле, хотя бы кругом его всё были хлебы. Это так, но что же вышло: вместо того чтоб овладеть свободой людей, ты увеличил им ее еще больше!"

the power to unite. In many ways, Zosima and the Inquisitor agree that modern science and atheistic socialism are powerless to unite humankind because they do not address the "spiritual" need in humankind:

> Look at the worldly and at the whole world that exalts itself above the people of God: are the image of God [лик божий] and his truth not distorted in it? They have science, and in science only that which is subject to the senses. But the spiritual world [же духовный], the higher half of man's being [высшая половина существа], is altogether rejected, banished with a sort of triumph, even with hatred.[135]

The freedom of living only for our materialistic needs and basing societal "happiness" on science, argues Zosima (and Ivan), are insufficient to unify humanity. According to Zosima, the increase of wealth and the advancement of technology will also not truly satisfy humanity's hunger for "heavenly bread": "We are assured that the world is becoming more and more united [единится], is being formed into a brotherly communion [братское общение], by the shortening of distances, by the transmitting of thought through the air. Alas, do not believe in such a union of people."[136] In fact, such materialistically focused living will "distort their nature, for they generate many meaningless and foolish desires, habits, and the most absurd fantasies in themselves." Such "unity," suggests Zosima, will only lead to "blood" and human sacrifice: "These, following science, want to make a just order for themselves by reason alone, but without Christ now, not as before, and they have already proclaimed that there is no crime, there is no sin. . . . In Europe the people are rising up against the rich with force, and popular leaders everywhere are leading them to bloodshed and teaching them that their wrath is righteous."[137]

135. Dostoevsky, *Brothers Karamazov*, 313. In the Russian, "Посмотрите у мирских и во всем превозносящемся над народом божиим мире, не исказился ли в нем лик божий и правда его? У них наука, а в науке лишь то, что подвержено чувствам. Мир же духовный, высшая половина существа человеческого отвергнута вовсе, изгнана с некиим торжеством, даже с ненавистью."

136. Dostoevsky, *Brothers Karamazov*, 313. In the Russian, "Уверяют, что мир чем далее, тем более единится, слагается в братское общение тем, что сокращает расстояния, передает по воздуху мысли. Увы, не верьте таковому единению людей."

137. Dostoevsky, *Brothers Karamazov*, 314. In the Russian, "е вослед науке хотят устроиться справедливо одним умом своим, но уже без Христа, как прежде, и уже провозгласили, что нет преступления, нет уже греха. Да оно и правильно по-их-нему: ибо если нет у тебя бога, то какое же тогда преступление? В Европе восстает народ на богатых уже силой, и народные вожаки повсеместно ведут его к крови и учат, что прав гнев его."

The Inquisitor might agree with Zosima, but Zosima's path (which we will examine in another chapter) is insufficient from Ivan's perspective. Beyond "earthly" bread, a higher "image" is necessary to pacify the moral and spiritual conscience of humanity.

Second, this leads the Inquisitor to the question of moral conscience, the concept of the higher "good" and how this "sovereignty" is mystically mediated in the human, collective conscience. According to the Inquisitor, the majority of humanity cannot bear the burden of freedom of will and the conscience. The freedom of conscience, the moral aspect of human nature is both a seduction, but also a torment: "Did you forget that peace and even death are dearer to man than free choice in the knowledge of good and evil [добра и зла]? There is nothing more seductive for man than the freedom [свобода] of his conscience [совести], but there is nothing more tormenting either."[138] The image of miracle, mystery, and authority are "powers" which are "capable of conquering and holding captive forever the conscience of these feeble rebels."[139] In order to appease the mystery of the conscience, the torment of freedom which they cannot bear, the Grand Inquisitor and his colleagues will become the mediators that will appease their consciences: "Oh, we will allow them to sin too; they are weak and powerless, and they will love us like children for allowing them to sin. We will tell them that every sin will be redeemed if it is committed with our permission; and that we will allow them to sin because we love them."[140] They will be the divine representatives on earth and be perceived as "gods" to the people: "They will marvel at us, and look upon us as gods, because we, standing at their head, have agreed to suffer freedom and to rule over them—so terrible will it become for them in the end to be free! But we shall say that we are obedient to you and rule in your name."[141] Indeed, the whole "mystery"

---

138. Dostoevsky, *Brothers Karamazov*, 254. In the Russian, "Или ты забыл, что спокойствие и даже смерть человеку дороже свободного выбора в познании добра и зла? Нет ничего обольстительнее для человека, как свобода его совести, но нет ничего и мучительнее."

139. Dostoevsky, *Brothers Karamazov*, 255.

140. Dostoevsky, *Brothers Karamazov*, 259. In the Russian, "О, мы разрешим им и грех, они слабы и бессильны, и они будут любить нас как дети за то, что мы им позволим грешить. Мы скажем им, что всякий грех будет искуплен, если сделан будет с нашего позволения; позволяем же им грешить потому, что их любим, наказание же за эти грехи, так и быть, возьмем на себя. И возьмем на себя, а нас они будут обожать как благодетелей, понесших на себе их грехи пред богом."

141. Dostoevsky, *Brothers Karamazov*, 253. In the Russian, "Они бу дут дивиться

that overcomes human freedom is embodied in this totalitarian religious state, a state that provides not just "earthly bread," but a sense of moral and communal cohesion through the name of Christ. That is, it suggests a messianic appeal. The Inquisitor's solution to the problem of conscience is that they—the one percent who rule—will offer themselves as an earthy messianism, who will "suffer" the truth of the lie for the sake of the happiness and peace of society. They uphold the "mystery of Christ" as a transcendent illusion to appease and assure the moral conscience of humanity. It will attend to the "spiritual" aspect of humankind, but it will be rooted in a lie. In the end, argues the Inquisitor, humanity will not be able to endure the "immanent materialism" of the socialist state: "The beast will come crawling to us and lick our feet and spatter them with tears of blood from their eyes. And we shall sit upon the beast and raise the cup, and on it will be written: 'Mystery! [Тайна]'"[142]

As I suggested above, this image of the woman corresponds to symbolism of the Apocalypse, whereby authority is sustained by the beast of the earth that is a parody of the "lamb." It seeks to bring unity to society as the image of worship and devotion. The failure of secular socialism, argues the Grand Inquisitor, to bring unity to heaven and earth is because it does not sufficiently address the inner transcendent need of humanity. Since there is no God, modernist atheist humanism denies the existence of sin or evil. All that is needed is the political organization to ensure the satisfaction of material necessity. The Inquisitor, however, is "realistic" and knows that humans need the myth of mystery to appease their consciences in their inability to love one another and unify humanity. They are enslaved to the Karamazovian "will to power" and they despair in this awareness. Therefore, the deceptive illusion of a transcendent "mystery" becomes a political necessity to assuage the conscience of humanity, tormented in their freedom, by inducing people to hand over their freedom to a mystical earthly power that also satisfies their needs for justice, security, and immediate "happiness." Yet as I argued above, this "happiness" is proposed in contrast to freedom.

на нас и будут считать нас за богов за то, что мы, став во главе их, согласились выносить свободу и над ними гос подствовать—так ужасно им станет под конец быть свободными! Но мы скажем, что послушны тебе и господствуем во имя твое. Мы их обманем опять, ибо тебя мы уж не пустим к себе."

142. Dostoevsky, *Brothers Karamazov*, 258. In the Russian, "Но тогда-то и приползет к нам зверь, и будет лизать ноги наши, и обрызжет их кровавыми слезами из глаз своих. И мы сядем на зверя и воздвигнем чашу и на ней будет написано: „Тайна!"

It stems from a retributive desire to assure "justice" through human sovereignty and not through the mediation of Christ.

Of course, the Inquisitor represents the "church." The Inquisitor prophesies the return to supremacy of the church in the wake of the failure of the socialist experiment. This, we suggest, and explore in the next section on the theme of authority, is the veiled critique of Roman Catholicism, or at the least what Dostoevsky perceived to be the antichristian principle of Christian Romanism. As Berdyaev asserts, for Dostoevsky "French socialism today is nothing but the direct and faithful sequel of the Catholic idea, its full and final expression, it is the inevitable conclusion elaborated through the ages. For French socialism is essentially the *compulsory* union of men, an idea inherited from ancient Rome which Catholicism kept integrally."[143] That is, the socialism that Dostoevsky perceived creeping into Russian society in this context was a "variant reincarnation of the old Roman formula of a universal union, and the same formula would govern the coming social upheaval."[144]

Third, the demonic alignment of the Inquisitor is further expressed in the final image and temptation. The final image of authority pertains to the use of Caesar's sword to ensure the order, peace, and harmony of the state. At this point, Dostoevsky's critique of the corrupt spiritual principle he perceived at the root Roman Catholicism as complicit with the evil one is exposed: "Listen, then: we are not with you, but with him, that is our secret! For a long time now—eight centuries already—we have not been with you, but with *him*. Exactly eight centuries ago we took from him what you so indignantly rejected, the last gift he offered you when he showed you all the kingdoms of the earth: we took Rome and the sword of Caesar [меч кесаря] from him, and proclaimed ourselves sole rulers of the earth [царями земными], the only rulers, though we have not succeeded in bringing our cause to its conclusion."[145] In this

---

143. In the same breath, Berdyaev admits, "Dostoevsky's knowledge of Catholicism was neither deep nor exact." Berdyaev, *Dostoevsky*, 146.

144. Dostoevsky, *Brothers Karamazov*, 146.

145. Dostoevsky, *Brothers Karamazov*, 257. In the Russian, "Может быть, ты именно хочешь услышать ее из уст моих, слушай же: мы не с тобой, а с ним, вот наша тайна! Мы давно уже не с тобою, а с ним, уже восемь веков. Ровно восемь веков назад как мы взяли от него то, что ты с негодованием отверг, тот последний дар, который он пред лагал тебе, показав тебе все царства земные: мы взяли от него Рим и меч кесаря и объявили лишь себя царями земными, царями едиными, хотя и доныне не успели еще привести наше дело к пол ному окончанию."

profound historical "cue," Ward suggests that the controversy between the East and West is alluded to, regarding the "papal claims to authority, an issue that was in turn closely linked to a problem of trinitarian theology—the status of the *filioque*."[146] Although Dostoevsky was not a trained theologian, he breathed the environment of the Russian Orthodox tradition, influenced by Slavophil theologians, such as Aleksei Khomyakov, who stressed the unity of the church rooted in the doctrine of God. Khomyakov argued that the catholicity of the church (*sobornaya*) is universal: "She belongs to the whole world, not to any particular locality; because by her is sanctified the whole human race and the whole earth."[147] Russian Orthodoxy held strongly to the *mysterion* expressed in the Niceno-Constantinopolitan Creed.

According to Khomyakov, the deviation of the creed by the Roman Catholic Church was perceived as deriving from a "different spirit." He states, "As of the pride of the particular Churches which dared to alter the creed of the whole church without their assent of their brethren, was inspired by another spirit, than the spirit of love, and was a crime before God and before the Holy Church; so also their blind wisdom unable to reach the mysteries of God, was a corruption of the Faith, for Faith is not preserved there, where there has been a failure of love."[148] As we see in this text, the primary accusation of the alteration of the confession is an act of sovereignty that is not consistent with the spirit of love. The aspirations of the Roman bishops expressed the imperial spirit of pagan Rome, not the spirit of Christian catholicism united in the mystery of the love of Christ. In the Grand Inquisitor, Dostoevsky expresses the spirit of imperial Romanism that asserts sovereignty in opposition to the spirit of love. Far from bringing universal reunion to humanity, it has only brought further division, violence, and suffering.

Moreover, according to Khomyakov, the addition of the *filioque*:

> Expresses an imaginary dogma unknown to any of the Godly writers, or bishops, or successors of the Apostles who lived in the first ages of the Church, nor uttered by Christ our Saviour. As Christ plainly spoke, so the Church plainly confessed from the beginning and still confesses that the Holy Spirit proceeds from the Father, for not only the outward, but also the inward

---

146. Ward, *Redeeming the Enlightenment*, 8.
147. Khomyakov, *Orthodox Doctrine*, 4.
148. Khomyakov, *Orthodox Doctrine*, 10.

mysteries of God were revealed by Christ and by the Holy Spirit to the holy Apostles and the Church.[149]

As Ward points out, the heart of the controversy was the question of how transcendence and immanence are related.[150] The *filioque*, according to some Orthodox critiques of the doctrine, suggest that if the Spirit is sent by both Father and Son, the church, who represents the Son, has divine sovereignty over all temporal and political affairs, as well as the spiritual.[151] It represents the sovereign conjoining of the spiritual and temporal affairs through the church. Khomyakov suggests as much in his critique of the Roman Catholic amendment to the creed, at least the emphasis on the temporal mission of the Son and the church. The *filioque* gave focus on the external *immanence* side of the mystery: "He who has renounced the spirit of love and has deprived himself of the gifts of grace cannot any longer possess the inner knowledge, that is to say—Faith (in its true sense), but he limits himself to mere outward knowledge, and so he can know only the outward, but not the inward mysteries of God."[152] That is, there is an inordinate focus on immanence at the expense of an "inner" transcendent experience of the mystery of Christ.

According to Khomyakov, this had implications for the Roman mission of the church as well: "Those Christian communities, which severed themselves from the Holy Church, could no longer confess (nor could they mentally comprehend) the process of the Holy Spirit from the Father only, within the Godhead itself, but they were obliged thenceforth

---

149. It goes beyond this project to consider the theological differences between the Russian Orthodox and Catholic understanding of the Trinity. However, Khomyakov states, "The church does not deny, that the Holy Spirit is sent not only by the Father, but also by the Son; the Church does not deny, that the Holy Spirit is communicated to all the reasonable creation, not from the Father only, but also through the Son: but the Church denies that the Holy Spirit has His processional origin in the Deity itself not from the Father only, but also from the Son." Khomyakov, *Orthodox Doctrine*, 11.

150. Khomyakov, *Orthodox Doctrine*, 8.

151. According to Timothy Ware, there are stricter Orthodox critiques, such as the Russian, Vladimir Lossky, who "argues that the imbalance in the Western doctrine of the Trinity has also led to an imbalance in the doctrine of the Church; the filioque, as he sees it, is closely linked to the Roman Catholic emphasis on Papal claims." Ware, however, asserts that "there are 'droves' [of Orthodox] who advocate a more lenient position. While they deplore the unilateral insertion of the Filioque into the text of the creed on part of the West, they do not consider the Latin doctrine of the Double Procession is in itself heretical." Ware, *Orthodox Church*, 207.

152. Khomyakov, *Orthodox Doctrine*, 8.

to confess only the outward mission of the Holy Spirit to all creation."[153] That is, it is a mission, "which is not from the Father only, but also through the Son. The outward law they kept, but the inward sense and the grace of God they lost in their creed as well as their life."[154] This seems to imply, that in losing the "inward" sense of the mystery of God, the Roman Catholic church then focused upon the "outward" mission. It justifies the church—and the pope—as the sovereign head of the outward, external state. Dostoevsky's allusion to this event in the Grand Inquisitor coincides with the advent of political sovereignty of the Roman Catholic church through the reign of the Frankish emperor, Charlemagne.[155] Perhaps this, according to Dostoevsky, is where the real "modernist" drift began, contra de Lubac, centuries prior to a misinformed interpretation of Thomas Aquinas. The Roman Catholic rift with the Orthodox Church meant, at least from the Russian Orthodox perspective, a drift toward an emphasis on immanence at the expense of the inner transcendent mystery of Christ. With the inherent need of humanity for unity, the subtle theological shift of the Trinity occurred to justify the necessity of political ordering through coercion in the name of unification.

Of course, considering what we developed in de Lubac's conception of the priesthood and the *corpus mysticum*, de Lubac would contest Dostoevsky's perception of such an inner spiritual principle of the Roman Catholic church. According to de Lubac, the mystery of the sacrament mediated by the priesthood is the embodiment of incarnate love, uniting all humanity in Christ. Moreover, de Lubac himself is critical of conceptions of papal authority that sovereignly preside over temporal affairs. As we saw in the previous chapter, his conception recognizes the inherent tension introduced by the Gospel as embodied by the church, a tension that Dostoevsky also seems to affirm. De Lubac attempts to recover the "inner transcendent" reality of the Eucharist, as well as affirm its visible reality. Yet, as both de Lubac and Berdyaev maintain, Dostoevsky's critique of the Roman Catholic church was nuanced and complex. For de Lubac, Dostoevsky uses the Roman Catholic as a symbol, "but nothing

---

153. Khomyakov, *Orthodox Doctrine*, 8.

154. Khomyakov, *Orthodox Doctrine*, 8.

155. As Pevear notes, "Exactly eight centuries ago . . . : in 755 A.D., eight centuries before the Inquisitor's time . . . Pepin the Short, king of the Franks, took the Byzantine exarchate of Ravenna and the Pentapolis . . . from the Lombards and turned the territories over to Pope Stephen II, thus initiating the secular power of the papacy." In Dostoevsky, *Brothers Karamazov*, 786.

more."[156] For de Lubac, Roman Catholicism may have been the starting point of Dostoevsky's reflection, but poetically bears little resemblance to it, just as he depicted socialism in *Demons*, "with Russian terrorists as its starting point."[157] In fact, for de Lubac, the Grand Inquisitor bears more resemblance to the "'servants of humanity' that Auguste Comte dreamed of, 'men of noble ambition' who 'take possession of the world of human society, not in virtue of any right, but because of an obvious duty'—for the purpose of organizing 'final order.'"[158] What Dostoevsky was attempting to discern was the demonic spirit that seeks to pervert even that which is meant to represent the divine, the church. The outcome of this evil spirit embodied in the Grand Inquisitor is a "*libido dominandi*" that justifies its sovereignty by deference to a higher transcendence in the deceptive guise of a messianic love for humanity. The church, whether Roman Catholic, Orthodox, or Protestant, is not immune from the spirit of "non-being" as imaged in the portrait of the Grand Inquisitor.

What is important to stress here is that Dostoevsky attempts to apocalyptically expose the spiritual meaning of all political theories of totalitarianism, be they "religious" or "secular."[159] For in reality, all things—even atheistic humanism and its forms of political embodiment—have a deeper spiritual and mystical meaning. The universalist, totalitarian aim of this political vision is made clear: "Had you accepted that third council of the mighty spirit, you would have furnished all that man seeks on earth, that is: someone to bow down to, someone to take over his conscience, and a means of uniting everyone at last into a common, concordant, and incontestable anthill—for the need for universal union is the third and last torment of man."[160] We have already seen the need for the spiritual unity

---

156. De Lubac acknowledges what Dostoevsky wrote in his journal, that "Roman Catholicism sold Christ in exchange for a kingdom on earth." De Lubac, *Drama of Atheist Humanism*, 327.

157. De Lubac, *Drama of Atheist Humanism*, 328.

158. De Lubac examines Auguste Comte as well in *Drama of Atheist Humanism* (328). Moreover, in demonstrating the more nuanced view of Roman Catholicism in relation to Russian Orthodoxy, Ward and Kroeker have suggested that the elder Zosima reflects Francis of Assisi more than any Russian Orthodox priest. Kroeker and Ward, *Remembering the End*, 78.

159. For instance, "Great conquerors, Tamerlanes and Genghis Khans, swept over the earth like a whirlwind, yearning to conquer the cosmos, but they, too, expressed, albeit unconsciously, the same great need of mankind for universal and general union." Dostoevsky, *Brothers Karamazov*, 257.

160. Dostoevsky, *Brothers Karamazov*, 257. In the Russian, "Приняв этот третий

of humanity, but what is stressed here is the necessity of compulsion over freedom to ensure this unity. According to Berdyaev, "Dostoevsky hotly denounces every tendency of Christianity to become a religion of obligation and constraint."[161] It was a controlling idea of Dostoevsky that "there would be no world harmony except through an experience of freedom that embraced both good and evil, that it could not be based on compulsion, whether theocratic or socialistic."[162] For Dostoevsky, truth cannot be coerced or manipulated, but must safeguard the spiritual principle of freedom in humankind. As we argue above, this "freedom" is fundamental to the meaning of the "image of God" in humankind. It is a mystery and must be respected as a sacred and holy dignity. Otherwise, as Berdyaev asserted, "there lies the whole secret of Christianity, and every time in history that man has tried to turn crucified Truth into coercive truth has betrayed the fundamental principle of Christ."[163] This has happened whenever "churchmen" or "priests," have "assumed the mask of earthly sovereignty and laid hands on the sword of Caesar."[164]

Atheistic Humanism as Disincarnate Sovereignty

With the Inquisitor, we are presented with Dostoevsky's conception of the antichrist. Ivan's atheistic humanism seeks, ultimately, to "correct the deed" of Christ. It represents a critique of not only an extreme form of Romanism, but also of atheistic socialism, the human attempt to eradicate the image of Christ in humankind. Dostoevsky's poetic is a powerful critique of the humanistic attempt to reunify "transcendence" and "immanence" apart from the rightful mediation of the Christ, thereby becoming essentially antichrist. It depicts the distorted demonic desire for the "beauty" of unity and social and political harmony, but in the denial of the proper image of God and of divine love of which humanity was created. The Inquisitor—and Ivan—though claiming to have a "love for humankind," only scorns humanity in its freedom. The creation of a

---

совет могучего духа, ты восполнил бы всё, чего ищет человек на земле, то есть: пред кем преклониться, кому вручить совесть и каким образом соединиться наконец всембесспорный общий и согласный муравейник, ибо потребность всемирного соединения есть третье и последнее мучение людей."

161. Berdyaev, *Dostoevsky*, 77.
162. Berdyaev, *Dostoevsky*, 77.
163. Berdyaev, *Dostoevsky*, 198.
164. Berdyaev, *Dostoevsky*, 198.

"higher image" focused on materialism, beyond that of the "whole" of Christ only creates another demonic image. The political totalitarianism expressed in the Grand Inquisitor is really the spirit of retribution that demands "immanent" punishment to enforce unity. Dostoevsky is attempting to express symbolically that the possessive, impatient, immanent desire for justice only unleashes a new moral chaos into the world, despite that it becomes systemic and institutional.

However, for Dostoevsky, this antichristian ethic, the creation of the image of the human-made-divine, only leads to isolation and despair. It is spiritual suicide. This is expressed in the degeneration of Ivan's mind, especially where he is tormented by his "double," the devil. Ivan is tormented by the thought that his antichristian teaching inspired the actual murder of his father by Smerdyakov: "You yourself kept saying then that everything is permitted [всё позволено], so why are you so troubled now, you yourself, sir?"[165] Lest we think that the spirit of the antichrist is only expressed in the heady intellectualism of Ivan, perhaps that precise intellectualism is only a mask. Smerdyakov explicitly accuses Ivan that he is guilty of the murder of his father, "Therefore, I want to prove it to your face tonight that in all this the chief murderer is you alone, sir, and I'm just not the real chief one, though I did kill him. It's you who are the most lawful murderer."[166] In fact, Smerdyakov reveals to Ivan his true essence and he is not different from the Karamazovian earthy force of his shameless father:

> You love money, that I know sir, you also love respect, because you're very proud, you love woman's charms exceedingly, and most of all you love living in peaceful prosperity, without bowing to anyone—that you love most of all sir . . . You're like Fyodor Pavlovich most of all, it's you of all his children who came out resembling him most, having the same soul as his.[167]

As we discussed above, the soul of Fyodor is an isolated, shameless, "sponger." It is these interactions with Smerdyakov that leads to a

---

165. Dostoevsky, *Brothers Karamazov*, 632.

166. Dostoevsky, *Brothers Karamazov*, 627.

167. Dostoevsky, *Brothers Karamazov*, 632. In the Russian, "Деньги любите, это я знаю-с, почёт тоже любите, потому что очень горды, прелесть женскую чрезмерно любите, а пуще всего в покойном довольстве жить и чтобы никому не кланяться—это пуще всего-с. Не захо‑ю т и т е вы жизнь навеки испортить, такой стыд на суде приняв. Вы как Федор Павлович, наиболее-с, изо всех детей наиболее на него похожи вышли, с одною с ними душой-с."

scene where Ivan, under the weight of his conscience, the thought that he is somehow responsible for the murder of his father, begins to mentally disintegrate. Despite Ivan's intent to confess at the trial that he is responsible, the devil appears to Ivan in a hallucination, an expression of "brain fever."[168] What is interesting is the similarity between the portrait of the father and the devil in Ivan's hallucination: "such spongers, gentlemen of agreeable nature, who can tell a story or two and play a hand of cards, and who decidedly dislike having any tasks thrust upon them."[169] In other words, careless, irresponsible, aristocratic, arrogant, self-absorbed. It is in the everyday, materialistic form that the "devil" is revealed, the "antichrist." And if Fyodor represents the moral and intellectual decadence of a progressive modern Russian, landowner class, then Ivan, despite his attempt to rebel in retribution against the buffoonery of his father, still derives from the same *seed*. It is a similar message, but in a more extreme form as *Demons*, Ivan represents too those "possessors" who are rushing down the hill into destruction. It is a prophetic caution regarding the impending catastrophe of Russian society. The story of Ivan exposes the spiritual root of such destiny. The devil mockingly exposes the spiritual source and aim of the "spirit of non-being," that endeavours to completely eradicate the image of God in humankind, exalting the human ego above all else. In Ivan's hallucination, the devil asserts that his "dream is to become incarnate [Моя мечта это—воплотиться], but so that it's final, irrevocable."[170] That is, the devil's desire to incarnate humanity means the dissolution of humanity. It means that the "spirit of non-being" comes to take sovereign residence in the heart of humanity. It means that the soul of humanity itself remains incomplete, broken, fragmented, at war with itself. Bodily passional, sensual eroticism becomes lord of the soul, governing the conscience. Whereas Fyodor Karamazov runs free in his buffoonery and provocative scandal scenes that often end in violence, Ivan's Inquisitor becomes a necessity for any semblance of "order" and "justice" to govern (rather than redeem) Karamazov "baseness." In either case, Satan is the result of a mystical immanentism, in which humanity itself becomes a reflection of the image of Satan—either as liar or as prosecuting authority. It is like a serpent beginning to devour its own tail. In the end, humanity becomes only the devil: "Once incarnate, I accept the

---

168. Dostoevsky, *Brothers Karamazov*, 634.
169. Dostoevsky, *Brothers Karamazov*, 636.
170. Dostoevsky, *Brothers Karamazov*, 638–39.

consequences. Satan *sum et nihil humanum a me alienum puto.*"¹⁷¹ That is, "Satan am I and nothing human is alien to me."¹⁷²

Despite the reality of retributive desire that drives Ivan, we must state that in the portrait of Ivan, and his "devil" in particular, there is another factor to consider that increases the complexity. The chapter, "the Devil," concludes with another "text" that Ivan wrote entitled the "Geological Cataclysm," which imagines a future whereby a happiness without God will be achieved, "people will come together in order to take from life all that I can give, but, of course, for happiness and joy in this world only."¹⁷³ It is a picture of an earthly mysticism, whereby a new humanity will "experience such lofty delight as will replace for him all his former hopes of heavenly delight."¹⁷⁴ The devil even attempts to prophesy an existence that transcends the desire retribution, "out of pride he will understand that he should not murmur against the momentariness of life, and he will love his brother then without any reward. Love will satisfy only the moment of life, but the very awareness of its momentariness will increase its fire, inasmuch as previously it was diffused in hopes of an eternal love beyond the grave . . ."¹⁷⁵ In this text, we get a bit closer to Nietzsche's vision of the Übermensch, which will be examined in the next chapter. Ivan's devil seems to imagine that the retributive desire that drives the socialist materialist vision will eventually overcome that retribution to enjoy a unity and happiness of humanity that have themselves become god-like, "conquering nature" and appreciating each moment of existence.

171. Dostoevsky, *Brothers Karamazov*, 639. In the Russian, "Почему же и нет, если я иногда воплощаюсь. Воплощаюсь, 20 так и принимаю последствия. Сатана sum et nihil humanum a me. alienum puto."

172. This is also the conclusion of Zosima's teaching, where the soul, which is created in the image of God, eternally refuses the eternal love: "'What is hell?' And I answer thus: 'The suffering of being no longer able to love.'" For Zosima, "hell" is the outcome to a self-will such that he rejected the image of Christ: "There are those who remain proud and fierce even in hell, in spite of their certain knowledge and contemplation of irrefutable truth; there are terrible ones, wholly in communion with Satan and his proud spirit [приобщившиеся сатане и гордому духу его все цело]. For them hell is voluntary and insatiable; they are sufferers by their own will." This is the mystical dissolution of humanity beyond the Incarnate love of Christ. The soul's proudful wrath eternally resists and grasps for more than the "whole" for which it has been created. Dostoevsky, *Brothers Karamazov*, 332–34.

173. Dostoevsky, *Brothers Karamazov*, 649.

174. Dostoevsky, *Brothers Karamazov*, 649.

175. Dostoevsky, *Brothers Karamazov*, 469.

However, this vision of the future still comes from the mouth of the "devil," a deceiver, who torments Ivan. Can the devil, especially about speaking about a "love" beyond that of the Christian God, be trusted? Is it possible to create the "man-god," a materially oriented existence that will bring a universal unity and happiness to humanity? And what political violence justifies the movement toward the actualization of such an "eschatological" vision? As I indicated above, Ivan succumbs to "brain fever," especially in relation to his "conscience," the guilt he experiences knowing it was his ethical "theory" that inspired the murder of his father. This is how Alyosha concludes with Ivan's dilemma: "'The torments of a proud decision, a deep conscience!' God, in whom he did not believe, and his truth were overcoming his heart, which still did not want to submit." That is, even within Ivan, the latent higher image disturbs him deeply within. Yet Alyosha holds hope for Ivan: "'God will win!' he thought. 'He will either rise into the light of truth, or . . . perish in hatred, taking revenge on himself and everyone for having served something he does not believe in,' Alyosha added bitterly, and again prayed for Ivan."[176] As de Lubac asserts with respect to Ivan's "Euclidean mind" in resistance to the higher spiritual transcendent reality, "Dostoevsky does not abandon the hope of opening minds to an idea of this kind," that humanity and Western society in particular *needs* God to be made "whole."[177]

---

176. Dostoevsky, *Brothers Karamazov*, 655.
177. De Lubac, *Drama of Atheist Humanism*, 348.

3

Dionysian Desire and the Church and the Modern State in *Zarathustra*

Introduction

IN THE PREVIOUS CHAPTER, we examined Dostoevsky's critique of all attempts of church and state to unite the transcendent and immanent through the Karamazovian force that is atheistic nature. The Inquisitor is presented as the epitome of this "rebellion," a deceptive mediation through the images of "bread," "mystery" and "authority" which is parody and perversion of the *Mysterium crucis*. In this chapter, we will examine Nietzsche *Thus Spoke Zarathustra*. In the next chapter, we will consider the inspiration behind the creation of Zarathustra in greater depth. In this chapter, I focus on the antagonist of the drama, such as the dragon in the section, "On Three Metamorphoses," which represents the "last god." I interpret Nietzsche's *Zarathustra* as a critique of the underlying spirit and ideal of cultural Christianity as he experienced it in late nineteenth-century Christendom. I demonstrate that what is at stake for Nietzsche is the corrupted, resentment rooted conception of existence and in the body and the "natural" desires, such as the "will to power." Moreover, I explore Nietzsche's conception of the church and state in *Zarathustra*, especially in the sections, "The New Idol" and "On Great Events." That is, I demonstrate that Nietzsche's critique of the church and state are superficial attempts engender human, cultural transformation that suffocates the necessary Dionysian power to create the Übermensch.

The Desire for a New Image

Now that we have examined Dostoevsky's expression of the mystical immanentism of atheistic humanism and its political embodiment, we will turn to Nietzsche. According to de Lubac, Nietzsche poses the deepest challenge to Christianity and the church. In Nietzsche, the image of the Incarnation in humankind is directly overthrown. What is at stake in the Nietzschean drama of atheist humanism is "the Christian conception of life, Christian spirituality, the inward attitude which, more than any particular act or outward gesture, bespeaks the Christian—that is what is at stake."[1] This is what Nietzsche intended to do, to go after and to eradicate the "Christian ideal": "Hostile to Christianity from the time when, at about the age of twenty, he lost his faith, Nietzsche opposed it with an absolute No. . . . For him, as for men like Comte and Feuerbach, Christianity was dead and done with."[2] We see at the heart of *Zarathustra*, whereby Christianity is essentially a "shadow" following Zarathustra, "I am a wanderer who has already walked a great deal at your heels—always on my way, but without any home; so that I really lack little being the Eternal Jew, unless it be that I am not eternal, and not a Jew?"[3] That is, as we will see, for Nietzsche, Western Christianity and its affirmation of the sovereign transcendence of the divine in the Incarnation is an insubstantial imitation of the reality of the form of immanence-transcendence poetically depicted in Zarathustra.

In the next chapter, we will examine how Nietzsche came to the idea of "Zarathustra" as a "redemptive vision," but for our purposes here, I explore his critique of Western attempts to unify and mediate the transcendent and the immanent through the political embodiments of the church and modern political state. According to de Lubac, for Nietzsche, "God is nothing more than the mirror of man, who, in a certain intense, exceptional state, becomes aware of the power that is in him or of the love that exalts him."[4] Religion, belief in God, is a debasement of human-

1. De Lubac, *Drama of Atheist Humanism*, 113.
2. De Lubac, *Drama of Atheist Humanism*, 114–15.
3. Nietzsche, *Zarathustra*, 386.
4. Yet de Lubac interprets Nietzsche's atheism as more indebted to Feuerbach than he would admit, "more, I dare say, than he thought—through his two masters,

kind, for it robs humanity of its own power. It is a kind of duplication. As we will interpret it, this "duplication" for Nietzsche is a false mediation, a deceptive attempt to unite the transcendent and the immanent. And for Nietzsche, what is at stake is unmasking the false mediation of the particular "God" as represented in Western Christendom. As I will demonstrate below, Nietzsche is still very much interested in "God," but in a much more "thinkable" one in opposition to the God of the Western church and the modern idealists in the wake of Christianity. Like Dostoevsky, Nietzsche is concerned with demonstrating the false, sick image of God, as represented in the Christianity of the Western church and the underlying values that are then transmitted and reflected in the idealism of modernist political ethics.

According to de Lubac, however, the language of the "death of God" takes on something new in Nietzsche. The expression "God is dead" certainly had "its place in the most traditional theology as signifying what happened on Calvary."[5] This can be seen from Luther's chorale "God himself is dead" to Hegel's taking of this idea, turning it into "one of the essential categories of his own thought, applying it both to Christ who dies and comes to life again and to human reason, which must pass through the moment of negation in order to join the universal spirit."[6] The same expression is found in such mystics as Jacob Boehme and Angelus Silesius: "Through love, the latter sang, 'God is led into dying', 'God dies in order to live in thee.'"[7] However, this is not how Nietzsche understood it. For Nietzsche, the "death of God" is not a mere statement of fact, nor is it a lament, nor is a sarcastic expression: it states a choice. It is a brutal act of will.[8] For de Lubac, Nietzschean atheism is an act, "as definite and brutal as that of a murderer."[9] What is needed is courage to

---

Schopenhauer and Wagner." Wagner stated that Feuerbach was the "only real philosopher of modern times" and the "representative of the radical and categorical liberation of the individual." De Lubac observes that it is not surprising to find that before madness overtook him, "Nietzsche's notes for the great synthesis on *Der Wille zur Macht* (The Will to Power)—a project he was continually postponing—included an explanation of belief in God that comes close to Feuerbach's, but with an added element of passion." De Lubac, *Drama of Atheist Humanism*, 44.

5. De Lubac, *Drama of Atheist Humanism*, 47.
6. De Lubac, *Drama of Atheist Humanism*, 47.
7. De Lubac, *Drama of Atheist Humanism*, 47.
8. De Lubac, *Drama of Atheist Humanism*, 49.
9. De Lubac's comments are based on Nietzsche's *Joyful Science*, where the madman proclaims the death of God and it is "we" who have murdered God. De Lubac, *Drama of Atheist Humanism*, 47.

"stand firm" against God.[10] In other words, for de Lubac, Nietzschean atheism is rooted in the heroic strength of the will to overcome the "God" of Western Christendom. At stake is a "spiritual battle" for the heart and will of Western culture.

The War against the Dragon, the "Last God"

In the "myth" of *Zarathustra*, Nietzsche presents us with another "image," new symbols that might awaken in the reader a new desire, emboldening the will to overcome the weakness of the Christian will. This Nietzschean "inner struggle" is formulated in the symbolic language of metamorphosis. In this way, the dramatic mythic depiction of Zarathustra is a form of mediation, but one that intends to initiate and inspire a new kind of human "becoming." That is, his vision for humanity is focused on the importance of *transformation*. At the outset of book I in the section, "On the Three Metamorphoses" (*Von den drei Verwandlungen*), Nietzsche provides a window into the meaning of the entire work of *Zarathustra*.[11] We could even go so far as to say that this section contains in a symbolic nutshell the entire thrust of Nietzsche's philosophy: "Of the three metamorphoses of the spirit I tell you: how the spirit becomes a camel; and the camel, a lion; and the lion finally a child."[12] *Thus Spoke Zarathustra* is the poetic expression of this dramatic transformation of soul, which moves toward a more authentic embodiment of the divine on earth through the overcoming and victory over the "God" of the West. The camel spirit embodies, according to Gooding-Williams, who uses the language of *The Genealogy of Morals* to interpret this text: "an attitude according to which nothingness, or the ascetic ideal, is the purpose of human existence."[13] That is, the seduction of the "thou shalt" is, as a form of transcendent valuation, in actuality, a "will to nothingness."[14] That the camel, seduced by the deceptive values of the dragon, embodies an ascetic ideal that denies the body and the material in time and space. Therefore, a metamorphosis

10. De Lubac, *Drama of Atheist Humanism*, 76.

11. Nietzsche, *Zarathustra*, 137.

12. According to Robert Gooding-Williams, the speech in this section is significant because it expresses the plot structure of *Zarathustra*. For him the three metamorphoses describe "modes of action" which poetically inspire the creation of new values. Gooding-Williams, *Zarathustra's Dionysian Modernism*, 31.

13. Gooding-Williams, *Nietzsche's Dionysian Modernism*, 34.

14. Gooding-Williams, *Nietzsche's Dionysian Modernism*, 34.

is necessary, "In the loneliest desert, however, the second metamorphosis occurs: here the spirit becomes a lion who would conquer his freedom and be master in his own desert. Here he seeks out his last master: he wants to fight him and his last god; for ultimate victory he wants to fight with the great dragon."[15]

As Gooding-Williams has noted, the image of the dragon is a nuanced symbol for Nietzsche. While it may be an allusion to Wagner's *The Ring of the Nibelung*,[16] it certainly echoes the imagery of the Apocalypse, the "great dragon," the "great serpent, called the devil, or Satan, who leads the whole world astray" (Rev 12:9). Dostoevsky also employs the imagery of the Apocalypse in the Grand Inquisitor. The demonic figure of the beast was connected to deceptive totalitarianism of the Inquisitor, who sought to overcome the freedom of humanity and to unite humanity through the cynical use of the "three images" under the guise of the "love of humanity." In this way, Dostoevsky expressed the demonic spirit that corrupts the purity of the image of Christ in humanity and in the church. We argue that it was a deceptive attempt to unite the transcendent and the immanent, but through a profound dehumanization. In Nietzsche's use of the dragon, the same impetus exists to limit the freedom of humanity. However, rather than a mutated and corrupt form of Christianity, Nietzsche's use of the dragon is to critique the nature of the Christian spirit itself. We see this in the text itself: the dragon is a great lord and god, who represents the "thou shalt (*du-sollst*)." This signifies a transcendent moral imperative that is imposed on humanity. In more concrete terms, the "thou shalt" signifies the command of God through Christ, particulary, the Christian affirmation to "love God" and to "love thy neighbour." We will examine further the nature of Nietzsche's critique of Christian ethics below, but for now, we observe how this "valuation," this form of spirituality is really a camel-spirit enslaved and seduced by the draconian spirit that has sickened the human will and its heroic potential. The text itself uses the language of "values" that subdue the "*ich will*" of the lion spirit:

> "Thou shalt" [du sollst] is the name of the great dragon. But the spirit of the lion says, 'I will' [ich will]. 'Thou shalt' [du sollst] lies in his way, sparkling like gold, an animal covered with scales; and on every scale a golden "thou shalt" [du-sollst]. Values, thousands of years old, shine on these scales; and thus, speaks the mightiest of dragons: "All values have long been created, and

---

15. Nietzsche, *Zarathustra*, 137.
16. Gooding-Williams, *Nietzsche's Dionysian Modernism*, 35.

I am all created value. Verily, there shall be no more, 'I will' [ich will]. Thus, speaks the dragon.[17]

It is this symbolic context that governs the entire narrative of Zarathustra and is an important clue to the meaning of *Zarathustra*. At stake, pertaining to the theme of the "will," is the question of sovereignty, "who decides on the exception." However, the "thou shalt" of the dragon, argues Zarathustra, is powerfully seductive, threatening to withhold the spirit from transforming from a camel-spirit to the lion-spirit and ultimately the child. At stake is the question of the power and strength of desire to overcome the dragon to become the lion. It is a question of sovereign power of the human spirit to overcome itself in the "desert." In other words, the central conflict in the poetics of *Zarathustra* could be formulated, is it possible for humanity to create a form of divine sovereignty beyond the transcendence of the divine will as embodied in the Western ecclesial and political culture? This desire to rise above the false transcendence of Western modern culture is expressed in Zarathustra's critique of the "last man" in the prologue: "The time has come for man to set himself a goal: the time has come to plant the seed of his highest hope. His soil is still rich enough. But one day this soil will be poor and domesticated, and no tall tree will be able to grow in it."[18] Zarathustra endeavours to awaken the "last man" to transform itself beyond the domesticated, barren, and hollow ascetic ideal that modernism has inherited from Western Christianity. Again, to reformulate the question: Can humanity create a higher image for itself beyond the image enforced by the dragon of the god of Christendom, create an image that is a more authentic reflection of the true reality of existence, a truer reflection of how the immanent might move toward the transcendent?

As stated, in *Zarathustra*, Nietzsche creates a new image, which will stir in humanity a new desire to overcome the deceptive allure of the dragon. It is the "ich will" of the Lion that will overcome the "thou shalt" of the dragon. This is war of the spirit—a "spiritual battle"—as de Lubac frames it.[19] in the Prologue, Nietzsche describes this image as the Übermensch, a vision of the divine-human being that is more "faithful to the earth": "Behold, I teach you the overman. The overman is the meaning of the earth. Let your will say: the overman shall be the meaning of the earth!

17. Nietzsche, *Zarathustra*, 138–39.
18. Nietzsche, *Zarathustra*, 129.
19. De Lubac, *Drama of Atheist Humanism*, 112.

I beseech you, my brothers, remain faithful to the earth, and do not believe those who speak to you of otherworldly hopes!"[20] The Übermensch is the aim of humanity, the overcomer of the dragon, the embodiment of the Lion-spirit. Yet, what precisely is this aim? What is the Übermensch moving toward? In the section, "On the Three Metamorphoses," this overman is imaged as the lion that moves toward the transformation of the church, which is an image of sovereignty: "The child is innocence and forgetting, a new beginning, a game, a self-propelled wheel, a first movement, a sacred, 'Yes.'" That is, the child embodies the movement of an immanence toward the transcendent, yet the child remains "faithful to the earth." Nietzsche is attempting to present a poetic vision of the possibility of a new kind of human existence beyond Western Christianity. It is an open question among scholars whether within the narrative, Zarathustra becomes the "child" (*Das Kind*).[21] Nonetheless, in the image of the "child," we see Nietzsche's creative aim: "Why must the preying lion still become the child? The child is innocence and forgetting, a new beginning, a game, a self-propelled wheel, a first movement, a sacred 'Yes.'"[22] In other words, the child is a sovereign, a divine-like agent who has the power to create "new values." New values engender new forms of "being," transforming the person at the deepest levels of the human psyche. It is a vision of the metamorphosis of the human heart. The is not necessarily the recovery of a lost innocence or the redemption of a lost paradise. It is future oriented, moving forward to an unknown form of becoming. That is, the child signifies the possibility of a new potential still unimagined, a form of becoming that has not yet existed. The climactic point of overcoming the camel-spirit as the lion-will, making ways for the new child is found in book III, where Zarathustra becomes the prophet of the eternal return. We will devote special attention to this in the next chapter.

The death of this "*letzten Gotte*" of Christendom is precisely what we emphasized above in our initial reflection in the section "On the Three

---

20. Nietzsche, *Zarathustra*, 124.

21. Gooding-Williams argues that the problem resides in how scholars interpret the children in relation to Romanticism. For instance, Erich Heller interprets the child as a "kind of symbol of a paradise regained (or attained)." That is, the child is a figure of naïveté, a "unity with nature that signify a dissolution of self-consciousness." This interpretation would place Nietzsche's child in the tradition of Rousseau, Schiller, and Hegel. For a summarization of the debate see *Zarathustra's Dionysian Modernism*, 40–44.

22. Nietzsche, *Zarathustra*, 139. In the German, "*Was muss der raubende Löwe auch noch zum Kinde werden? Unschuld ist das Kind und Vergessen, ein Neubeginnen, ein Spiel, ein aus sich rollendes Rad, eine erste Bewegung, ein heiliges Ja-Sagen.*"

Metamorphoses." This theme pervades the entire narrative and is crucial for understanding Nietzsche. We also see it in the prologue: the entire narrative of Zarathustra is premised on the "death of God." As Zarathustra descends from the mountain, leaving his solitude, to "become human" again (*wieder Mensch werden*), he is confronted with a hermit. The hermit recognizes Zarathustra and also recognizes that something has transformed in him, something has changed in his solitude on the mountain apart from the masses: "No stranger to me is this wanderer: many years ago, he passed this way. Zarathustra he was called, but he has changed... Zarathustra has changed [*Verwandelt*], Zarathustra has become a child [*Kind*], Zarathustra is an awakened [*Erwachter*] one."[23] Zarathustra has become an "enlightened one." Yet Zarathustra in the end will keep his distance from the hermit. Although they have both left the marketplace for the solitude of the mountain, Zarathustra is disturbed by how vastly different they are. They are both "mystics," but "united" to something entirely different. For the hermit, "I make songs and sing them; and when I make songs, I laugh, cry, and hum: thus, I praise God... I praise the God who is my God."[24] But when Zarathustra leaves the hermit, he "spoke thus to his heart: 'Could it be possible? This old saint in the forest has not yet heard anything of this, that *God is dead!*'"[25] The old hermit has not yet heard the frantic message of the madman who proclaimed the death of God of Western Christendom.

The above analysis helps us to understand the meaning of the "death of God" in the thought of Nietzsche, especially as expressed in *Zarathustra*. The death of God as symbolized in the "*ich will*" in direct opposition to the "*du-sollst*" of the dragon is also the direct opposition to the values as embodied in the church and the modern political state. It is a direct assault on the underlying values and acestic spirit of Christianity, as Nietzsche understood it, a denial of our existence in time and space. Gooding-Williams suggests that, as Nietzsche wrote within the German, Protestant context, the expression of the "pure" natural will is meant to replace Luther's emphasis on the sovereign will of God revealed in Christ.[26] In light of de Lubac's concerns, Nietzsche represents the most

23. Nietzsche, *Zarathustra*, 123.
24. Nietzsche, *Zarathustra*, 124.
25. Nietzsche, *Zarathustra*, 124. In the German, "*Als Zarathustra aber allein war, sprach er also zu seinem Herzen: „Sollte es denn möglich sein! Dieser alte Heilige hat in seinem Walde noch Nichts davon gehört, dass Gott todt ist!"*"
26. Gooding-Williams, *Zarathustra's Dionysian Modernism*, 37.

explicit attempt to affirm the "natural" will and desire freed from the draconian metaphysical presuppositions that have shaped the concept of the sovereignty of God and the valuations that undergird the crucified Christ. As we will see in the following sections, *Zarathustra* is Nietzsche's poetic attempt to expose and unveil the "spiritual" or perhaps better "psychological" reasons for the creation of the sovereignty of God and the "thou shalt" of the dragon. As we will see, even the modernist, Platonic assumption of "justice" rooted in human "transcendent" rationality, which also attempts to order and unite humanity, is deeply suspect for Nietzsche. Above all, the Christian, socialist, and democratic emphasis on compassion and equality—neighbour-love—is the most grotesque lie and distortion of all, a deceptive mask of the underlying "will to power," a cloaked expression of the *"libido dominandi,"* or Dostoevsky's poetic formulation, the Karamazovian desire.

The Image of a Tortured God: Bodily Despair and Nihilism

In the sections "On the Afterworldly" [*Von den Hinterweltlern*] and "On the Blessed Isles" (*Auf den glückseligen Inseln*), Zarathustra gives us further rationale for the death of God. In these sections, Nietzsche exposes the psychological roots of the reason for the sovereignty of the dragon, the Western Christian god of the West. The assertion of the sovereignty of God is less about a metaphysical argument than an expression of the sickness of *desire* [*Lust*]. It is desire that has been distorted by a false and deceptive image of God and the world. The desire for God reflects an unhealthy and sick desire for the transcendent, which distorts one's perception of the natural world. What is interesting is how Zarathustra articulates this as a "confession": "At one time Zarathustra too cast his delusion [*Wahn*] beyond man, like all the afterworldly. The work of a suffering [*leidenden*] and tortured [*zerquälten*] god, the world then seemed to me."[27] The concept of God made the soul "drunk" so as to escape the suffering pains and limitations of the experience of life: "Drunken *desire* [*Trunkne Lust*] it is for the sufferer to look away from his suffering and to lose himself. Drunken joy and loss of self the world once seemed to me. This world, eternally imperfect [*ewig unvollkommene*], the image

---

27. Nietzsche, *Zarathustra*, 143. In the German, "*Einst warf auch Zarathustra seinen Wahn jenseits des Menschen, gleich allen Hinterweltlern. Eines leidenden und zerquälten Gottes Werk schien mir da die Welt.*"

of an eternal contradiction [*Widerspruches Abbild*], an imperfect image [*unvollkommnes Abbild*]—a drunken joy for its imperfect creator: thus, the world once appeared to me."[28] For Zarathustra, this delusion of the "afterworld," and of "God," was the creative invention of himself that derived from a sickened ego, overcome with suffering: "It was suffering [*Leiden*] and incapacity [*Unvermögen*] that created all afterworlds—this and that brief madness of bliss which is experienced only by those who suffer most deeply."[29] It was weariness and bodily fatigue of life that created "God":

> Believe me, my brothers: it was the body [*Leib*] that despaired [*verzweifelte*] of the body and touched the ultimate walls with the fingers of a deluded spirit ... it was the body that despaired of the earth [*Erde*] and heard the belly of being [*den Bauch des Seins*] speak to it. It wanted to crash through these ultimate walls with its head, and not only with its head—over there to "that world.[30]

That world, for Zarathustra, is an "inhuman world" [*unmenschliche Welt*] that has caused people to sacrifice their lives for "nothing" [*Nichts*]: "It was the sick and decaying who despised body and earth and invented the heavenly realm and the redemptive drops of blood [*erlösenden Blutstropfen*]."[31] This despairing body, in other words, gave rise to the nihilism of God.

What is necessary, argues Zarathustra, is not to deny the creative power of the will, the same will that created "God." The creative will to power pertains, as we saw in the previous section, to a metamorphosis of

28. Nietzsche, *Zarathustra* 143. In the German, "*Trunkne Lust ist's dem Leidenden, wegzusehn von seinem Leiden und sich zu verlieren. Trunkne Lust und Selbst-sich-Verlieren dünkte mich einst die Welt. Diese Welt, die ewig unvollkommene, eines ewigen Widerspruches Abbild und unvollkommnes Abbild—eine trunkne Lust ihrem unvollkommnen Schöpfer:—also dünkte mich einst die Welt.*"

29. Nietzsche, *Zarathustra*, 143. In the German, "*Leiden war's und Unvermögen—das schuf alle Hinterwelten; und jener kurze Wahnsinn des Glücks, den nur der Leidendste erfährt.*"

30. Nietzsche, *Zarathustra*, 143–44. In the German, "*Glaubt es mir, meine Brüder! Der Leib war's, der am Leibe verzweifelte,—der tastete mit den Fingern des bethörten Geistes an die letzten Wände. Glaubt es mir, meine Brüder! Der Leib war's, der an der Erde verzweifelte,—der hörte den Bauch des Seins zu sich reden. Und da wollte er mit dem Kopfe durch die letzten Wände, und nicht nur mit dem Kopfe,—hinüber zu „jener Welt".*"

31. Nietzsche, *Zarathustra*, 144. In the German, "*Kranke und Absterbende waren es, die verachteten Leib und Erde und erfanden das Himmlische und die erlösenden Blutstropfen.*"

the will. It means creating a "brighter flame": "I overcame myself [überwand mich], the sufferer; I carried my own ashes to the mountains; I invented [erfand] a brighter flame [hellere Flamme] for myself."[32] Zarathustra is interested in the healing of those sick with desire for the transcendent beyond this life: "Zarathustra is gentle [Milde] with the sick . . . May they become convalescents, men of overcoming [Überwindende], and create a higher body [höhren Leib] for themselves!"[33] This "brighter flame" and "higher body" is the "overman." They must learn to create beyond the conjecture of eternal transcendence: "God is a conjecture [eine Muthmaasung]; but I desire that your conjectures should not reach beyond your creative will. Could you create [schaffen] a god? Then do not speak to me of any gods. But you could well create the overman [Übermensch]."[34] To create the overman is to create what is "thinkable": "God is a conjecture but I desire that your conjectures should be limited by what is thinkable [Denkbarkeit]. Could you think [denken] a god? But this is what the will to truth [Wille zur Wahrheit] should mean to you: that everything be changed into what is thinkable for man, visible for man, feelable by man."[35] In this text, we see a "mystical immanentism" whereby the rejection of God is premised on the *desire to be a god*: "But let me reveal my heart to you entirely, my friends: if there were gods, how could I endure not to be a god! Hence there are no gods. Though I drew this conclusion, now it draws me."[36] Resisting the God of the Christianity and the West does not mean "atheism" in the modernist sense, but even, as de Lubac suggests, a "growing in stature."[37] That is, humanity can grow

---

32. Nietzsche, *Zarathustra*, 143. "*Ich überwand mich, den Leidenden, ich trug meine eigne Asche zu Berge, eine hellere Flamme erfand ich mir. Und siehe!*"

33. Nietzsche, *Zarathustra*, 145. "*Milde ist Zarathustra den Kranken. Wahrlich, er zürnt nicht ihren Arten des Trostes und Undanks. Mögen sie Genesende werden und Überwindende und einen höheren Leib sich schaffen!*"

34. Nietzsche, *Zarathustra*, 198. In the German, "*Gott ist eine Muthmaassung; aber ich will, dass euer Muthmaassen nicht weiter reiche, als euer schaffender Wille. Könntet ihr einen Gott schaffen?—So schweigt mir doch von allen Göttern! Wohl aber könntet ihr den Übermenschen schaffen.*"

35. Nietzsche, *Zarathustra*, 198. In the German, "*Gott ist eine Muthmaassung: aber ich will, dass euer Muthmaassen begrenzt sei in der Denkbarkeit. Könntet ihr einen Gott denken?—Aber diess bedeute euch Wille zur Wahrheit, dass Alles verwandelt werde in Menschen—Denkbares, Menschen—Sichtbares, Menschen—Fühlbares!*"

36. Nietzsche, *Zarathustra*, 198. In the German, "*Aber dass ich euch ganz mein Herz offenbare, ihr Freunde: wenn es Götter gäbe, wie hielte ich's aus, kein Gott zu sein! Also giebt es keine Götter.*"

37. De Lubac, *Drama of Atheist Humanism*, 55.

as the Übermensch. In "On the Blessed Isles," what we see in Nietzsche's fundamental denial of all things "permanent" and "absolute" is a desire instead for the impermanent and "becoming":

> God is a thought that makes crooked [*krumm*] all that is straight [*Gerade*], and makes turn [*drehend*] whatever stands [*steht*]. How? Should time be gone, and all that is impermanent be a mere lie? To think this is a dizzy whirl for human bones, and a vomit for the stomach; verily, I call it the turning sickness to conjecture this. Evil I call it, and misanthropic—all this teaching of the One [*Einen*] and the Plenum [*Vollen*] and the Unmoved [*Unbewegten*] and the Sated [*Satten*] and the Permanent [*Unvergänglichen*]. All the permanent—that is only a parable. And the poets lie too much. It is of time [*Zeit*] and becoming [*Werden*] that the best parables should speak: let them be a praise and justification of all impermanence [*Vergänglichkeit*].[38]

The theological critique issued here pertains to the abstract, idealist God as represented in medieval theological concepts such as the "One," or the "Plenum," or the "Unmoved," influenced by the tradition of natural theology. Zarathustra critiques a formulation of transcendence that stands outside time and space, eternally fixed and immovable. At best, these theological constructs are themselves false images and parables of an authentic "transcendence," the "eternal return." What Zarathustra critiques is the concept of a fixed and eternal permanence, which then justifies and forms the basis of the moral sovereignty, the "thou shalt" of the dragon. And as we have seen in the section, "On the Afterworldly," the source of the creation of false transcendence, the idea of an "eternal" God or Ideal that stands outside nature, derives from a deep form of human suffering, a psychological torment of embodied immanent existence and the desire for an escape from reality into a metaphysical, transcendent delusion.

---

38. Nietzsche, *Zarathustra*, 198–99. In the German, "*Gott ist ein Gedanke, der macht alles Gerade krumm und Alles, was steht, drehend. Wie? Die Zeit wäre hinweg, und alles Vergängliche nur Lüge? Diess zu denken ist Wirbel und Schwindel menschlichen Gebeinen und noch dem Magen ein Erbrechen: wahrlich, die drehende Krankheit heisse ich's, Solches zu muthmaassen. Böse heisse ich's und menschenfeindlich: all diess Lehren vom Einen und Vollen und Unbewegten und Satten und Unvergänglichen! Alles Unvergängliche—das ist nur ein Gleichniss! Und die Dichter lügen zuviel. ber von Zeit und Werden sollen die besten Gleichnisse reden: ein Lob sollen sie sein und eine Rechtfertigung aller Vergänglichkeit!*"

The Sovereignty of Dionysian, Bodily Desire, and the Death of God

For Nietzsche, no more confusion between immanence and theological transcendence as expressed in absolute terms, body and spirit, must be admitted if humanity is to become healthy: "The overman is the meaning [*Sinn*] of the earth . . . remain faithful to the earth [*bleibt der Erde treu*], and do not believe those who speak to you of otherworldly hopes! Poison-mixers are they, whether they know it or not."[39] Zarathustra models greater "godlike desires" [*göttlichen Begierden*] whereby he seeks the immediacy of impermanence, beyond any mediation of an absolute, transcendent: "We loathe these mediators [*Mittlern*] and mixers [*Mischern*], the drifting clouds that are half-and-half and have learned neither to bless nor curse from the heart."[40] There is no fixed transcendent point that determined "good" and "evil." There is only "pure nature," which has no absolute divine destiny, but it is in perpetual motion: "Verily, it is a blessing and blasphemy when I teach: 'Over things stand the heaven Accident [*Zufall*], the heaven Innocence [*Unschuld*], the heaven Chance [*Ohngefähr*], the heaven Prankishness [*Übermuth*].'"[41] The concept of "Purpose" (*Zwecke*) or a higher absolute "Rationality" (*Vernünftigkeit*) is an impossibility: "I delivered them from their bondage under Purpose. This freedom and heavenly cheer I placed over all things like an azure bell when I taught them and through them no 'eternal will' wills ['*ewiger Wille*' *will*]. This prankish folly I have put in the place of that will when I taught: 'In everything is impossible: rationality.'"[42] However, like Ivan,

---

39. Nietzsche, *Zarathustra*, 125. In the German, "*Seht, ich lehre euch den Übermenschen! Der Übermensch ist der Sinn der Erde. Euer Wille sage: der Übermensch sei der Sinn der Erde! Ich beschwöre euch, meine Brüder, bleibt der Erde treu und glaubt Denen nicht, welche euch von überirdischen Hoffnungen reden! Giftmischer sind es, ob sie es wissen oder nicht.*"

40. Nietzsche, *Zarathustra*, 277. In the German, "*Diesen Mittlern und Mischern sind wir gram, den ziehenden Wolken: diesen Halb- und Halben, welche weder segnen lernten, noch von Grund aus fluchen.*"

41. Nietzsche, *Zarathustra*, 278. In the German, "*Wahrlich, ein Segnen ist es und kein Lästern, wenn ich lehre: „über allen Dingen steht der Himmel Zufall, der Himmel Unschuld, der Himmel Ohngefähr, der Himmel Übermuth.*"

42. Nietzsche, *Zarathustra*, 278. In the German, "*Von Ohngefähr*"—*das ist der älteste Adel der Welt, den gab ich allen Dingen zurück, ich erlöste sie von der Knechtschaft unter dem Zwecke. Diese Freiheit und Himmels-Heiterkeit stellte ich gleich azurner Glocke über alle Dinge, als ich lehrte, dass über ihnen und durch sie kein „ewiger Wille"—will. Diesen Übermuth und diese Narrheit stellte ich an die Stelle jenes Willens, als ich lehrte: „bei Allem ist Eins unmöglich—Vernünftigkeit!*"

in Zarathustra there is an erotic will to life, *a will to power*, that governs all life and "natural" existence. This is the Karamazovian force that animates and compels people to create, even beyond themselves. As we saw stated above, Ivan's solution was a cynical totalitarian governance that intentionally uses religious deception and physical force. Nietzsche acknowledges this force, describing it as "Dionysian," but as we will see below, does not share Ivan's atheistic cynicism and therefore justification of political coercion. Nonetheless, this is the creative force of Dionysus, the chaotic, creative, subterranean power of existence that mysteriously exists. However, the intent is to create a "higher image" than the image of God derived from the despairing body. As de Lubac argues, for Nietzsche, "bereft of the God in whom it used to repose, to whom it used to appeal, [humankind] must henceforth go forward and upward. It is forced into creating."[43] That is, in the radical renunciation of the God of the Christian West, Nietzsche "must produce from himself—out of nothingness—something with which to transcend humanity."[44] This sounds, of course, similar to the devil in the hallucination of Ivan. However, the difference stems from the desire for retribution. As we saw above, Ivan's devil also intends to eradicate the image of God in humankind and create a higher image, a new humanity. However, the difference is that Ivan's atheism is rooted in a retributive desire under the confines of the "Euclidean" mind. Nietzsche's Zarathustra is an "atheism" that endeavours to create an image that goes beyond retribution and the desire for revenge. Ivan's Grand Inquisitor gives worship to the spirit of "non-being," who cynically uses religion to enforce a false and deceptive peace, while Zarathustra's intent is to unify the West with a more authentic conception of "god," a "thinkable one" that celebrates and lives godlike, but in a celebration that fully affirms existence in the body with all its suffering. For Nietzsche, this means delving and plunging more deeply and passionately into the immanent Dionysian "will to power," in order to affirm it and through such affirmation, transform it—transcendence. However, Nietzsche provides no rationale as to *why* we exist, why the will to power exists. For him, the Christian modernist "will to truth" only leads to absurd conclusions. Perhaps at best, we can say that the will to power exists for itself. The power of life and death exists. We must learn to live to affirm it.

---

43. De Lubac, *Drama of Atheist Humanism*, 55.
44. De Lubac, *Drama of Atheist Humanism*, 56.

The human body, argues Zarathustra, is the conduit and mediator of such will to power. In the sections "On the Despisers of the Body" [*Von den Verächtern des Leibes*] and "On Enjoying and Suffering the Passions" [*Von den Freuden und Leidenschaften*], we see the basis of Nietzsche's mystical immanentism, which goes beyond reason: "The awakened and knowing say: body am I entirely [*Leib bin ich ganz*], and nothing else; and soul [*Seele*] is only a word for something about the body."[45] The body is a "great reason [*grosse Vernunft*], a plurality with one sense, a war and a peace, a herd and shepherd. An instrument [*Werkzeug*] of your body is also your little reason, my brother, which you call 'spirit'—a little instrument and toy of your great reason."[46] According to Zarathustra, all that exists is the sensual, the feeling, the passion, and the body: "behind your thoughts and feelings, my brother, there stands a mighty ruler [*Gebieter*], an unknown sage—whose name is self [*Selbst*]. In your body he dwells; he is your body."[47] It is the body that causes humans to feel pleasure and pain. Out of these sensations of the body came human reason and morality: "Once you suffered passions [*Leidenschaften*] and called them evil. But now you have only your virtues [*Tugenden*] left: they grew out of your passions. You commended your highest goal to the heart of these passions: then they become your virtues and passions you enjoyed."[48] We see in this text a direct opposition not only to Christian asceticism and the higher spiritual self, but also to Plato's conception of the higher eternal ideal of the rational. If there is no higher transcendent sovereignty, then "divine" sovereignty is in the immanent. And the immanent pertains to the body. Before we develop reason, we are bodily desire.

---

45. Nietzsche, *Zarathustra*, 146. In the German, "*Aber der Erwachte, der Wissende sagt: Leib bin ich ganz und gar, und Nichts ausserdem; und Seele ist nur ein Wort für ein Etwas am Leibe.*"

46. Of course, this anticipates Freud's conception of the "ego," as the irrational desire of the self in relation to sexual desire. In the German, "*Der Leib ist eine grosse Vernunft, eine Vielheit mit Einem Sinne, ein Krieg und ein Frieden, eine Heerde und ein Hirt.*" Nietzsche, *Zarathustra*, 146.

47. Nietzsche, *Zarathustra*, 146. In the German, "*Hinter deinen Gedanken und Gefühlen, mein Bruder, steht ein mächtiger Gebieter, ein unbekannter Weiser—der heisst Selbst. In deinem Leibe wohnt er, dein Leib ist er.*"

48. Nietzsche, *Zarathustra*, 148. In the German, "*Einst hattest du Leidenschaften und nanntest sie böse. Aber jetzt hast du nur noch deine Tugenden: die wuchsen aus deinen Leidenschaften. Du legtest dein höchstes Ziel diesen Leidenschaften an's Herz: da wurden sie deine Tugenden und Freudenschaften.*"

Dionysian Desire and the Church and the Modern State

In other words, what is "sovereign" and "divine" is the body and its desires. Zarathustra becomes more specific than this. The passional desires of the body are clarified further in the section, "On Three Evils" (*Von den drei Bösen*) where Zarathustra seeks to bless lust (*Wollust*), desire for power (*Herrschsucht*—lord/master-seeking), and selfishness (*Selbtsucht*—self-seeking), three desires that have been despised by the "preachers of death" (*Von den Predigern des Todes*).[49] We see all of these desires reflected in *The Brothers Karamazov*, akin to the "sensuality" of the Karamazovian force that drives the family. Nietzsche focuses on these desires that have been denounced as the "sinful nature" by Christianity. The ethical ideal of the Incarnation is that the desires of the flesh must be crucified, so that humanity might be reunited to eternal love. Nietzsche interprets this as the strict denial of the body. As I shall argue in chapter 5, Dostoevsky's vision of asceticism pertains more to the transformation of desire, than to a strict denial of erotic desire and the body. For Nietzsche, however, this desire for self-renunciation is an expression of a sick desire which has created the illusion of absolute transcendence. The "preachers of death" have rejected the desires that are the true source of becoming greater than human. In this sense, they are in "rebellion" against the god Dionysus. The preachers of death are in "rebellion" against their own nature as the living, conscious, embodiment of the will to power. These three "powers" are present for the overman to utilize in the process of becoming. The pure natural "law" or force of life is for the "will to power" (*Wille zur Macht*): "This is your whole will, you who are wisest: a will to power—when you speak of good and evil too, and of valuations [*Werthschätzungen*]."[50] The body and its desires are the expression of this will to power. The Übermensch is the one who has developed the power to conquer and use his own desires, not in self-renunciation, but by blessing them and using them for a greater and higher aim. One must learn how to command oneself, but this is difficult and risky and only a task for the few who have the strength to do so.

---

49. Nietzsche, *Zarathustra*, 300.

50. Nietzsche, *Zarathustra*, 225. In the German, "*Das ist euer ganzer Wille, ihr Weisesten, als ein Wille zur Macht; und auch wenn ihr vom Guten und Bösen redet und von den Werthschätzungen.*"

Tragic *Kenosis* and the Annihilation of Humanity

Again, it is not simply the general concept of the image of God in humankind that comprises the essential critique of *Zarathustra*, it is the radical revaluation of God as revealed in Christ, the Incarnation of God. As de Lubac argues, Nietzsche represents the most radical attack against the Christian conception of life, spirituality, and "ideal."[51] What Nietzsche fought was "trustfulness, ingenuousness, simplicity, patience, love for one's neighbours, resignation, submission to God, a sort of disarming and repudiation of own's own ego."[52] These are the very temptations of an inner "enemy" that has withheld humanity from self-becoming. With Nietzsche, argues de Lubac, "eternal paganism proudly lifts its head, but brings with it, new equipment. It prepares to remold individual life and intimate feelings just as much as public life and the exercise of power. It takes charge of man's destiny, with a view to new conquests."[53] In an active "no"—or the *"ich will"* of the lion—to Christianity, Nietzsche charts the way forward into the tragedy, the harnessing of the will to power to create new forms of valuation beyond humanity. This, in effect, means the annihilation of humanity as conceived under the valuation of the dragon god of the Western Christianity.

What Nietzsche expresses in his prologue to Zarathustra, of course, is that a profound transformation has occurred in his soul. He has moved beyond the Christian desire for God and created a new god for himself in the overman, the "incarnation" of Dionysus. What we see at the beginning of the prologue is an inversion of the basic concept of image of God, and the *kenotic* emptying of Christ expressed in Philippians 2:2–7 is parodied and its meaning transformed.[54] Zarathustra leaves his home at the age of thirty, the same age that Jesus began his ministry, and lives in a cave on the mountain with his animals.[55] As it says in the prologue,

---

51. De Lubac, *Drama of Atheist Humanism*, 113.

52. De Lubac, *Drama of Atheist Humanism*, 116.

53. De Lubac, *Drama of Atheist Humanism*, 117.

54. Paul's ethic is expressed Christologically, "Have this mind among yourselves which is yours in Christ Jesus, who, though he was in the form of God, did not count equality with God something to be grasped, but emptied (*kenosis*) himself by taking the form of a servant, being born in the likeness of humanity" (ESV).

55. Nietzsche's view of Christianity in relation to the "historical" Jesus is more complex than a simple rejection of Jesus. Nietzsche's critique is focused on the "belief" structure that was built around faith in Jesus. For instance, in *the Antichrist*, Nietzsche argues, "I shall now relate the *real* history of Christianity.—the word "Christianity is already a

"When Zarathustra was thirty years old he left his home and the lake of his home and went into the mountains. Here he enjoyed his spirit and his solitude, and for ten years did not tire of it. But at last a change came over his heart, and one morning he rose with the dawn, stepped before the sun, and spoke thus."[56] This is a parody of both Christianity and the Platonic tradition as embodied in patristic and medieval Christian thought. In Plato, the sun is symbolic of the light of God, the "Good beyond being," the source of all things and the source of pure knowledge.[57] The human soul is elevated and purified in a process of ascent toward the light of God. In the Platonic-Christian view, the transcendent, eternal God is reflected in creation, especially in the image of humankind.

However, in Nietzsche's *Zarathustra*, while Zarathustra worships and praises the sun, the sun revolves around and reflects him and not the reverse, "You great star, what would your happiness be had you not those for whom you shine? For ten years you have climbed to my cave: you would have tired of your light and of the journey had it not been for me and my eagle and my serpent."[58] Zarathustra becomes that which the "sun" reflects. Zarathustra is the new image. That which is "Zarathustra" is what humanity itself must ascend toward to overcome itself and attain the divine. The revolving sun reflects Zarathustra's desire to overflow with "light": "I would give away and distribute, until the wise among men find joy again in their folly, and the poor in their riches. For that I must descend to the depths, as you do in the evening when you go behind the sea and still bring light to the underworld, you overrich star."[59]

---

misunderstanding—in reality there has been only one Christian, and he died on the Cross." It was the apostolic community that misunderstood Jesus, "Clearly the little community had *failed* to understand precisely the main thing, the exemplary element in his manner of dying, the freedom from, the superiority *over* every feeling of resentment: a sign of how little they understood him at all!" See *Antichrist*, 163–65.

56. Nietzsche, *Zarathustra*, 121.

57. See Plato, *Republic*, bk. 7, 514a–518c.

58. Nietzsche, *Zarathustra*, 121. In the German, "*Du grosses Gestirn! Was wäre dein Glück, wenn du nicht Die hättest, welchen du leuchtest! Zehn Jahre kamst du hier herauf zu meiner Höhle: du würdest deines Lichtes und dieses Weges satt geworden sein, ohne mich, meinen Adler und meine Schlange.*"

59. Nietzsche, *Zarathustra*, 122. In the German, "*Ich möchte verschenken und austheilen, bis die Weisen unter den Menschen wieder einmal ihrer Thorheit und die Armen wieder einmal ihres Reichthums froh geworden sind. Dazu muss ich in die Tiefe steigen: wie du des Abends thust, wenn du hinter das Meer gehst und noch der Unterwelt Licht bringst, du überreiches Gestirn!*"

Zarathustra's descent from the mountain is presented as a parody of the concept of *kenosis* in Christianity. Zarathustra is portrayed as an "awakened one" basking in his own light as reflected in the sun that revolves around him in his solitude. However, something has also changed in his spirit and the plenitude of the divine that Zarathustra spills out and overflows. Zarathustra desires to share this "gift" (*Geschenk*) with humanity, and so he risks becoming "human" again, in a process of "emptying" himself: "'Bless the cup that wants to overflow [überfliessen], that the water may flow from it golden and carry everywhere the reflection of your delight. Behold this cup wants to become empty again [*wieder leer werden*], and Zarathustra wants to become man again [*wieder Mensch werden*].' Thus, Zarathustra began to go under [*Untergang*]."[60] However, Zarathustra's self-emptying descent, his impending "death" and "rejection" do not, as in Christianity, include the hope of a resurrection. Zarathustra's "mission" and "vocation" is a tragic one, as anticipated in the prologue.[61] Like the tightrope walker who is overcome by the jester, Zarathustra's self-emptying descent is a plunge into the death-filled "chaos" of the masses in the marketplace who do not understand him and therefore reject him: "This man, however, seeing his rival win, lost his head and the rope, tossed away the pole, and plunged into the depth even faster, a whirlpool of arms and legs. The marketplace became as a sea when the tempest pierces it: the people rushed apart and over one another, especially at the place where the body must hit the ground."[62] Zarathustra then goes to the dying body of the tightrope-walker, kneeling beside him as if in parody of a priest giving his parishioner the last rites. Zarathustra reaffirms the tragic character of life, that there is no "afterworld," but it is our vocation to create meaning where there is none. The man seems

---

60. Nietzsche, *Zarathustra*, 122. In the German, "'*Segne den Becher, welcher überfliessen will, dass das Wasser golden aus ihm fliesse und überallhin den Abglanz deiner Wonne trage! Siehe! Dieser Becher will wieder leer werden, und Zarathustra will wieder Mensch werden.' Also begann Zarathustras Untergang.*"

61. Gooding-Williams suggests that Kaufmann's translation of *Untergang* as "going-under" can be also translated as "ruin" or "destruction." Zarathustra's going-under resembles "the death-dealing incarnation of Paul's Christ: it is descent into a ruinous fate that inevitably awaits him once he embraces the human condition." Gooding-Williams, *Zarathustra's Dionysian Modernism*, 56.

62. Nietzsche, *Zarathustra*, 131. In the German, "*Dieser aber, als er so seinen Nebenbuhler siegen sah, verlor dabei den Kopf und das Seil; er warf seine Stange weg und schoss schneller als diese, wie ein Wirbel von Armen und Beinen, in die Tiefe. Der Markt und das Volk glich dem Meere, wenn der Sturm hineinfährt: Alles floh aus einander und übereinander, und am meisten dort, wo der Körper niederschlagen musste.*"

to despair over the meaningless of life: "If you speak the truth ... I lose nothing when I lose my life. I am not much more than a beast that has been taught to dance by blows and a few meager morsels."[63] Zarathustra assures him, "By no means ... You have made danger [*Gefahr*] your vocation [*Beruf*]; there is nothing contemptible in that. Now you perish of your vocation: for that I will bury you with my own hands."[64]

The tightrope-walker represents Zarathustra's ambivalent attitude toward his vocation to teach the overman. On the one hand, it represents his own skepticism with respect to his task of persuading the people in the marketplace to overcome "God," especially the values of Christianity that are politically embodied in the world. As we see at the end of the prologue, after leaving the body to decay in the hollow of a tree, Zarathustra revaluates his mission and recognizes he must not go after the "herd," but seek companions.[65] Zarathustra will call out a "remnant" from the masses: "An insight has come to me: companions [*Gefährten*] I need, living ones—not dead companions and corpses whom I carry everywhere I want to. . . . let me speak not to people, but to companions. Zarathustra shall not become a shepherd or a dog of the herd."[66] Indeed, if there is any form of "social ethic" in Zarathustra, this is one of the first places to look. Zarathustra's audience throughout his drama are his "brothers" and "disciples," fellow "creators [*der Schaffende*] . . . who write new values on new tablets."[67] This anticipates Nietzsche's "aristocratic anarchism," which we will explore further in the next chapter. At this point, we note

---

63. Nietzsche, *Zarathustra*, 132. In the German, "*Der Mann blickte misstrauisch auf. „Wenn du die Wahrheit sprichst, sagte er dann, so verliere ich Nichts, wenn ich das Leben verliere. Ich bin nicht viel mehr als ein Thier, das man tanzen gelehrt hat, durch Schläge und schmale Bissen."*

64. Nietzsche, *Zarathustra*, 132. In the German, "*Nicht doch, sprach Zarathustra; du hast aus der Gefahr deinen Beruf gemacht, daran ist Nichts zu verachten. Nun gehst du an deinem Beruf zu Grunde: dafür will ich dich mit meinen Händen begraben."*

65. Nietzsche, *Zarathustra*, 135. In the German, "*Ein Licht gieng mir auf: Gefährten brauche ich und lebendige,—nicht todte Gefährten und Leichname, die ich mit mir trage, wohin ich will. Sondern lebendige Gefährten brauche ich, die mir folgen, weil sie sich selber folgen wollen—und dorthin, wo ich will. Ein Licht gieng mir auf: nicht zum Volke rede Zarathustra, sondern zu Gefährten! Nicht soll Zarathustra einer Heerde Hirt und Hund werden!"*

66. Nietzsche, *Zarathustra*, 135. In the German, "*Ein Licht gieng mir auf: nicht zum Volke rede Zarathustra, sondern zu Gefährten! Nicht soll Zarathustra einer Heerde Hirt und Hund werden!"*

67. Nietzsche, *Zarathustra*, 136. In the German, "*Die Mitschaffenden sucht der Schaffende, Die, welche neue Werthe auf neue Tafeln Schreiben."*

that the path that Zarathustra outlines is really for "everyone" and for "no one." That is, while available for all, it is only for Zarathustra, a path that he must follow to engender its possibility for others. Zarathustra cannot but help but be a type of messianic hope.

On the other hand, the death of the tightrope-walker represents the tragic nature of the *attempted* "going under." Zarathustra is a parody of Christ, more tragic in that there is no "afterlife," no "resurrection," no power of God to raise to life. The hermit warns Zarathustra that he is like an arsonist and will not be received well by those in the marketplace. In fact, he encourages Zarathustra not to trouble himself with humanity, for they are not worth it. But the spirit of Zarathustra compels him out of "love" for humankind. It is not a "love" for what they are currently, but the desire to give them the "gift" of self-overcoming, to become as he strives to be, an overman. And perhaps, as we see in *Zarathustra*, it pertains not just to our attitude toward life, but to the inevitability of death. Interestingly, when Zarathustra speaks explicitly about the "historical" Jesus, in a section entitled "On Free Death" (*Von Freien Tode*), Zarathustra teaches about how best to die, or to be more specific, the "right time to die."[68] No one has yet, argues Zarathustra, learned to see death as a "festival." To truly overcome the despair of life is to embrace death itself so that it "consummates [*vollbringenden*]—a spur and a promise to the living [*Lebenden*]."[69] To "squander" the soul in "becoming" and "overcoming" as a heroic and noble victor means to make death a festival that engenders and nourishes a future beyond oneself. Zarathustra perceives his impending death as a "festival," a feast for the living to eat his body and create a "higher flame" for themselves. We could go as far as to assert that the tragic death of those who lived courageously, dangerously, attempting to become an overman, becomes a kind of mystical form of mediation for those of the "lower" type to "transcend" to the "thinkable" higher type, the self-becoming, value-creating god. However, in the process, the "last man" of modernism, the secular vestige of Christianity, is exposed as a threat and obstacle to Zarathustra's divine intention to "go under" in order to go over humanity to become the "Übermensch." The spirituality of the death of God means the death of humanity, but the possibility of giving birth of a new kind of humanity, the "child," we saw above in the section "On the Three Metamorphoses." As de Lubac interprets Nietzsche,

---

68. Nietzsche, *Zarathustra* 183.

69. Nietzsche, *Zarathustra*, 184. In the German, "*Den vollbringenden Tod zeige ich euch, der den Lebenden ein Stachel und ein Gelöbniss wird.*"

"Invention and creation: these are the two words that henceforth define the task of the genuine philosopher, who is to be the 'bad conscience of his age.'"[70] That is, as de Lubac interprets Nietzsche's project, the genuine philosopher will "make hay of accepted values, overthrowing them, and scrapping them so that something new can be got out of them."[71] Yet this is not simply philosophical opportunism, but a genuine struggle for a spiritual authenticity of a creative explosive power, creating a higher and better image that people can strive to attain. It is a vision of sovereignty, embracing the will to power to create a new culture and civilization. As Nietzsche declared in *Ecce Homo*, the philosopher's mission is "to command and lay down the law; his research is creation, his creation is legislation, his will to truth is will to power."[72]

The Politics of the Church and State

So far in this examination we have focused somewhat abstractly on Nietzsche's critique of the Christian moral ideal as embodied in the cross. For Nietzsche this is as much a political problem as an ethical and philosophical one. As we saw in *The Brothers Karamazov*, the question of the state and the nature of political power is an underlying theme. For Nietzsche, as with Dostoevsky, the theme of the "State" (*Staat*) as an "anthropological" problem of "humanity as a whole" is clearly seen in *Zarathustra*. In fact, in the section "On Great Events" (*Von grossen Ereignissen*), the church itself is regarded as a form of "state" in rivalry with the modern state. For Nietzsche, both church and state reflect a distorted systemic creation of humanity that is rooted in a spirit of revenge, an unhealthy expression of the will to power. However, let us first examine the meaning of "the state" in *Zarathustra*. We will go beyond the analysis of de Lubac, who does not address the problem of "resentment" or the explicit critique of the church and state in *Zarathustra*.[73] But to properly appreciate and understand Nietzsche's vision of the "child," his redemptive vision of Western culture in comparison with Dostoevsky, we must return to this theme in *Zarathustra*.

70. De Lubac, *Drama of Atheist Humanism*, 63.

71. Nietzsche, *Zarathustra*, 63.

72. Nietzsche, *Ecce Homo*, 101.

73. As de Lubac stated, "I do not propose to embark upon another exposition of Nietzschean anti-Christianism . . . the accusation of "resentment" brought against the founders of Christian ethics and their precursors." De Lubac, *Drama of Atheist Humanism*, 119.

However, we continue to interpret Nietzsche's critique of the church and state with de Lubac's theological formulation in mind, the human desire to unite the immanent with the transcendent. In the next chapter, we will consider de Lubac's interpretation of Nietzsche as the heroic mystic through an analysis of the eternal return.

In Part I, Zarathustra describes the state as the "new idol" (*Vom neuen Götzen*). It is the name of the "coldest of all cold monsters" (*kalten Ungeheuer*).[74] Nietzsche is referring to the external political expression of the "will the power" in its most unrefined form. The politicians of the state are the "swift monkeys" that "all want to get to the throne (*Thron*)."[75] In other words, the state, and those concerned with the state, are competitively seeking for political sovereignty. It is in the desire to dominate the political sphere that they assert their "good and evil." While the phenomenon of the state "precedes" modern embodiments of political power, in *Zarathustra* its latest manifestation is the modern rationalistic, democratic "last man" (*letzte Mensch*) of the marketplace in the prologue, who reject and oppose Zarathustra's teaching of the overman.[76] To be clear, this refers not only to the external impositions of the state, be they through the enforcement of law or political economy. It is the underlying valuations that lead to the embodiment and justification of such compulsion and enforcement.[77]

According to Zarathustra, the modern European state is a monster the stalks, kills, and destroys the possibility of creating new values. The state is the "death of peoples": "Coldly it tells lies too; and this lie crawls out of its mouth; 'I, the state, am the people.'"[78] In this sense, the state is the logic of cold rationalization that seeks to "unify" humanity, but in doing so actually annihilates the potential for becoming an overman. That is, the state is in direct opposition to the freedom of humanity to

---

74. Nietzsche, *Zarathustra*, 160.

75. Nietzsche, *Zarathustra*, 162.

76. Nietzsche, *Zarathustra*, 129–30.

77. In *Untimely Meditations*, Nietzsche argues, "Here, however, we are experiencing the consequences of the doctrine, lately preached from all the rooftops, that the state is the highest goal of mankind and that a man has no higher duty than to serve the state: in which doctrine I recognize a relapse not into paganism but into stupidity." Nietzsche, *Untimely Meditations*, 148.

78. Nietzsche, *Zarathustra*, 160. In the German, "*Staat? Was ist das? Wohlan! Jetzt thut mir die Ohren auf, denn jetzt sage ich euch mein Wort vom Tode der Völker. Staat heisst das kälteste aller kalten Ungeheuer. Kalt lügt es auch; und diese Lüge kriecht aus seinem Munde: „Ich, der Staat, bin das Volk."*"

overcome itself. Furthermore, the externalized form of the will to power is the manifestation of the "preachers of death," who renounce bodily desire.[79] The state is a corporate body that forces itself on "peoples" as the highest value and meaning of existence. The state becomes an annihilator (*Vernichter*) that enforces a unity through violence and through false desires: "They have a sword [*Schwert*] and a hundred appetites [or desires, *Begierden*] over them."[80] Certainly, as we will see in the next chapter, Nietzsche proposes a vision of sovereignty that has political implications. But this text demonstrates that Nietzsche opposes the Hobbesian—and the Grand Inquisitor's—justification of hanging a sword over the heads of society even if "the people" chose one in the form of a social contract. The state, enforced by compulsory methods and techniques, always seeks to take more liberty than what is given. It is driven by the will to power. The state is an imposed sovereignty through the threat of coercion, but also the promise of fulfillment. It presumes to be the highest destiny and aim of humanity and enforces this through the imposition of the "law." However, the state is fundamentally a "lie"; it is an illusionary myth that falsely claims to be the meaning of human existence: "I, the state, am the people."[81] The authority of the state thus falsely claims to reflect the "image of God."

Deceptive Mediation: The Sovereign Claims of the Church and State

For Nietzsche, this means that the value that the state claims to represent is morally absolute. The state, as a cold monster, steals from peoples their language of "good and evil": "This sign [*Zeichen*] I give you: every people speaks its tongue of good and evil, which the neighbour does not understand . . . But the state tells lies in all the tongues of good and evil; and whatever it says it lies—and whatever it has it has stolen . . . Confusion of tongues [*Sprachverwirrung*] of good and evil [*des Guten und Bösen*]: this sign I give you as the sign of the state."[82] Zarathustra alludes here to

79. Nietzsche, *Zarathustra*, 162.
80. Nietzsche, *Zarathustra*, 161.
81. Nietzsche, *Zarathustra*, 161.
82. Nietzsche, *Zarathustra*, 161. In the German, "*Dieses Zeichen gebe ich euch: jedes Volk spricht seine Zunge des Guten und Bösen: die versteht der Nachbar nicht. Seine Sprache erfand es sich in Sitten und Rechten. Aber der Staat lügt in allen Zungen des Guten und Bösen; und was er auch redet, er lügt—und was er auch hat, gestohlen*

the tower of Babel whereby humanity sought to create a "name" for itself in the world of its own image (Gen. 11). In the biblical narrative, humanity resisted the freedom of divinely mandated "multiplication" and therefore sought to remould itself into monolithic unity. What Nietzsche attends to here is the possessive imperialistic desire of human nature for a "unity." Like Dostoevsky's "Grand Inquisitor," the political state power seeks to conjoin the transcendent and the immanent. It claims to mediate sacred, divine sovereignty. To assert its moral and existential sovereignty, the state claims a divine status. It assumes a "divinity" that authorizes its will as sovereign: "'On earth there is nothing greater than I: the ordering [*ordnende*] finger of God am I'—thus roars the monster."[83] In fact, even the humanistic atheists have worshipped this new idol: "Indeed, it detects you too; you vanquishers of the old god. You have grown weary with fighting, and now your weariness still serves the new idol."[84] In reality, the secular worship of the new idol of the state is a new form of the "preachers of death," who preach the "renunciation of life."[85] Indeed, the politics of atheistic humanism still presumes a "transcendent" status to assert its will. It still reflects the "ascetic" spirit of the camel.[86] The state presumes to be the new "god" and, therefore that which sovereignly defines "good and evil." Morality is measured through obedience to the will of the state, since it is the highest value. At bottom, however, those who assume the sovereignty of the "state" are only expressing a possessive desire for power over others: "Watch them clamber, these swift monkeys! They clamber over one another and thus drag one another into the mud and the depth. They all want to get to the throne: that is their madness—as if happiness sat on the throne."[87] The state, therefore, reflects the will to power—a power that has not gone far enough. It has not thoroughly "gone under" in order to break free of the spirit of revenge.

---

hat er's. Falsch ist alles an ihm; mit gestohlenen Zähnen beisst er, der Bissige. Falsch sind selbst seine Eingeweide. prachverwirrung des Guten und Bösen: dieses Zeichen gebe ich euch als Zeichen des Staates. Wahrlich, den Willen zum Tode deutet dieses Zeichen! Wahrlich, es winkt den Predigern des Todes!"

83. Nietzsche, *Zarathustra*, 161. In the German, "*Auf der Erde ist nichts Grösseres als ich: der ordnende Finger bin ich Gottes*"—*also brüllt das Unthier.*"

84. Nietzsche, *Zarathustra*, 161.

85. Nietzsche, *Zarathustra*, 138.

86. Nietzsche, *Zarathustra*, 156.

87. Nietzsche, *Zarathustra*, 162.

Dionysian Desire and the Church and the Modern State 139

In the section "On Great Events," we see the modern state and the church as rivals for the "throne." As a parody, perhaps, of Jesus descent into hell, Zarathustra goes down to the devil.[88] His disciples are dismayed, thinking that the devil has taken him, but he returns five days later and reports his conversation with the "fire hound."[89] The fire hound represents the passional violence of modern revolutionaries and their "great [political] events": "'The earth,' he said, 'has a skin and this skin has diseases. One of these diseases, for example, is called "man" [*Mensch*]. And another one of these diseases is called "fire hound" [*Feuerhund*]'"[90] This fire hound is a "mystery" [*Geheimniss*] to Zarathustra and so he goes "over the seas" and now sees the naked truth concerning all "scum and overthrowdevils."[91] What concerns the revolutionary is "freedom" (*Freiheit*), for "freedom is what all of you like best to bellow."[92] As we have seen, it is for "freedom" that Zarathustra goes into the wilderness to battle the "last god." But according to Zarathustra, the freedom of the modern revolutionary does not go deep enough into the "heart of the earth [*dem Herzen der Erde*]"[93] This freedom is expressed in the political revolution of "great events," the overcoming of the ecclesial state church and the monarchy in order to construct a new society in the name of freedom. Both the state and church claim to speak from the "belly of being," which therefore give significance the sovereign intention of particular "political events."[94] This text is comparable to Dostoevsky's chapter "*So Be It! So Be It!*" where Miusov is astonished at the far-reaching universal intentions of the "aims" of the Russian church, as expressed by Ivan. Both Miusov and Rakitin represent the modernist French revolutionaries in the tradition of Rousseau seeking the modernization of the state through the secularization of its institutions. The rivalry pertains to who will dissolve whom, the church into the state or the state into the church.

---

88. Nietzsche, *Zarathustra*, 242.
89. Nietzsche, *Zarathustra*, 242.
90. Nietzsche, *Zarathustra*, 242.
91. Nietzsche, *Zarathustra*, 243.
92. Nietzsche, *Zarathustra*, 243.
93. Nietzsche, *Zarathustra*, 244. "*Ja, auch euch erräth er, ihr Besieger des alten Gottes! Müde wurdet ihr im Kampfe, und nun dient eure Müdigkeit noch dem neuen Götzen!*"
94. Elsewhere Nietzsche makes the statement, "every philosophy which believes that the problem of existence is touched on, not to say solved, by a political event is a joke—and a pseudo-philosophy." Nietzsche, *Untimely Meditations*, 147–48.

According to Zarathustra, however, the modern political revolutionary is superficial, not plunging into the depths of the "earth" sufficiently: "At most, I take you as earth's ventriloquist; and whenever I have heard overthrow- [*Umsturz-*] and scum-devils talking, I found them like you: salty, mendacious, superficial."[95] The revolutionary does not realize that as soon as one form of sovereignty replaces another, the dead one becomes even more "seductive": "the statue lay in the mud of your contempt; but precisely this is its law, that out of contempt life and living beauty come back to it. It rises again with more godlike features, seductive through suffering."[96] Nietzsche understood the power of *mystique*. Old idols that have been sacrificed by the new idols become mythological and therefore seductive. Zarathustra then counsels "kings and churches and everything that is weak with age and weak in virtue: let yourselves be overthrown—so that you might return to life, and virtue return to you."[97] I maintain that this statement connects with the larger drama of *Zarathustra*, especially as we see in book IV, where kings and popes seek after Zarathustra in the wake of the death of the Christian god of Western culture. It is Zarathustra's invitation to go beyond the atheism of modernism and secular state and to "go under" so as to become an Übermensch. And like Dostoevsky, Nietzsche is not just concerned with the political theory, but what the power-grasping church and state represent. For Nietzsche, the systemic forms of the state are the embodiment of false values that are rooted in a deceptive metaphysic of the despairing body. Although the external systemic violence of the state are expressions of denial, they are creative expressions of the very "will to power," of "Dionysus," the underlying subterranean power that it seeks to escape from. In the denial of and the attempt to "rein in" the chaotic desires of embodied existence and the chaos and suffering that such desire creates, an enforced politics of denial and illusion is the result. This denial results in a sick and perverted embodiment of sovereignty. Yet the irony is that these perverted

---

95. Nietzsche, *Zarathustra*, 243. In the German, "*Höchstens für den Bauchredner der Erde halt' ich dich: und immer, wenn ich Umsturz- und Auswurf-Teufel reden hörte, fand ich sie gleich dir: gesalzen, lügnerisch und flach.*"

96. Nietzsche, *Zarathustra*, 243. In the German, "*Im Schlamme eurer Verachtung lag die Bildsäule: aber das ist gerade ihr Gesetz, dass ihr aus der Verachtung wieder Leben und lebende Schönheit wächst! Mit göttlicheren Zügen steht sie nun auf und leidend-verführerisch.*"

97. Nietzsche, *Zarathustra*, 242. In the German, "*Diesen Rath aber rathe ich Königen und Kirchen und Allem, was alters- und tugendschwach ist—lasst euch nur umstürzen! Dass ihr wieder zum Leben kommt, und zu euch—die Tugend!*"

political and ecclesial expressions are themselves the result of the "will to power," the very power it seeks to sovereignly control through systemic and external measures. We could say, they are false mediators—idols—of the "mystery" of Dionysus.

The Church and Modern State as the "Religion of Pity"

We will now take a closer look at Zarathustra's critique of the church. At the mention of the church, the fire hound takes offence: "Church [*Kirche*]? What is that?" In reply, Zarathustra asserts that even the church "is a kind of state—the most mendacious kind."[98] The "state" claims to speak out of the "belly of reality" (*dem Bauch der Dinge*) for the state "wants to be by all means the most important beast [*Thier*] on earth."[99] As we saw above, to speak out of the "belly of reality" is to claim to know and to represent the transcendent meaning of the immanent. That is, the unity of the state claims to represent the meaning of existence. But the church is a particularly insidious monster that has enslaved the West. Despite its varying expressions, the church is the corporate body that has most corrupted and sickened the human mind and spirit, preventing it from overcoming itself so as to become a creator of new values. The Western modern state is simply the secular form of the church, the Holy Roman Church, including its Protestant deviations. Interestingly, in the section, "On Priests" (*Von den Priestern*) Zarathustra admits that his "blood is related" to the priests of the church, and even as he has compassion for them, he also is repulsed by them.[100] Zarathustra relates to the priest, I suggest, because the priest is primarily intended to be a representative and mediator of the divine image. We saw this in de Lubac's formulation of the priesthood as expressed in the *corpus mysticum*. In fact, the priest embodies divine sovereignty in the form of the servant. As we saw in de Lubac, it is a vocation vested to the priest by Christ himself. The priesthood, symbolized in the unity of the pope, administers the Eucharist, which mediates Christ to the new humanity. The priest is also a moral teacher, who instructs the ecclesial body in the values of their God. In

---

98. Nietzsche, *Zarathustra*, 244. In the German, "*Das ist eine Art von Staat, und zwar die verlogenste.*"

99. Nietzsche, *Zarathustra*, 244.

100. In fact, we see Zarathustra parody a priestly role in the prologue when he spoke to the dying tightrope-walker before his death. Nietzsche, *Zarathustra*, 203.

this sense, the traditional priestly role is less superficial than the modern rationalist moral-political technician. Zarathustra, however, is a kind of priestly anti-priest, who seeks to live and embody a new form of the divine reflecting the immanence of "life"—Dionysus.[101]

In contrast to his own project, Zarathustra perceives the priests of the church as enslaved to the myth of the "Redeemer" (*Erlöser*): "He whom they call Redeemer has put them in fetters: in fetters of false values and delusive words. Would that someone would yet redeem them from their Redeemer!"[102] In an allusion to the "last god" of the dragon in the section "On the Three Metamorphoses," the church and its mediational role through the priests is a "state" that embodies the "sleeping monster" (*ein schlafendes Ungeheuer*): "False values and delusive words: these are the worst monsters for mortals; long does calamity sleep and wait for them."[103] For Zarathustra, what is particularly destructive about the church and its priesthood is the psychological state of guilt it imposes on the spirit: "Behold these huts which these priests built! Churches they call their sweet-smelling caves. Oh, that falsified light! That musty air! Here the soul is not allowed to soar to its height. For thus their faith commands: 'Crawl up the stairs on your knees, ye sinners [*Sünder*]!'"[104] Nietzsche is particularly critical of the concept of sin as an unhealthy symptom of the spirit of revenge. We shall explore his critique of "revenge" further below. However, the picture we see here is that the church, rather than the fiery bellow of the modern revolutionary, is a dying and decaying "body." The church's conception of "God" has made the church melancholic. The worship of the "Redeemer" is only revealing how the spirit of the church and its priests are "drowned in their pity [*Mitleiden*]."[105]

The church and its priests, of course, celebrate the Eucharist whereby God became flesh in order to redeem sinful humanity. That is, the

---

101. See Gooding-Williams, *Zarathustra's Dionysian Modernism*, 50–64.

102. Nietzsche, *Zarathustra*, 203. In the German, "*In Banden falscher Werthe und Wahn-Worte! Ach dass Einer sie noch von ihrem Erlöser erlöste!*"

103. Nietzsche, *Zarathustra*, 203. In the German, "*Falsche Werthe und Wahn-Worte: das sind die schlimmsten Ungeheuer für Sterbliche,—lange schläft und wartet in ihnen das Verhängniss.*"

104. Nietzsche, *Zarathustra*, 203. In the German, "*Oh seht mir doch diese Hütten an, die sich diese Priester bauten! Kirchen heissen sie ihre süssduftenden Höhlen. Oh über diess verfälschte Licht, diese verdumpfte Luft! Hier, wo die Seele zu ihrer Höhe hinauf—nicht fliegen darf! Sondern also gebietet ihr Glaube: „auf den Knien die Treppe hinan, ihr Sünder!*"

105. Nietzsche, *Zarathustra*, 204.

Dionysian Desire and the Church and the Modern State 143

church worships a God who "pitied" humankind and therefore sacrificed his life for his love for humankind. The entire institution of the church thus functions as a kind of "state" that seeks to "unify" humanity in a particular moral form: love of God and neighbour. This "love" unites a particular concept of transcendence—a loving God—and a particular conception of immanence—humanity created in the image of a loving God. The uniting of the two in Christ is therefore how the divine redeems the existence of humanity. However, the fundamental presupposition, argues Nietzsche, is that according to Christianity there is something fundamentally wrong with our *existence as it is*. It presupposes an "original sin," that life is essentially cursed. Sin assumes the idea that all life is tainted by the corruption of a metaphysical evil. It is what we saw at the outset of our examination of *Zarathustra*, the despair of our own existence. Humanity has conceived itself as in need of something transcendent, beyond life itself, to redeem its existence. It is this tragic deception that is persistently represented in the very founding embodiment of the church: the Eucharist.

However, according to Nietzsche, love as reflected in Western Christianity is the refusal and denial of the tragic element of life and its suffering. The creation of a God of the cross is an existential, psychological reflex that seeks an escape from suffering and not just suffering, but from life itself. This theme is further developed in *Zarathustra* Part IV, in the section "Retired" (*Ausser Dienst*—off duty!) where Zarathustra converses with a former "Pope" and "Church Father."[106] He has become "higher man" (*höheren Mensch*) and is seeking for "Zarathustra" because of the death of the Christian God: "And I served that old god until his last hour. But now I am retired, without a master, and yet not free, nor cheerful except in my memories."[107] This retired pope represents someone who is in nihilistic despair. He has left "god," but has now "climbed these mountains, that I might again have a festival at last."[108] In particular, this is a comment on modern Westerners are no longer persuaded the church speaks with authority from the "belly of reality," but who have found no

---

106. Nietzsche, *Zarathustra*, 371.

107. Nietzsche, *Zarathustra*, 371. In the German, "*Und ich diente diesem alten Gotte bis zu seiner letzten Stunde. Nun aber bin ich ausser Dienst, ohne Herrn, und doch nicht frei, auch keine Stunde mehr lustig, es sei denn in Erinnerungen.*"

108. Nietzsche, *Zarathustra*, 371. "*Dazu stieg ich in diese Berge, dass ich endlich wieder ein Fest mir machte, wie es einem alten Papste und Kirchen-Vater zukommt: denn wisse, ich bin der letzte Papst!—ein Fest frommer Erinnerungen und Gottesdienste.*"

divine substitute. In the language of *The Gay Science*, the Western world has murdered God but has not yet created festivals that are worthy of the deed.[109] More broadly, what we see here is an intrinsic desire of humanity, which is seeking for the transcendent, for a "festival." Modern Europeans, argues Nietzsche, have still not overcome this desire for a god or for symbols that might unite humanity as one. Here Zarathustra assures the pope that it was "pity" that killed God: "You know how he died? It is true what they say, that pity strangled him, that he saw how man hung on the cross and that he could not bear it, that love of man became his hell, and in the end his death?"[110] In the section "On the Pitying" (*Von den Mitleidigen*) Zarathustra says, "Thus spoke the devil to me once: 'God too has his hell: that is his love for man.' And most recently I heard him say this: 'God is dead; God died of his pity for man.'"[111] That is, the proposed "redemption" has now been revealed as having been a curse on life all along.

Yet, even while now stripped of the myth of the cross, the modern state continues to embody the "religion of pity."[112] The modern revolutionaries may have fought for their freedom from the church, but in its place, there remains the religion of pity displayed in the attempt to alleviate and to escape from all suffering. Whereas the church promised such alleviation of suffering in an "afterlife," the modern state will seek for comfort with its science and technology. Using technique, it will organize itself in ways that alleviate all suffering. Whether in the form of socialism, communism, or the secular democratic state, humanity will avoid its suffering at all costs. What remains is a domesticated society where people seek "comfort" and escape from all suffering: "'We have invented happiness,' say the last men, and they blink. They have left the regions where it was hard to live, for one needs warmth. One still loves one's neighbour and rubs against him, for one needs warmth."[113] The modern state refuses to acknowledge what Ivan's "Grand Inquisitor" does, namely

---

109. Nietzsche, *Gay Science*, 181.

110. Nietzsche, *Zarathustra*, 372. In the German, "*Du dientest ihm bis zuletzt, fragte Zarathustra nachdenklich, nach einem tiefen Schweigen, du weisst, wie er starb? Ist es wahr, was man spricht, dass ihn das Mitleiden erwürgte,* dass er es sah, wieder Mensch am Kreuze hieng, und es nicht ertrug, dass die Liebe zum Menschen seine Hölle und zuletzt sein Tod wurde?"

111. Nietzsche, *Zarathustra*, 202. In the German, "*Also sprach der Teufel einst zu mir: „auch Gott hat seine Hölle: das ist seine Liebe zu den Menschen." Und jüngst hörte ich ihn diess Wort sagen: „Gott ist todt; an seinem Mitleiden mit den Menschen ist Gott gestorben.*"

112. Nietzsche, *Zarathustra*, 129.

113. Nietzsche, *Zarathustra*, 130.

that the secularized morality of Christianity now forms the politics of the modern state: "No shepherd and one herd! Everyone wants the same, everybody is the same: who still wants to rule? Who obey? Both require too much exertion."[114] This "education" of the last man has not gone far enough with the death of God. "God" is still expressed in the "preachers of equality," who seek to alleviate all difference and distinction. However, this notion of equality is still premised on the sick Christian notion of humanity created in the image of God.

Furthermore, the concept of equality—rooted in the concept of the image of God—is for Nietzsche a false "myth." For Nietzsche, human life has no inherent, intrinsic, and transcendent meaning in and of itself. Life is fundamentally unequal. It is governed by the life-force of the will to power. The chaos of Dionysus is sovereign. Therefore, in striving to worship the new idol over against the "reality" of the will to power, Zarathustra foresees only further violence and disaster: "On a thousand bridges and paths they shall throng to the future, and ever more war and inequality shall divide them: thus, does my great love make me speak. In their hostilities they shall become inventors of images and ghosts, and with their images and ghosts they shall yet fight the highest fight against one another."[115] War and violence are the result of a "pity" rooted in a metaphysical lie, attempting to deny the reality of Dionysus. Moreover, humans cannot escape the inequality and unfairness and suffering of life. Yet the superficiality of the religion of pity, embodied in the modern state, as inherited from Christianity, is only the mask of a more insidious reflection of humanity's nature: the spirit of revenge.

The Revenge of the Devil: The Birth of a Slave Morality

According to Zarathustra, the corporate bodies of the church and the modern state are enslaved to a sick moralism of the spirit of revenge. We may also describe it as retributive desire. The religion of pity, the struggle to alleviate and escape from suffering, is revenge against life itself. In the section "On the Tarantulas" (*Von den Taranteln*), Zarathustra seeks to expose the spirit of revenge that lies behind the modern preachers of equality:

---

114. Nietzsche, *Zarathustra*, 130.
115. Nietzsche, *Zarathustra*, 213.

> Thus, I speak to you in a parable—you who make the souls whirl, you preachers of equality [*Prediger der Gleichheit*]. To me you are tarantulas, and secretly vengeful [*Rachsüchtige*]. But I shall bring your secrets to light ... Therefore, I tear at your webs, that your rage may lure you out of your lie-holes and your revenge may leap out from behind your word justice [*Gerechtigekeit*]. For *that man be delivered from revenge [der Rache], that is for me the bridge to the highest hope, and a rainbow after long storms.*[116]

The desire for justice and equality, rooted in the love of neighbour, is really only a mask on the desire for power: "You preachers of equality, the tyrannomania of impotence clamors thus out of you for equality: your most secret ambitions to be tyrants thus shroud themselves in the words of virtue. Aggrieved conceit, repressed envy—perhaps the conceit and envy of your fathers—erupt from you as a flame and as the frenzy of revenge." What the "son" seeks against the father (the church?) is power: "Mistrust all in whom the impulse to punish [*strafen*] is powerful. . . . Mistrust all who talk much of their justice [*Gerechtigkeit*]! Verily, their souls lack more than honey. And when they call themselves the good and the just, do not forget that they would be Pharisees, if only they had—power [*Macht*]."[117] To reiterate, it is the erotic Karamazovian force that seeks to extend itself even if that means in forms of violent domination. Everything still flows from Dionysus.

But this tarantula, this "old enemy" of Zarathustra, is the spirit of revenge. In the section "On Redemption," the meaning of revenge is elaborated more fully. Here we see that revenge reflects humanity's deepest desire to escape material existence as experienced in time and space: "'It was' [*Es war*]—that is the name of the will's gnashing of teeth and most secret melancholy [*einsaste Trübsal*]. Powerless against what has

---

116. Nietzsche, *Zarathustra*, 211. In the German, "*Also rede ich zu euch im Gleichniss, die ihr die Seelen drehend macht, ihr Prediger der Gleichheit! Taranteln seid ihr mir und versteckte Rachsüchtige! Aber ich will eure Verstecke schon an's Licht bringen: darum lache ich euch in's Antlitz mein Gelächter der Höhe. Darum reisse ich an eurem Netze, dass eure Wuth euch aus eurer Lügen-Höhle locke, und eure Rache hervorspringe hinter eurem Wort „Gerechtigkeit." Denn dass der Mensch erlöst werde von der Rache: das ist mir die Brücke zur höchsten Hoffnung und ein Regenbogen nach langen Unwettern.*"

117. Nietzsche, *Zarathustra*, 212. In the German, "*Also aber rathe ich euch, meine Freunde: misstraut Allen, in welchen der Trieb, zu strafen, mächtig ist! Das ist Volk schlechter Art und Abkunft; aus ihren Gesichtern blickt der Henker und der Spürhund. Misstraut allen Denen, die viel von ihrer Gerechtigkeit reden! Wahrlich, ihren Seelen fehlt es nicht nur an Honig. Und wenn sie sich selber „die Guten und Gerechten" nennen, so vergesst nicht, dass ihnen zum Pharisäer Nichts fehlt als—Macht!*"

Dionysian Desire and the Church and the Modern State   147

been done, he is an angry spectator of all that is past. The will cannot will backwards [*Nicht zurück kann der Wille wollen*]; and that he cannot break time and time's covetousness [*der Zeit Begierde*], that is the will's loneliest melancholy."[118] It is the psychological anguish of imprisonment within time itself and the inability to undo the events and actions of the past. This anguish results in the desire to punish: "That time does not run backwards, that is his wrath, 'that which was' is the name of the stone he cannot move. And so, he moves stones out of wrath and displeasure, and he wreaks revenge on whatever does feel wrath and displeasure as he does. Thus, the will, the liberator, took to hurting." Moreover, "the spirit of revenge [*der Geist der Rache*], my friends, has so far been the subject of man's best reflection; and where there was suffering, one always wanted punishment [*Strafe*] too."[119] As "On Redemption" demonstrates, it is primarily revenge against "existence" (*Dasein*) itself, since existence is maddeningly perceived as itself a form of divine punishment.[120]

Seen in the light of Zarathustra's critique of the church and the modern state, the morality of punishment—of revenge—undergirds them both. The church and modern state are the political embodiment of a revenge against existence. Humanity is punished for its natural desires. For the modern state, it is the punishment of actions against the intrinsic, transcendent dignity and value of humankind. However, the church's punishment is greater for it is explicitly conditioned by a false eternal: "Can there be redemption [*Erlösung*] if there is eternal justice [*ewiges Recht*]? Alas, the stone *It was* cannot be moved: all punishments must be eternal too."[121] The church has placed an eternal weight on actions conducted in time and space. The consciousness of sin places a heavy psychological burden on the human mind and spirit. The fear of eternal justice and punishment—hell—is a particular form of psychological torture and madness. Therefore, the church as state is more "mendacious"

---

118. Nietzsche, *Zarathustra*, 251. In the German, "*Es war: also, heisst des Willens Zähneknirschen und einsamste Trübsal. Ohnmächtig gegen Das, was gethan ist—ist er allem Vergangenen ein böser Zuschauer. Nicht zurück kann der Wille wollen; dass er die Zeit nicht brechen kann und der Zeit Begierde,—das ist des Willens einsamste Trübsal.*"

119. Nietzsche, *Zarathustra*, 252. In the German, "*Der Geist der Rache: meine Freunde, das war bisher der Menschen bestes Nachdenken; und wo Leid war, da sollte immer Strafe sein.*"

120. Nietzsche, *Zarathustra*, 252. In the German, "*Sittlich sind die Dinge geordnet nach Recht und Strafe. Oh wo ist die Erlösung vom Fluss der Dinge und der Strafe 'Dasein'?*"

121. Nietzsche, *Zarathustra*, 252. "*Kann es Erlösung geben, wenn es ein ewiges Recht giebt? Ach, unwälzbar ist der Stein „Es war": ewig müssen auch alle Strafen sein!*"

than the modern state. The modern revolutionary may execute a punishment against an action that violates a law of love for the neighbour, a law that violates "human rights," but the church continues to perpetuate the lie that we have also violated a greater law against God himself and therefore deserve an eternal punishment. We have transgressed against our neighbour *and God*. In *On the Genealogy of Morals*, Nietzsche argues that the memory of the substitutionary sacrifice of Christ only continues to remind us of our previous guilt always holding the mind in a state of indebtedness.[122] One cannot ever remove the "It was." The Christian message of forgiveness only reinforces the false moralism of the necessity of eternal retribution. The entire existence of the church continues to perpetuate this insidious lie and deception. Therefore, it is a sick institutional monster that steals, kills, and destroys.

While Ivan may share with Zarathustra a "mystical immanence," a love for life that precedes an intellectual apprehension of it, they differ on the proper relation toward life as pertains to the meaning of justice. Ivan demands retribution for the suffering of the innocent. This is rooted in his concept of self-will and moral determination. It affirms the sovereignty of the self and its measure of justice. It locates sovereignty in the immanent, Euclidean sphere, in opposition to a divine transcendent reality. Nonetheless, Ivan's demand for the immanence of human retribution still does not fully acknowledge, at least from a Zarathustrian perspective, the complete sovereignty of Dionysus. With Ivan, there is still a presupposition of some form of judgement against oppression. Ivan does not escape the desire for punishment against the wrongdoer to satisfy an innate, human need for justice. In this way, Ivan is still vengeful against the "It was." It is precisely this desire for retribution that creates the political theory of the Grand Inquisitor. From a Zarathustrian perspective, Ivan is still ensnared in a particular conception of time, the "it was" of the actions of the oppressor, craving "drops of blood." Ivan does not respect human freedom, but despises it. This is not to say that Zarathustra would welcome the oppression of the innocent. We will grapple with his solution to "retribution" in the next chapter. Nonetheless, Zarathustra may stand before the Grand Inquisitor in silence just as did Christ, but his "silence" is for a very different reason.

---

122. Nietzsche, *On the Genealogy of Morals*, 62–67.

Interlude

At this point in our analysis, it is appropriate to briefly summarize the results of the previous three chapters in a comparative manner. While I have touched on various points of connection between Dostoevsky and Nietzsche as well as in relation to de Lubac, I will do so more explicitly here. First, we see particular attention to the reality of how *desire* is embodied in a "theological-political" nexus, between the desire of the heart and sociological and political praxis. When we use the language of "Karamazovian desire" and the "will to power," we must recognize the incredible complexity implicit in these terms. Returning to our comments in chapter 1, as de Lubac has observed, both Nietzsche and Dostoevsky are deeply attuned to the chaotic Dionysian element of bodily life. There is an intrinsic power latent in human nature rooted in a desire for the transcendent, but not disconnected from the "desires of the flesh." The human heart and its desire are fundamentally a mystery, a desire for beauty that, for Dostoevsky and de Lubac, has one foot on the earth and another in the eternal. For Dostoevsky, as we saw in our examination of Fyodor, shame is the source of retributive desire as the self-succumbs to deception that denies its essential nature as created in the image of God. Moreover, as complex as desire is, it is also mediational, moving the self in a particular trajectory toward divinity in a movement of transformation and becoming. However, Dostoevsky is not just speaking about individuals, but also nationalist personality as well. Desire has power to mediate peoples, cultures, nations, and political movements toward specific transcendent ends. However, Dostoevsky and de Lubac are in basic agreement that this human desire is connected both to the body and the spirit as created in the image of God, and therefore is essentially theological in character. Humanity intrinsically desires to be whole and unified. We may call this "justice" in the fullest sense of the term. As created in the image of God, the latent desire within the body is infused with desire for the divine and provides the clue for not only the redemption, but the future destiny of humanity, and by implication, social and political embodiment as well. For Dostoevsky, the secular atheism as embodied in the drama of Ivan Karamazov is the "end" of a long process in Western culture whereby the Western church, then modern political revolutionism, severed itself from "higher" aspects of this desire, denying the fundamental spirit of divine love for which it was created. As we see in Ivan's story, the spirit of modernist retribution derives from moral protest against the inherent "desire" and the freedom of which humans have to exercise the baser elements of the "Karamazovian force." As the Grand Inquisitor suggests, and as the medieval church discovered, physical coercion and political violence are necessary to "rein" in desire and limit this dangerous freedom.

Nietzsche passionately affirms latent desire as well, describing it as Dionysian, the fundamental will to power that drives and creates all of life. Furthermore, Nietzsche too is deeply attuned to the spiritual nature of this desire that longs for the transcendent. That is, Nietzsche attests to the desire for the eternal. However, while Dostoevsky lays more stress on shame as the source of retributive desire, Nietzsche emphasizes more the despair of the suffering body. For Nietzsche it was despair that engendered a revenge against life in the body, yearning for a corrupted desire for transcendence. While the longing for transcendence is natural, argues Nietzsche, within Western culture, especially through Plato and Christianity, this desire became sick and corrupted. In contrast to Dostoevsky and de Lubac, this desire for transcendence is not given from a divine presence that exists above time and space, but it rises up through nature itself. We can discover the power of the divine within the latent power of the body as we attune ourselves more closely to the passional impulse of Dionysian desire. Nietzsche is not simply an "atheist," but rather affirms that body and the spirit are so intricately linked. What is necessary to reform the passional desire for transcendence within the body into a new image that will mediate this desire in a healthier, "thinkable," incarnational way beyond the abstract conception of the eternal as constructed by Plato and Christianity. According to Nietzsche, we must pay close attention to the desires of the body for these are powers that engender the possibility of overcoming false conceptions of humanity that we have inherited from Western European Christianity. The Western church has denied its most powerful resources for the possibility of becoming more than what and who we are in the present moment. Through a despairing body which has created a spirit of revenge, Western culture, since the time of Plato and Jesus, has been in a process of decadence. The spirit of revenge is a particular desire that seeks to eliminate itself from the fundamental gift of life and existence itself. Revenge is a protest aginst suffering and has created theologies and ideologies that are fundamentally life denying. Out of this despairing revenge against existence, a political culture has evolved that uses coercion and violence to limit and control Dionysian desire. The personalist aspect of revenge, punishment for the "wrong-doer," is transformed, projected into the politic of retribution. Dostoevsky and Nietzsche are in basic agreement as to the coercive aspects of the politics of the church and state in Western culture that endeavour to suppress of freedom. Moreover, they both seem to suggest an irony: even the retributive desire that endeavours to overcome the chaotic desire of the body, derives from the same source of bodily desire. Nonetheless, as shown above, the reasons for this retributive politics are vastly different, and therefore it follows that their respective responses to the problem of the spirit of retribution are distinct. As indicated in the introduction, I will consider how Zarathustra and Alyosha Karamazov are used to portray an alternative embodiment of desire as a contrast to the politics of Christendom and the secularist state.

4

Eternal Return and the Politic of Friendship in *Zarathustra*

Introduction

IN THIS CHAPTER AND in chapter 5, we examine and compare the political visions of Nietzsche and Dostoevsky in relation to de Lubac's sacramental ecclesiology of the *corpus mysticum*. We will begin with Nietzsche because his answer to the political problem is vastly different from those of Dostoevsky and de Lubac. As we established in the introduction chapter, it is a question of the Christ versus the antichrist, or in Nietzsche's formulation in *Ecce Homo*, "Dionysus versus the Crucified."[1] In the previous chapter, we identified that what is at stake for Nietzsche and Dostoevsky is how our Western politics are informed by our conception of the "whole" of humanity in relation to (the Christian) "God." For Dostoevsky, while created in the image of God, Westerners have succumbed to the demonic pretention of creating a "higher image" for themselves, a higher "justice" apart from what is revealed in Christ. This spiritual state of soul has engendered a politics of retribution as expressed in the "Euclidean" immanence of Ivan, the demonic political aspect laid bare in the "Grand Inquisitor." For Nietzsche, the spirit of revenge against Dionysian life is the twisted, sick, and corrupted "spirit" that has created

---

1. Nietsche, *Ecce Homo*, 332–35.

a politics of revenge, expressed in the church and the modern secular political embodiments of retribution. The poetic conceptions of Dostoevsky and Nietzsche are of importance to de Lubac because they are prophetic thinkers who reflected on humanity's "transcendent" destiny as it is embodied in the immanent. Nietzsche, for instance, radically opposed the concept of the image of God in humankind, interpreting the desire for transcendence as an expression of the sickness of the soul and the desire for retribution as flowing from despair over embodied life in the face of suffering and death. For Dostoevsky, by contrast, while not denying or escaping the despair of suffering, acknowledges a profound mystery that intrinsically links the transcendence of "other worlds" with our own earthly, embodied existence. What we discovered in that chapter, in relation to de Lubac's thought, was that a politics of retribution, according to both Dostoevsky and Nietzsche, does not "unite" humanity. It does not mediate a politics of reunion that will bring "happiness" to society. In fact, as a spiritual, psychological sickness, retribution only engenders further violence and suffering. The "authority" of the sword, the illusions of the blank, impenetrable "mystery," and the pretension of the "miracle" are false mediations of a distorted and sick nature. They create a cold, monstrous politic that enslaves more than liberates. Moreover, Dostoevsky's conception does not imply escapism, but like Nietzsche, *transformation*. With Nietzsche, we may use the term *transvaluation*. These next chapters compare their respect visions of political transformation.

The Dramatic Embodiment of the Eternal Return

Zarathustra was written with a "grand politics" in view, as an alternative, educative "myth" for the new philosophers of the future. I affirm Robert Gooding-Williams' interpretation that Nietzsche's *Beyond Good and Evil* is written from "the perspective of Zarathustra's expectation, at the end of *Zarathustra*, that the advent of his children is imminent."[2] In particular, we see this anticipation in the section entitled "The Sign," the recognition that the higher men are still "asleep" in "distress"; yet Zarathustra, awakened, cries out, "My children are near, my children."[3] *Zarathustra* is intended to engender new forms of evaluation and judgment, new forms of "sovereignty" that will awaken a new future for Europe.

---

2. Gooding-Williams, *Zarathustra's Dionysian Modernism*, 304.
3. Nietzsche, *Zarathustra*, 438.

Gooding-Williams connects "The Sign" with the preface to *Beyond Good and Evil*, where Nietzsche presents himself as awakened, and ready to move beyond the modernist "nightmare" that a Christianized Platonism created: "But the fight against Plato, or, to speak more clearly and for the 'people,' the fight against the Christian-ecclesiastical pressure of millennia—for Christianity is Platonism for 'the people'—has created in Europe a magnificent tension the like of which has never yet existed on earth: with so tense a bow, we can now shoot for the most distant goals."[4] Here we see again that the "church" of European Christendom is the incarnate form of the disease of Socrates and Plato that we explored in the previous chapter, an otherworldly rationalism that has now infected the masses. *Zarathustra* presents a different vision that goes beyond the Platonic sickness, a vision for a "free Europe": "But we, who are neither Jesuits, nor democrats, nor even sufficiently German, we *good Europeans*, and free, *very* free spirits—we have it still, all the distress of spirit and all the tension of its bow! And perhaps also the arrow, the duty, and, who knows? *The goal to aim at* . . ."[5]

What Nietzsche presents is an alternative political philosophy of a new nobility that is both anarchistic *and* aristocratic in character. *Zarathustra* presents the "far sighted view," while *Beyond Good and Evil* is "near sighted, for it attempts to realize what is possible by transforming what is actual."[6] *Beyond Good and Evil* is designed to help fulfill the political aim of *Zarathustra*. Gooding-Williams relates *Beyond Good and Evil* to the genre of political tracts known as "advice books," or "mirrors-for-princes."[7] According to Gooding-Williams, these texts emerged in the thirteenth century, and they focused on educating and training young rulers in the virtues for leadership. Interestingly, in *Beyond Good and Evil*, Nietzsche praises Machiavelli's advice book, *The Prince*, for "presenting the most serious matters in a boisterous *allegrissimo*."[8] Gooding-Williams notes both the stylistic and thematic affinities. Machiavelli wrote *The Prince* with the aim of attending to Italian political realities, envisioning "a prince-legislator who would unite Italy and save it from barbarism

---

4. Nietzsche, *Beyond Good and Evil*, x.

5. Nietzsche, *Beyond Good and Evil*, x.

6. Gooding-Williams, *Zarathustra's Dionysian Modernism*, 307.

7. Gooding-Williams, *Zarathustra's Dionysian Modernism*, 308.

8. Gooding-Williams, *Zarathustra's Dionysian Modernism*, 308. See also Nietzsche, *Beyond Good and Evil*, 41.

and chaos."[9] As in *Beyond Good and Evil*, "Nietzsche envisions, on a much grander scale, a new caste of philosophers who would unite Europe and promote a 'great politics' that displaced the 'petty politics' of splinter states."[10] It is a politics aligned with the Dionysian will to power that is the expression of a master morality: "I have learned much, far too much, about the philosophy of this God, and, as I said, from mouth to mouth—I, the last disciple and initiate of the God Dionysus: and perhaps I might at last begin to give you, my friends, as far as I am allowed, a little taste of this philosophy?"[11] It is a philosophy aimed at preparing a new philosopher for sovereignty, developed for a higher rank than the masses: "The noble type of man regards *himself* as a determiner of values; he does not require to be approved of; he passes judgment: 'What is injurious to me is injurious in itself.'"[12] The sovereign will decide what is justice, but without resentment.

However, it remains to be seen upon what basis Nietzsche establishes his philosophy of the sovereign. We have already caught a glimpse of this in the previous chapter, in the learning to recognize and discern the nihilistic sickness of modernism and to affirm the Dionysian *will to power*. Zarathustra is calling Western society to leave the valuations of the Christian church behind to create a "higher type" of self that overcomes that deformed conception of humanity. Nietzsche perceived with acuity where the war against the spirit of revenge is fought, that is, how to wage war against the values of Western society as expressed in both the state and the church. But we return to the question stated in the introduction: Nietzsche affirms the "death of God," but what will fill the void? What festivals must be invented, feasting on the decomposing corpse of the Christian god? As Camus states, Nietzsche did not simply want to overcome the nihilism of Western culture and society, he wanted to construct a new edifice upon it.[13]

According to de Lubac, the possibility of going beyond Christendom and its modernist counterparts lies in Nietzsche's mystical vision of the eternal return. To create new values means to create the possibility of a new politics of eternal return. And, argues de Lubac, it is a politics

---

9. Gooding-Williams, *Zarathustra's Dionysian Modernism*, 308.
10. Gooding-Williams, *Zarathustra's Dionysian Modernism*, 308.
11. Nietzsche, *Beyond Good and Evil*, 146.
12. Nietzsche, *Beyond Good and Evil*, 127.
13. Camus, *Rebel*, 68.

that endeavours to mystically unite immanence with a conception of transcendence. Despite his emphasis on being "faithful to the earth," in *Zarathustra*, Nietzsche is still deeply interested in eternity: "O Eternity, I love you!"[14] Nietzsche cannot escape the longing for a "transcendence," albeit a "thinkable" one. We will examine de Lubac's critical assessment of Nietzsche below, but it suffices to say here that Nietzsche's poetic vision of political redemption attempts to replace that of Christ, mystically uniting the transcendent with the immanent, the eternal with the temporal, and being with becoming, in a creative, paradoxical way. Again, it is not the mystery of revelation enveloping and transforming nature, but nature rising in reconceiving of the conception of the eternal through the creation of a new myth. It is transvaluation—the creation of new perceptions of "life," "time," and "being"—that will better orient the self in relation to them to become a "higher" human. More specifically, for Nietzsche it is the creative myth of *Zarathustra* that he hopes will shape the future of Europe; what is most politically transformative is not "great events," but the "stillest hour," where a new thought is conceived: "The greatest events and thoughts—the greatest thoughts, however, are the greatest events—are longest in being comprehended."[15] For Nietzsche, the greatest transformative thought occurred in solitude and suffering of a wandering philosopher who affirmed the courage to live and write on his own terms. To this "thought" we now turn.

The Mystical Inspiration of the Eternal Return

In *The Drama of Atheist Humanism*, de Lubac employs the phrase "mystical immanentism" to describe the atheistic humanist phenomenon, especially with respect to Nietzsche, whom he interprets as a "mystic."[16] His interpretation derives from an examination of Nietzsche's primary texts, but also a consideration of letters to personal friends, where Nietzsche describes the experience of the inspiration of the "eternal return." The teaching of the eternal return is the climax of *Zarathustra*, where Zarathustra's animals declare that his destiny is to become the teacher of eternal recurrence, "for your animals know well, O Zarathustra, who you are and must become: behold, you are the teacher of the eternal

---

14. Nietzsche, *Zarathustra*, 340.
15. Nietzsche, *Zarathustra*, 142.
16. De Lubac, *Drama of Atheist Humanism*, 11, 469.

recurrence—that is your destiny!"[17] According to Nietzsche's friend Lou Andreas-Salomé, something changed in Nietzsche after completing *The Gay Science* in 1882. She writes that Nietzsche perceived himself as disembarking "onto the shores of an unknown world, a formidable one, a nameless one, about which he knew nothing yet, except that he found himself beyond what can be attacked or destroyed by thought."[18]

Moreover, Nietzsche himself wrote to his mother, "My hour has come . . . In me can be found today the culminating point of Europe's thought and moral effort and many other things besides."[19] De Lubac also underscores the language of a "new vision" that Nietzsche uses in a letter to his friend, Peter Gast, in describing the inspiration behind Zarathustra.[20] What we have, argues de Lubac, is "an ecstasy, an illumination, a thundering intuition."[21] Following de Lubac, we will interpret Nietzsche's philosophy of the eternal return as mystical, for the vision goes far beyond conventional rational or scientific analysis. It is rooted in an intuitive inspiration that seeks to unify the two seemingly contradictory mysteries of the eternal return and the overman. That is, how can the concept of eternal recurrence, the idea in the eternal repetition of all things be reconciled to the desire for the freedom of creation, especially the creation of new values that have not yet existed? Nietzsche's *Zarathustra* is the poetic expression of this inspired intuition.

The precise time and location of the illumination is debated. Whether it occurred at Rapallo, Italy or Sils Maria, Switzerland, or a combination is unknown, but taken as a whole, "there is no contradiction here, seeing that Nietzsche manifestly did not claim to determine and date this memory in a unique way but rather to analyze a certain kind of experience that could be reproduced more than one time with variations."[22] Nonetheless, de Lubac associates Nietzsche's time at Sils Maria as the primary inspiration of the thought of eternal return and

17. Nietzsche, *Zarathustra*, 332.

18. De Lubac, *Drama of Atheist Humanism*, 469. See Lou Andreas-Salomé's *Nietzsche* (French translation of *Friedrich Nietzsche in seinen Werken*), 159.

19. De Lubac, *Drama of Atheist Humanism*, 470. De Lubac quotes the texts from Ernst Bertram, *Nietzsche, essai de mythologie* (French trans. of *Nietzsche: Versuch eiener Mythologie*), 873.

20. De Lubac, *Drama of Atheist Humanism*, 470. A letter from Sils Maria, Switzerland, August 14, 1881. In Nietzsche, *Lettres choisies*, edited by Walz, 327.

21. De Lubac, *Drama of Atheist Humanism*, 471.

22. De Lubac, *Drama of Atheist Humanism*, 471.

his time in Rapallo as the place where *Zarathustra* as the overman and teacher of the eternal return took shape. De Lubac stresses the mystical nature of the inspiration that Nietzsche's language betrays as he explains the origins of the thought of eternal return. It is not based on scientism and rationalism, but an intuitive experience: "There was no companion to witness it. No direct document relates it to us."[23] Nietzsche attempts to describe in his final work, *Ecce Homo*, the nature of the experience. We will quote selected aspects of his own descriptions:

> Suddenly, with sureness, with indescribable delicacy, a thing makes itself heard. It shakes you, it overwhelms you right to your innermost depths . . . a thought blazes forth like a flash of lightning. . . . I never had to choose it. It is an ecstasy whose formidable tension resolved at intervals in a torrent of tears. . . . You are raptured, taken outside yourself, and you maintain a clear consciousness of an infinity of delicate thrills and cascades that run through you right to the tops of your toes and fingers. . . . All of this, which is involuntary to the highest degree, is accompanied by a tumultuous feeling of liberty, of independence, of divinity. . . . There you have my experience of the inspiration.[24]

What Nietzsche refers to is his experience of inspiration at the idea of the eternal return of the same. If the initial inspiration came to him in Sils Maria, the forming of the idea came in Rapallo, where Nietzsche would go for long walks along the bay.[25] According to de Lubac, it is within this framework that a new and mysterious event took place. In a letter to Lou Andreas-Salomé, Nietzsche wrote, "I was sitting and waiting, without waiting for anything, / beyond good and evil, tasting / light and sometimes shade, / absorbed by this brew, / become the sea, noonday, and pure duration, without design, / when suddenly, my friend, what was one became two, / and Zarathustra passed before me . . ."[26] Zarathustra thus becomes the medium through which to communicate the inspiration he received at Sils Maria. This mystical inspiration culminates in the narrative climax of *Zarathustra* in book III in the recognition that

---

23. De Lubac, *Drama of Atheist Humanism*, 471.

24. De Lubac, *Drama of Atheist Humanism*, 471. See Nietzsche, *Ecce Homo*, 300–301.

25. De Lubac, *Drama of Atheist Humanism*, 474.

26. Poem to Lou Andreas-Salomé and published in the second edition of *The Gay Science*. De Lubac, *Drama of Atheist Humanism*, 474.

Eternal Return and the Politic of Friendship

Zarathustra is the prophet of eternal recurrence of the same.[27] As Nietzsche saw it, this "teaching" is at the centre of his work and the essential meaning of becoming the overman. The two concepts, fate and freedom, are intrinsically linked.

Zarathustra is not the first utterance of the doctrine of the eternal return of the same.

The first communication is in *The Gay Science* (*Die fröhliche Wissenschaft*).[28] Nietzsche laments the dying Socrates' concession of perceiving life as sickness and his imminent death as a redemption.[29] As we know, Nietzsche perceived the Greek philosophy of Socrates and Plato as a sign of decadence, where the tragic element of life was giving way to a rationalist conception that was rooted in a resentment of life.[30] It is in this context that Nietzsche introduces the "greatest weight (*das grösste Schwergewicht*):"

> What, if some day or night a demon [*ein Dämon*] were to steal after you into your loneliest loneliness [*Einsamkeit*] and say to you: 'This life as you now live it and have lived it, you will have to live once more and innumerable times more; and there will be nothing new in it, but every pain and every joy and every thought and sigh and everything unutterably small and great in your life will have to return to you, all in the same succession and sequence—even this spider and this moonlight between the trees, and even this moment and I myself. The eternal hourglass

---

27. For Heidegger, when Nietzsche creates "poetically the figure of Zarathustra, he creates the thinker, creates the other kind of humanity which, in opposition to humanity heretofore, initiates the tragedy by positing the tragic spirit in being itself." That is, Zarathustra is the supreme "yes" to the extreme "no." See Heidigger, *Nietzsche*, 32.

28. Nietzche, *Gay Science*, 273. In the German, "*Wie, wenn dir eines Tages oder Nachts, ein Dämon in deine einsamste Einsamkeit nachschliche und dir sagte: „Dieses Leben, wie du es jetzt lebst und gelebt hast, wirst du noch einmal und noch unzählige Male leben müssen; und es wird nichts Neues daran sein, sondern jeder Schmerz und jede Lust und jeder Gedanke und Seufzer und alles unsäglich Kleine und Grosse deines Lebens muss dir wiederkommen, und Alles in der selben Reihe und Folge—und ebenso diese Spinne und dieses Mondlicht zwischen den Bäumen, und ebenso dieser Augenblick und ich selber. Die ewige Sanduhr des Daseins wird immer wieder umgedreht—und du mit ihr, Stäubchen vom Staube!*"

29. Nietzsche, *Gay Science*, 272. In the German, "*Würdest du dich nicht niederwerfen und mit den Zähnen knirschen und den Dämon verfluchen, der so redete? Oder hast du einmal einen ungeheuren Augenblick erlebt, wo du ihm antworten würdest: „du bist ein Gott und nie hörte ich Göttlicheres!*"

30. Nietzsche, *Gay Science*, 322.

of existence is turned upside down again and again, and you with it, speck of dust.[31]

This is the nucleus of the thought, the concept of a universal and eternal return of one's life, every detail of life, every suffering, experienced over and over again. In this context, Nietzsche is more concerned with the reader's response to such an utterance: "Would you not throw yourself down and gnash your teeth and curse the demon who spoke thus? Or have you once experienced a tremendous moment when you would have answered him: 'You are a god [*du bist ein Gott*] and never have I heard anything more divine [*Göttlicheres*]."[32] The "function" of the teaching, then, is meant to be a kind of cure for the decadence of life-denying philosophy. The role of the eternal return is to combat and ultimately replace what, as we examined in the previous chapter, are metaphysical conceptions that derive from the spirit of revenge in the form of pity and the desire to escape from suffering. We cannot understand the meaning of Nietzsche's teaching of the eternal return apart from his critique of Western, Platonic, and Christian shaped morality. According to de Lubac, what is whispered in *The Gay Science* bursts out in a "lyrical gushing forth" in *Zarathustra*. As de Lubac notes, the inspiration overflows like a river: "'It is a poem and a fifth Gospel,' he writes to his publisher."[33] According to Nietzsche, *Zarathustra* is the epitome and summit of his work, and a work that precedes all religious and philosophic works before it: "There is no doubt, moreover, that it must be understood, in the thought of Nietzsche, that this fifth gospel abolishes the preceding ones, the four Christian Gospels."[34]

The question, however, according to de Lubac, is how the idea of eternal return and the sovereign freedom of the overman who creates new values can be reconciled and unified. They seem to be contradictory "mysteries." As stated above, it is how the "mystery" of the endless eternal return of life is reconciled with the "mystery" of freedom and the creation of new values. It is the mystery of an eternal recurring immanence. *Zarathustra* is the poetic creation to express these images, a symbolic mediation that will engender a form of willing that assists the reader in becoming the overman. It is the intentional creation of *myth* that will engender new forms of

---

31. Nietzsche, *Gay Science*, 273–74.
32. Nietzsche, *Gay Science*, 274.
33. De Lubac, *Drama of Atheist Humanism*, 476.
34. De Lubac, *Drama of Atheist Humanism*, 477.

desire: "I love the great despisers because they are the great reverers and arrows of longing for the other shore."[35] However, to become absolutely "free," one must come to affirm the eternal return of the same. As de Lubac questions, "How could Nietzsche have believed in the newness of the discovery? And how could he have found a source of exaltation in a thought pattern that was really quite oppressive? How, moreover, did he, who was so perspicacious, not discover its incoherences? And how did he not see at least that his ideal of the overman, incarnated in Zarathustra, stood in contradiction to his faith in the Eternal Return?"[36]

According to de Lubac, the idea of the eternal return, of eternal becoming, could be seen in the ancient Greeks whom Nietzsche admired—Anaximander, Heraclitus, and also Pythagoras.[37] It was also at the centre of the Stoic cosmology, and it could be found in India.[38] Moreover, how could such an idea inspire the concept of freedom and the creation of new values at the heart of the vision of Zarathustra? As de Lubac questions, if I have to do what I have done and am doing innumerable times again, as I have before, is it not "impossible for me to imagine that I might be able in any way whatsoever to create myself or change myself, to take the least bit of initiative, to effect the least the bit of real progress?"[39] Moreover, the idea of the overman was not necessarily new either, as "Herder and Goethe, among others, had already conceived of it."[40] Nonetheless, "it is not in any case clear that it is necessary to choose between two things: either a resigned acceptance of a cycle that will always bring back the same unchanged elements, making the same progressions succeed the same instances of decay, or else a being's effort to grow, to contrive new values, to surpass itself always, and ever to impose its law?"[41]

There can be no superficial reconciliation of the contradiction and paradox between the inescapable fate of the eternal return and the free-creating sovereignty of the overman. De Lubac affirms an interpretation of Daniel Halévy who finds, in the doctrine of the eternal return,

---

35. Nietzsche, *Zarathustra*, 127.
36. De Lubac, *Drama of Atheist Humanism*, 477.
37. De Lubac, *Drama of Atheist Humanism*, 478.
38. De Lubac, *Drama of Atheist Humanism*, 478.
39. De Lubac, *Drama of Atheist Humanism*, 478.
40. De Lubac, *Drama of Atheist Humanism*, 479.
41. De Lubac, *Drama of Atheist Humanism*, 480.

a "metaphysics that is new bound up with a myth that is ancient."[42] That is, argues de Lubac, "it is true that Nietzsche has an idea of eternity that did not exist at all in this guise among the ancients. It is also true that in that union he conceived of becoming and eternity, he put the accent on the later term . . . It is true as well that this insistence arises from a profound yearning, 'For I love you, O Eternity.'"[43] The climax of book III of *Zarathustra* betrays a deep longing for the eternal. Still, how did Nietzsche understand the relationship between the two realities that seem to him united? How does "eternity for him prevail over becoming? How can each of the moments that the cosmic wheel of becoming brings back indefinitely be truly, in his eyes, 'an eternal thing' itself?" It is here in these questions where the "essential element of Nietzsche's intuition is touched," where the Eternal Return and the overman, the "two mysteries meshed with one another."[44] In the following sections, we will delineate an exegesis of *Zarathustra* that will explore the relational tension, but also the mutual development of these themes. In this way we hope to provide an account that is lacking in de Lubac.

The Mystical Dance: The Transvaluation of Life

We will build on the reading of de Lubac with reference to the work of Kathleen Higgins, who argues that it is best to understand the doctrine of eternal return as the attempt to articulate a proper relation to life. She does not use the term "mystic," but I suggest that her interpretation is consistent with de Lubac's interpretation of Nietzsche as a mystic. We could also use the term *existential*, if by existential we mean the personal appropriation of our existence in relation to life itself. As Higgins asserts, "I view the doctrine of eternal recurrence as an interpretive scheme, accepted on faith rather than proof, that elaborates the implications of a basic worldview with respect to a specific subject matter . . . I shall treat the doctrine as a kind of expression for a fundamental orientation toward one's life, rather than as a cosmological thesis or a practical imperative."[45] By contrast, though not necessarily incompatibly, we will interpret this

---

42. De Lubac, *Drama of Atheist Humanism*, 482.

43. De Lubac, *Drama of Atheist Humanism*, 483. See also Nietzsche, *Thus Spoke Zarathustra*, 340.

44. De Lubac, *Drama of Atheist Humanism*, 483.

45. Higgins, *Nietzsche's Zarathustra*, 104–5.

teaching as mystical in the sense that it is Nietzsche's attempt to reimagine a renewed relation via the overman to eternal Dionysian life. However, we also want to note Paul S. Loeb's approach to *Zarathustra* as not a "doctrinal" explanation of eternal recurrence, but that "Nietzsche constructed these aspects so they would embody and enact his thought of eternal recurrence."[46] Loeb's interpretation of Zarathustra as the "embodiment and enactment" of eternal recurrence is not incompatible with an understanding of a "mystic," for it is the narrative itself that dramatizes the movement of Nietzsche's philosophical conception of life. Loeb himself quotes Nietzsche in a manner that seems to support reading *Zarathustra* in this mystical embodied way: as a "philosopher of Dionysus," Nietzsche states, "I have discovered the Greeks: they believed in eternal recurrence! This is the mystery-faith!"[47] As Loeb rightly maintains, the mystery-cults of the Greeks were more concerned with "ritualistic enactment" than with doctrinal formulation. Thus, we may read Zarathustra as a poetic enactment of the mystery of Dionysus as enfleshed and embodied in the narrative of Zarathustra, the prophet of eternal recurrence.[48]

In relation to the fundamental orientation inherited in Christendom, based upon Plato and Christianity, Nietzsche's teaching is intentionally transvaluative. That is, Nietzsche desires that we have a proper valuation of life itself. This is the first "medical treatment" of the sick self of Western Christendom. While there may be ethical implications that follow, Nietzsche's stress is on a relation, or a proper *unification* with life. Nietzschean mysticism is "demonic," as Stefan Zweig asserts, in that the doctrine is an expression of "the unrest that is in us all, driving each of us out of himself into the elemental."[49] In particular, Nietzsche depicts

46. Paul S. Loeb distinguishes his interpretation from a "doctrinal" approach, "some kind of explication and defense of the thought of eternal recurrence. Or more recently, and in a more literary vein, they have interpreted the narrative of Zarathustra as a kind of *Bildungsroman* in which Zarathustra learns how to awaken, confront, teach, and affirm his thought of eternal recurrence" (1). In contrast to the idea that Zarathustra is a "useful fiction, mythic image" or even an incommunicable "mystical insight." Loeb, *Death of Nietzsche's Zarathustra*, 2.

47. Loeb, *Death of Nietzsche's Zarathustra*, 3.

48. Loeb argues that when we "consider *Zarathustra's* pervasive allusions to the myth of Dionysus (Lampert, 1986; Del Caro, 1988; Gooding-Williams, 2001), as well as Nietzsche's identification of Zarathustra with Dionysus, it seems very likely that the Greek mystery-cult performance of Dionysus' eternally recurring life actually served as a model for Nietzsche's invention and enactment of Zarathustra's eternally recurring life." Loeb, *Death of Nietzsche's Zarathustra*, 3.

49. Zweig, *Struggle with the Daemon*, 11.

this revaluation of mystical relation to life as an *erotic* dance with life that resists the spirit of gravity. In the section "The Dancing Song" (*das Tanzleid*), Zarathustra and his followers walk through a forest where they encounter girls dancing with each other:

> Do not cease dancing, you lovely girls! No killjoy has come to you with evil eyes, no enemy of girls. God's advocate [*Fürsprecher*] am I before the devil: but the devil is the spirit of gravity [*der Geist der Schwere*]. . . . And with tears in his eyes he shall ask you for a dance, and I myself will sing a song for his dance: a dancing and mocking song on the spirit of gravity, my supreme and most powerful devil, of whom they say that he is "the master of the world [*der Herr der Welt*]."[50]

Zarathustra calls himself God's advocate before the devil, who is the spirit of gravity. This represents a nice reversal of the biblical pattern, where the devil advocates for justice before God in the heavenly court (Job 1–3). Zarathustra is the mediator of the divine that seeks to overcome the regnant "master of the world." Dancing signifies the perpetual, non-static, *movement* that creatively aligns itself with the beauty of life's rhythms and melodies. To dance with life means to respond lightly and with agility to her movements. First, to dance is a bodily movement. It is sensual. It is physical. It is dynamic. Second, dancing can also be an "erotic" activity as it is an expression of the *desire* of the body. The girls represent the erotic, but also the innocence of life with which Zarathustra seeks to be enjoined. For Zarathustra, however, there is no guilt in the erotic mysticism of life: "How could I, you light-footed ones, be an enemy of godlike dances? Or of girls' feet with pretty ankles?"[51] That is, to learn how to dance with the eroticism of life is a godlike activity, a holy innocence. Moreover, in this movement, there is an immanent mystical experience with life itself. "Life" (*das Leben*) is personified as a wild, unfathomable wisdom:

---

50. Nietzsche, *Zarathustra*, 219. In the German, "*Lasst vom Tanze nicht ab, ihr lieblichen Mädchen! Kein Spielverderber kam zu euch mit bösem Blick, kein Mädchen-Feind. Gottes Fürsprecher bin ich vor dem Teufel: der aber ist der Geist der Schwere. Wie sollte ich, ihr Leichten, göttlichen Tänzen feind sein? Oder Mädchen-Füssen mit schönen Knöcheln?*" As well as, "*Und mit Thränen im Auge soll er euch um einen Tanz bitten; und ich selber will ein Lied zu seinem Tanze singen: Ein Tanz- und Spottlied auf den Geist der Schwere, meinen allerhöchsten grossmächtigsten Teufel, von dem sie sagen, dass er „der Herr der Welt sei."*

51. Nietzsche, *Zarathustra*, 220.

> In your eyes I looked recently, O life [*oh leben*]! And into the unfathomable I then seemed to be sinking. But you pulled me out with a golden fishing rod; and you laughed mockingly when I called you unfathomable. . . . And when I talked in confidence with my wild wisdom [*Weisheit*] she said to me in anger, "You will [*willst*], you want [*begehrst*], you love [*liebst*]—that is the only reason why you praise [*lobst*] life."[52]

Zarathustra's revaluated mystical relation to life is one of adoration, love, and worship. It is in praise of life. It is the worship of life of which Zarathustra is a part. As we see in Zweig's interpretation, "it seems as if nature implanted into every mind an inalienable part of the primordial chaos, and as if this part were interminable striving—with tense passion—to rejoin the superhuman, suprasensual medium whence it derives."[53] That is, a healthy demonic desire strives for a "higher reconciliation" with life.[54] Yet, what exactly *is* life? What is the *wisdom* that knows life? As we see in this text, life herself is playful, mocking, and wild. We cannot tame or domesticate life. There is an admission here of ignorance with respect to the meaning of life, a *docta ignorantia*. The kind of wisdom that dances with life is seductive, yet illusive. What does it mean to "know" this life? According to Zarathustra, we cannot really "know" or apprehend the meaning of life:

> When life asked me, "Who is the wisdom [*Weisheit*]?" I answered fervently, "Oh yes, wisdom! One thirsts [*dürstet*] after her and is never satisfied; one looks through veils, one grabs through nets. Is she beautiful? How should I know? . . . She is changeable and stubborn; often I see her bite her lip and comb her hair against the grain. Perhaps she is evil and false and a female in every way; but just when she speaks ill of herself she is most seductive [*verführt*]."[55]

---

52. Nietzsche, *Zarathustra*, 220. In the German, "*In dein Auge schaute ich jüngst, oh Leben! Und in's Unergründliche schien ich mir da zu sinken. Aber du zogst mich mit goldner Angel heraus; spöttisch lachtest du, als ich dich unergründlich nannte. So geht die Rede aller Fische, sprachst du; was sie nicht ergründen, ist unergründlich.*" As well as, "*Und als ich unter vier Augen mit meiner wilden Weisheit redete, sagte sie mir zornig: „Du willst, du begehrst, du liebst, darum allein lobst du das Leben!"*"

53. Zweig, *Struggle with the Daemon*, 11.

54. Nietsche, *Zarathustra*, 253.

55. Nietzsche, *Zarathustra*, 221. In the German, "*Und als mich einmal das Leben fragte: Wer ist denn das, die Weisheit?—da sagte ich eifrig: „Ach ja! die Weisheit! Man dürstet um sie und wird nicht satt, man blickt durch Schleier, man hascht durch Netze. Ist sie schön? Was weiss ich!* As well as, "*Veränderlich ist sie und trotzig; oft sah ich sie*

In this text, Nietzsche expresses the desire for the wisdom of life, but acknowledges both its seduction, and its illusiveness. We lose ourselves in our erotic desire for life. Our experience with life is a mystical unification that surpasses what philosophy can apprehend rationally. With the wisdom of life, we can sink into the unfathomable. As we saw in the previous chapter, life is incomprehensible because there is no intrinsic meaning or purpose in it. Life is an accident and a meaningless prankster. Nonetheless, Nietzsche perceives a beauty in life even though life is "changeable and stubborn." We do not know what life is, nor do we need to know this. We do not know if life is "good" or "evil." We do not know if life is really "ugly" or "beautiful." We only have our personal mystical relation to life. We exist in life, and we can either love or despise life, but we really cannot "know" life. All we have is the immanence of the present moment. Certainly, this does not preclude the fact that we can "remember" past events or anticipate future events. As we saw earlier, the spirit of revenge is precisely the spirit's wrath against the memory of past events and the inability to "will backwards." This leads to the next section, the question of the transvaluation of the embodied spirit in time.

The Mystical Vision and the Riddle: The Transvaluation of Time

For Nietzsche, the mystical relation with life is an affirmation of time and our embodied existence in time. What does it mean to dance with life? What does it mean to exist in a healthy mysticism of life? In "On Redemption," Nietzsche criticizes a Christian rooted, linear concept of time that is interpreted from a perspective of a transcendent, eternal perspective. The spirit of revenge is the spirit against the "it was," whereby we are powerless to change or undo the actions of the past. Under the possession of the spirit of revenge and retribution is a despair of existence of life itself as imprisonment within time, and from which one seeks eternal release. One despises one's own life and gnashes one's teeth against the "stone" that cannot be removed. The linear conception of time is rooted in a metaphysical deception, whereby the eternal stands in relation to time consisted of a past, present, and future.[56] As we saw in the previous

---

sich die Lippe beissen und den Kamm wider ihres Haares Strich führen. Vielleicht ist sie böse und falsch, und in Allem ein Frauenzimmer; aber wenn sie von sich selber schlecht spricht, da gerade verführt sie am meisten."

56. Nietzsche, *Zarathustra*, 251–53.

chapter, it is the vengeful that are filled with despair and loathing for their existence and therefore take to "hurtdoing."[57]

The issue at stake metaphysically for Nietzsche is the misconception that one can stand abstracted outside of time itself. Therefore, if the conception of linear time and history is the result of the spirit of revenge and the creation of a metaphysical lie, then Nietzsche seeks to create a new conception of time, and therefore, a new conception of "history." Nietzsche's concept of the eternal return emerges more explicitly in the section "On the Vision and the Riddle" (*Von Gesicht und Räthsel*):

> Then something happened that made me lighter, for the dwarf jumped from my shoulder, being curious; and he crouched on a stone before me. But there was a gateway [*Thorweg*] just where we had stopped. "Behold this gateway, dwarf!" I continued. "It has two faces. Two paths meet here; no one has yet followed either to its end. This long lane stretches back for an eternity [*Ewigkeit*]. And the long lane out there, that is another eternity. They contradict [*widersprechen*] each other, these paths; they offend each other face to face; and it is here at this gateway that they come together. The name of the gateway is inscribed above: 'Moment' [*Augenblick*]. But whoever would follow one of them, on and on, farther and father—do you believe, dwarf, that these paths contradict each other eternally?"[58]

In this mystical vision, Nietzsche poeticizes the eternal contradiction between the past and future, linked in the "moment," that time itself is an eternal circle. Of course, there is debate with respect to the proper interpretation of the "moment" (*Augenblick*). Does it represent, as Heidegger suggests, the present movement with the past flowing one way and the future the other?[59] Or alternatively, Paul S. Loeb has argued, that

57. Nietzsche, Zarathustra, 252.

58. Nietzsche, Zarathustra, 268. In the German, "*Da geschah, was mich leichter machte: denn der Zwerg sprang mir von der Schulter, der Neugierige! Und er hockte sich auf einen Stein vor mich hin. Es war aber gerade da ein Thorweg, wo wir hielten. „Siehe diesen Thorweg! Zwerg! sprach ich weiter: der hat zwei Gesichter. Zwei Wege kommen hier zusammen: die gieng noch Niemand zu Ende. Diese lange Gasse zurück: die währt eine Ewigkeit. Und jene lange Gasse hinaus—das ist eine andre Ewigkeit. Sie widersprechen sich, diese Wege; sie stossen sich gerade vor den Kopf:—und hier, an diesem Thorwege, ist es, wo sie zusammen kommen. Der Name des Thorwegs steht oben geschrieben: „Augenblick". Aber wer Einen von ihnen weiter gienge—und immer weiter und immer ferner: glaubst du, Zwerg, dass diese Wege sich ewig widersprechen?*"

59. As Heidegger argues, "the gateway 'Moment,' with its avenues stretching infinitely onward and counter to one another, is the image of time running forward

it is a "symbol for the presently experienced moment of death," a "poetic device for suggesting Zarathustra's dying prophetic vision?"[60] That is, it is a poetic description of the enactment of the ritual of the dying Dionysus-Zarathustra in the moment prior to death. For Loeb, the reference to the "*Augenblick*" alludes to *The Gay Science*, where Nietzsche states regarding the dying Socrates, "Whether it was death or the poison or piety or malice—something loosened his tongue that moment [Augenblick] and he said, 'O Crito, I owe Asclepius a rooster.'"[61] Nietzsche's conclusion is that Socrates suffered from the spirit of revenge: "Socrates suffered life! And he then still revenged himself—with this veiled, gruesome, pious, and blasphemous saying."[62]

I am persuaded by the compelling interpretation of Loeb, that Zarathustra's interaction with the dwarf at the gate represents the moment of death, as poetic enactment of the death of Zarathustra as an image of Dionysus. Yet, as a poetic text that dramatizes the movement to affirm eternal recurrence, the rhetorical effect of the drama forces the reader to consider one's own future moment of death in the present moment. The "moment" of death is not the literal death of Zarathustra, per se, but is symbolically a kind of death of a "sick self" with its soul weighed down by the spirit of revenge and gravity. It is the mystical death of the "old" self with its deceitful desires shaped by Platonic and Christian metaphysical assumptions. It forces the reader to consider the enactment of such a death of the sickness of that desire to give birth to new desire to affirm the mystery of life through the thought of eternal recurrence. In this way, the text engenders the process of "going under" in a tragic, mystical conjoining with life itself. The text expresses the *death of a metaphysical desire* that seeks to transcend time, a desire that seeks "afterworldly" solace and comfort. It is the death of the desire to "crash through these ultimate walls with its head."[63]

Moreover, as I interpret this text, even if Nietzsche is attempting to create a "near death" experience, the text may also be interpreted mystically, as a transvaluation of a particular relation with *time*. That is, to

and backward into eternity. Time itself is viewed from the 'moment,' from the 'now.'" Heidegger, *Nietzsche*, 2:41.

60. See Loeb, *Death of Nietzsche's Zarathustra*, 45.

61. Nietzsche, *Gay Science*, 340. See also Loeb's analysis in *Death of Zarathustra*, 47.

62. Nietzsche, *Gay Science*, 272.

63. Nietzsche, *Zarathustra*, 143.

affirm the "moment" means the confirmation that there is no metaphysical reality outside the circle of time. There is no break between the past, present, and future. It is as if history repeats itself for all eternity. In this way the eternal circle of time as cosmological reality is incomprehensible. As Higgins suggests, it is taken on "faith."[64] Yet, Nietzsche might argue that it is more "thinkable" than the eternal God of the natural philosophers and of the revelation of God in the Bible. Time itself as embodied life itself, the eternal return, is in this way *divine*. It is all there is. This is the mysterious immanent experience of the will to power, and there is no ontological substance outside it. Time is what it mysteriously is and we only experience it in the gateway of the present, which is a kind of *image* and *reflection* of the eternity of and in time. This may be more "thinkable," but it remains incomprehensible. We cannot comprehend life; therefore, we cannot rationally comprehend an inner purpose in time and history since this "purpose" remains transcendent. Time itself is beyond discernable good and evil, meaning, and purpose, beyond all knowable transcendent destiny.

In this text, of course, Zarathustra is in conversation with the dwarf, also identified as the "spirit of gravity, my devil and archenemy."[65] Interestingly, the dwarf parrots the same teaching as Zarathustra, namely, that time itself is a circle: "All that is straight lies," the dwarf murmured contemptuously. "All truth is crooked [*Alle Wahrheit ist krumm*]; time itself is a circle [*die Zeit selber ist ein Kreis*]."[66] In this way, the dwarf is a kind of "double" of Zarathustra, like Ivan Karamazov's devil. He takes what Zarathustra says, but reinterprets it in way that Zarathustra has not intended:

> "You spirit of gravity [*der Schwere*]," I said angrily, "do not make things too easy for yourself! Or I shall let you crouch where you are crouching, lamefoot; and it was I that carried you to this height.
>
> "Behold," I continued, "this moment [*Augenblick*]! From this gateway, a long, eternal lane lead backwards: behind lies an eternity. Must not whatever can walk have walked on this lane before? Must not whatever can happen have happened, have been done, have passed before? And if everything has been there before—what do you think, dwarf, of this moment? Must not this gateway too have been there before?

---

64. Higgins, *Nietzsche's Zarathustra*, 122.
65. Nietzsche, *Zarathustra*, 268.
66. Nietzsche, *Zarathustra*, 270.

"And this slow spider, which crawls in the moonlight, and this moonlight itself, and I and you in the gateway, whispering together, whispering of eternal things—must not all of us have been there before? And return and walk in that other lane, out there, before us, in this long dreadful lane—must we not eternally return [*ewig wiederkommen*]?"[67]

Exegetically we observe an allusion to the first utterance of the eternal return of the same in *The Gay Science*, the "slow spider" and the "moonlight."[68] In consideration of that context, especially in relation to the death of Socrates, Loeb argues that the conceptual background is Plato's *Phaedo*. This lends credibility to the idea "On the Vision and the Riddle" articulates the near-death experience of Zarathustra.[69] However, the emphasis of the text intends to evoke for the reader a mystical relation to life as it is experienced in time, a Dionysian embodiment with time and not in revenge against the "It was." There is no metaphysical reality beyond time, nor is there an immortal soul beyond time. According to Nietzsche, Socrates represents a sick soul that longs for death and despises existence in the body and in time. Socrates is a nihilist, representing the decay of Western culture.

According to Higgins, the argument between the dwarf and Zarathustra at first seems strange, for they each hold an account of the cyclical theory of time. What is at issue? The "apparent similarity of their view makes the passage important: the passage pinpoints what Nietzsche takes

---

67. Nietzsche, *Zarathustra*, 269–70. In the German, "*Du Geist der Schwere! sprach ich zürnend, mache dir es nicht zu leicht! Oder ich lasse dich hocken, wo du hockst, Lahmfuss,—und ich trug dich hoch! Siehe, sprach ich weiter, diesen Augenblick! Von diesem Thorwege Augenblick läuft eine lange ewige Gasse rückwärt: hinter uns liegt eine Ewigkeit. Muss nicht, was laufen kann von allen Dingen, schon einmal diese Gasse gelaufen sein? Muss nicht, was geschehn kann von allen Dingen, schon einmal geschehn, gethan, vorübergelaufen sein? Und wenn Alles schon dagewesen ist: was hältst du Zwerg von diesem Augenblick? Muss auch dieser Thorweg nicht schon—dagewesen sein? Und sind nicht solchermaassen fest alle Dinge verknotet, dass dieser Augenblick alle kommenden Dinge nach sich zieht? Also—sich selber noch? Denn, was laufen kann von allen Dingen: auch in dieser langen Gasse hinaus—muss es einmal noch laufen! Und diese langsame Spinne, die im Mondscheine kriecht, und dieser Mondschein selber, und ich und du im Thorwege, zusammen flüsternd, von ewigen Dingen flüsternd—müssen wir nicht Alle schon dagewesen sein? und wiederkommen und in jener anderen Gasse laufen, hinaus, vor uns, in dieser langen schaurigen Gasse—müssen wir nicht ewig wiederkommen?*"

68. See Nietzsche, *Gay Science*, 272.

69. Loeb, *Death of Nietzsche's Zarathustra*, 47. See also, Nietzsche, *Gay Science*, 272.

to be significant about his cyclical time theory."⁷⁰ While the "dwarf is content with the view that 'time itself is a circle,'" Zarathustra objects to this declaration, which "approaches time with the detachment of a God who has synoptic vision and who is not himself involved in the temporal sequence."⁷¹ The spirit of gravity within Zarathustra, symbolized by the dwarf, seeks to make the doctrine of the eternal return of the same into a theory, which can be understood as a cosmological doctrine. This entails the possibility of abstracting oneself metaphysically from the circle itself and examining it from the vantage point of an eternity outside the circle. To "rationalize" the theory of the eternal return would go against the whole meaning of the teaching. Zarathustra argues that we cannot abstract ourselves or devise a theory of knowledge that will transcend time itself. The teaching of the eternal return is not an eternal rational ideal.

The essential point of Zarathustra here is to embrace the reality of the concept of the eternal return in the same way that we are to dance with life. Mystically speaking, there is a fundamental ambiguity. Even in this "gateway," the "thou shalt" of the dragon whispers and taunts Zarathustra in the form of the dwarf. Zarathustra overcomes the oppression of the dwarf through the courage to consider the thought of the eternal return: "Courage [*Muth*], however, is the best slayer [*Todtschläger*—death slayer]—courage, which attacks: which slays even death itself, for it says, 'Was that life? Once more!'"⁷² In this text, therefore, we see the "negation of the negation." Yet, not as the negation of existence, but the negation of the desire to transcend existence. If the vision represents the mystery of the eternal return, the "riddle" signifies the courageous freedom of the overman to address it or "resolve" it in his own way. Here we see a vision of Zarathustra's metamorphoses, becoming the lion-spirit that will slay the dragon, and breaking the tablets of Platonic and Christian values through the strength of the strong courageous will. It is the courage to overcome the conventional "humanity" of the "last man," which seeks a false transcendence. It is a vision of tragic sovereignty. It is the sovereignty of courage to "forgive" the sufferings of life, to embrace and to affirm life as it is experienced in the moment with all its suffering and ambiguity. The "vision" of the eternal return shifts the "riddle" of the young shepherd, and thus anticipates the climax of *Zarathustra*:

70. Higgens, *Nietzsche's Zarathustra*, 113.
71. Higgens, *Nietzsche's Zarathustra*, 113.
72. Nietzsche, *Zarathustra*, 269.

> Verily, what I saw—I had never seen the like. A young shepherd [*Hirten*] I saw, writhing, gagging, in spasms, his face distorted, and a heavy black snake hung out of his mouth. Had I ever seen so much nausea and pale dread on one face? He seemed to have been asleep when the snake [*Schlange*] crawled into his throat, and there bit itself fast. My hand tore at the snake and tore in vain; it did not tear the snake out of his throat. Then it cried out of me: "Bite! Bite its head off! Bite!" Thus, it cried out of me—my dread [*Grauen*], my hatred [*Hass*], my nausea [*Ekel*], my pity [*Erbarmen*], all that is good and wicked in me cried out of me with a single cry.[73]

The young shepherd is a kind of Nietzschean messianic figure that stems from biblical imagery, a classic imagery of the sovereign. It signifies the mythic battle between the Messiah and the serpent. It is a vision of sovereignty that overcomes the deception of the spirit of heaviness. This text anticipates the section 'The Convalescent," whereby Zarathustra affirms the eternal return of the same. The young shepherd is Zarathustra's imagined self as sovereign master over the spirit of gravity. It is a prophetic vision of Zarathustra overcoming the spirit of revenge and retribution. In this text, Nietzsche poetically expresses his redemption vision, that even amid our tremendous suffering we must summon the courage to bite the head of the snake that threatens to suffocate us.

The Mystery of the Eternal Return: The Transvaluation of Being

The section "On the Vision and the Riddle" anticipates the climax of book III, a vision of redemption from the spirit of gravity in the affirmation of life through the teaching of the eternal return. In "On Old and New Tablets" (*Von alten und neuen Tafeln*), Zarathustra identifies himself as a "firstling" of the future, which is always "sacrificed": "We, however, are firstlings. All of us bleed at the secret sacrifice altars [*Opfertischen*]; all

---

73. Nietzsche, *Zarathustra*, 271. In the German, "Und, wahrlich, was ich sah, desgleichen sah ich nie. Einen jungen Hirten sah ich, sich windend, würgend, zuckend, verzerrten Antlitzes, dem eine schwarze schwere Schlange aus dem Munde hieng. Sah ich je so viel Ekel und bleiches Grauen auf Einem Antlitze? Er hatte wohl geschlafen? Da kroch ihm die Schlange in den Schlund—da biss sie sich fest. Meine Hand riss die Schlange und riss:—umsonst! sie riss die Schlange nicht aus dem Schlunde. Da schrie es aus mir: „Beiss zu! Beiss zu! Den Kopf ab! Beiss zu!"—so schrie es aus mir, mein Grauen, mein Hass, mein Ekel, mein Erbarmen, all mein Gutes und Schlimmes schrie mit Einem Schrei aus mir."

of us burn and roast in honour of the old idols [*Gotzenbilder*]."[74] However, the will to sacrifice for life is the best kind of sacrifice: "But thus our kind wants it; and I love those who do want to preserve themselves. Those who are going under [*Untergehenden*] I love [*liebe*] with my whole love: for they cross over [*gehen hinüber*]."[75] This is not love of proximate "neighbour," but rather love of the farthest, the love of those who are yet to come. It is love for the overcomers, who have the courage to slay the dragon and to "go under." It is a love for Zarathustra's coming "children" who go beyond the humanism of Christianity and modernism. Zarathustra's aim is to negate the old tablets that negated Dionysian life. It is the aim to create a new nobility who alone may become sowers of the future. This is not for everyone, but for those who are able to achieve it through self-overcoming. To break the old and new tablets is to seek for the joy of life in opposition to the world-weary.[76] It is for those who have learned how to dance the Dionysian dance. Zarathustra seeks to slay the dragon to experience the third metamorphosis, the innocence of the child: "The child is innocence and forgetting, a new beginning, a game, a self-propelled wheel, a first movement, a sacred 'Yes.' For the game of creation, my brothers, a sacred 'Yes' is needed: the spirit now wills his own will, and he who had been lost to the world conquers his own world."[77]

How does one overcome oneself, redeem oneself from the nausea of the snake that clings to the throat? The sections "The Convalescent" (*Der Genesende*) and "The Seven Seals" (*Die Sieben Siegel*) express the apocalyptic breakthrough from sick desire to a healthy desire and a love for a more authentic lived, embodied, this-worldly "eternity." Of course, the thought of the eternal return, of a determined fate which our lives endlessly repeat is for Zarathustra an abysmal and horrific thought. Zarathustra cries out and roars like a madman, like a lion, summoning the courage to awaken and raise up the "abysmal thought," the thought of the eternal return of the same:

> You are stirring, stretching, wheezing? Up! Up! You shall not wheeze but speak to me. Zarathustra, the godless [*Gottlose*],

---

74. Nietzsche, *Zarathustra*, 312.
75. Nietzsche, *Zarathustra*, 312. See also section 4 in the prologue, 126–28.
76. Nietzsche, *Zarathustra*, 312.
77. Nietzsche, *Zarathustra*, 139. "*Unschuld ist das Kind und Vergessen, ein Neubeginnen, ein Spiel, ein aus sich rollendes Rad, eine erste Bewegung, ein heiliges Ja-sagen. Ja, zum Spiele des Schaffens, meine Brüder, bedarf es eines heiligen Ja-sagens: seinen Willen will nun der Geist, seine Welt gewinnt sich der Weltverlorene.*"

summons you! I, Zarathustra, the advocate [*Fürsprecher*] of life [*lebens*], the advocate of suffering [*Leidens*], the advocate of the circle [*Kreises*]; I summon you, my most abysmal thought [*abgründlichsten Gedanken*]!

Hail to me! You are coming, I hear you. My abyss *speaks*, I have turned [*gestülpt*] my ultimate depth inside out into the light. Hail to me! Come here! Give me your hand! Huh! Let go! Huhhuh! Nausea [*Ekel*], nausea, nausea—woe to me![78]

As in "The Dancing Song," Zarathustra identifies himself as an advocate, but this time with more clarity. Zarathustra is the advocate of life, of suffering, and of the circle. Zarathustra, the godless, is becoming godlike in his commanding of the abysmal thought. Zarathustra is taking command, becoming a sovereign and master over his sick desire. He becomes the overman by *freely* embracing the abysmal thought of the eternal return. Nonetheless, it requires a struggle with nausea. Zarathustra must heed his own command to the young shepherd, to bite the head off the snake. Whereas in "The Vision and the Riddle" we see Zarathustra revaluating time, in this text, time is connected the eternal becoming of being. Being is not an eternal absolute, but it is a constant and eternal becoming. Nonetheless, after Zarathustra speaks these words, he falls down as one dead "and long remained as one dead."[79] Again, I interpret this death mystically. That is, it is as if the thought of the eternal return of the same has destroyed the one who seeks to bear this greatest weight. Its meaning and implication are too heavy to bear. After he regains his senses, he remains lying there, without eating or drinking. This is no eudaemonian vision of life. This coma lasts for seven days. This is a significant number, the same period that God takes to create the world in Genesis.[80] Nietzsche is indeed attempting to poetically express a kind of death and rebirth of the self. It is the desire to express a new creation, a new way of "being" that goes beyond the "being" of the sickness of Christianity and modernism.

---

78. Nietzsche, *Zarathustra*, 327. In the German, "Du regst dich, dehnst dich, röchelst? Auf! Auf! Nicht röcheln—reden sollst du mir! Zarathustra ruft dich, der Gottlose! Ich, Zarathustra, der Fürsprecher des Lebens, der Fürsprecher des Leidens, der Fürsprecher des Kreises—dich rufe ich, meinen abgründlichsten Gedanken!

Heil mir! Du kommst—ich höre dich! Mein Abgrund **redet**, meine letzte Tiefe habe ich an's Licht gestülpt! Heil mir! Heran! Gieb die Hand—ha! lass! Haha!—Ekel, Ekel, Ekel—wehe mir!"

79. Nietzsche, *Zarathustra*, 328.

80. See Gen 1–2.

Moreover, during this time his animals, the eagle and serpent, do not leave him. Perhaps this is another allusion to the Genesis narrative, since after the seven days Zarathustra "raised himself on his resting place, took a rose apple into his hand, smelled it, and found its lovely fragrance."[81] Zarathustra will eat of the knowledge of the tree of good and evil and become a creator of good and evil, for this is the path back to innocence. The animals speak to Zarathustra: "It is now seven days that you have been lying like this with heavy eyes; won't you at last get up on your feet again? Step out of your cave: the world awaits you like a garden."[82] Not only does it remind the reader of Genesis, but stepping out of the cave is also reminiscent of the myth of the cave in Plato's *Republic*.[83] Zarathustra is stepping out of the world of shadows into the brightness of the midday sun, where there is no shadow. Only Zarathustra now seems to exist: "To every soul there belongs another world; for every soul, every other soul is an afterworld. . . . For me—how should there be any outside myself?"[84] With this the animals speak again about the wheel of being: "O Zarathustra," the animals say,

> To those who think as we do, all things themselves are dancing [*tanzen alle Dinge selber*]: they come and offer their hands and laugh and flee—and come back. Everything goes, everything comes back; eternally rolls the wheel of being [*das Rad des Seins*]. Everything dies, everything blossoms again, eternally runs the year of being [*das Jahr des Seins*]. Everything breaks, everything is joined anew; eternally the same house of being is built [*Haus des Seins*]. Everything parts, everything greets every other thing again; eternally the ring of being [*der Ring des Seins*] remains faithful [*treu*] to itself. In every Now, being begins; round every Here rolls the sphere There. The centre is everywhere. Bent is the path of eternity.[85]

81. Nietzsche, *Zarathustra*, 328.

82. Nietzsche, *Zarathustra*, 328. "*Oh Zarathustra, sagten sie, nun liegst du schon sieben Tage so, mit schweren Augen: willst du dich nicht endlich wieder auf deine Füsse stellen? Tritt hinaus aus deiner Höhle: die Welt wartet dein wie ein Garten.*"

83. Plato, *Republic*, bk. 7, 514a–15b.

84. Nietzsche, *Zarathustra*, 329. "*Zu jeder Seele gehört eine andre Welt; für jede Seele ist jede andre Seele eine Hinterwelt.*" As we all "*Für mich—wie gäbe es ein Ausser-mir?*"

85. Nietzsche, *Zarathustra*, 329. In the German, "*Oh Zarathustra, sagten darauf die Thiere, Solchen, die denken wie wir, tanzen alle Dinge selber: das kommt und reicht sich die Hand und lacht und flieht—und kommt zurück. Alles geht, Alles kommt zurück; ewig rollt das Rad des Seins. Alles stirbt, Alles blüht wieder auf, ewig läuft das Jahr des Seins. Alles bricht, Alles wird neu gefügt; ewig baut sich das gleiche Haus des Seins. Alles*

This text brings us full circle to the heights of the mountain where Zarathustra communes with his animals, the serpent, and the eagle. As Heidegger shows, when Zarathustra speaks to his heart in the midday, he hears the piercing cry of the bird, looking into the sky: "And behold! An eagle soared through the air in vast circles, and a serpent hung suspended from him, not as his prey but as though she were his friend: for she had coiled about his neck."[86] According to Heidegger, this image is already an emblem of the new pride and wisdom of the doctrine of the eternal return of the same.[87] In "The Convalescent," Zarathustra's animals speak to him of what they themselves symbolize, the eternal return of the same. This is the enlightenment of the "enlightened one." It goes beyond the conception of time rooted in a theological metaphysic of being or transcendence. It dances over the despair of Christian morality and its love of neighbour. It goes beyond the humanity still possessed by the spirit of revenge. It goes beyond the modernism of the "last man" with his doctrine of equality. It goes beyond the despairing body and its nihilistic desire to escape from the body and revolt against life itself.

What does it mean to go beyond all this? What does it mean to transcend the desire to transcend? What does it mean to negate the power that negates? How does Zarathustra overcome the nihilism that he perceives at work in the small man, the last man, the dwarf, the dragon, the jester, that oppose him? And by implication, how does one overcome the draconian systemic violence of the church and the modernist state? How does one overcome the politics of retribution? Somehow it also means affirming the eternal recurrence of those very things that oppose Zarathustra and life in nihilistic revolt:

> The great disgust [Überdruss] with man [Menschen]—this choked me and had crawled into my throat; and what the soothsayer [der Wahrsager] said: "All is the same, nothing is worthwhile, knowledge chokes." A long twilight limped before me, a sadness, weary to death, drunken with death, speaking with yawning mouth. "Eternally recurs the man of whom you are weary, the small man [kleine Mensch]"—thus yawned my

---

scheidet, Alles grüsst sich wieder; ewig bleibt sich treu der Ring des Seins. In jedem Nu beginnt das Sein; um jedes Hier rollt sich die Kugel Dort. Die Mitte ist überall. Krumm ist der Pfad der Ewigkeit."

86. Nietzsche, *Zarathustra*, 136–37.

87. In the lecture "The Eternal Recurrence of the Same." Heidegger, *Nietzsche*, 2:46.

sadness and dragged its feet and could not go to sleep...."Alas, man recurs eternally! The small man recurs eternally!"[88]

The great disgust and nausea that Zarathustra experiences, the snake that crawls into his mouth and choked him, is the great contempt for humanity, the "small man," who believes that he is "created in the image of Christ." To overcome the nausea of the eternal thought, Zarathustra must *affirm* the "small man" as an intrinsic aspect of life itself in the process of becoming. He must affirm him eternally. More specifically, Zarathustra must affirm and "will" an eternal struggle and opposition to the man possessed by the spirit of revenge. This does not mean pitying the small man, but it means contending with him eternally. It means even to affirm and find "joy" in this struggle. It means squandering oneself eternally in the "descent" of the mountain, "emptying oneself" and annihilating oneself to contend with the dragon with no hope of resurrection from the struggle. It means to affirm life as *tragic*.

Zarathustra must eternally struggle with the spirit of revenge and retribution. To overcome the spirit of revenge, Zarathustra must overcome his revenge against revenge. In order to overcome the spirit of gravity, the melancholy of the soothsayer, Zarathustra must overcome his weariness with weariness. This does not mean that Zarathustra must "love" the world weary, the despairing, and the vengeful, but he must learn to love what they might become as he contends with them. However, it does mean that he must say "Yes" to life, which has produced its own disease. Zarathustra must affirm the life that created Plato and Jesus, for Plato, Jesus, and their followers, as embodied in the church and the modern state, will recur eternally. Even as Zarathustra entertains the abysmal thought of the eternal recurrence of the small man, his animals urge him on—Zarathustra's pride and wisdom of the knowledge of the eternal return of the same. This is the great "contempt" that overcomes "contempt" with life itself. Zarathustra must cure his own soul and learn to sing and dance again in the knowledge of the eternal return of the

---

88. Nietzsche, *Zarathustra*, 331. In the German, "*Der grosse Überdruss am Menschen—der würgte mich und war mir in den Schlund gekrochen: und was der Wahrsager wahrsagte: „Alles ist gleich, es lohnt sich Nichts, Wissen würgt." Eine lange Dämmerung hinkte vor mir her, eine todesmüde, todestrunkene Traurigkeit, welche mit gähnendem Munde redete. „Ewig kehrt er wieder, der Mensch, dess du müde bist, der kleine Mensch"— so gähnte meine Traurigkeit und schleppte den Fuss und konnte nicht einschlafen.* As well as, "*Ach, der Mensch kehrt ewig wieder! Der kleine Mensch kehrt ewig wieder!*"

small man. Zarathustra contends with his animals in this, but they only urge him on:

> "Do not speak on!" his animals answered him again; "rather even, O convalescent, fashion yourself a lyre first, a new lyre! For behold, Zarathustra, new lyres [*neuer Leiernare*] are needed for your new songs [*neuen Liedern*]. Sing and overflow [*brause über*], O Zarathustra, cure your soul with new songs that you may bear your great destiny [*Schicksal*], which has never yet been any man's destiny. For your animals know well, O Zarathustra, who you are [*du bist*] and must become [*werden must*]: behold, you are the teacher of the eternal recurrence [*der ewigen Wiederkunft*]—that is your destiny [*Schicksal*]!"[89]

The animals affirm Zarathustra's prophetic destiny as the teacher of the eternal recurrence. It is this mystical thought—more than a thought, a re-evaluation of the self's relation to life as an eternally recurring circle of becoming, yet never "arriving." Thus, the present moment will always be forward and future looking, as it strives with all innocence in a willful "forgetting" of the past. This is Nietzsche's formulation of an ethic of "forgiveness" founded upon *immanence*. This is a teaching that is more than an intellectual apprehension of life, as if life could be objectified or rationalized. Rather it is a teaching which involves the entirety of the self that is existentially and mystically engaged with life in all its pleasure and erotic joy, but also in all its suffering and pain. Perhaps it is Nietzsche's intention that by affirming such a tragic view of life, people might learn how to love life again. Loeb is correct, *Zarathustra* is literally about the death of Zarathustra: "Now I die and vanish . . . and all at once I am nothing . . . I spoke my word, I break of my word: thus, my eternal lot wants it; as a proclaimer I perish. The hour has now come when he who goes under should bless himself. Thus, *ends* [*endet*] Zarathustra's going under [*Untergang*]."[90] On the other hand, this also means, with Heidegger, that

---

89. Nietzsche, *Zarathustra*, 332. In the German, "*Sprich nicht weiter, antworteten ihm abermals seine Thiere; lieber noch, du Genesender, mache dir erst eine Leier zurecht, eine neue Leier! Denn siehe doch, oh Zarathustra! Zu deinen neuen Liedern bedarf es neuer Leiern. Singe und brause über, oh Zarathustra, heile mit neuen Liedern deine Seele: dass du dein grosses Schicksal tragest, das noch keines Menschen Schicksal war! Denn deine Thiere wissen es wohl, oh Zarathustra, wer du bist und werden musst: siehe, du bist der Lehrer der ewigen Widerkunft—das ist nun dein Schicksal.*"

90. Nietzsche, *Zarathustra*, 333. In the German, "*Dass ich wieder das Wort spreche vom grossen Erden- und Menschen-Mittage, dass ich wieder den Menschen den Übermenschen künde. Ich sprach mein Wort, ich zerbreche an meinem Wort: so will es mein*

Zarathustra discovers the "becoming of his being."[91] The animals speak this to Zarathustra, but he remains silent. Zarathustra is not "dead," but in this silence he is "conversing with his soul." It is the paradox of finding "peace" in an eternal striving with and against the spirit of gravity. It means affirming that life is not static, but wild, dangerous, unfathomable, and constantly moving and changing in an eternal circle of life and death. It means affirming that there is no ultimate, transcendent morality, no intrinsic meaning, no purpose unless we create it:

> Then life answered me thus, covering her delicate ears: "'O Zarathustra, don't crack your whip so frightfully! After all, you know that noise murders thought—and now such tender thoughts are coming to me. We are both two real good-for-nothings [*Thunichtgute*] and evil-for-nothings [*Thunichtböse*]. Beyond good and evil [*Jenseits von Gut und Böse*] we found our island and our green meadow—we two alone. Therefore, we had better like each other."[92]

The Sovereignty of Affirming the Mystery of Fate and Freedom

I contend that this mystical interpretation of Nietzsche's engagement of the two mysteries of eternal return and the overman is consistent with Henri de Lubac's more general reading. There is no Hegelian "synthesis" that emerges, but rather a mystical tension that embraces the paradox. The best interpretive path is to acknowledge it as transvaluation of a relation to life and death, as difficult and affirming as this paradox might be. As de Lubac argues, Nietzsche is not advocating a "naïve optimism that humanity has, which could see in the endless return of the ages a means of constantly recommencing anew an animal existence that epitomizes for it all that is good."[93] Nietzsche understands the ambiguity of reality:

---

ewiges Loos—, als Verkündiger gehe ich zu Grunde! Die Stunde kam nun, dass der Untergehende sich selber segnet. Also—endent Zarathustras Untergang."

91. In particular the chapter, "Nietzsche's Fundamental Metaphysical Position," Heidegger, *Nietzsche*, 2:198.

92. Nietzsche, *Zarathustra*, 338. In the German, *"Oh Zarathustra! Klatsche doch nicht so fürchterlich mit deiner Peitsche! Du weisst es ja: Lärm mordet Gedanken,—und eben kommen mir so zärtliche Gedanken. ir sind Beide zwei rechte Thunichtgute und Thunichtböse. Jenseits von Gut und Böse fanden wir unser Eiland und unsre grüne Wiese—wir Zwei allein! Darum müssen wir schon einander gut sein!"*

93. De Lubac, *Drama of Atheist Humanism*, 483.

"It does not escape him that, depending on the way one becomes aware of it, the Eternal Return can appear by turns as the most exalting reality or, on the contrary, as the most crushing reality."[94] A person can "be carried away passively in an immense and desperate rotation, or, on the other hand, he can participate in the dominating force that thus move the whole cosmos."[95] Furthermore, "he can suffer the iron law of universal determinism, but he can, on the other hand, be himself this very law of freedom . . . for such a being the circle of iron becomes a ring of gold. 'Fatum [fate]' concludes Nietzsche, 'is an exalting thought for whoever has come to understand that he is part of it himself.' *Amor fati. Ego Fatum.*"[96]

This, argues de Lubac, is "rightly a mystical experience." Quoting Henri Delacroix, the "mystic is present at the genesis of things. He places himself at the heart of the source and lets himself be carried by it. Thus, he traverses all the forms of being without leaving being."[97] However, with Nietzsche, it is more than permitting oneself to be carried by the "source," for he "feels in himself the Force that produces everything and that finds itself intact, unchanged, free and sovereign in each instant of universal becoming. For him, existence is a circle whose centre really 'is everywhere.' Nothing weighs on him, because 'at every moment existence commences.'"[98] This, to be sure, is an "extreme reconciliation of the world of becoming with the world of Being."[99] Yet, if coming to the mystery of eternity "from the side of becoming, nothing is more horrible, than Nietzsche's vision of the world."[100] And Nietzsche would be the first to acknowledge this. This awareness is sufficiently demonstrated in the section "The Convalescent," where Nietzsche summons the abysmal thought. However, the vision of the overman at Rapallo will "expel the doubts" that the thought of the eternal return instigated: "He participates actively, freely in *Fatum*. He himself is part of it."[101] Nietzsche knows that

> he is the Overman, he whose lawless will engenders worlds.
> He is what he has perceived. . . . He can henceforth pronounce

---

94. De Lubac, *Drama of Atheist Humanism*, 484.
95. De Lubac, *Drama of Atheist Humanism*, 484.
96. De Lubac, *Drama of Atheist Humanism*, 484–85.
97. De Lubac, *Drama of Atheist Humanism*, 485.
98. De Lubac, *Drama of Atheist Humanism*, 485.
99. De Lubac, *Drama of Atheist Humanism*, 486.
100. De Lubac, *Drama of Atheist Humanism*, 486.
101. De Lubac, *Drama of Atheist Humanism*, 486.

without hint of a lie the word *amor Fatum* (I am Fate). The new Prophet has thus received his investiture. He escapes the common humanity. He arises therefore, he is going to pronounce the new gospel, calling on a new 'metanoia' in order to enter into a new kingdom.[102]

Moreover, according to de Lubac, Nietzsche's new vision goes beyond Spinoza's "universal Necessity," a kind of mystical intuition, a "third-degree" knowledge of one who is "no longer in himself one of the innumerable elements that go to make up *natura naturata* (literally, 'natured nature'). He participates in *Natura naturans* (literally, 'naturing Nature.')."[103] There is an analogy here to Nietzsche, but with Nietzsche there is no *Natura naturans*, no "divinity, there are no objective essences, no eternal ideas. There is nothing that resembles a Platonic world. As a result, there is no ontology."[104] The mystery of *Fatum* is:

> Pure contingency, because it is pure invention, a throw of the dice, a divine fantasy, a dance in the middle of an empty sky.... And when Zarathustra discovers that he coincides with such a principle, he discovers rather, to put it plainly, that there is no superior principle to which he needs to be linked. The law of the world is completely, at every moment, sprung from his arbitrariness. He is eternal in himself, not by participation. Or rather he makes himself eternal. All value proceeds from his will.[105]

It as if Nietzsche takes the concept of "pure nature" as far as it will go in the direction of contingency, to the breaking point of affirming a radical eternal determinism, but without creating an abstract theory of this "nature." The paradox is that in affirming fate freely, the overman exercises his radical sovereignty of freedom. There is no intrinsic moral valuation, but the mystical alignment of desire with an essentially meaningless existence. What is "miraculous" is that such nature has produced a creature that consciously wills such an existence and attributes a meaning to it. In overcoming a conception of humanity that falsely assumes that it reflects the divine, the overman then becomes the divine consciousness of nature itself. The overman is the divine image that reflects nature's meaning back

---

102. De Lubac, *Drama of Atheist Humanism*, 486–87.
103. De Lubac, *Drama of Atheist Humanism*, 487.
104. De Lubac, *Drama of Atheist Humanism*, 488.
105. De Lubac, *Drama of Atheist Humanism*, 488.

to itself. The overman is mystically at the centre. The overman is naturally divine, the value-making apex of chaotic, meaningless existence.

Interestingly, what is most analogous to Nietzsche's mystical vision, argues de Lubac, is Buddhism, for "Sakyamuni" is also the "protagonist of a mysticism without God."[106] We know that Nietzsche wanted to establish a "European Buddhism." For Nietzsche, asserts Lou Andreas-Salomé, "the highest ideal is not called nirvana but *samsara*. The supreme end of life is not to deliver oneself from the cycle of reincarnations but to accept it with joy."[107] Nietzsche's eternity is entirely in becoming, to the point that there is nothing but becoming: "His eternity prevails over becoming."[108] In fact, the closest Buddhist analogy to Nietzschean mysticism of becoming is the "*bodhisattva*" who, "by virtue of his vow of charity, delays indefinitely his entry into nirvana, even though he has already achieved all the conditions to enter it."[109] However, with Nietzschean "Buddhism," there maintains the tragic element; never does it throw off that "shudder of joy mingled with tears."[110] The symbol that Nietzsche uses to express the mystical tragedy of eternal becoming is that of Dionysus. Furthermore, Nietzsche is not attempting to overcome all "desire," as in Buddhism, but to exalt it to acknowledge that he is eternal Fate: "And the god of ecstasy and orgiastic life will seem to him more apt for defining his frenetic opposition to him whose image will not cease to torment him right to the end. Zarathustra is opposed above all to the Galilean prophet. Dionysus, in his mystic passion, is opposed to the Crucified One at Calvary."[111] Again, we cannot understand the thought of eternal return without acknowledging the sickness that Nietzsche perceived to be that of Christianity.

To understand Nietzsche the thinker, argues de Lubac, we must understand that he is "intimately dependent on Nietzsche the mystic. The value of the former hangs on the authenticity of the latter."[112] His philosophy goes further than the claims of a thinker, but he "invites us to a renewed existence whose announcer and exemplar he supposes himself

---

106. De Lubac, *Drama of Atheist Humanism*, 490.
107. De Lubac, *Drama of Atheist Humanism*, 490.
108. De Lubac, *Drama of Atheist Humanism*, 490.
109. De Lubac, *Drama of Atheist Humanism*, 490.
110. De Lubac, *Drama of Atheist Humanism*, 492.
111. De Lubac, *Drama of Atheist Humanism*, 493.
112. De Lubac, *Drama of Atheist Humanism*, 494.

to be."[113] However, along with Loeb, this experience of Zarathustra, the "death" of Zarathustra, is embodied in the drama of the text. In other words, to understand it, we must delve into the narrative of *Zarathustra*, as the narrative mediates the path to such a perception of freedom and the affirmation of life. *Zarathustra* is not an abstracted "mysticism," but one embodied in the drama of *Zarathustra*. And in this way, *Zarathustra* demands to be lived and experienced as much as "understood."

Moreover, de Lubac does not question the sincerity of Nietzsche's mystical exuberance: "The solitary of Sils Maria truly believed that the emotional shock that disturbed him so deeply was produced by his contact with a marvelous reality and that this contact opened him up to a new world, which offered itself to him like a grace."[114] However, according to de Lubac, what Nietzsche did in this situation, in fact, "was only construct, for better or worse, a mysticism of replacement, to fill the dreadful emptiness that had opened up in him."[115] His true experience was the emptiness expressed in *The Gay Science*, which is foundational for all that would follow. In *The Gay Science*, it is not the positive overflowing of joy, but a negative one of terror: "To escape the despair engendered by the decisive No even while maintaining this No without weakness, he invents the Eternal Return."[116] Nietzsche knew that the void of the death of God must be filled, a new myth must replace the old one, a myth of the overman, a "thinkable" god who affirms the eternal return. As de Lubac puts it, "'If we do not wish to fall prey again to the old idea of the Creator,' we must put another thing in his place. . . . Whether one wishes to or not, this paradox must be upheld, since 'he who refuses to believe that the universe is marked by a circular process is constrained to believe in a sovereign, absolute God.'"[117]

113. De Lubac, *Drama of Atheist Humanism*, 494.
114. De Lubac, *Drama of Atheist Humanism*, 494.
115. De Lubac, *Drama of Atheist Humanism*, 494.
116. De Lubac, *Drama of Atheist Humanism*, 496.
117. The conclusion of de Lubac, unfortunately, ends on a critical note assuming the failure of Nietzsche's mysticism as an expression of resentment against Christianity. Despite his intended positive affirmation of life, de Lubac contends that Nietzsche could not escape the spirit of resentment and revenge, for "Nietzsche will not stop being haunted, right to his last day, by the figure of Jesus." A new Dionysian kingdom is not discovered, but "what comes first is an anxiousness to antagonize in the very act of imitation, through the need to play an analogous and superior role. It is not enough for Nietzsche to make himself the announcer of a new gospel. He aspires to the title of Redeemer." In final analysis, argues de Lubac, Nietzsche is envious and resentful of Jesus and cannot escape him. De Lubac, *Drama of Atheist Humanism*, 496.

Beyond this contention regarding Nietzsche's own resentment, de Lubac is critical of Nietzsche's theory of the paradoxical unity between the overman and the Eternal Return. De Lubac observes that these two "mysteries" are tendencies in Nietzsche's thought that "are expressed with equal force, which pull the prophet in two opposing directions."[118] That is, between "a violent passion and an immense nostalgia."[119] On the one hand there is the passionate cry "nothing but earth," "remain faithful to the earth."[120] Such "declarations have often caused Nietzsche's doctrine to be taken for crude biologism, an exaltation of strength and animal life . . . but the excess nature itself of these declarations causes us to entertain doubts. There is a tone of defiance in them, a willful arrogance, which is the sign of a turbulent soul, a fragmented one."[121] The other tendency is the longing for the eternal: "Deep is sadness, Joy deeper than affliction. Sadness says: pass one and die! But all joy wants eternity, wants deep, deep eternity!" That is, "between this 'deep eternity' that all joy wants and the height 'of sexual instinct, of rapture, of cruelty,' into which the Dionysiac plunges, 'the ring of becoming and return' has not affected a unity. This 'nuptial ring' has remained a beautiful symbol—a beautiful powerless symbol."[122]

However, de Lubac's critical assessment does not stand up for the following reason. It seems that de Lubac makes the same error that Loeb

---

118. De Lubac, *Drama of Atheist Humanism*, 501.

119. De Lubac, *Drama of Atheist Humanism*, 501.

120. De Lubac, *Drama of Atheist Humanism*, 501.

121. De Lubac, *Drama of Atheist Humanism*, 502.

122. I also cannot affirm de Lubac's critical psychological interpretation of Nietzsche. De Lubac argues that in the end, Nietzsche could not overcome the nihilism of the death of God: "The Eternal Return is the most extreme form of nihilism: eternal nothingness (absurdity)." His ambiguous confidence in the Eternal Return is reflected in *Zarathustra*: "In truth, I advise you, get far away from me, defend yourself against Zarathustra! Better still, be ashamed of him. Perhaps he has deceived you. . . . You venerate me, but what would happen if your veneration was destroyed one day? Take care not to be crushed by a statue . . ." Of course, Nietzsche may respond that "prophetic men are beings who suffer much." But de Lubac insists, "He is neither unified nor free." For de Lubac, "in reality Nietzsche destroys himself. He has not risen above the despair of the 'madman' who looks everywhere with his lantern for the body of the murdered God." Nietzsche was "'stoned to death by his own hand.' He suffered the mortal fall of the rope dancer 'who does not want be excelled in his leaping jumps.' He suffered a fall that is all too real, 'an all too commonplace physiological shipwreck.'" This seems to be de Lubac's own assessment that goes beyond what we see in Nietzsche's text. De Lubac, *Drama of Atheist Humanism*, 502.

is critical of, a doctrinal reading of *Zarathustra* and the thought of eternal return rather than recognizing the dramatic enactment of the embodiment of eternal recurrence. Nietzsche is not attempting to reconcile two "mysteries," but rather to poetically embody a dramatic movement of Zarathustra's affirmation of life through the depiction of his dying with the hope of life again recurring. It is meant to be a more authentic "image" of the eternal within the confines of human experience in time. It is meant as a transvaluation of the Christian conception of time in relation to the eternal. It cannot be refuted on rational, theoretical ground, just as de Lubac's affirmation of the dramatic image of the Incarnation, the *Mysterium crucus* as embodied in the Eucharist is also beyond rational or theoretical disputation. It means affirming the messianic mystery through faith. What Nietzsche attempts to dramatize in the narrative of Zarathustra is, through re-envisioning the death and dying of Dionysus, is another "gospel" that affirms the tragic. Nietzsche's hope, I argue, is to provide a more authentic possibility of cultural transformation for Western Christianity and the secularizing of Christianity as embodied in modernism. How the "performance" of Zarathustra might be enacted as a political possibility for Western culture will be considered in the next section.

Beyond Resentment: The Way of the Warrior and Friend

Nietzsche, as we have seen, also viewed *Zarathustra* as Europe's highest moral point. What is the "moral" meaning of *Zarathustra*? There is no "practical" agenda here, the formulation of a social or political program to be implemented externally and technically. Yet, the vision is profoundly political, for it is a vision of the affirmation of power in its deepest sense, the formation of particular kind of person, an *Übermensch*, prepared to shape the future destiny of Western culture. As Gooding-Williams demonstrates, Nietzsche's political thought shifted from the writing of the *Birth of Tragedy* to *Thus Spoke Zarathustra*. In comparison between these two works, Gooding-William concludes, "In *The Birth of Tragedy*, Nietzsche's historical, dialectical explanation of the possibility of cultural interruption rests on an interpretation of the German nation as a self-purging Dionysian spirit."[123] That is, while still a "transnational" political vision, Nietzsche, still influenced by Wagner, believed that "the German nation could serve as the agent of historical challenge leading to the

123. Gooding-Williams, *Zarathustra's Dionysian Modernism*, 117.

Dionysian transformation of European humanity."[124] This view Nietzsche later repudiated. Rather, argues Gooding-Williams, in *Zarathustra*, the focus becomes on the physical and psychological healthy of the body, "the possibility of cultural interpretation rests on an interpretation of the healthy body as (potentially) a value-creating Dionysian body."[125] This is, of course, consistent with what we developed in chapter 3 in our section on Dionysian desire. *Zarathustra* pertains radical call to be "faithful to the earth," and to resist the sickness that comes from poison mixing, allowing our desires to be shaped (and deformed) by false illusions and deceptions. After the failure of Zarathustra to bring the teaching of the overman to the masses in the marketplace, Zarathustra resolves to seek "companions."[126] His purpose is to "lure many away from the herd, for that I have come."[127] As we saw in the third chapter, the lie of the dragon still enslaves the peoples of the West, even modern atheists who have "vanquished the old god."[128] The mass of moderns worship the state and its coercive, vengeful, "doctrine of equality."[129] Therefore, Zarathustra seeks companions who will be "fellow creators." Zarathustra intends to prepare for the future, beyond modernism:

> Wake and listen, you that are lonely [*Einsamen*]! From the future come winds with secret wing-beats; and good tidings are proclaimed to delicate ears. You that are lonely today, you that are withdrawing, you shall one day be a people [*ein Volk*]: out of you, who have chosen yourselves [*selber auswähltet*], there shall grow a chosen people—out of them, the overman [*der Übermensch*]. Verily, the earth shall yet become a site of recovery [*Gensung*]. Even now a new fragrance surrounds it, bringing salvation [*Heil bringender*]—and a new hope [*eine neue Hoffnung*].[130]

124. Gooding-Williams, *Zarathustra's Dionysian Modernism*, 117.
125. Gooding-Williams, *Zarathustra's Dionysian Modernism*, 117.
126. Nietzsche, *Zarathustra*, 135.
127. Nietzsche, *Zarathustra*, 135.
128. Nietzsche, *Zarathustra*, 161.
129. Nietzsche, *Zarathustra*, 212–13.
130. Nietzsche, *Zarathustra*, 189. In the German, "*Wachet und horcht, ihr Einsamen! Von der Zukunft her kommen Winde mit heimlichem Flügelschlagen; und an feine Ohren ergeht gute Botschaft. Ihr Einsamen von heute, ihr Ausscheidenden, ihr sollt einst ein Volk sein: aus euch, die ihr euch selber auswähltet, soll ein auserwähltes Volk erwachsen:—und aus ihm der Übermensch. ahrlich, eine Stätte der Genesung soll noch die Erde werden! Und schon liegt ein neuer Geruch um sie, ein Heil bringender,—und eine neue Hoffnung!*"

This text gives evidence of the larger political aims of *Zarathustra*. That is, as Gooding-William observes, "Zarathustra suggests that the self-overcoming is not an end in itself but a means to the end of the transforming humanity into a *people*."[131] It was what Nietzsche later will call, the "great politics," the international political vision envisaged in *Beyond Good and Evil*.[132] In order for the future of the overman to come, Zarathustra emphasizes that the awakened individuals enter into a friendship. Zarathustra may be, as Barth argues, a vision of man "without the fellowman." That is, Zarathustra eliminates all notion of a universal Übermenschen *Gemeinde*. If Zarathustra is not interested in the "state" per se, at least as he understands it in *Zarathustra*. As we have seen, for Nietzsche the state and its external systemic institutions are mediations of violence and the sickness of revenge. However, this does not mean that Nietzsche-Zarathustra is not interested in politics. As others have argued and Nietzsche himself affirmed, if there is a political philosophy embedded within *Zarathustra*, Georg Brandes described as "radical aristocracy."[133] However, while this description remains rather vague, our interpretation focuses on the poetic language of Zarathustra. That is, *Zarathustra* seeks to engender a new form of *education* for those with the nobility to become companions in the creation of new values. It is an elite alternative community made up of philosophers and educators, but not of the conventional varieties. It cannot be enforced as the "state," since this is the outcome of revenge. But it will engender a path whereby people follow Zarathustra to learn how to "follow themselves." *Zarathustra* is, above all, a vision of individualist *sovereignty*, not as a transcendent moral right, but as a decision that emanates from one's own personal will. One takes full responsibility for oneself and one's own destiny. It is a sovereignty that "decides" on the exception. It is a sovereignty that rules, however, not through extrinsic institutions, but through the invitation to an individual struggle that is nevertheless tied to a broader culture.

131. Gooding-Williams, *Zarathustra's Dionysian Modernity*, 142.

132. Gooding-Williams, *Zarathustra's Dionysian Modernity*, 143. See also Nietzsche, *Beyond Good and Evil*, 142.

133. Nietzsche wrote to Georg Brandes, who coined the term in relation to his interpretation of Nietzsche's writings: "The expression 'aristocratic radicalism,' which you use, is very good. That is, if I may say so, the shrewdest remark that I have ever read about me. How far this way of thinking has already guided my thoughts, how far it will still guide me—I'm almost afraid to imagine. But there are paths that don't permit one to turn back; and so I go forward, because I *must* go forward." See thenietzschechannel.com.

Zarathustra is populated with priests, popes, kings, and the "rabble" in the marketplace because these remain his political rivals, and there is no way "out" of the struggle. Zarathustra's aim is to prepare his "children" for the future, who will be prepared to rule because they have learned how to rule themselves: "Whenever I found the living, there I learned also the speech on obedience. Whatever lives, obeys. And this is the second point: he who cannot obey himself is commanded. That is the nature of the living."[134] Zarathustra, we contend, is a political vision as much as a mystical dramatic one.

The Way of the Warrior: An Honest Affirmation of the Will to Power

To be sure, the vision of *Zarathustra* is, as Barth and de Lubac agree, radically individualist. Even more so, it is the annihilation of the individual. Yet, the entire narrative of Zarathustra presupposes a community of those who have separated themselves from the masses to mystically affirm a more authentic and healthier attitude toward life. Zarathustra has followers whom he counsels: "Now I bid you lose [*verlieren*] me and find [*finden*] yourselves; and only when you have all denied me will I return to you."[135] This means that fellow overcomers must become "hard" toward one another in the perpetual self-denying war against the lie of Western Christianity and modernist political culture. This process of metamorphoses that Zarathustra initiated is the path to the new politics. The character of this nobility of friendship consists in what we have outlined in this chapter: the perpetual contention with the spirit of gravity or heaviness. It means eternal war against revenge. It means becoming an enemy to your companions in order to assist them to overcome, to become the lion, to strive toward the sovereign innocence of the child. As Zarathustra asserts in the section "On War and Warriors" (*Vom Krieg und Kriegsvolke*):

> My brothers in war, I love you thoroughly; I am and I was of your kind. And I am also your best enemy.... You should have eyes that always seek an enemy—*your* enemy [*eurem Feind*] ...

---

134. Nietzsche, *Zarathustra*, 226.

135. Nietzsche, *Zarathustra*, 190. In the German, "*Nun heisse ich euch, mich verlieren und euch finden; und erst, wenn ihr mich Alle verleugnet habt, will ich euch wiederkehren.*"

> Your enemy you shall seek, your war you shall wage—for your thoughts [*für eure Gedanken*]. And if your thought be vanquished, then your honesty [*Redlichkeit*] should still find cause for triumph in that. You should love peace [*Frieden*] as means to new wars [*neuen Kriegen*]—and the short peace more than the long. To you I do not recommend peace, but victory. Let your work be a struggle [*Kampf*]. Let your peace be a victory![136]

This text describes Nietzsche's vision of friendship as the perpetual struggle and battle for one's "thoughts." It is not necessarily a "non-violent" political vision, but it certainly intends to go beyond the question of political compulsion, coercion, and violence. Through the affirmation of the tragic, Higgins interprets Nietzsche's vision as, interestingly, deeply humane. It does not mean the "love" of atrocity: "He is not lecturing that hurtful events are in themselves good. Instead, he is singing, and to our ears, the song he sings is not from the blues."[137] Nietzsche's politic was neither nationalist nor imperialistic, but he was attempting to address the deeper desires that produced such politics. In fact, one might insinuate from *Zarathustra*, only those who have undergone the necessary overcoming of the "dragon" and the values associated with the church and state as they have been embodied in the West, are able to adequately assume the mantle of leadership, a political leadership that goes beyond the limited vision of the "last man" of modernity. That is, proper political leaders must necessarily consider the meaning of what it means to become an Übermensch, which means addressing the desire of the "will to power," to which we now turn.

With respect to self-overcoming, Nietzsche takes the suffering of the neighbour seriously, and permits the person to experience their suffering to learn, grow, and become. Nietzsche's intent is to create resilience and courage to face honestly the embodied experience of life and death, but also to destroy the illusions and lies rooted in revenge that keeps us from the consideration of life and death. It is an ethic that seeks to engender a personalist nobility in "the other," even if this means to radically question, oppose, and challenge the heart and thought of the friend. However,

---

136. Nietzsche, *Zarathustra*, 158. In the German, "*Euren Feind sollt ihr suchen, euren Krieg sollt ihr führen und für eure Gedanken! Und wenn euer Gedanke unterliegt, so soll eure Redlichkeit darüber noch Triumph rufen! Ihr sollt den Frieden lieben als Mittel zu neuen Kriegen. Und den kurzen Frieden mehr, als den langen. Euch rathe ich nicht zur Arbeit, sondern zum Kampfe. Euch rathe ich nicht zum Frieden, sondern zum Siege. Eure Arbeit sei ein Kampf, euer Friede sei ein Sieg!*"

137. Higgins, *Nietzsche's Zarathustra*, 127.

this first pertains to the question of "self-overcoming." As we see in the section "On War and Warriors," the war of Zarathustra in overcoming the dragon engenders a deeper form of authority and obedience within the self, the alignment the command and the obedience in the inner will, "Your nobility should be obedience. Your very commanding should be an obeying. To a good warrior 'thou shalt' sounds more agreeable than 'I will.' And everything you like you should first let yourself be commanded to do."[138] This endeavour to embody the alignment between commanding and obeying is, as we have developed in chapter 3, connected to the war against the values inherited within Christendom and modernity. With Gooding-Williams, I interpret this text ironically: "Paradoxically, obeying *this* "thou shalt' [of the overman] ... would involve a leonine repudiation of *all* 'thou shalt.'"[139] The inner voice of the dragon must be exorcized through the metamorphoses from camel-spirit to lion-spirit. The will must ally itself in obedience to the higher will of the overman. This implies the third metamorphosis, the conjoining of the will with the inner movement of Dionysian desire, striving to become the "thinkable" god of the Übermensch, "Your love of life shall be love of your highest hope; and your highest hope shall be the highest thought of life. Your highest thought; however, you should receive as a command from me—and it is: man is something that shall be overcome."[140] This concept of is further elaborated in the section, "On Self-Overcoming," where the theme of the "command" (*Befehlen*) addressed, "This, however, is the third point that I heard: that commanding is harder than obeying; and not only because he who commands must carry the burden of all who obey, and because this burden may easily crush him."[141] The relation of the command with obedience, according to Zarathustra, is the mystery of *the will to power*, "Hear, then, my word, you who are wisest. Test in all seriousness whether I have crawled into the very heart of life and into the very roots of its

138. Nietzsche, *Zarathustra*, 160. In the German, "*Eure Vornehmheit sei Gehorsam! Euer Befehlen selber sei ein Gehorchen! Einem guten Kriegsmanne Klingte 'du sollst' angenehmer, also 'ich will.' Und Alles, was euch lieb ist, sollt ihr euch erst noch befehlen lassen.*"

139. Gooding-Williams, *Zarathustra's Dionysian Modernism*, 137.

140. Nietzsche, *Zarathustra*, 160. In the German, "*Eure Liebe zum Leben sei Liebe zu eurer höchsten Hoffnung: und eure höchste Hoffnung sei der höchste Gedanke des Lebens! Euren höchsten Gedanken aber sollt ihr euch von mir befehlen lassen—und er lautet: der Mensch ist Etwas, das überwunden werden soll.*"

141. Nietzsche, *Zarathustra*, 226. In the German, "*Dies aber ist das Dritte, was ich hörte: dass Befehlen schwerer ist, als Gehorchen. Und nicht nur, das der Befehlende die Last aller Gehorchenden trägt, und dass leicht ihn diese Last zerdrückt.*"

heart. Where I found the living, I found the will to power; and even in the will of those who serve I found the will to be master."[142] The mystery, for Zarathustra, is that the weaker yield to the stronger because of their desire for greater power, "and where men make sacrifices and serve and cast amorous glances, there too is the will to be master. Along stealthy paths the weaker steals into the castle and into the very heart of the more powerful—and there steals power."[143] The honest way of the warrior is to acknowledge and affirm this fundamental reality of the will to power, exposing one's own desire to be master and not only confess it, but affirm it. It is, in other words, the acceptance of the *libido dominandi*, but also its transformation, for this power is now used for a higher purpose. This "law" of the "will to power" compels Zarathustra to oppose and overcome his weaker will in a movement toward the Übermensch, engaged in the perpetual, even eternal, struggle to overcome, "And life itself confided this secret to me: 'Behold,' it said, 'I am that *which must always overcome itself*. Indeed, you call it a will to procreate or a drive to an end, to something higher, farther, more manifold: but all this is one, and one secret."[144] That is, the *will to power* is the only pure, natural, creative movement that connects humanity to what we experience in existence. It is beyond "good" and "evil." In consideration of the implications of this, every human society and culture are manifestations of the will to power, expressed in the moral "esteeming," "Zarathustra saw many lands and many peoples: thus, he discovered the good and evil of many peoples . . . no people could live without first esteeming."[145] All religious, political, and social practices are particular embodiments of the *will to power*, even Christianity with its assertion of the renouncement of power. Again, as we saw in chapter 3, this explains why Nietzsche holds Christianity in

---

142. Nietzsche, *Zarathustra*, 226. In the German, "*Hört mir nun mein Wort, ihr Weisesten! Prüft es ernstlich, ob ich dem Leben selber in's Herz Kroch und bis in die Wurzeln seines Herzens! Wo ich Lebendiges fand, da fand ich Willen zur Macht; and noch im Willen des Dienenden fand ich den Willen, Herr zu sein.*"

143. Nietzsche, *Zarathustra*, 227. In the German, "*Und wo Opferung und Dienste und Liebesblicke sind: auch das ist Wille, Herr zu sein. Auf Schleichwegen schleicht sich da der Schwächere in die Burg und bis in's Herz dem Mächtigeren—und stiehlt da Macht.*"

144. Nietzsche, *Zarathustra*, 227. In the German, "*Und diess Geheimniss redete das Leben selber zu mir. 'Siehe, sprach es, ich bin das, was sich immer selber überwinden muss. Freilich, ihr heist es Wille zur Zeugung oder Trieb zum Zwecke, zum Höheren, Ferneren, Vielfacheren: aber all diess ist Eins und Ein Geheimniss.*"

145. See the section "On the Thousand and One Goals" in Nietzsche, *Zarathustra*, 170.

such suspicion. It is the most insidious and sick expression of the will to power because it is the most blind by its own desire for such power, despite the assertion of renunciation of power and its ascetic practices. Christianity is the epitome of the camel-spirit and the spiritual parent of secular modernity. The power of Zarathustra's teaching is the *exposing* of the will to power embodied in the church and the modern state, to name the archenemy so that it can be exorcised from Western culture. The way of the warrior pertains, as we saw in the previous section, especially in our analysis of the "Vision and the Riddle," the courageous act of biting off the serpent's head and struggling with the "small man," even if this means an eternal war. This is a Nietzschean version of the "monastic path." It means attuning oneself to the energies of the Dionysian body and becoming a creative of new values, of new forms of "good" and "evil" that could unite Western Europe with a new goal and aim, to overcome the "old" self shaped by Christianity and the church and modern state. Zarathustra endeavours to shape a community of "warriors" who have the take upon themselves, voluntarily and in freedom, as individuals, to assume this new moral responsibility which is also a political one. That is, those who *desire* it and have the moral strength to *will* it into reality. That is, *Zarathustra* is a vision of a new kind of political leadership.

Solitude and the Friend: An Intimacy of Adversaries

Nietzsche does not prescribe a particular "Zarathustrian" form of society.[146] The narrative of *Zarathustra* begins and ends with him in solitude.[147] Zarathustra relates most to the hermit, the monk, and the saint, who have departed human society for the wilderness, pursuing redemption and confronting the greater demonic battle within the soul. In the section, "On Three Metamorphoses," it is in the *loneliest desert* that the lion spirit engages in battle with the "last god."[148] However, there is strong evidence that Nietzsche does not intend for the path of Zarathustra to be walked in isolation. Solitude, yes; isolation, no. As we see in prologue,

---

146. I am borrowing the phrase "intimacy of adversaries" from Gooding-Williams, *Zarathustra's Dionysian Modernism*, 141.

147. Of course, what I refer to is the beginning of the Prologue after Zarathustra has spent ten years in solitude. The narrator tells us that a change came over his heart and sought to bring his gift to humankind. Depending on how one views the "end" of Zarathustra, either book III or IV, we see Zarathustra alone in solitude.

148. Nietzsche, *Zarathustra*, 138.

when he recognizes his failure in reaching the masses in the marketplace, a "new truth" came to his heart, "an insight has come to me: Let Zarathustra speak not to people but to companions. Zarathustra shall not become the shepherd and dog of herd. To lure many away from the herd, for that I have come."[149] We could also suggest, by implication, this suggests at least one reason Nietzsche wrote *Zarathustra*, to seek a readership of companions, who would struggle with him with the possibility of overcoming Western cultural Christianity. It is possible that Nietzsche intended to persuade a few who were worthy to join him as forerunners of a new post-Christendom, postmodernist philosophy whereby more honest philosophers pave the way for the possibility of a new future.

Furthermore, we see further evidence of space for community in the section "On the Friend" (*Vom Freunde*] Zarathustra asserts:

> "There is always one too many around me"—thus thinks the hermit. "Always one times one—eventually that makes two." I and me are always in deep conversation: how could one stand that if there were no friends? For the hermit the friend is always the third person: the third is the cork that prevents the conversation of the two from sinking into the depths. Alas, there are too many depths for all hermits; therefore, they long so for a friend and his height.[150]

That is, a friend can assist in the depth of dialogue that occurs with the soul, a conversation that is itself reflected in *Zarathustra*, conflicting wills and desires. It is the conversation that occurs in the "Stillest Hour."[151] Of course, Zarathustra does not pursue the cheap comfort of a friend that will remove or alleviate his struggle or suffering, for the

---

149. Nietzsche, *Zarathustra*, 135. In the German, "*Ein Licht gieng mir auf: nicht zum Volke rede Zarathustra, sondern zu Gefährten! Nicht soll Zarathustra einer Heerde Hirt und Hund werden! Viele wegzulocken vond der Heerde—dazu kam ich. Zürnen soll mire Volk und Heerde: Räuber will Zarathustra den Hirten heissen.*"

150. Nietzsche, *Zarathustra*, 167–68. In the German, "'*Einer ist immer zu viel um mich*'—*also denkt der Einsiedler. 'Immer Einmal Eins—das giebt auf die Dauer Zwei!' Ich und Mich sind immer zu eifrig im Gespräche: wie wäre es auszuhalten, wenn es nicht einen Freund gäbe? Immer ist für den Einsiedler der Freund der Dritte: der Dritte ist der Kork, der verhindert, dass das Gespräch der Zweie in die Tiefe sinkt. Ach, es giebt zu viele Tiefen für alle Einsiedler. Darum sehnen sie sich so nach einem Freunde und nach seiner Höhe.*"

151. At the end of book II, the section "The Stillest Hour," provides a good example of this inner dramatic dialogue within Zarathustra as he moves closer to embracing the thought of the eternal return. Nietzsche, *Zarathustra*, 257–59.

longing for friend is also "our betrayer. And often love is only a device to overcome envy."[152] And we see in book IV that "pity for the higherman" because Zarathustra's last temptation. What Zarathustra seeks in a friend is a warrior who can also be his enemy: "If one wants to have a friend one must also want to wage war for him; and to wage war, one must be capable of being an enemy. In a friend, one should have one's best enemy. You should be closest to him with your heart when you resist him."[153] In other words, to love your friends, you must spur them on to overcome themselves. This form of friendship is beyond slavery and tyranny, "Are you a slave? Then you cannot be a friend. Are you a tyrant? Then you cannot have friends."[154] Nonetheless, for Zarathustra, the way of the friend is not about "equality" either. There is no inherent equality in society, rather the many serve the few that have ability to go beyond themselves. Among those with such power, it means learning to struggle with each other to overcome the humanity as shaped by Western Christian culture, in an honest, mystical new relation to the "eternal" immanence of life. The way of the friend is the way of noble warrior that I examined above, it is the learning to master desire in a way that does not deny the will to power, but divinely creates something higher than we have yet imagined. A friend is a *spur* to move one another forward in process of transformation through transvaluation. But the way of the friend is treacherous and not for the faint of heart. As a warrior-friend, this means the challenging to unmask the "clothes" that we put on to mask our true desire and true self. How much does one expose?

> You do not want to put on anything for your friend? Should it be an honor that you give yourself to him as you are? But he sends you to the devil for that. He who makes no secret of himself, enrages so much reason have you for fearing nakedness. Indeed, if you were gods, then you might be ashamed of your clothes. You cannot groom yourself to beautifully for your friend: for you shall be to him an arrow and a longing for the overman.[155]

152. Nietzsche, *Zarathustra*, 168.

153. Nietzsche, *Zarathustra*, 168. In the German, "*Will man einen Freund haben, so muss man auch für ihn Krieg führen wollen: und um Krieg zu führen, muss man Feind sein können ... In seinem Freunde soll man seinen besten Feind haben. Du sollst ihm am nächsten mit dem Herzen sein, wenn du ihm widerstrebst.*"

154. Nietzsche, *Zarathustra*, 169. In the German, "*Bist du ein Sclave? So kannst du nicht Freund sein. Bist du ein Tyrann? So kannst du nitcht Freunde haben.*"

155. Nietzsche, *Zarathustra*, 168. In the German, "*Du willst vor deinem Freunde kein Kleid tragen? Es soll deines Freundes Ehre sein, dass du dich giebst, wie du bist? Aber er wünscht dich darum zum Teuful! Wer aus sich kein Hehl macht, empört: so sehr habt*

In other words, friendship is not an aim, but can function as a kind of catalyst for self-becoming. As Nietzsche imagines it, the friend is a fellow warrior who will be an arrow, a model, and an instigator to become an overman. The friend will courageously expose your self-delusions and tear you down, if necessary, if one lapses again into the way of the camel-spirit or worse, one of the political actors in the marketplace. Moreover, the way of the friend is contrasted with the Christian moral teaching on neighbour-love. In the section "On Love of Neighbour" Zarathustra declares, "I teach you not the neighbour [*Nächsten*], but the friend [*Freund*]. The friend should be the festival [*Fest*] of the earth to you and an anticipation of *the overman* [des Übermenschen]."[156] This vision of friendship is a gift-giving one, an overflow of the wisdom that is attained in the solitude of the heart, a solitude that consisted in a struggle to overcome the dragon, "I teach you the friend and his overflowing heart. . . . I teach you the friend in whom the world stands completed, a bowl of goodness—the creating friend who always has a completed world to give away."[157] A Nietzschean friend is gift-giving friend, who loves what is still furthest in you, "Let the future and the farthest be for you the cause of your today: in your friend you shall love the overman as your cause."[158] Zarathustra, of course, is the model of such friendship. As the one who intended to bring a "gift" to humankind in the prologue, learns through rejection and suffering that humanity, at least people who have been shaped by the values of Christianity and modernism, are not prepared for this gift. Nonetheless, the narrative of *Zarathustra*, anticipates that there will those who seek after the friendship of Zarathustra.

---

ihr Grund, die Nachtheit zu fürchten! Ja, wenn ihr Götter wäret, da dürftet ihr euch eurer Kleider schämen! Du kannst dich für deinen Freund nicht schön genug putzen: den du sollst ihm ein Pfeil und eine Sehnsucht nach dem Übermenschen sein."

156. Nietzsche, *Zarathustra*, 173. We observe that in the German, it is the plural overmen. "Nicht den Nächsten lehre ich euch, sondern den Freund. Der Freund sei euch das Fest der Erde und ein Vorgefühl des Übermenschen."

157. Nietzsche, *Zarathustra*, 174. In the German, "Ich Lehre euch den Freund und sein übervolles Herz. Aber man muss verstehn, ein Schwamm zu sein, wenn man von übervollen Herzen geliebt sein will. Ich Lehre euch den Freund, in dem Welt fertig dasteht, eine Schale des Guten, den schaffenden Freund, der immer eine fertige Welt zu verschenken hat."

158. Nietzsche, *Zarathustra*, 174. In the German, "Die Zukunft und das Fernste sei dir die Ursache deines Heute: in deinem Freunde sollst du den Übermenschen also deine Ursache lieben."

Eucharistic Mockery and Ambiguity of the Future

In book IV, we see a picture of an emerging community of "friends" as the higher men seek for Zarathustra on the mountain. This is Zarathustra's last temptation, the pity for the higher men. The temptation is to love the "farthest" as if he "loves the neighbour." That is, it is the temptation to respond to the "cry of distress" of the higher men by removing their "suffering."[159] The "final sin" of Zarathustra, is, of course, ironic, since "sin" belongs to the moral worldview that he has rejected. Nonetheless, the "sin" is Zarathustra's compassion for the higher men that seemingly leads to failure.[160] The higher men struggle to overcome the spirit of revenge and gravity. We see the ambiguity of Zarathustra's project to eradicate Christ and Christian conscience from the "higher man" (*höheren Mensch*) in book IV. The higher men are those who are seeking the way of Zarathustra, those who are experiencing the "great nausea" of the "small man." However, even while they are celebrating "the last supper" (*das Abendmahl*) in Zarathustra's cave, while Zarathustra steps outside, the higher men begin to sing a song of worship to God revealed in the Christ, a parody of the Gospel: "Amen! And praise and honour and wisdom and thanks and glory and strength be to our god, from everlasting to everlasting! But the ass brayed: Yea-Yuh. He carries our burden, he took upon himself the form of a servant, he is patient of heart and never says No; and whoever loves his God, chastises him. But the ass brayed: Yea-Yuh."[161]

While at first Zarathustra chastises the higher men for this act of worship, this is soon applied to Zarathustra himself: "And whoever has too much spirit might well grow foolishly fond of stupidity and folly itself. Think about yourself, O Zarathustra! You yourself—verily, overabundance and wisdom could easily turn you into an ass."[162] That is, Zarathustra must hold to his own teaching and vocation as the teacher of the eternal recurrence with ironic ambivalence. As Higgins asserts, Zarathustra confronts his own folly at the ass festival: "The ass festival disturbs

---

159. Nietzsche, *Zarathustra*, 352.

160. Nietzsche, *Zarathustra*, 354.

161. Nietzsche, *Zarathustra*, 396, 422. In the German, "*Amen! Und Lob und Ehre und Weisheit und Dank und Preis und Stärke sei unserm Gott, von Ewigkeit zu Ewigkeit! Der Esel aber schrie dazu I-A. Er trägt unsre Last, er nahm Knechtsgestalt an, er ist geduldsam von Herzen und redet niemals Nein; und wer seinen Gott liebt, der züchtigt ihn. Der Esel aber schrie dazu I-A.*"

162. Nietzsche, *Zarathustra*, 427.

Eternal Return and the Politic of Friendship

him because he is viewing his doctrine of the death of God as a value to preserve, when honesty forces him to acknowledge, at least to himself, that the Ugliest man is right, that no one does know how dead God is, and that if God is really dead no ass festival can represent a spiritual or cultural danger."[163] However, if one is to kill God, it must not come from wrath, but from *laughter*: "Not by wrath does one kill, but by laughter [*Lachen*]—thus you once spoke. O Zarathustra, you hidden one, you annihilator without wrath, you dangerous saint—you are a rogue!"[164]

The section "The Ass Festival" (*das Eselfest*) concludes with Zarathustra making light of the foolishness of the higher men and his own foolishness. Is this not all nonsense anyway? The dance with life means the laughter that slays the spirit of gravity and revenge. This requires applying this laughter to ourselves. We must not take ourselves too seriously. We must become like children in order to become true "overmen": "To be sure, except ye become like children, ye shall not enter the kingdom of heaven [*Himmelreich*]. . . . But we have no wish whatever to enter the kingdom of heaven: we have become men [*Männer sind wir worden*]: so, we want the earth."[165] As I signalled at the introduction of this chapter, *Zarathustra* concludes with the section "The Sign" (*das Zeichen*). In a sense, Zarathustra comes full circle, from where he was in the prologue. He is on the mountain and leaves his cave in the morning to greet the sun. Another change comes over his heart: "The sign is at hand" (*Das Zeichen kommt*).[166] Zarathustra sees a great lion appear, that laughs. Indeed, the imagery of the lion refers to the section "The Three Metamorphoses," where the camel-spirit must become the lion to defeat the dragon. Zarathustra has overcome the dragon of pity for the higher men. When the higher men "reached the door of the cave and the sound of their steps ran ahead of them, the lion started violently, turned away from Zarathustra suddenly, and jumped toward the cave, roaring

---

163. Higgins, *Nietzsche's Zarathustra*, 150.

164. Nietzsche, *Zarathustra*, 427–28. In the German, "*Nicht durch Zorn, sondern durch Lachen tödtet man*"—*so sprachst du einst. Oh Zarathustra, du Verborgener, du Vernichter ohne Zorn, du gefährlicher Heiliger,—du bist ein Schelm!*"

165. Nietzsche, *Zarathustra*, 428. In the German, "*Freilich: so ihr nicht werdet wie die Kindlein, so kommt ihr nicht in das Himmelreich. (Und Zarathustra zeigte mit den Händen nach Oben.) Aber wir wollen auch gar nicht in's Himmelreich: Männer sind wir worden, so wollen wir das Erdenreich.*"

166. Nietzsche, *Zarathustra*, 436.

savagely."[167] When they heard the roar, they disappeared. Nonetheless, we surmise that *Zarathustra* ends with Zarathustra having transformed into the second metamorphosis, that of the lion and not yet child, although he perceives it in the horizon: "My children are near, my children" (*meine Kinder sind nahe*)[168] Near, but not yet born. "Maturity" in the Dionysian mystical dramatic existence has not yet arrived. Nonetheless, Nietzsche has given Western culture, and all who read *Zarathustra*, a new heroic image to consider as a possible medium of which to overcome oneself and use the passions of the body to create oneself, and possible a new culture and politic, beyond the humanity as shaped by the resentment of the Western church and state. The question remains is whether any in the "marketplace" have heard the call and are willing to step out from the "herd" and follow Zarathustra into the wilderness.

167. Nietzsche, *Zarathustra*, 438.
168. Nietzsche, *Zarathustra*, 438.

5

The Mysticism of Resurrection and the Sacrament of Friendship in *The Brothers Karamazov*

Introduction

As we turn to Dostoevsky, we will examine how the "whole" of humanity as created in the image of God is brought together through the messianic political vision that undergirds *The Brothers Karamazov*. As I will demonstrate, there is an underlying vision of the *mystical body of Christ* in *The Brothers Karamazov*. As Ward suggests, Dostoevsky's vision of Christ culminates the "church idea": "The claim that *the* masterpiece of modern literature, regarded as such by Einstein, Wittgenstein, Freud, Heidegger, and Levinas, *inter alia*, is devoted to the unfashionable subject of the church might well appear ridiculous, at least to Western critics."[1] Nonetheless, Ward also quotes the Russian philosopher Vladimir Soloviev: "The overall point of Dostoevsky's entire activity . . . consists in a solution of the twofold problem concerning a higher societal ideal and an actual path to its attainment. . . . If we want to specify and designate the social idea at which Dostoevsky arrived with a single word, then this word will not be the nation, but the *Church*."

---

1. Soloviev, "Three Speeches in Memory of Dostoevks," 8–11, cited by Ward, *Redeeming the Enlightenment*, 215.

Considering these statements, the question we aim to explore here is, how does Dostoevsky convey the church, the "societal ideal," as political community that overcomes the spirit of retribution, as reflected in Ivan and the Grand Inquisitor? I will demonstrate that Alyosha, the "hero" of the novel, is the character that Dostoevsky uses to display his poetic vision of a political community that embodies the ideal of the image of Christ. At the end of the novel, as Ward contends, we see an "image" of the church in the chapter "Ilyushechka's Funeral. The Speech at the Stone." Ward observes how there were "about twelve boys altogether," perhaps an allusion to the biblical image of the people of God. The chapter concludes the novel with the theme of unity rooted in the resurrection and redemptive love.[2] It is expressed in their commitment to remember the dead Ilyusha:

> "Karamazov!" cried Kolya, "can it really be true as religion says, that we shall rise from the dead, and come to life, and see one another again, and everyone, and Ilyushechka?"
> "Certainly, we shall rise, certainly we shall see and gladly, joyfully tell one another all that has been," Alyosha replied, half laughing, half in ecstasy. . . ."Now let's end our speeches and go to his memorial dinner. Don't be disturbed that we'll be eating pancakes. It's an ancient, eternal thing, and there's good in that too," laughed Alyosha. "Well, let's go! And we go like this now, hand in hand."[3]

In this text, we catch a glimpse of Dostoevsky's vision of the mystical community that, rooted in resurrection, transcends death itself in an eternal reality. There is a sense of joyful, almost cathartic relief in this text, as they grieve the death of their young friend, Ilyushechka. The memory

---

2. Ward comments that the opening phrase of Alyosha's speech, "Let us agree here," appeals to a "spiritual unity, or harmony ('Let us agree,' *soglasimsia*—literally, a 'joining of voices'), composed of people who are friends to each other ('one another,' *drug o druge*—literally 'friend of friend')." This is multi-voiced unity that enhances unique personhood. Ward, *Redeeming the Enlightenment*, 217.

3. Dostoevsky, *Brothers Karamazov*, 776. In the Russian, "—Вечная память!—подхватили снова мальчики.—Карамазов!—крикнул Коля,—неужели и взаправду религия говорит, что мы все встанем из мертвых, и оживем, и увидим опять друг друга, и всех, и Илюшечку?—Непременно восстанем, непременно увидим и весело; радостно расскажем друг другу всё, что было,—полусмеясъ% полу в восторге ответил Алеша.—Ах, как это будет хорошо!—вырвалось у Коли. ю—Ну, а теперь кончим речи и пойдемте на его поминки. Не сму щайтесь, что блины будем есть. Это ведь старинное, вечное, и тут есть хорошее,—засмеялся Алеша.—Ну пойдемте же! Вот мы теперь и идем рука в руку."

of their friend is celebrated and experienced in the most human and mundane way, the eating of pancakes. In the church, death does not have the final word: Alyosha and his boys will enjoy reunion with their friend again in an eschatological hope of life eternal. It is this hopeful anticipation of resurrection that unites them in a common journey of friendship: "And we go like this now, hand and hand." In *Drama*, de Lubac asserts that Dostoevsky is the prophet of "unity, which presupposes a breach to be healed; the prophet of the Resurrection, which presupposes the experience of death."[4] The sacramental mystery is that transcendence is united with the immanent as persons freely participate in the mystery of the death and resurrection of Christ.

Yet how does mystical vision of resurrection connect to the story of Alyosha? And more precisely, especially considering chapter 2, how does Dostoevsky envision the church as a mystical political community overcoming and go beyond the spirit of retribution, as reflected in Ivan and the Grand Inquisitor? How does the church overcome the power of the Karamazovian force? In the novel, no one is exempt from the temptation of the "spirit of non-being," as the Grand Inquisitor describes him. The devil tempts Alyosha too, the hero of the novel, to take vengeance into his own hands. We see this spiritual crisis at the beginning of part III of the novel in the chapters "The Odor of Corruption" and "An Opportune Moment." Alyosha's beloved elder, his idol Zosima, dies, and rather than the miracle as anticipated, the pungent odor of corruption whiffs up from his body. The stench of a decaying body is the most natural thing, but in Zosima's case, the smell of death was a sign of God's judgment on Zosima, and, therefore, his teaching and the institution of elders. According to Father Ferapont, "The deceased, your saint here . . . denied devils. He gave purgatives against devils. They've bred here like spiders in the corners. And on this day he got himself stunk. In this we see a great sign from God."[5] Although Alyosha also anticipated the miracles, he was more cut to the heart because of the false accusation against the elder, whom he loved with his whole heart. As a result, what Alyosha yearned for was justice, a "higher justice," a vindication for his beloved elder. "Again, it was not miracles he needed, but only a 'higher justice [высшей справедливости],' which, as he believed, had been violated—it was this that wounded his heart so cruelly and suddenly . . . But it was

---

4. De Lubac, *Drama of Atheist Humanism*, 393.
5. Dostoevsky, *Brothers Karamazov*, 335.

justice [справедливости], justice he thirsted [жаждал] for, not simply miracles!"⁶ It is interesting that what causes Alyosha to stumble is the spiritual failure of the monastic community itself which succumbed to "revenge" and "retribution" as expressed in the ascetic arrogance of Father Ferapont.

Despite the fact that in his diverse writings Dostoevsky's political theology sometimes seems at odd with itself, at least within *Brothers Karamazov*, we observe the vision of an "alternative society, or community, acknowledging the higher world and preoccupied with realizing justice in this world."⁷ As we consider how this is developed in *The Brothers Karamazov*, we see reflected here de Lubac's conception of the church as *corpus mysticum*, the mystical mediation of transcendence and immanence. Dostoevsky of course provides a stronger poetic vision for how the reality of Christ is to be embodied in this world, with a focus on redemption, especially on overcoming the evil spirit of retribution. I suggest that what *The Brothers Karamazov* displays here is an apocalyptic ecclesiology that unites the divine and the human in the imitation of Christ, a participation in divine active love. The cruciform image of such a political ethic is expressed in the Johannine epigraph of the novel. To repeat once more, "Verily, verily, I say unto you, except a corn of wheat fall into the ground and die, it abideth alone: but if it dies, it bringeth forth much fruit" (Jn. 12:24)." That is, humanity as a "whole" is mystically reunited when one dies to self, renewing the soul and uniting it with Christ and the mystical body. This attainment of this higher societal ideal is signified in the life and teachings of the elder Zosima, and the path of the monk as represented in Alyosha. The rest of this chapter on Dostoevsky will examine the theme of the church as a messianic community that gives witness to the redemptive from the spirit of retribution.

While *The Brothers Karamazov* is, as Bakhtin rightly argues, a "polyphonic" novel, this does not mean that Dostoevsky's own voice does not bleed through.⁸ As the preface of the novel suggests, the novel

---

6. De Lubac, *Drama of Atheist Humanism*, 339.

7. Ward compares Dostoevsky's varying views with the various options envisaged by Rousseau, "(1) the church and society, theology and politics, are completely integrated . . . (2) the church is entirely spiritual in orientation . . . (3) the church forms a parallel society, pretending to be spiritual but in actuality adopting the power mechanism of the state." According to Ward, *The Brothers Karamazov* articulates a fourth option as alternative society. Ward, *Redeeming the Enlightenment*, 218–19.

8. Bakhtin, *Problems of Dostoevsky's Poetics*, 5.

centers on the youngest brother, Alyosha, the monastic devotee of the elder Zosima. To be sure, Alyosha is not as an "original" a character as Ivan or as passionately erotic and explosive as Mitya. Yet according to the preface, Alyosha is the proper "hero" of the novel. Commentators have wondered at this, even disagreeing with the author, given how undeveloped he seems to be.[9] However, on closer inspection, Alyosha is the glue that brings everything and everyone together. He often functions as "go-between," a "mediator" between people. As Richard Pevear notes, the narrator or other characters often describes him as an angel: "He has the function of an *angelos*, a messenger, in the most literal sense."[10] Moreover, according to Pevear, in the deeper sense Alyosha is a "hearer of words, and he is almost the only one in the novel who *can* hear. That is his great gift: the word can come to life in him."[11] In light of Kroeker and Ward's interpretation of "spiritual causality," Alyosha is the receptor of the agency of the Word made flesh, and in turn becomes a sower of the Word in the world.[12] Alyosha represents the mission of the redemptive Word. According to the elder Zosima, Alyosha must not remain hidden in the cloister; Zosima *sends* him into the world. Therefore, our strategy is simply to follow his story. The first section will explore the redemptive metaphysical and moral implications of Dostoevsky's conception of Alyosha, the "societal ideal" of the church as Soloviev formulates it, and the second section will focus on "the actual path of its attainment."

9. According to de Lubac, Shestov took little interest 'in this character, calling him common place, unreal, tiresome, according to them the author's failure to make him stand out is a sign that Dostoevsky did not put any of his profound ideas into Alyosha.' Moreover, de Lubac quotes Shestov, who argued that Dostoevsky was afraid of 'soiling with his impure hands the beautiful modern icon' (in Les Révélations, 118–19). De Lubac, *Drama of Atheist Humanism*, 386.

10. Dostoevsky, *Brothers Karamazov*, xviii.

11. Dostoevsky, *Brothers Karamazov*, xviii.

12. According to Kroeker and Ward, "we would rather argue that his poetics bears testimony to the spiritual causality characterized by the mysterious enactment of the extraordinary in the world." Could we say, the mysterious enactment of divine transcendence in the immanent? To provide another quote: "Faith is somehow beyond reason or that sacred history is detached from secular, mundane history or from nature. Rather it claims that the truth of the world is made, named, and sustained by divine agency—an agency that human action (in keeping with its created status in *imago dei*) is to imitate in certain regards, if it is to find happiness and true life." Kroeker and Ward, *Remembering the End*, 18.

Out of the Darkness into the Light of Love

How precisely is Alyosha portrayed? The narrator does not describe Alyosha as a "mystic" per se, but gives his "full opinion" at the outset of the novel: "He was simply an early lover of mankind, and if he threw himself into the monastery path, it was only because it alone struck him at the time and presented him, so to speak, with an ideal way out for his soul struggling from the darkness of worldly wickedness towards the light of love."[13] As Pevear notes at the end of his translation of *The Brothers Karamazov*, the designation "lover of mankind" is an epithet for Christ in various Orthodox liturgical prayers.[14] That is, the character of Alyosha is intended to be an iconic figure who mediates the image of Christ, an image of a lover of humankind. However, Alyosha does not represent the perfection of Christ, but the movement of an embodied soul that is struggling out of the dark and into the light of love. The embodiment of divine love is a movement, not a static, abstract essence. Nonetheless, this movement is not without struggle and suffering. To understand Alyosha means to understand this struggle as defined by the narrative itself as Alyosha seeks to move toward the light of love out of the "den of iniquity into which he was born." We explored the source of the struggle in the second chapter, the Karamazovian force, especially as it is reflected in the spirit of retribution in Ivan and his literary creation of the Grand Inquisitor. That, too, is a movement, but in the opposing direction, toward the elimination of the image of Christ in humankind to exalt the sovereignty of humanity. Alyosha's character is designed to reflect a movement of resistance against the spirit of "non-being," unveiled in Ivan's hallucination of the devil. In the narrative of Alyosha, we capture a glimpse of Dostoevsky's redemptive metaphysic, the mediation of a transcendent divine love incarnated in an embodied soul as it struggles against the spirit of "non-being," a spirit of retribution.

In the chapter "Alyosha" we see that the spiritual struggle toward the light of love was first bestowed to him through the memory of his

---

13. Dostoevsky, *Brothers Karamazov*, 18. In the Russian, "Прежде всего объявляю, что этот юноша, Алеша, был вовсе не фанатик и, по-моему, по крайней мере, даже и не мистик вовсе. Заранее скажу мое полное мнение: был он просто ранний человеколюбец, и если ударился на монастырскую дорогу, то потому только, что в то время она одна поразила его и представила ему, так сказать, идеал исхода рвавшейся из мрака мирской злобы к свету любви души его."

14. See the notes section in *The Brothers Karamazov*.

mother when he was a young child. The narrator provides us with an image which profoundly shaped Alyosha:

> He remembered a quiet summer evening, an open window, the slanting rays of the setting sun (these slanting rays he remembered most of all), an icon in the corner of a room, a lighted oil-lamp in front of it, and before the icon, on her knees, his mother, sobbing as if in hysterics, with shrieks and cries, seizing him in her arms, hugging him so tightly that it hurt, and pleading for him to the Mother of God, holding him out from her embrace with both arms towards the icon, as if under the protection of the Mother of God.[15]

This memory of Alyosha's mother reflects the meaning of transcendence touching the immanent, whereby the divine intersects with the human. It is not necessarily in the peaceful serenity of meditation that the transcendent is mediated. Rather it is mediated through the agony of struggle and suffering, with "shrieks and cries," and the violence of love, "hugging him so tightly that it hurt." Of course, this dramatic scene contains a serene poetic image of divine light, "the slanting rays of the setting sun," yet the rays of light illuminate the picture of his crying mother, who passionately intercedes before the icon of the Mother of God, for the protection of her son. As suggested in the story, divine light is revealed in the agony of love as expressed in the love Sophia Ivanovna possessed for her son. Perhaps it is not coincidence either, that Alyosha's mother's name derives from the Greek term, *sophia*, which means "wisdom." Like the beauty of "Madonna," that we explored in the second chapter, Sophia, like Mary, represents the wisdom of humble, servant love, which gives birth to the divine into the world. According to Ware, if Christ represents the new Adam, "Mary is the new Eve, whose obedient submission to the will of God counterbalanced Eve's disobedience in Paradise."[16] Dostoevsky links Alyosha's earliest memory to the *theotokis*, the intercession of the mother of God, who is also an image of *Panagia*, the "supreme example

---

15. Dostoevsky, *Brothers Karamazov*, 18–19. In the Russian, "Так точно было и с ним: он запомнил один вечер, летний, тихий, отворенное окно, косые лучи заходящего солнца (косые-то лучи и запомнились всего более), в комнате в углу образ, пред ним зажженную лампадку, а пред образом на коленях рыдающую как в истерике, со взвизгиваниями и вскрикиваниями, мать свою, схватившую его в обе руки, обняв шую его крепко до боли и молящую за него богородицу, протяги-вающую его из объятий своих обеими руками к образу как бы под покров богородице... и вдруг вбегает нянька и вырывает его у нее в испуге."

16. Ware, *Orthodox Church*, 251.

of synergy or cooperation between the purpose of the Deity and human freedom."[17] In light of Dostoevsky's emphasis on the christological basis of human freedom, echoing the image of the mother of God in relation to Alyosha's mother is highly relevant to this theme. Yet with this image, there is greater focus on the struggle and agony in the care and love of her innocent child. Furthermore, motherhood, and Mary in particular, are symbols of the church.[18] Perhaps the theme of motherly suffering love for the child is intended as counterpoint to the protest of Ivan in the chapter "Rebellion" where we are given pictures of the exploitation and desecration of the innocent.

Interestingly, in the chapter "Women of Faith" we see the kind of agonized love exhibited by Alyosha's mother expressed in other "peasant" women, the women of the Russian people. It is in this text, I suggest, that we also are given another clue into Dostoevsky's inspiration for the character of Alyosha. In that chapter, the narrator informs us of a peasant woman, who weeps over the death of her child: "I pity my little son, dear father, he was three years old, just three months short of three years old. I grieve for my little son, father, for my little son."[19] It is not out of the realm of possibility that the repetition of "three" is an echo to the Orthodox understanding of the divine as trinitarian, a faint suggestion that Dostoevsky seeks to help us poetically grasp the nature of the divine triune love, as revealed in motherly love. Moreover, in response to her suffering in grief for her dead son, Zosima does not offer cheap "comfort," but affirms her grief, linking the suffering of the mother to the cry of Rachel, "this is Rachel of old, 'weeping for her children, and she would not be comforted, because they are not.' This is the lot that befalls you, mothers, on earth. And do not be comforted, you should not be comforted, but weep."[20] As Zosima interacts with the grieving mother, it is revealed that the name

---

17. Ware, *Orthodox Church*, 251.

18. In the chapter, "So Be It! So Be It!," Zosima states, "But the Church, like a mother, tender and loving, withholds active punishment." Dostoevsky, *Brothers Karamazov*, 65.

19. Dostoevsky, *Brothers Karamazov*, 48.

20. Dostoevsky, *Brothers Karamazov*, 50. The larger text in Russian is "А это,— проговорил старец,—это древняя «Рахиль пла чет о детях своих и не может утешиться, потому что их нет», и таковой вам, матерям, предел на земле положен. И не утешайся, и не надо тебе утешаться, не утешайся и плачь, только каждый раз, когда плачешь, вспоминай неуклонно, что сыночек твой—есть единый от ангелов божиих—оттуда на тебя смотрит и видит тебя, и на твои слезы радуется, и на них господу богу указывает."

The Mysticism of Resurrection and the Sacrament of Friendship 207

of the dead son is Alexei, a name shared with Alyosha. Zosima clarifies, "A lovely name! After Alexei, the man of God?" "Of God, dear father, of God. Alexei, the man of God."[21] In the novel, Alyosha is referenced often as "the man of God." It is plausible that Dostoevsky was inspired by the legend of the fourth century ascetic, St. Alexei, celebrated in the Russian monastic tradition. Alexei, the man of God, is famed for his renunciation of his worldly status in Rome, giving up even his own name, serving Christ in anonymity, seeking to serve others in humble love.[22]

However, with respect to the theme of motherly suffering love, Alyosha's mother, Sophia, exhibits the same passional, protective, humble love that cries out to the divine for the protection of her child. In the novel, it seems to function as a kind of sacrament, mediating the agony and suffering love of the divine. It reflects a metaphysic that is not the abstract idealism of Plato, nor the creation of a Dionysian transcendence within immanent, but a divine transcendence that envelops the immanent through the suffering of familial love, the "natural" love of a mother for her son.

As I indicated above, the narrator emphasizes, of course, the significance of the serene image of "the slanting rays" of the sun, an image of light piercing darkness. However, this also provides us with a literary clue as to the theological meaning of this early memory of Alyosha's suffering mother. In the chapter "From the Life of the Hieromonk and elder Zosima" we see that Zosima's teaching on the meaning of the biblical character of Job assists us in our interpretation of the meaning of Alyosha's memory of his mother, Sophia. Here we observe another reference to the "slanting rays of the setting sun." Reflecting on his love of the story of Job, Zosima responds to the problem of "scoffers and blasphemers . . . : how could the Lord hand over the most beloved of saints for Satan to play with him?"[23] For Zosima, there is no rationalized theological answer to this question of suffering, but only a mystery to wonder at: "But what is great here is this very mystery—the passing image and eternal truth here

---

21. Dostoevsky, *Brothers Karamazov*, 50. In the Russian, "Алексеем, батюшка.— Имя-то милое. На Алексея человека божия?—Божия, батюшка, божия, Алексея человека божия!—- Святой-то какой! Помяну, мать, помяну и печаль твою."

22. According to the legend, the version known in the Russian tradition, Alexei eventually returned home to serve his family in anonymity, having to suffer in silence even as he heard the grief of his mother and his fiancée. For one version of the story, see http://www.fatheralexander.org/booklets/english/saints/alexis_manofgod.htm.

23. Dostoevsky, *Brothers Karamazov*, 292.

touched each other. In the face of earthly truth, the enacting of eternal truth is accomplished."[24] The mystery consists in learning to bless and affirm God and life amid the suffering, a new kind of education through suffering which matures the soul:

> But it is possible, it is possible: the old grief, by a great mystery of human life, gradually passes into quiet, tender joy, instead of young, ebullient blood comes a mild, serene old age: I bless the sun's rising each day and my heart sings to it as before, but now I love its setting even more, its long slanting rays, and with them quiet, mild, tender memories, dear images from the whole of a long and blessed life—and overall is God's truth, moving, reconciling, all-forgiving.[25]

This is not a perverse celebration of suffering, but how the grief that derives from suffering is transformed into a deeper affirmation of life, even during suffering. It is the ability to bless life because of the mediation of the divine through the "tender memories, dear images from the whole of a long and blessed life." That is, as the embodied soul struggles in suffering, in the transformative movement from darkness to the divine light of love, memories are created that are sacred and sacramental, and continue to powerfully mediate the transcendence of God in the immanence of life. The result is the blessed affirmation of life in the immanent, not a cursed resentment of life. Of course, Alyosha, at least at the outset of the novel, has not reached this "quiet, tender joy." Alyosha is still only twenty years old, but he has lived long enough that memories such as the one he had of his mother has the power to form the trajectory and movement of his life toward the divine "light of love." To pursue this "ascent" from darkness to light, Alyosha will attach himself to Zosima and the path of monasticism as the "ideal way out for his soul." Nonetheless, the memory of his mother's suffering and struggle, calling out to the Mother of God for the protection of her son in the "den of iniquity" in which he was born, is the mysterious sacramental mediation of the transcendent

24. Dostoevsky, *Brothers Karamazov*, 292.

25. Dostoevsky, *Brothers Karamazov*, 292. In the Russian, "Но можно, можно: старое горе великою тайной жизни человеческой переходит постепенно в тихую умиленную радость; вместо юной кипучей крови наступает кроткая ясная старость: благословляю восход солнца ежедневный, и сердце мое по-прежнему поет ему, но уже более люблю закат его, длинные зэ косые лучи его, а с ними тихие, кроткие, умиленные воспоминания, милые образы изо всей долгой и благословенной жизни—а надо всем-то правда божия, умиляющая, примиряющая, всепрощаю щая!"

in the immanent. It is reflected in a passionate and even desperate desire expressed in her intercession for the protection of her son. In Sophia's shrieks, we catch a glimpse of the "beauty" of Madonna, of Mary, the Mother of God. As a result of being touched by this memory, Alyosha becomes focused on a particular "inner preoccupation, as it were, strictly personal, of no concern to others."[26] The memory serves to nurture a particular sensitivity toward the movement of divine love. Indeed, this inner preoccupation is precisely the spiritual struggle as outlined above, the movement of his soul from darkness to the light of love, which is a movement toward "God's truth, moving, reconciling, all-forgiving." It is modelled and mediated in the iconic, sacred image of the agony of his mother's love.

Morality and the *Kenotic* Will

Moreover, in the chapter "Alyosha," the author informs us that one of the chief characteristics of Alyosha, is that "he did not want to be a judge of men, that he would not take judgment upon himself and would not condemn anyone for anything. It seemed, even that he accepted everything without the least condemnation, though often with deep sadness."[27] I suggest that this preoccupation with the internal movement of his soul meant the authentic recognition of the darkness of his own heart and soul as he struggled toward the light. In this spiritual struggle, all sense of moral superiority is burned away and annihilated. That is, the transcendence of divine love as embodied in suffering love, a love that reflects the image of Christ, is a love that removes egotistical morality. As one who sought the path of the monastic, Alyosha sought to embody the teaching of love by Zosima: "A loving humility is a terrible power, the most powerful of all, nothing compares with it."[28] It is this struggle toward the light of love that engendered a particular love and trust in others. As the narrator states, this characteristic would awaken in others a "special love for himself."[29] We see this played out in the drama of the novel, as people are

26. Dostoevsky, *Brothers Karamazov*, 19.

27. Dostoevsky, *Brothers Karamazov*, 19. In the Russian, "Что-то было в нем, что говорило и внушало (да и всю жизнь потом), что он не хочет быть судьей людей, что он не захочет взять на себя осуждения и ни за что не осудит. Казалось даже, что он всё допускал, нимало не осуждая, хотя часто очень горько грустя."

28. Dostoevsky, *Brothers Karamazov*, 319.

29. Dostoevsky, *Brothers Karamazov*. In the Russian, "Так что дар возбуждать

drawn to Alyosha. We see in the chapter "Confession, In Verse," whereby Mitya confesses his longing for Alyosha: "I could take you, Alyoshka and press you to my heart until I crushed you, for in all the world . . . I really . . . re-al-ly . . . (understand?) . . . love only you!"[30] Mitya himself wonders about the mystery of this love: "Why was I longing and thirsting for you with every curve of my soul and even with my ribs?"[31] Mitya will go on to confess, as we saw in the previous chapter, the mystery of "beauty," between the beauty of "Madonna," the mother of God, which signifies divine, humble love in contrast with the twisted love of the "Sodom," an egotistical love that thirsts of self-pleasure, and feeds on pride. Mitya is drawn to the humility of Alyosha, the simplicity of divine love that is reflected in his character. I suggest that through Alyosha, engaged in the movement of divine, humble love that resists moral superiority, reflects the particular focus of "willing," rooted in a desire that has been touched by the image Christ, mediated through memory, as I outlined above. Alyosha reflects the particular form of willing and "desire" that mediates the divine in the immanent and forms character into a more authentic moral beauty.

This form of "willing," by which the embodied soul moves from darkness to the light of love, is initially outlined in the chapter "Elders" where the narrator is insistent that Alyosha is a "realist." In describing Alyosha's physiognomy as "well-built, red-cheeked," the narrator maintains, "Some will say, perhaps, that red cheeks are quite compatible with both fanaticism and mysticism, but it seems to me that Alyosha was even more of a realist than the rest of us."[32] By "realism," the narrator seems to mean, one who is radically committed to a particular "truth," a specific view of reality: "A true realist, if he is not a believer, will always find in himself the strength and ability not to believe in miracles as well, and if a miracle stands before him as an irrefutable fact, he will sooner doubt his own senses than admit the fact."[33] That is, the atheist, who is a realist, will

---

к себе особенную любовь он заключал в себе, так сказать, в самой природе, безыскусственно и непосредственно."

30. Dostoevsky, *Brothers Karamazov*, 104.
31. Dostoevsky, *Brothers Karamazov*, 105.
32. Dostoevsky, *Brothers Karamazov*, 25.
33. Dostoevsky, *Brothers Karamazov*, 25. In the Russian, "Истинный реалист, если он не верующий, всегда найдет в себе силу и способность не поверить и чуду, а если чудо станет пред ним неотразимым фактом, то он скорее не поверит своим чув ствам, чем допустит факт. Если же и допустит его, то допустит как факт естественный, но доселе лишь бывший ему неизвестным."

be committed to the principle of atheism regardless of all other evidence. Realism, therefore, at least as we see in this text, is a particular ideological commitment to which the will is firmly attached. However, if the "realist" is a believer, the possibility of divine interaction in the immanence must follow as a real possibility: "Faith is not born from miracles, but miracles from faith. Once the realist comes to believe, then, precisely because of his realism, he must also allow for miracles."[34] That is, divine intervention in the immanent world, even the resurrection from the dead, as the narrator's allusion to the Apostle Thomas suggests, is possible precisely because of a commitment of faith in the existence of the Christian God. If God exists, then miracles must also be a possibility. Yet Dostoevsky is not engaging the reader in a kind of rational apologetic. "Realism," in this context, is described as the resilience of commitment of the will to a particular ideal or, in Nietzsche's language, a form of valuation.[35] That is, it pertains to the inner, spiritual-psychological will to live in radical alignment with the ideal that one is committed to, to live out in action a particular ideal of "reality." Alyosha was committed to the path of monasticism because "at the time it alone struck him and presented him all at once with the whole ideal way out for his soul struggling from darkness to light."[36] This is the particular moral heroism of Alyosha, as a follower of Zosima, committed to a form of "willing" that moves toward the light of love. It is an ethic that reflects the cruciform nature of the image of Christ, as Alyosha reveals to Ivan that Christ is the one on whom "the structure is being built, and it is to him that they will cry out: 'Just art thou, O Lord, for thy ways have been revealed!'"[37] Alyosha is portrayed as a character who has freely chosen and committed to the structure of the crucified Messiah, who "can forgive everything, forgive all *and* for all,

---

34. Dostoevsky, *Brothers Karamazov*, 26. In the Russian, "В реалисте вера не от чуда рождается, а чудо от веры. Если реалист раз поверит, то он именно по реализму своему должен не пременно допустить и чудо."

35. To reiterate the importance of the commitment of the will, "in just the same way, if he had decided that immortality and God do not exist, he would immediately have joined the atheists and socialists." For Alyosha, there is no middle ground. That is, Alyosha would be committed to the transformation of the world through the socialist ideal as "the modern embodiment of atheism, the question of the Tower of Babel built precisely without God, not to go from earth to heaven but to bring heaven down to earth. Dostoevsky, *Brothers Karamazov*, 172.

36. Dostoevsky, *Brothers Karamazov*, 26.

37. Dostoevsky, *Brothers Karamazov*, 246.

because he himself gave his innocent blood for all and for everything."[38] The commitment to the struggle against darkness into the light of love is the characteristic that Ivan admired in Alyosha: "But in the end I learned to respect you: this little man stands his ground, I thought. . . . I love people who stand their ground, whatever they may stand upon, and even if they're such little boys as you are."[39] While this is a backhanded compliment, it also puts the entire chapters of "Rebellion" and "The Grand Inquisitor" into greater narrative insight. Ivan's design in these chapters is to challenge Alyosha's commitment to Christ as mediated through the monastic way of the elders. Ivan's intent is to expose the spirit of retribution in the heart of Alyosha, especially with respect to the examples of empirical "realism," that brutal, Karamazovian force, the image of the "devil," that is the true "structure" of which humanity is constituted. In response to the story of a brutal violence against a child, Ivan questions, "Well . . . what to do with him? Shoot him? Shoot him for our moral satisfaction? Speak Alyoshka!" Alyosha replies, "Shoot him!" And Ivan responds, "Bravo . . . If even you say so, then . . . A fine monk you are! See what a little devil is sitting in your heart, Alyoshka Karamazov!"[40]

The "realism" of Alyosha is confronted and challenged by the "realism" of Ivan, expressed in the impossibility of the divine love of humanity. This spirit of retribution will more greatly tempt Alyosha's commitment when the reputation of his idol, Zosima, is questioned, especially when the body of Zosima does not produce the expected miracles. We will examine Alyosha's struggle below; here I want to emphasize the "structure" of Christ, to which Alyosha has committed his will. This helps us to grapple with the conception of "morality" in the novel. As outlined in the chapter "Elders," the movement of the will toward the transcendent is not an abstract ideal or rational conception, but a living, humble love that eternally moves toward embodied incarnate action. That is, it is an eternal movement toward the "other" in a humble, non-coercive manner. It is a commitment to sacrifice the egotistical will for the sake of serving the other. The commitment to self-sacrifice as the embodiment of humble love is the expression of a dynamic, moving metaphysic. This, too, is reflected in the narrator's initial description of the character of Alyosha. His commitment to struggle toward the light of love meant the

---

38. Dostoevsky, *Brothers Karamazov*, 246.

39. Of course, Ivan is simultaneously belittling his younger brother. Dostoevsky, *Brothers Karamazov*, 229.

40. Dostoevsky, *Brothers Karamazov*, 243.

willingness to sacrifice his life, "in that belief demanding an immediate deed, with an unfailing desire to sacrifice everything for this deed, even life."[41] That is, the ideal of his faith must be embodied and enfleshed in the immanence of time and space, unveiled in the redemptive desire for the "other." The movement of his soul toward the light of love must be enfleshed through the "deed," an action that immanently reflects the soul's struggle in the movement from darkness to light. For Alyosha, there is no mediocre resolve if one is committed to an ideal: "So Alyosha said to himself: 'I cannot give two roubles instead of "all," and instead of "follow me" just go to the Sunday liturgy.'"[42] The mystery of the divine as imaged in the "slanting rays," touched the heart of Alyosha, creating a memory that formed a particular strength of inner resolve to maintain a movement of the soul toward the light of love as embodied in "sacrificial deeds." In this way, Alyosha strives to reflect the cruciform nature of Christ, suffering his will for the sake of the "love of humankind."

This embodiment of love is contrasted in the novel with a "lady of little faith," who is struggling in her faith in God. Indeed, this very woman, a rich landowner, is the potential mother-in-law of Alyosha, who confesses her "love for humankind," but it is an egotistical, abstract ideal of love that knows nothing of humble, active, suffering love. Zosima recalls the confession of a particular doctor: "'I love humankind,' he said, 'but I am amazed at myself: the more I love humankind in general, the less I love people in particular, that is, individually, as separate persons.'"[43] Even Ivan admits, perhaps one can love humanity "abstractly," but acknowledges the profound difficulty of the kind of love exhibited in humble, suffering love. On the example of the suffering love of "John the Merciful," he comments, "I'm convinced that he did it with the strain of lie, out of love enforced by duty, out of self-imposed penance."[44] Zosima accentuates the contrast between egotistical love and authentic humble, committed love:

---

41. Dostoevsky, *Brothers Karamazov*, 26. In the Russian, "Прибавьте, что он был юноша отчасти уже нашего последнего времени, то есть честный по природе своей, требующий правды, ищущий ее и верующий в нее, а уверовав, требующий немедлен ного участия в ней всею силой души своей, требующий скорого подвига, с непременным желанием хотя бы всем пожертвовать для этого подвига, даже жизнью."

42. Dostoevsky, *Brothers Karamazov*, 26.

43. Dostoevsky, *Brothers Karamazov*, 57.

44. Dostoevsky, *Brothers Karamazov*, 237.

> Love in dreams thirsts for immediate action, quickly performed, and with everyone watching. Indeed, it will go as far as the giving even of one's life, provided it does not take that long but is soon over, as on stage, and everyone is looking on and praising. Whereas active love is labor and perseverance, and for some people, a whole science.[45]

Again, as evidenced in Ivan's challenge, the question is, how is such an ethical way of life possible? This was the impossibility that Ivan confesses to Alyosha, as we saw in chapter 2. Indeed, Dostoevsky endeavours to poetically portray a possible pathway in *The Brothers Karamazov*, as to how the harsh labour of personalist, active love might be embodied. How does one achieve this? We will explore this further in the next section. What I am demonstrating is Alyosha's commitment of will to struggle toward the light of love, reflects a particular metaphysic of the divine in relation to the human, or the transcendent in connection to the immanent. The image of Christ in humankind is expressed. It is poetically iconic. Dostoevsky's conception of morality pertains to the significance of the will's commitment to the image of Christ as mediated in an embodied movement of action. For Alyosha, the way of monasticism, as practised by the elders, seemed the best available path forward to satisfy this desire. This institution forms an important background for the novel, anchoring the story deeply in the history of Eastern and Russian monasticism. Dostoevsky uses the institution to poetically express the kind of "morality" of the will as represented in Alyosha in the most dramatic way. We see characters such as Father Ferapont fiercely criticize the institution, describing it as a modern innovation. However, according to the narrator, "in the whole of Orthodox East, especially on Sinai and Athos, they have existed for well over a thousand years."[46] Dostoevsky alludes to an important Russian monastic figure, Paissy Velichkovsky and the

---

45. Dostoevsky, *Brothers Karamazov*, 58. In the Russian, "Жалею, что не могу сказать вам ничего отраднее, ибо любовь деятельная сравнительно с мечтательною есть дело жестокое и устрашающее. «Любовь мечтательная жаждет подвига скорого, быстро удовлетворимого и чтобы все на него глядели. Тут действительно доходит до того, что даже и жизнь отдают, только бы не продлилось долго, а поскорей совершилось, как бы на сцене, и чтобы все глядели и хвалили. Любовь же дея тельная—это работа и выдержка, а для иных так, пожалуй, с целая наука."

46. Dostoevsky, *Brothers Karamazov*, 28.

historic hermitage of Kozelskaya-Optina, where the institution of elders was practised.[47] The narrator provides us with a description:

> An elder is one who takes your soul, your will into his soul and into his will. Having chosen an elder, you renounce your will and give it to him under total obedience and with total self-renunciation. A man who dooms himself to this trial, this terrible school of life, does so voluntarily, in the hope that after the long trial he will achieve self-conquest, self-mastery to such a degree that he will, finally, through a whole life's obedience, attain to perfect freedom—that is, freedom from himself—and avoid the lot of those who live their whole lives without finding themselves in themselves.[48]

What is critical is the formation of a bond of obedience between the novice and the master, the renunciation of the will, a subjugation of the will to another, mature soul, who has earned the trust of such a responsibility. It is the renunciation of the desire of the will for sovereignty and placing it under the power of another will. The obedience to an elder supersedes all asceticism in importance and significance, as illustrated in the story of a particular "disciple" in early Christianity who failed to fulfill a certain obedience of his elder, despite living a life of asceticism and dying as martyr. Yet as he was being venerated in death at his funeral, "the coffin containing the martyr's body tore from its place and cast itself out of the church."[49] Not until the elder was summoned to absolve the man, could he be properly buried. While acknowledging the story as legend,

---

47. According to Timothy Ware, this movement was inspired in later modern Russian by St. Paissy Velichkovsky. According to Ware, "this monastic movement, while outward-looking and concerned to serve the world, also restored to the centre of the Church's life the tradition of the Non-Possessors, largely suppressed since the sixteenth century." According to Ware, the "first and greatest of the *startsy* of the nineteenth century was St. Seraphim of Sarov (1754–1833), who of all the saints of Russia is perhaps the most immediately attractive to non-Orthodox Christians." Ware, *Orthodox Church*, 114–15.

48. Dostoevsky, *Brothers Karamazov*, 28. In the Russian, "Итак, что же такое старец? Ста рец—это берущий вашу душу, вашу волю в свою душу и в свою волю. Избрав старца, вы от своей воли отрешаетесь и отдаете ее ему в полное послушание, с полным самоотрешением. Этот искус, эту страшную школу жизни обрекающий себя принимает добро-вольно в надежде после долгого искуса победить себя, овладеть собою до того, чтобы мог наконец достичь, чрез послушание всей жизни, уже совершенной свободы, то есть свободы от самого себя, избегнуть участи тех, которые всю жизнь прожили, а себя в себе не нашли."

49. Dostoevsky, *Brothers Karamazov*, 28.

the narrator stresses the spiritual power of such a binding of souls in a kind of covenant of obedience. It signifies the radical practice of the Christian ideal of crucifying the self to reach the perfection of Christ. It means that the movement toward spiritual freedom and thereby true "sovereignty" is achieved when all desire for the sovereignty of the will has been annihilated. It is the embodied and actualized death of all possessive desire, the "*libido dominandi*." It means the death of all egotistic desire. The text acknowledges the potential for demonic corruption of the monastic, ascetic practice: "It is also true, perhaps, that this tested and already thousand-year-old instrument for the moral regeneration of man from slavery to freedom to moral perfection may turn into a double-edged weapon, which may lead a person not to humility and ultimate self-control, but, on the contrary, to the most satanic pride—that is, to fetters not to freedom."[50] This practice is an instrument and is not an obligation, yet there is a poetic power in Dostoevsky using this practice to provide us an image of the kenotic, self-emptying will of Christ as lived out in his contemporary Russia.

To reiterate, the aim of the practice is what Alyosha desires and represents, the "ideal way from the worldly darkness to the light of love." It represents a pathway of the moral regeneration of the will that is rooted in a metaphysical movement, an ascent from darkness to light. And as expressed in the path of the elders with its focus on the obedience of the will, there is an inherent paradox. As indicated above, the path toward true freedom and sovereignty is only achieved when the desire for sovereignty is renounced and surrendered. It is the paradox that to ascend to the transcendent, the will must descend in humble, suffering love. Only in a committed "descent," mediated through the voluntary, non-coercive sacrifice of the will, is the transcendence of the divine experienced in the immanent. It is the way of the cross of Christ, as expressed in the Pauline hymn of Philippians 2:2–7:

> Let the same mind be in you that was in Christ Jesus, who, though he was in the form of God, did not regard equality with God as something to be exploited, but emptied himself, taking

---

50. Dostoevsky, *Brothers Karamazov*, 29. In the Russian, "Правда, пожалуй, и то, что это испытанное и уже тысячелетнее орудие для нравственного перерождения человека от рабства к свободе и к нравственному совершенствованию может обратить ся в обоюдоострое орудие, так что иного, пожалуй, приведет вместо смирения и окончательного самообладания, напротив, к самой сатанинской гордости, то есть к цепям, а не к сво боде."

The Mysticism of Resurrection and the Sacrament of Friendship 217

the form of a slave, being born in human likeness. And being found in human form, he humbled himself and became obedient to the point of death—even death on a cross.

According to Ware, it was this kenotic, self-emptying ideal that inspired and shaped the Russian monastic movement.[51] With respect to the institution of elders, Alyosha had not bound himself to this way, but he had attached himself to Father Zosima, who is an ideal character in the novel, reflecting that maturity of one who has attained "freedom from himself." That is, freedom from the egotistic will governed by the Karamazovian force, focused on the immediate sensual, immanent needs of the self. We will examine this further in the next section. For Alyosha, it is the elder Zosima who becomes the model that he endeavours to imitate, as Zosima imitates the way of the Christ. For Alyosha, Zosima is the ideal model of the kenotic, self-emptying ideal that is outward-focused, struggling forward to the "light of love." Indeed, for Alyosha, Zosima is a kind of loving embodiment of the hope of humankind. As the narrator characterizes Alyosha's love for Zosima:

> And generally, of late a certain deep, flaming inner rapture burned more and more strongly in his heart. He was not at all troubled that the elder, after all, stood solitarily before him: "No matter, he is holy, in his heart there is the secret of renewal for all, the power that will finally establish the truth on earth, and all will be holy and will love one another, and there will be neither rich nor poor, neither exalted nor humiliated, but all will be like the children of God, and the true kingdom of Christ will come." That was the dream in Alyosha's heart.[52]

---

51. According to Ware, the movement was modelled in the example of St. Anthony, "a Russian who had lived on Mount Athos," but reorganized by his successor St. Theodosius, who "followed Christ in his life of poverty and voluntary 'self-emptying' (*kenosis*)." Moreover, the same "ideal of kenotic humaility is seen in others, for example Bishop Luke of Vladimir (died 1185) who, in the words of the *Vladimir Chroncile*, 'borne upon himself the humiliation of Christ, not having a city here but seeking a future one.' It is an ideal found often in Russian folklore, and in writers such as Tolstoy and Dostoevsky." Ware, *Orthordox Church*, 76–77.

52. Dostoevsky, *Brothers Karamazov*, 31. In the Russian, "Не смущало его нисколько, что этот старец все-таки стоит пред ним единицей: «Всё равно, он свят, в его сердце тайна обновления для всех, та мощь, которая уста новит наконец правду на земле, и будут все святы, и будут лю бить друг друга, и не будет ни богатых, ни бедных, ни возвы- 40 шающихся, ни униженных, а будут все как дети божий и насту пит настоящее царство Христово». Вот о чем грезилось сердцу Алеши."

This text demonstrates that the characterization of Alyosha is as much a social and political image as that of an individual struggle. However, this "dream" will be tested, as we explore below. For Alyosha to move authentically, participating in the life of the divine love, he too must die to all human iconic figures, even Zosima, his idol. However, it expresses the social and political ideal embodied in the individual struggle to move from darkness to light. We have already addressed the struggle in which Alyosha was to engage, first through the temptation of the alternative "realism" of retribution of Ivan, but especially as the desire for retribution against the monastics that tainted the reputation of his idol, elder Zosima, as his bodied decayed, without producing the expected miracles.

The Temptation of Alyosha to Revenge

Part III, book 7 of *The Brothers Karamazov* is entitled "Alyosha," and narrates the temptation of Alyosha to abandon the path of humble, forgiving love for retribution. In these chapters, we are presented a picture of Dostoevsky's redemptive vision as embodied in the hero of the novel, the internal struggle of Alyosha coming out of the darkness and into the light of love. The crisis of faith for Alyosha is introduced in the chapter "The Odor of Corruption," where, after the death of Zosima, among the mourners the question "should they open in the windows in the room?" was raised.[53] Within the story, because of the fame and influence of the elder Zosima, to "expect corruption and the odor of corruption from the body of such a deceased person was a perfect absurdity, even deserving pity (if not laughter) with regard to the thoughtlessness and little faith of the one who had uttered the question."[54] However, the odor of corruption of the dead body of the elder occurred. This occasioned a "temptation" in the monastery, the rejoicing in the "fall" of the elder, his disgrace and humiliation in the fact that his body did not produce the expected miracle. The narrator also suggests that the reasons for the temptation derived from the various legends of other saints that did not produce the odor of corruption, but also from the "envy of the dead man's holiness, so firmly established while he lived that it was even forbidden, as it were, to question it.[55] The elder had attracted to himself, a "whole world of those who

53. Dostoevsky, *Brothers Karamazov*, 329.
54. Dostoevsky, *Brothers Karamazov*, 330.
55. Dostoevsky, *Brothers Karamazov*, 330.

The Mysticism of Resurrection and the Sacrament of Friendship   219

loved him," Alyosha among them.[56] However, this also produced many who also envied him, not only monastics, but also laymen. Therefore, the odor of corruption is interpreted as a sign of judgment from God for the supposed pride of the elder: "'He sat in pride,' the most malicious cruelly recalled, 'he considered himself a saint; when people knelt before him, he took it as his due.'"[57] As Father Ferapont, the fierce critic of Zosima, proclaimed to Father Paissy, "I am foul, not holy. I would not sit in an armchair; I would not desire to be worshipped like an idol!"[58]

This crisis within the monastery deeply affected Alyosha, engendering a crisis of faith: "'Have you too, fallen into temptation?' Father Paissy exclaimed suddenly. 'Can it be that you, too, are those with little faith?'"[59] The narrator acknowledges that Alyosha's faith, while pure, was immaturely overly focused on the hero-worship of Zosima, "that was just it, that the entirety of the love for 'all and all' that lay hidden in his young and pure heart, then and during the whole previous year, was at times as if wholly concentrated, perhaps even incorrectly, mainly on just one being, at least in the strongest impulses of his heart—on his beloved elder, now deceased."[60] That is, Alyosha idealized the elder to the point of idolization. The crisis of faith, therefore, was not that he expected the miracle, but in yearning for justice for the tarnished memory and reputation of his idol: "Again, it was not miracles he needed, but only a 'higher justice,' which he believed had been violated—it was this that wounded his heart so cruelly and suddenly."[61] For Alyosha, Zosima was a being who embodied the "whole," incarnated the ideal of the *kenotic*, suffering love of Christ on earth. And now he who, "was to have been exalted higher than anyone in the world, this very man, instead of receiving the glory that was due him, was suddenly thrown down and disgraced."[62] Ultimately,

56. Dostoevsky, *Brothers Karamazov*, 331.

57. Dostoevsky, *Brothers Karamazov*, 333.

58. Dostoevsky, *Brothers Karamazov*, 335. In the Russian, "Поган есмь, а не свят. В кресла не сяду и не восхощу себе аки идолу поклонения!—загремел отец Ферапонт."

59. Dostoevsky, *Brothers Karamazov*, 335.

60. Dostoevsky, *Brothers Karamazov*, 339.

61. Dostoevsky, *Brothers Karamazov*, 339. In the Russian, "Но не чудес опять-таки ему нужно было, а лишь «высшей справедливости», которая была, по верованию его, нарушена и чем так жестоко и внезапно было поранено сердце его."

62. Dostoevsky, *Brothers Karamazov*, 339. In the Russian, "И вот тот, который должен бы был, по упованиям его, быть вознесен превыше всех в целом мире,— тот самый вместо славы, ему подо- ю бавшей, вдруг низвержен и опозорен!

for Alyosha, where was "Providence and its finger? Why did it hide its finger 'at the most necessary moment' (Alyosha thought), as if wanting to submit itself to the blind, mute, merciless laws of nature?"[63] In other words, to formulate the temptation in another way, perhaps, questioned Alyosha, only the underlying chaos of Karamazovian force exists after all.

The narrator informs us that "a certain strange phenomenon" occurred in Alyosha's mind a day earlier: "This new *something* that appeared and flashed consisted of a certain tormenting impression from his conversation with his brother Ivan the day before, which Alyosha now kept recalling."[64] While his love for God was not shaken, "he suddenly murmured against him."[65] This mention of a "murmur" against the divine could be an allusion to the murmuring of the people of God in the wilderness when faced with suffering (Num 14). That is, while perhaps not outright rebellion, there is the subtle emergence of a resentment against the divine. Moreover, the presence of Rakitin, the disgruntled follower of Ivan, does not help. Rakitin is Alyosha's Judas, a betrayer who attempts to exploit Alyosha's heart for financial profit. In reaction to the sarcasm of Rakitin, Alyosha is tempted to Ivan's rebellion: "I do not rebel against my God, I simply 'do not accept his world.'"[66] With this reference, Dostoevsky connects the temptation of Alyosha to the entire argument developed in the chapter "Rebellion" where Ivan essentially presents the alternate "realism" of the Euclidean mind as a rejection of the "realism" of faith as represented in Zosima. Alyosha is tempted to embrace the

---

За что? Кто судил? Кто мог так рассудить?—вот вопросы, которые тотчас же измучили неопытное и девственное сердце его."

63. Dostoevsky, *Brothers Karamazov*, 340. In the Russian, "Где же провидение и перст его? К чему сокрыло оно свой перст «в самую нужную минуту» (думал Алеша) и как бы само захотело подчинить себя слепым, немым, безжалостным законам естественным?"

64. Dostoevsky, *Brothers Karamazov*, 340. In the Russian, "Это новое объявившееся и мелькнувшее нечто состояло в некотором мучительном впечатлении от неустанно припоминавшегося теперь Алешей вчерашнего его разговорас братом Иваном."

65. Dostoevsky, *Brothers Karamazov*, 340. The larger Russian text, "Именно теперь. О, не то чтобы что-нибудь было поколеблено в душе его из основных, стихийных, так ска зать, ее верований. Бога своего он любил и веровал в него незыб лемо, хотя и возроптал было на него внезапно. Но всё же какое-то смутное, но мучительное и злое впечатление от припоминания вчерашнего разговора с братом Иваном вдруг теперь снова заше велилось в душе его и всё более и более просилось выйти на верхее."

66. Dostoevsky, *Brothers Karamazov*, 341.

The Mysticism of Resurrection and the Sacrament of Friendship 221

atheistic spirit of retribution as articulated by Ivan, the presumption that there is no "higher justice" other than the immediate demand of retribution through human agency. In other words, there is no transcendent "light of love" that can redeem the Karamazovian, Dionysian power of nature, the "will to power."

As a result of this temptation, in the suffering and grief in the death of the elder, Alyosha allows himself to be led by Rakitin to the seductress, Grushenka, the "Russian beauty," who was at the centre of the scandal between the father, Fyodor, and Mitya. That is, what we observe in the section "Alyosha" in these chapters is a kind of possible "fall" of Alyosha, a descent away from the light of love and into the darkness and the "den of iniquity." Whereas the first temptation for retribution is influenced by the atheism of Ivan, it now further descends into the possibility of an unleashed "sensual" eroticism as represented in the debased desires of Mitya and ultimately, of the father, Fyodor. As the narrator unveils, both Rakitin and Grushenka were seeking the ruin and fall of Alyosha. However, what is interesting about this interaction with the seduction of Grushenka is that the greater love that he had for the elder, while perhaps misplaced, becomes the source of protection: "The great grief in his soul absorbed all the feelings his heart might have conceived, he would have understood that he was now wearing the strongest armour against any seduction and temptation."[67] In fact, we are told that in this moment of greatest temptation, as Grushenka sits on his lap, even Alyosha's fear of evil and sin was overcome: "This woman . . . now aroused in him the feeling of some . . . most pure-hearted curiosity, and without any fear now, without a trace of his former terror—that was the main thing, and it could not but surprise him."[68] What redeems the situation is Grushenka's sensitivity to the grief and suffering of Alyosha. When she learns of Zosima's death, Grushenka snaps out of her revenge-based seduction. Grushenka is an important figure in the novel, exploited by "Kuzma," using her "beauty" to elicit attention and money from masculine desire; she is the cause of the scandal between the father, Fyodor, and his first son, Mitya. The family is torn apart because of their inability to overcome

---

67. Dostoevsky, *Brothers Karamazov*, 349. In the Russian, "Великое горе души его поглощало все ощущения, какие только могли зародиться в сердце его, и если только мог бы он в сию минуту дать себе полный отчет, то и сам бы до- 40 гадался, что он теперь в крепчайшей броне против всякого соблазна и искушения."

68. Dostoevsky, *Brothers Karamazov*, 349.

their sensual desire for "beauty." Grushenka willingly uses her power of attraction, but in this scene, we see that the inner beauty reflected in the image of God shines through in her and becomes a turning point for the redemption of Alyosha's soul. The compassionate reaction of Grushenka lifted him out of temptation. As Alyosha says to Rakitin, "You'd do better to look here, at her: did you see how she spared me? I came here looking for a wicked soul—I was drawn to that, because I was low and wicked myself, but I found a true sister, I found a treasure—a loving soul . . . She spared me just now . . . I am speaking of you, Agrafena Alexandrovna. You restored my soul just now."[69] How so? The sensitive reaction of Grushenka to Alyosha's grief reveals the image of Christ still preserved in her soul, even hidden and buried under the shame of her sinful, exploitive way of life. She confesses how she despised Alyosha for not giving her the attention she desired. The turning point in this interaction between Alyosha and Grushenka is the alteration of the perception of the other through the respect for suffering. That is, rather than the relation of exploitation for the satisfaction of revenge, they perceive one another and their individual souls as intrinsically connected through active, living love: "'I will start crying, I will start crying!' Grushenka kept repeating. 'He called me his sister; I'll never forget it! Just know one thing, Rakitka, I may be wicked, but still I gave an onion.'"[70]

The "onion" signifies the moral action that is authentically rooted in divine love revealed in the image of Christ, the structure of which the new humanity built. Grushenka narrates the fable of a wicked woman, in hell for her wickedness, having died without any "good deeds." The demons take her to the lake of fire. Her guardian angel wonders what good deed he could remember to tell God. Then he remembers that she had given an onion to a poor woman. God told the angel, "Take that same onion, hold it out to her in the lake." If she can hold on to it, she will be

---

69. Dostoevsky, *Brothers Karamazov*, 351. In the Russian, "Ракитин,—проговорил он вдруг громко и твердо,—не ю дразни ты меня, что я против бога моего взбунтовался. Не хочу я злобы против тебя иметь, а потому будь и ты добрее. Я потерял такое сокровище, какого ты никогда не имел, и ты теперь не можешь судить меня. Посмотри лучше сюда на нее: видел, как она меня пощадила? Я шел сюда злую душу найти—так влекло меня самого к тому, потому что я был подл и зол, а нашел сестру искреннюю, нашел сокровище—душу любящую . . . Она сейчас пощадила меня . . . Аграфена Александровна, я про тебя говорю. Ты мою душу сейчас восстановила."

70. Dostoevsky, *Brothers Karamazov*, 352.

The Mysticism of Resurrection and the Sacrament of Friendship 223

saved.[71] The "onion" signifies the living active love that mediates divine sovereignty—the sacrificial love of Christ—in the world. Despite this, the woman in the fable is not transformed by love and so she kicks at the other sinners who are trying to pull her back into the fire. The mystery of grace, suggests Dostoevsky, is that divine transcendent love is so deeply woven into the fabric of our "deeds," that even "grace" and "deeds" are mystically united into the "whole" of the divine image. It is the earthly embodiment of divine love that manifests the eternal grace of God. There is no other reason to love, *but to love*: "You should love for no reason, like Alyosha."[72] It is this underlying light of love that exists for the sake of its own existence that transforms the relationship between Alyosha and Grushenka, creating a new sense of family. This is a poetic expression, I suggest, of the possibility of the "church." Considering the larger theme of the novel, the active, free, human love structured upon the divine love revealed in Christ is how the "church" becomes the higher type of society on earth. It is unlike the love of the "woman of little faith" who loves humanity and seeks equality abstractly, but an active living love that creates a new family. It is experienced in the solidarity of grief and suffering in the reality of mortality and death. This love transforms desire. Alyosha and Grushenka now see each other as brother and sister rather than as mutual objects of erotic desire. They share a common mission. Together they will attend to the "suffering" and redemption of Mitya.

The Mystical Experience of the Resurrection

While the encounter with Grushenka is the turning point for both her and Alyosha, in the chapter "Cana of Galilee" Dostoevsky provides a powerful poetic expression of a mystical experience of divine mediation. This text signifies Dostoevsky's attempt to poetically express the climactic point of regeneration and transformation of Alyosha that will overcome the spirit of retribution. To be sure, "Cana of Galilee" does not express an immediate experience of the divine. It is the reading of the Gospel and a mystical dream of the elder Zosima that mediates the redemptive presence of

---

71. Unfortunately, the woman doesn't make it. Dostoevsky, *Brothers Karamazov*, 353.

72. Dostoevsky, *Brothers Karamazov*, 353. In the Russian, "А ты ни за что люби, вот как Алеша любит."

divine love to Alyosha.[73] This scene occurs as Alyosha prays before the dead, decaying body of the elder and as Father Paissy reads the Gospel. The scene is anchored in an Orthodox eucharistic text of John 2, which narrates Jesus' first miracle, where Mary, the mother of God, commands the servants at the wedding to listen to Jesus when the wine runs out. It is a Gospel narrative that expresses the "new wine" of the messianic wedding feast between God and his people. It a "sign" that signifies the transformative event of the union between the divine and the human. This scene narrates Alyosha's inner experience in the form of broken, seemingly haphazard thoughts. It is interesting to compare this form of narration with Ivan's conversation with the devil, also narrated in the form of fragmented thoughts.[74] But whereas Ivan's dialogue with the devil unveils the further fragmentation and division within his soul, the scene with Alyosha unveils a divine mediation that reunites the self into the greater "whole," not just the whole of the self, but a sense of reunion with the divine in the immanence of all creation. That is, this climactic event in Alyosha's life brings together many of the novel's themes into a "whole."

As an expression of apocalyptic redemption, this text is designed as an alternative to the modernist attempt to reunite humankind. First, we observe a reference to Rakitin, the betrayer, who represents the modernist, revolutionary cry of "freedom, equality, and fraternity."[75] As Alyosha hears the first verses of the story read—"And the third day there was a marriage in Cana of Galilee"—his thought oscillates between the Gospel which he is hearing and the meaning of the betrayal of Rakitin: "Rakitin walked off into the alley. As long as Rakitin thinks about his grudges, he will always walk off into some alley."[76] The reference to the "alley" alerts the reader to the confession of Mitya. As we stated in chapter 2, the "riddle" of the Karamazovian force pertains to a movement toward the darkness of chaos, toward the "beauty" of Sodom and not the Madonna. This is linked to the mention of "grudges;" that is, to resentment and retribution. Is Dostoevsky making a comment about the betrayal of modernism, as represented by Rakitin, as a resentment that has perverted the beauty of the image of Christ? Again, as we expressed in the second chapter, the struggle between "God" and the "devil" resides in

---

73. Dostoevsky, *Brothers Karamazov*, 359.

74. See the chapter "The Devil. Ivan Fydorovich's Nightmare." Dostoevsky, *Brothers Karamazov*, 634.

75. Dostoevsky, *Brothers Karamazov*, 360.

76. Dostoevsky, *Brothers Karamazov*, 360.

the soul of humanity, reflected in the conflict of desire. Modernism, as represented in Rakitin, is the spiritual, atheistic perversion of the image of Christ reflected in humankind.

The redemption from the darkness is mediated, however, through the miracle of Jesus: "And when they wanted wine, the mother of Jesus saith unto him; They have no wine . . ." Alyosha overheard:

> Ah yes, I've been missing it and I didn't want to miss it, I love that passage: it's Cana of Galilee, the first miracle! Not grief, but men's joy [радость] Christ visited [посетил Христос] when he worked his first miracle, he helped men's joy [радости людской] . . ."He who loves men, loves their joy . . .» The dead man used to repeat it all the time, it was one of his main thoughts . . ."One cannot live without joy," says Mitya . . . All that is true [истинно] and beautiful [прекрасно] is always full of all-forgiveness [всепрощения]—that, too he used to say . . .[77]

While suffering is the reality of human experience, the coming of Christ in the Incarnation is intended for the restoration of the joy of life. Even amid death there is the possibility of joy in Christ. This reflects, I suggest, Dostoevsky's poetic expression of the rationale for the Incarnation, consisting of divine intent for the joy of humankind. For Dostoevsky, divine embodiment in the Incarnation of Christ unveils the intent of God, which is for the joy of humankind. In this context, Alyosha remembers Mitya, who suffers in his erotic passion for Grushenka and in his revenge against his father. Accused of murder, Mitya experiences the "torture" of guilt, not for committing the murder, but for the deception of a calculating thief.[78] His future is uncertain, as he faces the prospect of isolation in prison, separated from those he loves. The theme of the transformation of joy amid suffering is further elaborated in the chapter "A Hymn and a Secret" where Mitya sits in prison, accused of murdering his father. Mitya speaks of the "new man" that has "risen in me." Even though he didn't kill his father, he is still "guilty." He accepts his guilt before all

---

77. Dostoevsky, *Brothers Karamazov*, 360. In the Russian, "Ах да, я тут пропустил, а не хотел пропускать, я это место люблю: это Кана Галилейская, первое чудо . . . Ах, это чудо, ах, это милое чудо! Не горе, а радость людскую посетил Христос, в первый раз сотворяя чудо, радости людской помог . . ."Кто" любит людей, тот и радость их любит . . ." Это повторял покойник поминутно, это одна из главнейших мыслей его была . . . Без радости жить нельзя, говорит Митя . . . Да, Митя . . . Всё, что истинно и пре красно, всегда полно всепрощения—это опять-таки он говорил . . ."

78. Dostoevsky, *Brothers Karamazov*, 489.

and for all. There are many people like him in the "underground, with hammers in their hands."[79] Moreover, as Mitya states:

> Oh yes, we'll be in chains, and there will be no freedom, but then in our great grief, we will arise once more into joy, without which it's not possible for man to live, or for God to be, for God gives joy, it's his prerogative, a great one ... Lord, let man dissolve in prayer! How would I be there underground without God? Rakitin's lying: if God is driven from the earth, we'll meet him in the underground! It's impossible for a convict to be without God, even more impossible than for a non-convict! And then from the depths of the earth, we, the men underground, will start singing a tragic hymn to God, in whom there is joy! Hail to God and his joy! I love him![80]

There is an allusion here to the eradication of God, elaborated further in Ivan's hallucination of the devil, which we addressed in chapter 2. Despite the modernist construction of the "Tower of Babel," the delusion that humankind can destroy the idea of God, humanity will be driven to the "underground," a place of darkness. However, even in that darkness, humanity will rediscover God. The underground signifies the darkness of the soul in its death and suffering. It is the "earthly image" of human suffering. Echoing the Gospel of John read over the dead body of Zosima, Mitya proclaims that, even in the suffering and imprisonment of the underground, God will give joy. This is not to deny the tragedy of life, but it is the soul's resolution to worship God even in death, suffering, and grief. God is revealed in and through the transformation of human suffering. God has the power to transform the experience of suffering into a hymn of joy to God. How is it possible? It is a divine mystery, the mystery of the resurrection, the mystery of rebirth. There is no "Euclidean," rational explanation. It is a "miracle" of divine sovereignty. It is the divine mystery

---

79. Dostoevsky, *Brothers Karamazov*, 591.

80. Dostoevsky, *Brothers Karamazov*, 592. The full text in Russian, "А их ведь много, их там сотни, подземных-то, с молотками в руках. О да, мы будем в цепях, и не будет воли, но тогда, в великом горе нашем, мы вновь воскреснем в радость, без которой человеку жить невозможно, а богу быть, ибо бог дает радость, это его привилегия, великая ... Господи, истайо человек в молитве! Как я буду там под землей без бога? Врет Ракитин: если бога с земли изгонят, мы под землей его сретим! Каторжному без бога быть невозможно, невозможнее даже, чем некаторжному! И тогда мы, подземные человеки, запоем из недр земли трагический гимн богу, у которого радость! Да здравствует бог и его радость! Люблю его!"

The Mysticism of Resurrection and the Sacrament of Friendship 227

that intervenes, transforming the heart and soul of humankind amid tragedy. In light of the temptation and betrayal of the modernist Rakitin, who attempts to take Ivan's atheism to Mitya in prison, there is a deeper, more mysterious work of the divine that touches the immanence of the Karamazovian force, the will to power and erotic desire for dominance. The divine miracle of joy in tragedy through Christ is the "inner meaning" of history—joy is the "end" and "fulfillment" of history.

As Alyosha hears the Gospel, he drifts into sleep and in his dream receives a vision of Zosima inviting him to the eschatological messianic banquet that the wedding feast signifies. Zosima invites him to receive and experience "the new wine of the new and great joy."[81] Zosima too gave his "onion." That is, rooted in the divine love of Christ, Zosima lived the divine movement toward the light of life out of the darkness. Zosima is an image of one mystically united to Christ in the daily dying to self in the movement of active love. Zosima commends Alyosha for loving Grushenka even in her sin and awakening her soul to love as well. For those who lived a life of active love, they are called and invited to be guests of the messianic banquet, where they eternally rejoice: "See how many guests there are? Here are the bridegroom and the bride, here is the wise ruler of the feast, tasting the new wine. Why are you marveling at me? I gave a little onion, and so, I am here. And there are many here who gave an onion, my meek boy, today you, too, were able to give a little onion to a woman who hungered."[82] In other words, Alyosha has already moved into the divine world through his active love. Dostoevsky links this with the biblical poetic image of the messianic banquet, the "miracle" of the mystery revealed at the wedding in John 2. This story orients the vocation and destiny of Alyosha:

> "Begin, my dear, begin, my meek one, to do your work! And you do see our Sun, do you see him?"
>
> "I'm afraid . . . I don't care to look," whispered Alyosha.
>
> "Do not be afraid of him. Awful is his greatness before us, terrible is his loftiness, yet he is boundlessly merciful [милостив бесконечно], he became like [уподобился] us out of love, and

---

81. Dostoevsky, *Brothers Karamazov*, 361.

82. Dostoevsky, *Brothers Karamazov*, 361. In the Russian, "пьем вино новое, вино радости новой, великой; видишь, сколько гостей? Вот и жених и невеста, вот и премудрый архитриклин, вино новое пробует. Чего дивишься на меня? Я луковку подал, вот и я здесь. И многие здесь только по луковке подали, по одной только маленькой луковке . . ."

he is rejoicing with us, transforming [превращает] water into wine, that the joy of the guests may not end. He is waiting for new guests, he is ceaselessly calling [беспрерывно зовет] new guests, now and unto ages and ages. See, they are bringing the new wine, the vessels are being brought in . . .»

Something burned in Alyosha's heart, something suddenly filled him almost painfully, tears of rapture nearly burst from his soul . . . He stretched out his hands, gave a short cry, and woke up.[83]

Dostoevsky poetically expresses a vision of the redemptive purpose of cosmic history. It is a vision of the new resurrected life of Christ. According to Zosima, God became flesh because God is eternal love. God became flesh even in death to transform our suffering into eternal joy. Although not explicitly mentioned here, the decisive factor that makes this transformation possible is resurrection. Although the dead body of Zosima lies before Alyosha, in the dream, we see Zosima alive, inviting Alyosha to join him. Zosima as the "idol" of Alyosha is here transformed to Zosima as a fellow, equal guest in the messianic banquet. The spirit of resentment is not only overcome in Alyosha, but also the "higher justice" that he longs for is also fulfilled, but not in the expected way. We must not forget that this dream occurs while he grieves before the decaying body of Zosima. Zosima's accusers are still accusing. However, Alyosha is given a vision of the apocalyptic "end" of history, whereby the "dream" of equality is mystically perceived. Just as the seed must die so that much more fruit might come to life, so Zosima as an idol must die, so the soul of Alyosha might be attached to a purer image of the divine, an image that transcends all human form.

83. Dostoevsky, *Brothers Karamazov*, 361–62. In the Russian, "Веселимся,— продолжает сухенький старичок,—пьем вино новое, вино радости новой, великой; видишь, сколько гостей? Вот и жених и невеста, вот и премудрый архитриклин, вино 20 новое пробует. Чего дивишься на меня? Я луковку подал, вот и я здесь. И многие здесь только по луковке подали, по одной только маленькой луковке . . . Что наши дела? И ты, тихий, и ты, кроткий мой мальчик, и ты сегодня луковку сумел подать алчущей. Начинай, милый, начинай, кроткий, дело свое! . . . А видишь ли солнце наше, видишь ли ты его?—Боюсь . . . не смею глядеть . . .—прошептал Алеша.—Не бойся его. Страшен величием пред нами, ужасен высотою своею, но милостив бесконечно, нам из любви уподобился и веселится с нами, воду в вино превращает, чтобы не пресекалась зо радость гостей, новых гостей ждет, новых беспрерывно зовет и уже на веки веков. Вон и вино несут новое, видишь, сосуды несут . . ." Что-то горело в сердце Алеши, что-то наполнило его вдруг до боли, слезы восторга рвались из души его . . . Он простер руки, вскрикнул и проснулся . . ."

What does the death of Zosima signify? While the dream of Alyosha before the decaying body of the elder is a vision of the "end" of history, it is an "end" that is experienced in the present. The world of the divine and the human, the eternal and the mortal, the transcendent and immanent, while separate and distinct, commingle and overlap, requiring a specific form of spiritual discernment to affirm this particular expression of reality. The divine joy that transforms suffering is the soul's eternal enjoyment of the eternal presence of the God of self-giving, *kenotic* love. That is, eternal communion with God is experienced in the flesh through the mediation of the presence of the image of Christ. It is sacramental. God's sacrificial death in the Incarnation transforms all creation through resurrection. As the biblical story of the new wine that Dostoevsky employs signifies, it is given to humanity through the "bread" of the body of Christ and "wine" of his blood. As de Lubac states in a comment on this text, "the changing of the water into wine stands for process by which the human being becomes divine, the transition from natural life to life according to the spirit."[84] Therefore, the dream of Alyosha is deeply eucharistic, reflecting the "*corpus mysticum*," the heavenly community that exists in eternal communion with eternal, divine love. This Eucharist mystery is the "heart of the whole." This is the heavenly bread and the new wine that will unite humanity in the struggle out of the darkness of resentful, retributive will that refuses to die to itself. The messianic banquet of Christ mediated through death and resurrection cannot be "bought" with earthly bread. It cannot be mediated through a false "image" of "mystery." Moreover, it cannot be enforced through the fear of the sword. In other words, the state cannot regulate the messianic banquet. It remains hidden in the underground of the heart of humanity in their suffering, but also in their joy. It is certainly embodied in the flesh, but it is driven by the inner, transformed conscience, mediated by a new desire gifted by the divine. It must be freely received just as it is freely given. It is this hidden reality that must be dynamically expressed through active, living love, not through state-driven, externally enforced "law."

Dostoevsky recognizes the gift of grace in the new resurrection wine given to humankind in Christ. As the chapter "Cana of Galilee" comes to its conclusion, Dostoevsky gives expression to the inner transformation of Alyosha. The Word of the Gospel penetrates his heart:

What was he weeping for?

---

84. De Lubac, *Drama of Atheist Humanism*, 389.

Oh, in his rapture he wept even for the stars that shone on him from the abyss, and "he was not ashamed of this ecstasy [исступления]." It was as if threads from all those innumerable worlds of God all came together in his soul, and it was trembling all over, "touching other worlds [соприкасаясь мирам иным]." He wanted to forgive [Простить] everyone and for everything, and to ask forgiveness, oh, not for himself! But for all and for everything, "as others are asking for me," rang in his soul. But with each moment he felt clearly and almost tangibly something as firm and immovable as this heavenly vault descend into his soul. Some sort of idea [идея], as it were, was coming to reign in his mind [воцарялась в уме его]—now for the whole of his life and unto ages and ages. He fell to earth a weak youth and rose up a fighter, steadfast for the rest of his life, and he knew it and felt it suddenly, in that very moment [минуту] of his ecstasy [восторга]. Never, never in all his life would Alyosha forget that moment.

"Someone visited my soul in that hour," he would say afterwards, with firm belief in his words.[85]

The movement from leaving the space of bodily decay of Zosima into the open air is significant. This is not the denial of mortality and death, but through the mediation of the sacrament, a movement toward the eternal and the infinite, as expressed in the experience of ecstatic rapture "before the stars that shone on him from the abyss." Alyosha's experience in the immanent, the transcendent reality expressed in the teaching of Zosima, was "as if threads from all those innumerable worlds of God all came together in his soul." As de Lubac describes Alyosha's ecstasy, this text is a poetic expression of mystic transfiguration: "The earthly mystery borders upon that of the stars, and God envelops his creation

---

85. Dostoevsky, *Brothers Karamazov*, 363. In the Russian, "О чем плакал он? О, он плакал в восторге своем даже и об этих звездах, которые сияли ему из бездны, и «не стыдился исступления сего». Как будто нити ото всех этих бесчисленных миров божиих сошлись разом в душе его, и она вся трепетала, «соприкасаясь мирам иным». Простить хотелось ему всех и за всё и просить прощения, о! не себе, а за всех, за всё и за вся, а «за меня и другие просят»,—прозвенело опять в душе его. Но с каждым мгновением он чувствовал явно и как бы осязательно, как что-то твердое и незыблемое, как этот свод небесный, сходило в душу его. Какая-то как бы идея воцарялась в уме его—и уже на всю жизнь и на веки веков. Пал он на землю слабым юношей, а встал твердым на всю жизнь бойцом и сознал и почувствовал это вдруг, в ту же минуту своего восторга. И никогда, никогда не мог забыть Алеша во всю жизнь свою потом этой минуты. го «Кто-то посетил мою душу в тот час»,—говорил он потом с твердою верой в слова свои . . ."

as the tranquil night envelops the earth. In Alyosha's heart 'the whole universe throbs.' His ecstasy is supernatural, but the cosmos is transfigured with him."[86] It is an expression of *deification*, to be made as a kind of god—*theosis*.[87] The entirety of Alyosha's being is transformed in connection with the cosmos in an experience of ecstasy that will form a sacred memory, which will strengthen the will to engage in the movement "from darkness to the light of love." This means an immanent participation in divine transcendence. However, the movement toward divine transcendence through the resurrection of Christ also means to participate in the "end" of history, the anticipation of the eschatological redemption of all creation. As de Lubac states, "That ecstasy [of Alyosha], however, is not an ending. It is a dawn, a promise."[88] It is rooted in the hope of resurrection: "The mysticism of *The Brothers Karamazov* is the mysticism of the resurrection. It is eschatological. It is that of the Fourth Gospel but also that of the Apocalypse."[89]

Just as significant, in this mystical ecstasy, Alyosha experiences the freedom of retribution: "He wanted to forgive everyone for everything, and to ask forgiveness . . . for all and for everything." As Timothy Ware asserts, the Orthodox conception of deification does not mean union with God's "essence," but rather his "energies."[90] This means that the mystical union between God and humans does not annihilate human personhood: "Creator and creature do not become fused into a single being."[91] Moreover, because it is *by grace* that one is deified, this presupposes that deification includes a "continued act of repentance."[92] That is, redemption is the freedom of soul to align itself and embody the "light of love," as tangibly expressed in a new desire to be forgiven, but also to forgive. It is expressed in the new resolve of the will to embody the reality of the

---

86. De Lubac, *Drama of Atheist Humanism*, 390.

87. According to Timothy Ware, "Such, according to the teaching of the Orthodox Church, is the final goal at which every Christian must aim: to become god, to attain *theosis*, 'deification' or 'divinization.' For Orthodoxy our salvation and redemption means our deification." Ware, *Orthodox Church*, 225.

88. De Lubac, *Drama of Atheist Humanism*, 390.

89. De Lubac, *Drama of Atheist Humanism*, 390.

90. Ware states, "The idea of deification must always be understood in the light of the distinction between God's essence and His energies. Union with God means union with the divine energies, not the divine essence; the Orthodox Church, while speaking of deification and union, rejects all forms of pantheism." Ware, *Orthodox Church*, 226.

91. Ware, *Orthodox Church*, 226.

92. Ware, *Orthodox Church*, 230.

image of Christ to the very "end," which is the radical annihilation of the egotistical self that clings to its "grudges" like Rakitin and to the retribution of Ivan. However, for this regeneration to occur, the death of Zosima was necessary, that is, the death of Zosima as an idol. The paradox is that the decay and the odor of corruption of the body of Zosima, even the disgrace of his beloved mentor, sacramentally unleashes a process, a struggle with Alyosha's soul that must be overcome. The process is too complex to reduce to one or two factors, but we observe that even "darkness" and "death" are used to mediate divine grace that transforms the soul, from Rakitin's betrayal to Grushenka's seduction, to the memory of Mitya's erotic passion and accusation of the murder of his father, to the retribution of Ivan. All aspects of immanent existence are potentially transformed through the mystery of the divine resurrection power. These elements of darkness and death that are also within the soul and body of Alyosha are overcome by eucharistic mystery that cannot be explained rationally, but perhaps glimpsed and even received iconically. Christ takes root in Alyosha in an experience of mystical ecstasy. It embodies him "wholly," physically, emotionally, as expressed in his tears and his prostrate body before the cosmos. This a vision of cosmic apocalyptic redemption: "Then I saw a new heaven and a new earth" (Rev. 21:1). Material creation is transfigured along with Alyosha. It is expressed in rapture, but also as an "idea" that enters into Alyosha and begins to "reign" in him. That is, we observe the paradoxical theme of sovereignty actualized in Alyosha. As Alyosha dies to himself, and surrenders resentment, a new form of "sovereignty" emerges, a divine sovereignty of messianic, cruciform, forgiving love that redeems and governs the desire and the will of Alyosha. It is also earthly, experienced in the body: "He fell to the earth." Alyosha is now "solid" and "whole"; he "rose up a fighter, steadfast for the rest of his life . . ."[93] It is clear from this text that this dramatic event in the life of Alyosha is pivotal and climactic. Retribution is overcome. As the movement of the story proceeds, Alyosha will be about his mission, his "work," attending to the souls of his brothers and others, mediating the same divine, active love.

---

93. Dostoevsky, *Brothers Karamazov*, 363.

Beyond Retribution—The Kiss of Christ and the Eucharistic Community

In the above section, we interpreted the sections on Alyosha as Dostoevsky's poetic expression of the heroic will, which struggles in a movement from darkness into the light of love, but climaxes in a mystical experience of resurrection, where heaven and earth are united in an experience of ecstasy, mediated by the word of the Gospel. We also asserted that Alyosha serves Dostoevsky's poetic image of the church, an alternative community, embodying divine, humble, kenotic love in the world. In this section, we will further explore the political vision embodied in the novel through Alyosha, but also through the teachings of Zosima. While the teachings of Zosima are structurally set prior to the dramatic event of the wedding in Cana, they are presented to us as collected and organized by Alyosha.[94] That is, we may assume that, within the narrative world of the novel, Alyosha collected and organized these teachings after the death of Zosima and his mystical experience. Perhaps we may assume as well, that Alyosha collected the teachings of Zosima considering his conversation with his brother Ivan and the temptation of retribution at the event of the elder's death. The narrator of the story, therefore, places them in the same book as the Grand Inquisitor. This juxtaposition between Ivan's Grand Inquisitor and the elder's life and teaching is intentional. However, I will not interpret the political vision of Alyosha, as expressed in the teachings of Zosima, as a kind of apologetic in response to Ivan and the Grand Inquisitor. Rather, I interpret Alyosha's collection of Zosima's teaching as an alternative political vision that endeavours to go beyond the spirit of retribution. If the Grand Inquisitor represents a political vision rooted in the atheistic retribution of Ivan, the teachings of Zosima also embodies a political vision, but one that is rooted in the freedom of the silent Christ, the Christ that kissed the bloodless lips of the of the Grand Inquisitor: "The old man would have liked him to say something, even something bitter, terrible. But suddenly [Christ] approaches the old man in silence and gently kisses him on his bloodless, ninety-year-old lips. That is the whole answer. The old man shudders."[95]

94. Dostoevsky, *Brothers Karamazov*, 287 and 323. "Here ends the manuscript of Alexei Fyodorovich Karamazov."

95. Dostoevsky, *Brothers Karamazov*, 262. In the Russian, "Старику хотелось бы, чтобы тот сказал ему что-нибудь, хотя бы и горькое, страшное. Но он вдруг молча приближается к старику и тихо целует его в его бескровные девяностолетние уста. Вот и весь ответ. Старик вздрагивает."

What is the "whole" answer? What is signified in the silent kiss of Christ on the monstrous lips of evil incarnate, the embodiment of the "spirit of non-being"? We are told that the kiss "burns" the old man. It touches his soul, though he still clings to his cynical, atheistic spirit. What does this kiss mean? In the Orthodox tradition, the act of a holy kiss occurred during the Eucharist as a "sign of peace."[96] More specifically, it occurs between priests between the proclamation of the Word and the giving of the Eucharist. That is, Dostoevsky links the "whole answer" to the Grand Inquisitor to the liturgy of the church, which celebrates the communion of the saints at the altar of the Eucharist, where the real body and blood of Christ is materially mediated to the people of God. In this sense, Dostoevsky powerfully embeds the idea of the *corpus mysticum*, the mystical body of Christ as the "answer" to the modern, atheistic, political realism of Ivan. If this is the case, then the "kiss of Christ," as an echo of the liturgy of the Eucharistic church, which celebrates the sacrifice of Christ, is also the means to move beyond a politics of resentment and retribution that underlies Ivan's deep cynical attitude toward humanity.

However, this "answer" of the church is not an abstract apologetic that attempts to refute the argumentation of Ivan and the Grand Inquisitor. Rather, it embodies the appropriate response of the *spirit* that is moving from the darkness of revenge into the "light of love."[97] That is, as a kiss, it is incredibly close, intimate even, an act of vulnerability. It signifies communality and intimate fraternity. It signifies union. The silent Christ, in this sense, *loves* the Grand Inquisitor in a spirit of unity. Dostoevsky's strategic use of it here is profound, for it signifies the gift of peace even to the Grand Inquisitor. Perhaps it is also Dostoevsky's "answer" to his perceived corruption of the Roman Catholic church? It is a poetic expression that links the ancient tradition of peace mediated through the Eucharist, embedded within the horrific cynical political vision of the Inquisitor. Furthermore, what is peculiar is that the idea to include the holy kiss of peace is Ivan's idea. As I see it, while the inclusion of the kiss of Christ could be a cynical joke on the part of Ivan, perhaps Dostoevsky is attempting to say something about that inescapable image of God in which we are created and cannot escape, even in humanity's most rebellious attempts to eradicate God from the heart of humanity. Even Ivan, who

---

96. Ware, *Orthodox Church*, 274.

97. In addition, however, along with Kroeker and Ward, Alyosha's manuscript on Zosima's teaching is "Dostoevsky's apologia for the silent Christ." We will explore this teaching below. See Kroeker and Ward, *Remembering the End*, 77.

attempts to eradicate the image of Christ in humankind, cannot wholly negate the underlying freedom of Christ with which he is created. The image of Christ is still reflected in and through the atheistic modernist cynicism. As Alyosha observes in Ivan, after his mental breakdown and his tortured discourse with the devil, at stake in Ivan is the pride of a deep conscience that refuses to submit to his true nature as created in the image of God: "'The torments of a proud decision, a deep conscience!' God, in whom he did not believe, and his truth were overcoming his heart, which still did not want to submit."[98] However, in Alyosha's response to Ivan, perceiving the spiritual struggle within him—"Either he will rise into the light of truth, or . . . perish in hatred, taking revenge on himself and on everyone for having served something he does not believe in"—he remains committed to his brother and "again prayed for Ivan."[99]

Therefore, if this interpretation rings true, then we also cannot separate the vision of Ivan and Zosima so strictly, for the image of Christ, despite its demonic corruption, still resides within the heart of Ivan, who produced the most radical, atheistic, retributive politic. It is as if the riddle of beauty between "Sodom" and "Madonna" are coexistent within the complex matrix of human will and desire as expressed in Ivan. Nonetheless, as a response to the Grand Inquisitor, I suggest the silence of the holy kiss of Christ, as well as the prayer of Alyosha for his brother, signifies the divine redemption of forgiveness, extended in humble love to the Inquisitor. That is, Dostoevsky's poetic political vision pertains ultimately to the *redemption* of Ivan and the politics he represents. The alternative politic imagined in Alyosha and Zosima is not another retributive vision against the corruption of the church and state. There is no evidence that Dostoevsky rejects the "state" in the poetics of *The Brothers Karamazov*. Dostoevsky is not an anarchist. Rather the political vision embedded within the poetics of the narrative endeavours to image the *redemption* of the politics of the state, through the creative imaginative possibility of divine love touching and transforming the human heart and its desires. The kiss of the silent Christ is a prophetic hope of the redemption of the Inquisitor through the mediation of Eucharistic realism, the "dream" of Alyosha endeavouring to capture the imagination of the Russian and European readership for whom Dostoevsky writes.

---

98. Dostoevsky, *Brothers Karamazov*, 655.
99. Dostoevsky, *Brothers Karamazov*, 655.

Redeeming Russia and Beyond: Alyosha Sent into the World

As we saw in the previous section, although Alyosha represents a desire for the holiness of love and the radical will necessary to enter into the monastic bond of obedience with the elder, Zosima has another assignment for him. Alyosha is not to remain in solitude and isolation in the monastery, but to go into the world:

> "You are more needed there. There is no peace there. You will serve and be of use. If demons raise their heads, recite a prayer . . . For the time being your place is not here. I give you my blessing for a great obedience in the world. You still have much journeying before you. And you will have to marry—yes, you will. You will have to endure everything before you come back again. And there will be much work to do. But I have no doubt of you, that is why I am sending you. Christ is with you. Keep him, and he will keep you. You will behold great sorrow and, in this sorrow, you will be happy. Here is a commandment for you: seek happiness in sorrow."[100]

This text is cited immediately after the scandal between the father Fyodor and Mitya in the elder's cell and prior to Alyosha's conversation with Rakitin about the problem of "sensuality" that lies at the heart of the drama between the father and the brothers. We examined how Dostoevsky conceives of sensuality in chapter 2, but here we emphasize that this is precisely the world into which the elder is sending Alyosha as the embodiment of divine love. That is, Alyosha will fulfill his act of obedience to the elder through the intentional movement of solidarity with those who are under the power of the erotic, Karamazovian force. We see this as Alyosha engages with the tragedy of his brothers, Mitya and

---

100. Dostoevsky, *Brothers Karamazov*, 77. The entire text in Russian, "Ты там нужнее. Там миру нет. Прислужишь и приго дишься. Подымутся беси, молитву читай. И знай, сынок (старец любил его так называть), что и впредь тебе не здесь место. Запомни сие, юноша. Как только сподобит бог преставиться мне—и уходи из монастыря. Совсем иди. Алеша вздрогнул. ты? Не здесь твое место пока. Благословляю тебя па великое послушание в миру. Много тебе еще странствовать. И ожениться должен будешь, должен. Всё должен будешь пере нести, пока вновь прибудеши. А дела много будет. Но в тебе не сомневаюсь, потому и посылаю тебя. С тобой Христос. Сохрани его, и он сохранит тебя. Горе узришь великое и в горе сем счаст лив будешь. Вот тебе завет: в горе счастья ищи. Работай, неустанно работай. Запомни слово мое отныне, ибо хотя и буду еще бесе довать с тобой, но не только дни, а и часы мои сочтены."

Ivan, one who is accused of murdering his father, and the other who goes insane believing he is responsible for his father's death.

While all the other brothers in the novel head for disaster—Mitya's imprisonment, Ivan's mental breakdown, and Smerdyakov's suicide—Alyosha remains faithful to them in the action of humble, servant love. Practically speaking, the movement out of darkness into the light of love means descending into the darkness of his brothers precisely because this is the law of love. As we saw above, it is *kenotic*, self-emptying. Alyosha does not escape from the darkness and suffering of his brothers; he deeply enters it in loving solidarity. Moreover, within the story, Alyosha goes beyond the darkness of his brothers. While Mitya's impulsive violence leads to the humiliation of the impoverished Snegiryov, spiralling into a conflict among the schoolchildren, Alyosha attempts to bring a dignified redemption to the situation.[101] The novel culminates with the funeral of Snegiryov's son, Ilyushechka, and Alyosha's sermon on the "eternal memory" of the boy.[102] Thus, the novel ends with the cry for the eternal in the midst of death.

However, Dostoevsky has more in mind here, signified in Alyosha's movement of love toward the darkness of his brothers and lives of others. The character of Alyosha represents the possibility of the future of Russia that goes beyond the atheism of Ivan and the "flooding wind" of modernism, especially atheist socialism, that is sweeping across Russia in the nineteenth century. In this text, there is reflected here a societal and political ideal of equality, but one that is structured on the image of the suffering Christ. Alyosha, as one sent by Zosima, is meant to bring the monastic spirit of the *startsy* into the world as a redemptive influence that holds the possibility of the transformation of society. Alyosha's individual struggle embodies and provides the means for the national struggle. The teachings of Zosima, collected by Alyosha,[103] accentuate the importance of the individual struggle for the national soul: "Our own humble and meek ones, fasters and keepers of silence, will arise and go forth for a

---

101. See "He Gets Involved with Schoolboys," and the entire section of book 10, entitled "Boys." Dostoevsky, *Brothers Karamazov*, 172–75, and 515–62.

102. Dostoevsky, *Brothers Karamazov*, 776.

103. As Kroeker and Ward suggest, "just as the Grand Inquisitor is Ivan Karamazov's prophetic creation, so is Zosima, in a sense, the prophetic creation of Alyosha Karamazov." The narrator informs us that the teachings of the "Russian Monk," are based on a manuscript by Alyosha, who "wrote it all down from memory sometime after the elder's death." Kroeker and Ward, *Remembering the End*, 77.

great deed. The salvation of Russia is from the people. And the Russian monastery has been with the people from time immemorial."[104] Zosima's teachings in a sense are an intrinsic aspect of the poetic expression of the kind of metaphysic of love that Dostoevsky expresses in the novel. And in this sense, they reflect the "heart of the whole" of Alyosha; they constitute a reflection of Alyosha's vision for the world. The redemptive intent for the Russian people is clear in the final sentences of this section: "Remember that. The people will confront the atheist and overcome him, and there will be one Orthodox Russian. Watch over the people, therefore, and keep a watch on their hearts. Guide them in peace. Such is your monastic endeavour, for this is a God-bearing people."[105]

Of course, this raises the contentious notion of the "Russian Idea," and the nationalistic tendency in the thought of Dostoevsky, which is also reflected in *The Brothers Karamazov*. As James P. Scanlan states, "understandably, Dostoevsky's messianic nationalism is the most controversial feature of his intellectual outlook."[106] While acknowledging the xenophobic elements of Dostoevsky's thought, Scanlan also asserts that, "whatever the psychic roots of his nationalism, it was conceptually more complex than is often acknowledged."[107] It is, argues Scanlan, connected to his understanding of history, of the "relation between society and the individual, and of the realizability of the Christian ideal on earth."[108] At stake, argues Scanlan, is how various Russian streams of thought interpreted the term *pochvennichestvo*, which he defines more broadly as an "empirical theory about the impact of a nation's history and culture on not only the attitudes but the capacities and other traits of the individual—a theory that in itself was neutral with respect to the

---

104. Dostoevsky, *Brothers Karamazov*, 314. In the Russian, "Те же смиренные и кроткие постники и молчальники восстанут и пойдут на великое дело. От народа спасение Руси. Русский же монастырь искони был с народом."

105. Dostoevsky, *Brothers Karamazov*, 315. In the Russian, "Это помните. Народ встретит атеиста и поборет его, и станет единая православная Русь. Берегите же народ и оберегайте сердце его. В тишине воспитайте его. Вот ваш иноческий подвиг, ибо сей народ—богоносец." According to Berdyaev, Dostoevsky "did not feel called upon to idealize the Russia of before Peter the Great, but he gave enormous importance to his period and to the rise of Petersburg. What interested him was man's destiny in after-Peter Russia, the tragic and complicated ordeal of the men who were uprooted at the time." Berdyaev, *Dostoevsky*, 170.

106. Scanlan, *Dostoevsky*, 198.

107. Scanlan, *Dostoevsky*, 198–99.

108. Scanlan, *Dostoevsky*, 199.

relative merits of the nations."[109] The interpretation of *pochvennichestvo* could go in either a chauvinistic or a non-chauvinistic direction.[110] With respect to Russian "universality," Scanlan argues that Dostoevsky was "less concerned with the full realization of the ideal of Russia alone than what he saw as Russian's role in leading the way to the salvation of the entire world."[111] What does this mission look like in practice? Or in Scanlan's formulation, how concretely did Dostoevsky expect "Russia to fulfill her 'universal purpose?" Scanlan cites three forms that this took in the thought of Dostoevsky, the first one being most relevant for an interpretation of *The Brothers Karamazov*, "the least imperialistic vision limited the mission to moral example and peaceful suasion: Russia would simply bring humanity a 'new word,' as he frequently expressed it, in the form of Christ's teaching and brotherly love."[112] While acknowledging the complexity of Dostoevsky's thought, I interpret the poetic intention *The Brothers Karamazov*, as the mission to mediate the humble, suffering love of Christ as embodied in Alyosha. Alyosha represents the pathway of redemptive suffering, a kind of creation of a literary iconic figure, which embodies the entire Russian monastic tradition, but reimagined for the modern world. As Kroeker and Ward state, "Such freedom is made possible through spiritual rebirth in the image of Christ—that is, conformity to the 'form of the servant' of 'serf's garb' that builds up human community through deeds of humble love."[113] Therefore, the "whole" signifies

---

109. Scanlan, *Dostoevsky*, 200.

110. Scanlan provides a survey of Dostoesvky's respective attitudes toward Russian nationalism and its relationship to the world in the chapter "The Russian Idea." Scanlan, *Dostoevsky*, 200.

111. Scanlan, *Dostoevsky*, 212. Berdyaev too argued that "Dostoevsky's Russianist tendencies are especially seen in his diaries, but his poetics bears witness that he was able to go beyond such ethnonationalism as well. While Berdyaev acknowledges that Dostoevsky is a thoroughly Russian writer and carries with him all its Slavophil tendencies, Dostoevsky still "belonged to a new era that was sensible to change and looked for its religion in the Book of the Apocalypse. His conception of the people embraced their messianic relation to the whole world: the slavophils were still provincials compared with him." See Berdyaev, *Dostoevsky*, 170.

112. The second form articulated political aims, Russia's mission to lead the Slavs, which they would accept without coercion. And third and "most ambitious vision extended Russia's political efforts at unification to all of humanity, beginning with the world of Orthodoxy, and did not rule out the violence as a possible instrument." Scanlan, *Dostoevsky*, 219.

113. Kroeker and Ward, *Remembering the End*, 16.

the image of Christ or as we saw in de Lubac, the *mysterium crucis*, the mystery of the cross of Christ to redeem creation.

The Monastic Path: Uncovering the Paradise in the Heart

As stated above, the path of redemption exemplified in Alyosha and modelled by the monastic institution of elders is not for the individual alone; it is a means to participate in a greater redemptive movement for the Russian people and for the world. This is the path of "freedom" that we observed earlier in the section "Elders." The underlying ideological "plot" of *The Brothers Karamazov* is nothing other than the path for this redemption. Alyosha brings to the Russian people the way of the monastic as taught and practised by the elder Zosima. Who or what does Zosima represent? According Kroeker and Ward, while an Orthodox Russian Monk, "more importantly, he embodies a spiritual practice that predates the schism between Western and Eastern Christianity. The primary difference between him and the Grand Inquisitor is not identical with the divide between Roman Catholicism and Russian Orthodoxy, but rather with that between the hierarchical and spiritual strands of Christianity."[114] Moreover, he is not simply an "archaic figure," but Zosima's spirituality, while rooted in ancient practice, is "explicitly orientated toward engagement with the modern world."[115] In particular, the question of the meaning of modern freedom and equality is of particular interest in the teaching of Zosima, which I will delineate below. As Kroeker and Ward assert, especially in the climate of "all-consuming materialism, the notion of equality can be little more than expression of envy and resentment."[116] As developed in chapter 2, this form of freedom and the modernist permission to follow ones passional desires without limit, leads to the problem of the "Karamazov," as represented in the father, Fyodor, and of which each brother must contend. However, Zosima does not reject freedom, as the Inquisitor does, but seeks to appropriate it in the proper conception of the human, that is, the proper relation between the bodily, sensual aspect of the self, with that of the higher spiritual aspect. Freedom

---

114. Furthermore, as Kroeker and Ward state, on occasion Zosima is called, "Pater Seraphicus," a "name sometimes given to St. Francis of Assisi, a Western spiritual figure, with whom Zosima seems to have more in common than with many Russian Orthodox saints." Kroeker and Ward, *Remembering the End*, 78.

115. Kroeker and Ward, *Remembering the End*, 80.

116. Kroeker and Ward, *Remembering the End*, 81.

The Mysticism of Resurrection and the Sacrament of Friendship 241

is properly experienced with the lower aspect of the self comes under the reign of the higher, spiritual self. As we saw in the previous section in our examination of the chapter "Cana of Galilee," this necessitates a mystical experience with the resurrected Christ. However, we also argued that this also entails the ongoing commitment of the will toward the higher ideal of the image of Christ. This is how the "Karamazovian force" will be overcome and therefore, a new kind of politic engendered for the Russian people against the onslaught of the modern "flooding wind." How will the brute, chaotic force be overcome by the Spirit of God? How does the will unite itself to the way of the kenotic ideal of Christ?

First, solitude is necessary to attune the self toward the image of Christ. The solitude of the monks is ridiculed by Alyosha's father, who described them as parasites on the land, living off others. However, Zosima asserts that "the monk is reproached for isolation: 'You isolate yourself in order to save your soul behind monastery walls, but you forget the brotherly ministry to mankind.' We shall see, however, who is more zealous in loving his brothers."[117] The path of self-renunciation in order to achieve perfect freedom is the redemptive path for all of society and humankind: "People point less often to these monks, and even pass them over in silence, and how surprised they would be if I were to say that from these meek ones, thirsting for solitary prayer, will perhaps come once again the salvation of the Russian land!"[118] According to Zosima, this is because the monastic way is the attempt to preserve the *kenotic* image of the suffering love of Christ: "Meanwhile, in their solitude they keep the image of Christ fair and undistorted, in the purity of God's truth, from the time of the ancient fathers, apostles, and martyrs, and when the need arises they will reveal it to the wavering truth of the world. This is a great thought. This star will shine forth from the East."[119]

---

117. Dostoevsky, *Brothers Karamazov*, 314. In the Russian, "Инока корят его уединением: «Уединился ты, чтобы себя спасти в монастырских стенах, а братское служение человечеству забыл». Но посмотрим еще, кто более братолюбию поусердствует?"

118. Dostoevsky, *Brothers Karamazov*, 313. In the Russian, "А между тем сколь много в монашестве смиренных и кротких, жаждущих уединения и пламенной в тишине молитвы. На сих меньше ука зывают и даже обходят молчанием вовсе, и сколь подивились бы, если скажу, что от сих кротких и жаждущих уединенной молитвы выйдет, может быть, еще раз спасение земли русской!"

119. Dostoevsky, *Brothers Karamazov*, 313. Образ Христов хранят пока в уединении своем благолепно и неиска женно, в чистоте правды божией, от древнейших отцов, апостолов и мучеников, и, когда надо будет, явят его

This means that the ascetic path is critical for the redemption of modern Russia. It means the elimination of desires that are inordinately focused only on superfluous material needs. This connects again to the fundamental ontology of Zosima's conception of humankind, whereby the sensual immanent world of the senses is exalted above the higher spiritual aspect of humankind's being: "But the spiritual world, the higher half of man's being, is altogether rejected, banished with a sort of triumph, even with hatred."[120] The focus of monastic solitude is to give special attention to the higher half of our being, disciplining the desires of the lower self to come under the authority and sovereignty of the higher spiritual half of the self. The intent is to reunite the two halves of the self into a unified whole. This is the path, argues Zosima, that will unite humanity, as the monastic gives special attention to the higher spiritual aspect of our humanity. According to Zosima, the modern world has mistakenly interpreted freedom as the freedom to satisfy their immediate material needs, ignoring and even denying the higher spiritual half of the self:

> The world says: "You have needs, therefore satisfy them, for you have the same rights as the noblest and richest men. Do not be afraid to satisfy them, but even increase them"—this is the current teaching of the world. In addition, in this they see freedom. However, what comes of this right to increase one's needs? For the rich, *isolation* and spiritual suicide; for the poor, envy and murder, for they have been given rights, but have not yet been shown the way of satisfying their needs. We are assured that the world is becoming more and more united, is being formed into brotherly communion, by the shortening of distances, by the transmitting of thought through the air. Alas, do not believe in such a union of people. Taking freedom to mean the increase and prompt satisfaction of needs, they distort their own nature, for they generate many meaningless and foolish desires, habits, and the most absurd fancies in themselves.[121]

поколебавшейся правде мира. Сия мысль великая. От востока звезда сия воссияет."

120. Dostoevsky, *Brothers Karamazov*, 313.

121. Dostoevsky, *Brothers Karamazov*, 313–14. In the Russian, "бо мир говорит: «Имеешь потребности, а потому насыщай 20 их, ибо имеешь права такие же, как и у знатнейших и богатей ших людей. Не бойся насыщать их, но даже приумножай»—вот нынешнее учение мира. В этом и видят свободу. И что же выходит из сего права на приумножение потребностей? У бога тых уединение и духовное самоубийство, а у бедных—зависть и убийство, ибо права-то дали, а средств насытить потребности еще не указали. Уверяют, что мир чем далее, тем

Through the voice of Zosima, Dostoevsky advocates for the monastic way of solitude as a redemptive antidote against the distorted fragmentation of the individualist self in modern society. The modernist focus on materialist desire as the means to freedom only leads to isolation, spiritual suicide, envy, and violence. The monastic path does not mean the renunciation of all bodily desire, but its moderation, to attune the self to the "higher half of man's being."[122] As Zosima learned from the "mysterious visitor," the modernist focus on accumulation of superfluous desires and technological advancement is not the path to "universal brotherhood." With respect to isolation, the visitor testifies it is "that which is now reigning everywhere, especially in our age . . . For everyone strives most of all to separate his person, wishing to experience the fullness of life within himself, and yet what comes of all his efforts is not the fullness of life but full suicide, for instead of the fullness of self-definition, they fall into complete isolation."[123] The individual self cannot mediate its own "fullness," or its own fulfillment and self-definition. Why? It is because "men in our age are separated into units, each seeks seclusion in his own hole, each withdraws from others, hides himself, and hides what he has, and ends by pushing himself away from people and pushing people away from himself."[124] Consequently, "he has separated his unit

---

более единится, слагается в братское общение тем, что сокращает расстояния, передает по воздуху мысли. Увы, не верьте таковому единению людей. Понимая свободу как приумножение и скорое утоление потребностей искажают природу свою, ибо зарождают в себе много бессмысленных и глупых желаний, привычек и нелепейших выдумок."

122. Dostoevsky, *Brothers Karamazov*, 314.

123. Dostoevsky, *Brothers Karamazov*, 303. The fuller Russian text, "Чтобы переделать мир по-новому, надо, чтобы люди сами психически повернулись на другую дорогу. Раньше, чем не сделаешься в самом деле вся кому братом, не наступит братства. Никогда люди никакою наукой и никакою выгодой не сумеют безобидно разделиться в собственности своей и в правах своих. Всё будет для каждого зо мало, и всё будут роптать, завидовать и истреблять друг друга. Вы спрашиваете, когда сие сбудется. Сбудется, но сначала должен заключиться период человеческого уединения»,—«Какого это уединения?»—спрашиваю его. «А такого, какое теперь везде царствует, и особенно в нашем веке, но не заключился еще весь и не пришел еще срок ему. Ибо всякий-то теперь стремится отделить свое лицо наиболее, хочет испытать в себе самом полноту жизни, а между тем выходит изо всех его усилий вместо полноты жизни лишь полное самоубийство, ибо вместо полноты определения существа своего впадают в совершенное уединение."

124. Dostoevsky, *Brothers Karamazov*, 303. In the Russian, "Ибо все-то в наш век разделились на единицы, всякий уединяется в свою нору, всякий от другого

from the whole."[125] That is, the whole of the image of Christ that is the proper mediator of the "universal brotherhood" of humankind:

> Such will be the spirit of the time, and they will be astonished that they sat in darkness for so long, and did not see the light. Then the sign of the Son of Man will appear in the heavens . . . but until then we must keep hold of the banner, and every once in a while, if only individually, a man must suddenly set an example, and draw the soul from its isolation for an act of brotherly communion, though it be with the rank of holy fool.[126]

Of course, the "holy fool" here also needs interpretation. Father Ferapont represents extreme asceticism which denies the body for the immediate experience of the Spirit. He falsely perceives the demonic in the monasticism practised by Zosima because of the need for "bread": "I can do without their bread, I don't need it at all, I can go to the forest and live on mushrooms and berries, but they can't do without their bread here, that's why they're in bondage to the devil."[127] The redemptive path of Zosima does not deny the need for bread, nor does he despise the body, but emphasizes that the lower aspect of the self, the physical and the material, must exist in a proper relation to the higher aspect of the self, the "immortal soul" that exists in humanity, which is the image of Christ. As we saw above in "Cana of Galilee," the living Word mediates the conjoining of the lower and the higher, opening Alyosha beyond himself to a rapturous sense of connection to the universe as a whole. Alyosha felt more connected rather than isolated. Therefore, faithful attention to the living Word and the image of Christ is essential for the "reconciliation" of individual self to the "whole" of the divine as well as to the cosmos. This certainly fits well with the wholistic vision we saw in de Lubac in chapter 1. Here is another reference from de Lubac that is suitable in this context,

---

отдаляется, прячется и, что имеет, прячет и кончает тем, что сам от людей отталкивается и сам людей от себя отталкивает."

125. Dostoevsky, *Brothers Karamazov*, 303.

126. Dostoevsky, *Brothers Karamazov*, 304. In the Russian text, "Но непременно будет так, что придет срок и сему страшному уединению, и поймут все разом, как неестест венно отделились один от другого. Таково уже будет веяние времени, и удизятся тому, что так долго сидели во тьме, а света не видели. Тогда и явится знамение сына человеческого на небеси . . . ю Но до тех пор надо все-таки знамя беречь и нет-нет, а хоть единично должен человек вдруг пример показать и вывести душу из уедине ния на подвиг братолюбивого общения, хотя бы даже и в чине юродивого."

127. Dostoevsky, *Brothers Karamazov*, 168.

The Mysticism of Resurrection and the Sacrament of Friendship 245

the "same mysterious participation in God which causes the soul to exist effects at one and the same time the unity of spirits among themselves. Whence comes the notion, so beloved of Augustinianism, of one spiritual family intended to form the one city of God."[128]

The monastic way exemplified by Zosima aims to reconcile these two aspects together into a "whole," not just of the human self alone, but laying a foundation of which connects the self to the rest of the redeemed community in the city of God. As we saw with the Nietzschean concept of solitude, this is not isolationism, but the intent to connect the self to the higher "whole," and the cosmos itself, and ultimately, to reconcile and unite the body and its desires with Christ. In this way, the higher self must exercise sovereignty over the lower physical aspect of the self. And this sovereignty and mastery over the lower aspect of the self can only be accomplished through the way of the monastic: "Very different is the monastic way. Obedience, fasting, and prayer are laughed at, yet they alone constitute the way to real and true freedom: I cut away my superfluous and unnecessary needs. Through obedience, I humble and chasten my vain and proud will, and thereby with God's help, attain freedom of spirit, and with that, spiritual rejoicing!"[129]

The irony is that solitude meant is to overcome and resist the spiritual isolation of modernist individualism. Obedience, fasting, and prayer are the necessary means of self-renunciation in order to achieve freedom—the freedom from the self in order to reunite with the "whole" of humanity, as created in the image of Christ.[130] The purpose of fasting and prayer is to cut away superfluous needs and desires that create a social

---

128. Henri de Lubac, *Catholicism*, 29.

129. Dostoevsky, *Brothers Karamazov*, 314. In the Russian, "Другое дело путь иноческий. Над послушанием, постом и молит вой даже смеются, а между тем лишь в них заключается путь к настоящей, истинной уже свободе: отсекаю от себя потребности лишние и ненужные, самолюбивую и гордую волю мою смиряю и бичую послушанием, и достигаю тем, с помощью божьей, сво боды духа, а с нею и веселья духовного!"

130. Kroeker and Ward assert that the portrait of Zosima is more complex that simply the Russian orthodox spiritual tradition is the ultimate expression of Christianity, "To note one example of the sort of nuance this equation ignores: Zosima is on one occasion called 'Peter Seraphicus,' a name more striking in the original Russian text because of the contrast between the Roman letters in which it appears and the surrounding Cyrillic script. It is also striking because this was the name sometimes given to St. Francis of Assisi, a Western spiritual figure, with whom Zosima seems to have more in common than with many Russian Orthodox saint." Kroeker and Ward, *Remembering the End*, 78.

environment of envy: "They live only for mutual envy, for pleasure-seeking and self-display. To have dinners, horses, carriages, rank, and slaves to serve them is now considered such a necessity that for the sake of it, to satisfy it, they will sacrifice life, honour, the love of mankind, and will even kill themselves if they are unable to satisfy it."[131] This materialistic way of life only ends, argues Zosima, in greater disunity and isolation. In contrast, the solitude of the monk, which focuses on the higher spiritual self, connected to the image of Christ, is how humanity will be reunited, not only with God, but with one another. Zosima asks, "Which of the two is more capable of upholding and serving a great idea—the isolated rich man or one who is liberated from the tyranny of things and habits?"[132] As Kroeker and Ward argue, as Zosima understand it, "human freedom . . . is the reverse image of modern materialism: Rather than an aggrandizement of the self, it is the freedom *from* the self."[133]

We examined the significance of obedience above, but here we stress that its importance is essential because it directly counters the egotistic pride that desires to be a master, a sovereign. Obedience is the renunciation of self-sovereignty. It is humble in that it recognizes its fundamental dependency on the living Word for authentic freedom. It is the paradoxical path toward *theosis*, to *deification*. We noted above that the institution of elders practises the humble submission of obedience to an extreme. Nonetheless, the paradox of humility in obedience, the surrendering of proud, self-exaltation to sovereignty is that the aim is—sovereignty. That is, the divine sovereignty to exercise an authentic authority over the chaos of desires within the human heart. It is the sovereignty to resist an egoist sovereignty that is fundamentally self-serving. It is resistant to the "sovereignty" as expressed in the bestial desires of the father, Fyodor Karamazov, the reign of "sensuality." Alyosha wondered whether the Holy Spirit could reign in the earthy, Karamazovian force. Through faithful attention to the living Word, the Holy Spirit engenders the sovereignty of the higher self to master and control the bodily desires of the lower

---

131. Dostoevsky, *Brothers Karamazov*, 314. In the Russian, "Живут лишь для зависти друг к другу, для плотоугодия и чванства. обеды, выезды, экипажи, чины и рабов-прислужников считается уже такою необходимостью, для которой жертвуют даже жизнью, честью и человеколюбием, чтоб утолить эту необходимость, и даже убивают себя, если не могут утолить ее."

132. Dostoevsky, *Brothers Karamazov*, 314.

133. Kroeker and Ward, *Remembering the End*, 81.

Zosima's Sacrament of Radical Solidarity

self. This is the inner path of freedom and the redemption of the self, but also the redemption of Russia and the world beyond.

If the path of the monastic is the solitary path of renouncing superfluous desire to attend to the inner image of Christ, it also consists of an outward orientation toward the "other," rooted in "love of humankind." As we see in the teaching of Zosima, the social-economic concern is deeply reflected, addressing the arising issue of child labour in modern industrialism. In critiquing the injustices that are occurring in the growth of modern capitalism of the nineteenth century, Zosima observes, "I have seen ten-year-old children in the factories: frail, sickly, stooped, and already depraved."[134] Zosima shares the same concern for the suffering of children as Ivan, attending to the socialist solution to political and economic oppression of the innocent. As Kroeker and Ward suggest, Zosima's teaching is "close to the Marxist critique of the merely formal equality of capitalist liberalism."[135] That is, as we saw above, Zosima is critical of a capitalist culture that permits the unlimited freedom of excessively satisfying personal desires. However, in contrast to Marxism, Zosima rejects the atheistic foundation of socialism, the "modern embodiment of the tower of Babel": "These, following science, want to make a just order for themselves by reason alone, but without Christ now, not as before, and they have already proclaimed that there is no crime, there is no sin."[136] If there is no sin, there is no crime. We are only victims of social and political circumstance. Moreover, "if you have no God, what crime is there to speak of?"[137] According to Zosima, the socialist solution lays the ethical foundation for "everything is permitted." It results in Ivan's political logic of the Grand Inquisitor. However, according to Zosima, modernist atheism and revolutionary socialism engenders only a politic of retribution and violence: "In Europe the people are rising up against the rich with force, and popular leaders everywhere are leading

---

134. Dostoevsky, *Brothers Karamazov*, 315.

135. Kroeker and Ward, *Remembering the End*, 81.

136. Dostoevsky, *Brothers Karamazov*, 315. In the Russian, "Те вослед науке хотят устроиться справедливо одним умом своим, но уже без Христа, как прежде, и уже провозгласили, что нет преступления, нет уже греха."

137. Dostoevsky, *Brothers Karamazov*, 315.

them to bloodshed and teaching them that their wrath is righteous."[138] In contrast, Zosima asserts that the humble faith of the Russian people will engender the redemption of land: "Salvation will come from the people, from their faith and their humility."[139] Interestingly, Zosima does not point to the institution of the Russian Orthodox church, nor particularly to the monastic institution, as the future redemption of Russia, but to its people. That is, the immanence of the divine is revealed in the Russian people themselves. We have already observed examples of "the people," the humility of faith represented in "the women of faith," those who weep for their Russian children, like biblical Rachel weeping for her children. It is as if Dostoevsky is attempting to communicate that the faith that still exists in the motherland needs only to be fanned into flame by exemplars like Zosima and his followers, such as Alyosha.

However, what precisely is it about the kind of humble faith that will redeem Russia from modernist materialistic isolation? First, moving beyond the resentment of the wealthy and powerful means the mutual acknowledgement of the inherent dignity of a shared humanity. As Zosima articulates with respect to the wealthy: "You are noble, you are rich, you are intelligent and talented, very well, God bless you. I honour you, but I know that I, too, am a man. By honouring you without envy, I show my human dignity before you."[140] Zosima believes firmly in the power of humility for the creation of equality in society, "for it will come to pass that even the most corrupt of our rich men will finally be ashamed of his riches before the poor man, and the poor man, seeing his humility, will understand and yield to him in joy, and respond with kindness to his gracious shame."[141] This is because, as those created in the image of Christ, a common shared dignity is the ontological essence of humankind. This is the foundation for equality: "Equality is only in man's spiritual dignity, and only among us will that be understood. Where there

138. Dostoevsky, *Brothers Karamazov*, 315. In the Russian, "В Европе восстает народ на богатых уже силой, и народные вожаки повсеместно ведут его к крови и учат, что прав гнев его."

139. Dostoevsky, *Brothers Karamazov*, 315. In the Russian, "А Россию спасет господь, как спасал уже много раз. Из народа спасение выйдет, из веры и смирения его."

140. Dostoevsky, *Brothers Karamazov*, 316.

141. Dostoevsky, *Brothers Karamazov*, 316. In the Russian, "Мечтаю видеть и как бы уже вижу ясно наше грядущее: ибо будет так, что даже самый развращенный богач наш кончит тем, что устыдится богатства своего пред бедным, а бедный, видя смирение сие, поймет и уступит ему с радостью, и лаской ответит на благолепный стыд его."

The Mysticism of Resurrection and the Sacrament of Friendship 249

are brothers, there will be brotherhood; but before brotherhood they will never share among themselves. Let us preserve the image of Christ, that it may shine forth like a precious diamond to the whole world ... So be it, so be it!"[142] This reference connects to the chapter "So Be It!," where Zosima articulates the significance of the church over the state, the power of the image of Christ that can transform the inner desires of the self that will engender an authentic equality in the state and thus result in the transformation of society.

Zosima does not deny the hierarchical structure of society—"the world cannot do without servants"—but it is possible that the master seeks also to serve the servant. In this section "Some Words about Masters and Servants," Zosima alludes to the teaching in Mark 10, where Jesus deplores the desire for power and status of the disciples. On whether it is "possible" for masters and servants to "become brothers in spirit," Zosima asserts,

> This may be accomplished even now, but it will serve as the foundation for the magnificent communion of mankind in the future, when a man will not seek for servants for himself, and will not wish to turn his fellow man into servants, as now, but, on the contrary, will wish with all his strength to become himself the servant of all, in accordance with the Gospel.[143]

The allusion of this text addresses the theme of the kind of leadership necessary for the new society. In the Gospel, Jesus makes a stark contrast between the leadership of Rome, which lords its authority and sovereignty over its citizens with the kind of servant leadership that is required in the kingdom of God. In the Gospel, as in the teaching of Zosima, servanthood has a redemptive quality for people as a whole, "For the Son of Man did not come to be served but to serve, and to give his life as a ransom for many" (Mk. 10:45). Zosima dreams of this form of society, where the desire to be master, the *"libido dominandi,"* will be transformed

---

142. Dostoevsky, *Brothers Karamazov*, 316. In the Russian, "Лишь в человеческом духовном достоинстве равенство, и сие поймут лишь у нас. Были бы братья, будет и братство, а раньше братства никогда не разделятся. Образ Христов храним, и воссияет как драгоценный алмаз всему миру ... Буди, буди!"

143. Dostoevsky, *Brothers Karamazov*, 317. In the Russian, "Даже и теперь еще это так испол нимо, но послужит основанием к будущему уже великолепному единению людей, когда не слуг будет искать себе человек и не в слуг пожелает обращать себе подобных людей, как ныне, а, напротив, изо всех сил пожелает стать сам всем слугой по Еван-ю гелию."

into the desire to be the servant of all. For Zosima, this is an eschatological hope fulfilled by the people of God: "People laugh and ask: when will the time come, and does it look as if it will ever come? But I think that with Christ we shall bring about this great deed."[144] This, for Zosima, is the path to transform the world beyond the violence of retribution: "They hope to make a just order for themselves, but having rejected Christ, they will end by drenching the earth with blood, for blood calls to blood, and he who draws the sword will perish by the sword. And were it not for Christ's covenant, they would annihilate one another down to the last two men on earth."[145] That is, the end of human history, as Zosima interprets the socialist agenda, concludes with death and annihilation. The only hope for society, according to Zosima, is the humble way of Christ.

Still, how precisely is the way of transforming society into one of equality through the monastic attention to the image of Christ attained? How is the "holy kiss" of the silent Christ embodied? How is the "sacrament" of Christ mediated in the world? Zosima discusses the practices of prayer and love, which are oriented in a particular perception of the self in relation to the world. It is appropriate to interpret Zosima's teaching here as "sacramental," since these are the means to achieve unity between God and humanity. As de Lubac defines the term, "since the sacraments are the means of salvation they should be understood as instruments of unity."[146] The entire monastic way of life as expressed in *Brothers Karamazov* is in this since sacramental, for it is oriented toward a greater mystical unity with God and humanity. In this context, prayer and acts of love are particularly significant. Prayer is a form of mediation between the transcendent and the immanent for souls, even at the moment of death: "Remember also: every day and whenever you can, repeat within yourself: 'Lord, have mercy upon all who come before you today.'"[147] Prayer unites souls who die in isolation: "So many of them part with the earth in isolation, unknown to anyone, in sadness and sorrow."[148] Prayer is a form of

---

144. Dostoevsky, *Brothers Karamazov*, 317.

145. Dostoevsky, *Brothers Karamazov*, 318. In the Russian, "Мыслят устроиться справедливо, но, отвергнув Христа, кончат тем, что зальют мир кровью, ибо кровь го зовет кровь, а извлекший меч погибнет мечом. И если бы не обе тование Христово, то так и истребили бы друг друга даже до последних двух человек на земле."

146. De Lubac, *Catholicism*, 82.

147. Dostoevsky, *Brothers Karamazov*, 318. In the Russian, "Запомни еще: на каждый день и когда лишь можешь, тверди про себя: «Господи, помилуй всех днесь пред тобою представших»."

148. Dostoevsky, *Brothers Karamazov*, 318.

The Mysticism of Resurrection and the Sacrament of Friendship 251

intercession that is an expression of love for others, *uniting* people across time and space, beyond death itself: "Perhaps from the other end of the earth, your prayer for his repose will rise up to the Lord, though you did not know him at all, nor he you. How moving it is for his soul, coming in fear before the Lord, to feel at that moment that someone is praying for him, too, that there is still a human being on earth who loves him."[149] This, again, is consistent with de Lubac's vision of being united in the Spirit with an emphasis of the communion of the mystical body. However, while de Lubac lays more stress on the institution of the Eucharist, Dostoevsky's sacramental thought on Eucharistic mediation is intended as an expression outward toward others in the mundane of everyday. For instance, in *Catholicism*, de Lubac asserts that the unity of humanity is primarily experienced and actualized in the practice of the Eucharist and the liturgy of the Roman Catholic Church.[150] De Lubac quotes John Chrysostom to accentuate this point, "Let us learn the wonders of this sacrament, the purpose of its institution, the effects that it produces. We become one body, says the Scripture, members of his flesh, bone of his bones."[151] However, in Zosima's teaching, we see that the sacramental "instrument" of unity is actualized more in everyday expressions of prayer and humble love toward others. For example, we see this outward extension of the mystical unity in the Eucharist in Zosima's vision of love, which extends to all creation: "Love all of God's creation, both the whole of it and every grain of sand. Love every leaf, every ray of God's light. Love animals, love plants, love each thing. If you love each thing, you will perceive the mystery of God in things ... And you will come at last to love the whole world with an entire, universal love."[152] Like Nietzsche's vision of the Übermensch in *Zarathustra*, there is an overflow that spills out

---

149. Dostoevsky, *Brothers Karamazov*, 318. In the Russian, "И вот, может быть, с другого конца земли вознесется ко господу за упокой его и твоя молитва, хотя бы ты и не знал его вовсе, а он тебя. Сколь умилительно душе его, ю ставшей в страхе пред господом, почувствовать в тот миг, что есть и за него молельщик, что осталось на земле человеческое существо, и его любящее."

150. De Lubac, *Catholicism*, 82.

151. De Lubac, *Catholicism*, 91. See also John Chrysostom, *Hom. 46. In Joannem* (PG 59, 260).

152. Dostoevsky, *Brothers Karamazov*, 319. In the Russian, "Любите всё создание божие, и целое и каждую песчинку. Каждый листик, каждый луч божий любите. Любите животных, любите растения, любите всякую вещь. Будешь любить всякую вещь и тайну божию постигнешь в вещах. Постигнешь однажды и уже неустанно начнешь ее познавать всё далее и более, на всяк день."

toward the other. It is an overabundant love. However, unlike Zarathustra, it is a divine love that envelops and fills immanent existence. It is this love that affirms life and creation, overcoming resentment, even the desire for retribution against sin and evil itself: "One may stand perplexed before some thought, especially seeing men's sin, asking oneself: 'Shall I take it by force, or by humble love?' Always resolve to take it by humble love. If so, resolved once and for all, you will be able to overcome the whole world. A loving humility is a terrible power, the most powerful of all, nothing compares with it."[153] For it is this love in action, as discussed in the section above, that reflects the divine image in creation.

Finally, the only salvation from retribution and the disturbance of "sin" is to authentically assume a kind of radically responsibility for it: "There is only one salvation for you: take yourself up, and make yourself responsible for all the sins of men. For indeed it is so, my friend, and the moment you make yourself sincerely responsible for everything and everyone, you will see at once that it is really so, that it is you who are guilty on behalf of all and for all."[154] This directly counters the concept that "there is no sin." Equality and the redemption of the state begins with the individual self acknowledging responsibility for the sin of the world. It assumes a participation in a collective guilt, the "sin of humankind." This means a kind of solidarity of sin that refuses to condemn the other in their sin because it is deeply shared. Retribution assumes the moral superiority and the right to punish and condemn. This seems to be what the "pride of Satan" is for Zosima, the "strongest impulses of our nature that we cannot comprehend while on earth," the impulse to presume the moral right to punish and condemn. This interpretation of the pride of Satan seems to be justified by the consideration of the theme of the next section of Zosima's teaching, "Can One Be the Judge of One's

---

153. Dostoevsky, *Brothers Karamazov*, 319. In the Russian, "Пред иною мыслью станешь в недоумении, особенно видя грех людей, и спросишь себя: «Взять ли силой али смиренною любовью? » Всегда решай: «Возьму смиренною любовью». Решишься так раз навсегда и весь мир покорить возможешь. Смирение любовное—страшная сила, изо всех сильнейшая, подобной которой и нет ничего."

154. Dostoevsky, *Brothers Karamazov*, 320. In the Russian, "Одно тут спасение себе: возьми себя и сделай себя же ответчиком за весь грех людской. Друг, да ведь это и вправду так, ибо чуть только сделаешь себя за всё и за всех ответчиком искренно, то тотчас же увидишь, что оно так и есть в самом деле и что ты-то и есть за всех и за вся виноват."

Fellow Creatures?"[155] This does not mean that "judgment" does not exist or cannot occur, but that our practice of moral judgment and discernment must itself be redeemed by the reality that we are responsible for the sin of all. Zosima argues that humble love means that even before the criminal, one cannot presume to be judge, "for there can be no judge of a criminal on earth until the judge knows that he, too, is a criminal, exactly the same as the one who stands before him, and that he is perhaps most guilty of all for the crime of the one standing before him. When he understands this, then he will be able to be a judge."[156] This is the heart of Zosima's ethic, the forgiving spirit of Christ which can transform and regenerate the conscience in solidarity of guilt and the common hope of the Eucharistic mediation of Christ. With respect to the criminal, he contends, "And if, having received our kiss, he goes away unmoved and laughing at you, do not be tempted by that either: it means that his time has not yet come . . ."[157] I suspect there is a connection here to the kiss of the silent Christ and all that implies with respect to the Orthodox liturgical tradition. The mystical body of Christ is mediated on a particular spirit of humble love, that affirms the solidarity of guilt with the criminal: "Believe it, believe it without a doubt, for in this lies all hope and all the faith of the saints."[158] Indeed, one must strive to acknowledge one's deep participation in the guilt and sin of the world to resist the spirit of retribution and indignation:

> If the wickedness of people arouses indignation and insurmountable grief in you, to the point that you desire to revenge yourself upon the wicked, fear that feeling most of all; go at once and seek torments for yourself, as if you yourself were guilty of their wickedness. Take these torments upon yourself and suffer

---

155. Dostoevsky, *Brothers Karamazov*, 320.

156. Dostoevsky, *Brothers Karamazov*, 320–21. In the Russian, "Ибо не может быть на земле судья преступника, прежде чем сам сей судья не познает, что и он такой же точно преступник, как и стоящий пред ним, и что он-то за преступление стоящего пред ним, может, прежде всех и виноват. Когда же постигнет сие, то возможет стать и судиею."

157. Dostoevsky, *Brothers Karamazov*, 321. The entire Russian sentence, "Если же отойдет с целованием твоим бесчувственный и смеясь над тобою же, то не соблазняйся и сим: значит, срок его еще не пришел, но придет в свое время; а не придет, всё равно: не он, так другой за него познает, и пострадает, и осудит, и обвинит себя сам, и правда будет восполнена."

158. Dostoevsky, *Brothers Karamazov*, 321. In the Russian, "Верь сему, несомненно верь, ибо в сем самом и лежит всё упование и вся вера святых."

them, and your heart will be eased, and you will understand that you, too, are guilty, for you might have shone to the wicked, even like the only sinless One, but you did not.[159]

In this text, near the conclusion of the teaching of Zosima, there is mention of the "sinless One." As Alyosha confesses to Ivan, the redemption of the "whole" of humanity, the reconciliation between the oppressor and the oppressed, the victimizer and the victim, is structured upon the Messiah. Who has the divine right to forgive? As Alyosha asserts, "There is such a being, and he can forgive everything, forgive all *and* for all, because he gave his innocent blood for all and for everything."[160] It is the "structure" of Christ that engenders the possibility for the soul to engage in a movement from the darkness of isolation and the pride of the egotistical will into the divine light of love, where all creation, heaven and earth, transcendence and immanence, is connected as a "whole" through the incarnate image of Christ. It is this redemptive apocalyptic vision to which the people of God align their faith in the "realism" of love. Dostoevsky's poetic is designed to strengthen the will toward this radical redemptive commitment. As we see in the teaching of Zosima, he stresses a radical dependency on the "heavenly light," even beyond the apparent empirical evidence that suggests that the darkness cannot be overcome: "And even if you do shine, but see that people are not saved even with your light, remain steadfast, and do not doubt the power of the heavenly light; believe if they are not saved now, they will be saved later."[161] Even after death, the light of the saint continues to shed its light even more powerfully: "People are always saved after the death of him who saved them. The generation of men does not welcome its prophets and kills them, but men love their martyrs and venerate those they have tortured to death. Your work is for the whole, your deed is for the future."[162]

---

159. Dostoevsky, *Brothers Karamazov*, 323. In the Russian, "Если же злодейство людей возмутит тебя негодованием и скорбью уже необоримой^ даже до желания отомщения злодеям, то более всего страшись сего чувства; тотчас же иди и ищи себе мук так, как бы сам был виновен в сем злодействе людей. Приими сии муки и вытерпи, и утолится сердце твое, и поймешь, что и сам виновен, ибо мог светить злодеям даже как единый безгрешный и не светил."

160. Dostoevsky, *Brothers Karamazov*, 246.

161. Dostoevsky, *Brothers Karamazov*, 322. In the Russian, "И даже если ты и светил, но увидишь, что не спасаются люди даже и при свете твоем, то пребудь тверд и не усомнись в силе света небесного; верь тому, что если теперь ю не спаслись, то потом спасутся."

162. Dostoevsky, *Brothers Karamazov*, 322. In the Russian, "Не принимает род

The Mission of the Church: The "Ridiculous" Basis of Friendship

The "dream" of Zosima, remains, of course, unfulfilled. The novel does not conclude in triumph. Ivan's "conscience" is broken, and he is going insane. Mitya is on a journey toward redemption, but he is still in prison in the "underground." Nonetheless, as Alyosha tends to his brothers in love, there is hope. Alyosha, as representative of the "whole," draws to himself those out of the world, in the formation of a redemptively oriented "church." Alyosha carries forward the "dream" as expressed in the example of Zosima, a spiritual authority—sovereignty—that reflects the humble, servant love of the Messiah, the crucified Christ. Dostoevsky interprets history, therefore, not as a modernist movement whereby the church evolves into the state, from a "lower to a higher species, as it were, so as to disappear into [the state] eventually, making way for science, the spirit of the age, and civilization."[163] Dostoevsky exposes this modernist dream for what he perceives it is—the antichristian political vision of the man-god. This modernist vision is exposed in Ivan's devil, the eradication of the image of Christ in humankind. It ends in self-destructive annihilation of the human. For Dostoevsky, history means the inner meaning and working of the aims of Christ, transforming the world into the new creation of freedom in love.[164]

The elder sends Alyosha into the world, not to accuse it, but to actively and tenaciously love it, as reflected in his commitment to his tormented brother, Mitya, a representative of the "Russian people." Just as the elder bowed before Mitya in his cell, so now Alyosha must humble himself before the Russian people, beyond the political and intellectual elite and serve to bring to maturity their underlying faith in God. This is not the exaltation of Russian ethnocentrism, but its redemption.

людской пророков своих и избивает их, но любят люди мучеников своих и чтят тех, коих замучили. Ты же для целого работаешь, для грядущего делаешь."

163. Dostoevsky, *Brothers Karamazov*, 66.

164. "It is true," smiled the elder, "that now Christian society itself is not yet ready, and stands only one seven righteous men, but as they are never wanting, it abides firmly all the same, awaiting its complete transfiguration from society as still and almost pagan organization, into one universal and sovereign church. And so be it, so be it, if only at the end of time, for this alone is destined to be fulfilled! And there is no need to trouble oneself with times and seasons, for the mystery of the times and seasons is in the wisdom of God, in his foresight, and in his love. And that which by human reckoning may still be rather remote, by divine predestination may already be standing on the eve of its appearance, at the door. And be that too! So be it!" Dostoevsky, *Brothers Karamazov*, 66.

According to Ward, Dostoevsky's interpretation of historical Christianity, mostly expressed in his prose articles, "tended to focus on western deformations of the church idea—Roman Catholicism as compulsory communion that eclipsed personal freedom, Protestantism as anarchic freedom that undermined communion—and on Eastern Orthodoxy, at least its 'unofficial' spiritual strand, as most faithfully preserving freedom-in-communion of the original church idea."[165] We have addressed Dostoevsky's critique of Roman Catholicism in chapter 2. However, Dostoevsky does not wholly affirm the institutional or indeed the spiritual-ascetic elements of the Orthodox church either, at least he does not in his poetics. In *The Brothers Karamazov*, Dostoevsky reflects a compelling vision of the church, which according to Ward, is focused "on the tiny community of children founded by Alyosha."[166] This is the reason the elder Zosima had sent him out of the monastery and into the world. It is a vision of messianic redemption embodied in this humble character.

How will Alyosha tend to the redemption of the Russian people, and beyond Russia, all humanity? Considering the theme of the "fatherhood" in the novel, Zosima asserts in his teaching that the crucial element will be sowing the seed of the Word, thus creating redemptive memories in the children and youth of humanity and through them, reaching the "fathers." In this way, the Russian family might be restored. It is the sowing of the Word in youth so that, at the proper time, they might freely respond to the Word, "unless the seed dies . . ." According to Zosima, it is through the simple sharing of the stories of the Bible, which mediate the eucharistic embodiment of Christ. This need not be complicated: "If at first we were to gather just the children in his house, once a week, in the evening, the father would hear about it and begin to come. Oh, there's no need to build a mansion for such a purpose . . ."[167] What is needed is not modernist, sophisticated interpretation per se, but humbly and simply sharing the Word: "Were he to open this book and begin reading without clever words and without pretension, without putting himself above them, but tenderly and meekly, rejoicing that you are reading to them, and they are listening to you and understanding you; loving these words yourself."[168] Zosima is convinced the people will understand, the

---

165. Ward, *Redeeming the Enlightenment*, 216.
166. Ward, *Redeeming the Enlightenment*, 216.
167. Dostoevsky, *Brothers Karamazov*, 293.
168. Dostoevsky, *Brothers Karamazov*, 293.

"Orthodox heart" will understand everything. It will implant the Word in the heart, which will bear redemptive fruit in society.

Alyosha, therefore, plunges deeply into the lives of children and their families. We see this in his relationship to Kolya. As Kroeker and Ward assert, "Dostoevsky displays his approach to the 'social question' from the 'other end' in the educative exchange between Alyosha and the leader of the gang of boys, Kolya Krasotkin."[169] They interpret Kolya as "a double [of Ivan and the Grand Inquisitor] whose mimetic enactment (as a fatherless only child) of these models of desire becomes the occasion, in the novel, for revealing the capacity of Alyosha's contrasting 'authority,' modelled after the elder's."[170] That is, Alyosha models a different "sovereignty," the humble, active love of the divine Christ. Through his humble interaction with Kolya, Alyosha enables him to recognize the vanity and pride that consumed him. As Kolya says, "It was vanity that kept me from coming, egoistic vanity and base despotism, which I haven't been able to get rid of all my life."[171] This vanity causes him to fear what others think of him and incites in him violent revenge: "But I swear to you, I was in a hurry to show off, not out of vanity, but just, I don't know, for the joy of it . . . though it's an extremely disgraceful quality in a man to go throwing himself on everyone's neck out of joy. I know that . . . Oh, Karamazov, I'm profoundly unhappy. Sometimes I imagine God knows what, that everyone is laughing at me, the whole world, and then I . . . then I'm quite ready to destroy the whole order of things!"[172] That is, Kolya fears the social perceptions of being "ridiculous." As Alyosha observes, "Nowadays even children almost are beginning to suffer from it. It's almost madness. The devil has incarnated himself in his vanity and crept into a whole generation—precisely the devil."[173]

---

169. Kroeker and Ward, *Remembering the End*, 212.

170. Kroeker and Ward, *Remembering the End*, 212.

171. Dostoevsky, *Brothers Karamazov*, 556. In the Russian, "Не говорите мне! Вы меня растравляете. А впрочем мне поделом: я не приходил из самолюбия, из эгоистического само любия и подлого самовластия, от которого всю жизнь не могу избавиться, хотя всю жизнь ломаю себя."

172. Dostoevsky, *Brothers Karamazov*, 557. In the Russian, "Но клянусь вам, я торопился выста вить не от тщеславия, а так, не знаю отчего, от радости, ей-богу как будто от радости . . . хотя это глубоко постыдная черта, когда человек всем лезет на шею от радости. Я это знаю. Но я зато убежден теперь, что вы меня не презираете, а всё это я сам выду мал. О Карамазов, я глубоко несчастен. Я воображаю иногда бог зо знает что, что надо мной все смеются, весь мир, и я тогда, я просто готов тогда уничтожить весь порядок вещей."

173. Dostoevsky, *Brothers Karamazov*, 557. In the Russian, "Нынче даже почти

The key characteristic difference of Alyosha that disarms the "ridiculous" vanity of Kolya is that he *refuses to judge*. He refuses to stand in a position of moral superiority over others, because he genuinely believes that he is "guilty before all" and "responsible for all in all." Alyosha incarnates the mystery of Christ through a relational humility that places him at the same social standing as Kolya. That is, Alyosha's humility creates the space where Kolya can honestly address his "vanity," his self-accusations, his "passions," his "devils," without fear of the "accuser of the brethren." It means overcoming the fear of being "ridiculous" and recognizing the shame of our spiritual and social condition. As Zosima said to the father, Fyodor, everything stems from a sense of shame: "Be at ease, and feel completely at home. And above all do not be so ashamed of yourself, for that is the cause of everything."[174] While the problem of "guilt" is significant in Dostoevsky's thought, the question of honour and shame are no less important, for they determine how people perceive one another socially. Morality and ethics—and politics—are as much about personal relationships and social status. Revenge and retribution stem from taking offence socially. As Zosima says to Fyodor, "A man who lies to himself is often the first to take offense . . . And surely, he knows that no one has offended him, and that he himself has invented the offense and told lies just for the beauty of it . . ."[175] The spirit of the lie revels in offence and even finds beauty in retribution and revenge. Alyosha acknowledges even his own "ridiculous" shame before Kolya: "Oh, how I love you and value you right now, precisely because you, too, are ashamed of something with me! Because you're just like me! . . . You're a prophet. Oh, we will become close, Karamazov. You know, what delights me most of all is that you treat me absolutely as an equal. And we're not equal, no, not equal, you are higher!"[176] Alyosha is "higher" precisely because he does not act or

---

дети начали уж этим страдать. Это почти сумасшествие. В это самолюбие воплотился черт и залез во всё поколение, именно черт,—прибавил Алеша, вовсе не усмехнувшись, как подумал было глядевший в упор на него Коля."

174. Dostoevsky, *Brothers Karamazov*, 43.

175. Dostoevsky, *Brothers Karamazov*, 44.

176. Dostoevsky, *Brothers Karamazov*, 558. In the Russian, "О, как я вас люблю и ценю в эту минуту, именно за то, что вой вам чего-то стыдно со мной! Потому что и вы точно я!—в решительном восторге воскликнул Коля. Щеки его пылали, глаза блестели.—Послушайте, Коля, вы, между прочим, будете и очень несчастный человек в жизни,—сказал вдруг отчего-то Алеша.—Знаю, знаю. Как вы это всё знаете наперед!—тотчас же подтвердил Коля.—Но в целом все-таки благословите жизнь.—Именно! Ура! Вы пророк! О, мы сойдемся, Карамазов.

pretend to be. He is "kenotic," making himself in the form of a person at the level of Kolya, to actively love him and, in so doing, elevate him. Alyosha does this by becoming "ridiculous" with Kolya, acknowledging his own shame.

The Way of the Friend: Nietzsche and Dostoevsky Compared

I conclude this chapter with some comparative observations between Nietzsche and Dostoesvky on the concept of friendship. We will further compare their thought with de Lubac in the Conclusion, but it is appropriate to consider our findings here in a comparative manner. One of the essential aims of the poetics of *The Brothers Karamazov,* like that of *Thus Spoke Zarathustra,* but on a completely different foundation, is to express a community of "friendship," the possibility of a society that emerges "after modernity." The higher social order that Dostoevsky envisions is an "equality" of friendship or a new "brotherhood,"[177] whereby people reveal their shame and overcome it through a humility that is not pretentious, that does not pretend to be "higher" than others. It is this authentic humility that, in my estimation, at least provides a response to the critique of Nietzsche that Christian humility is a mask of revenge and the will to dominate. In the process of authentic confession, humility includes, by implication, the acknowledgement of the resentment and the desire for power. What is necessary is simply the courage to be honest. Friendship in this context is a shared mutual confession that endeavours to assist the friend in the movement "out of the darkness and into the light of love." The way to overcome resentment is to confess and expose it in a consideration of the underlying desire that has engendered resentment, such as the will to power and the experience of despair in suffering. As we saw in *Zarathustra,* especially in the section, "On the Afterworldly," Zarathustra too confesses his desire to create an unhealthy conception of the eternal and of God. This means, by inference, that Zarathustra, prior to his experience of solitude, was under the grip of the spirit of revenge. He had discovered the power of the lie of revenge within himself first before

---

Знаете, меня всего более восхищает, что вы со мной совершенно как с ровней. А мы не ровня, нет, не ровня, вы выше!"

177. It is clear that Dostoesvky includes women as well, as is seen in the redefined relationship between Alyosha and Gruschenka.

his consideration of its pervasive influence in Western culture. However, the enlightenment of Zarathustra engendered a process of which he will invite others into, "out of my ashes and fire this ghost came to me, and, verily it did not come to from beyond. What happened, my brothers? I overcame myself, the sufferer; I carried my own ashes to the mountains; I invented a brighter flame for myself."[178] That is, the friend is an exemplar, a model, and an embodied reflection, an "image," which then moves others in a process of emulation and imitation. In other words, the embodiment of the "image" in the friend, which represents a particular desire for the transcendence, is a spur and a catalyst, which endeavours to assist the friend into a process of becoming. However, for Dostoesvky, this means a development of becoming that moves further and more deeply into the *kenotic*, incarnate love of God. This is possible because of the "Sinless One," the Christ, who is the structure of which the new humanity is built. It is the mystery of God which envelopes and incarnates, engendering the possibility of a becoming that moves more deeply into the higher being of God. Whereas for Nietzsche, it is the process of becoming through the act of the creation of new values. In this way, more generally, we can suggest that, as Nietzsche and Dostoesvky envision it, the possibility of a higher "unity" is possible through the mediation of a particular embodiment of character through a mutual process of relationship that we may describe as friendship.

What might this entail with respect to the concept of "authority?" "Hierarchy" or "authority," therefore, is defined less in an external "positional" manner, but it is differentiated by the spiritual maturity as expressed in a particular kind of character. This is also the case in *Zarathustra*. The higher men in Book IV are drawn to Zarathustra not because positional power, but because of the spiritual prophetic power embodied in his message and character, which dramatically embodies the way of the Übermensch. Zarathustra invites them (former kings, popes, etc.) up to the mountain in order that they might overcome themselves and perhaps even go beyond that Zarathustra, becoming fellow creators. As we see here, there is an intrinsic irony embedded in the concept of spiritual authority, at least in Nietzsche and Dostoevsky's formulation. For Dostoevsky, friendship is eternally *kenotic*, never seeking to "possess" the other in a spirit of domination. That is, even within a particular hierarchical relation, for instance, between Elder and novice, there still exists

---

178. Nietzsche, *Zarathustra*, 143.

The Mysticism of Resurrection and the Sacrament of Friendship 261

the potential for mutual reciprocity in the spirit, which means authentic friendship. Friendship is an eternal orientation toward the "other" in a spirit that authentically seeks to elevate the friend through a radical embodied commitment. However, to what "aim?" Again, for Dostoevsky, it is assisting the friend in a process of maturing, embodying the image of Christ, the revelation of the divine apocalyptic Word. There is a *kenotic* movement in Zarathustra as well. As we see in the Prologue in *Zarathustra*, Zarathustra becomes "human" again, to give his gift to those who would receive.[179] The stark difference between them lies in the hope of resurrection, which Dostoesvky affirms, and Nietzsche does not. Moreover, this, we suggest, is the difference between the prophetic function of the concept of friendship in the poetics of Nietzsche and Dostoesvky. While the friend in Nietzsche's formulation stresses the courage to create and to affirm the divine in embodied life, Dostoesvky accentuates the courage to be faithful to the humble, incarnate Word, the mystery of divine love revealed in the image of Christ. As Kroeker and Ward argue, Dostoevsky's prophetic power is a *remembered* Word, a Word incarnated in the flesh.[180]

Furthermore, the portraits of Zarathustra and Alyosha as images of friendship have political implications. As I argued in the above chapter, Dostoevsky's vision of the universal "sovereign" church in the world, through the story of Alyosha, is an alternative to the politics of the Inquisitor. In a similar way, the community of friends envisioned by Nietzsche is presented as an alternative to the politics of the church and state, embodied in the "dragon" and the "cold monster." However, there is no prescribed "statecraft" or external program suggested in their poetics. The political nature of their poetics lies in their prophetic power, the ability to address the necessity of a personal, internal revolution, prior to or perhaps better, in substitution to the claim of the necessity of external revolution and managerial compulsion. That is, their poetics do not express the criterion of political violence in order achieve a higher transcendent unity and political identity. I do not argue that these poetic visions are pacifist, per se, but as the evidence stands, they do attempt to address—and overcome—the underlying desire for political unity that justifies violence, even systemic violence, to actualize a higher transcendent aim of society, whether in the form of the national state, a

---

179. Nietzsche, *Zarathustra*, 122–23.
180. Kroeker and Ward, *Remembering the End*, 2–3.

universal communism, or in the form of some other religious institution. In contrast to political coercion, friendship implies an acknowledgement of an inherent freedom of the individual person to freely embrace or to reject the "message" offered by Zarathustra or Alyosha. This "either/or" predicament requires the direct personal, individualist response of the will to freely engage as friend in the new community, seeking to either create the new image, as in *Zarathustra*, or press in more deeply into the image of Christ, as in *The Brothers Karamazov*. The choice and possibility of such a new kind of non-coercive politic depends on the response of the reader. It is interesting that both narratives conclude with hope and anticipation, but also deeply tinged with a sense of uncertainty and ambiguity regarding the future destiny of their respective heroes. Nietzsche and Dostoesvky were both passionately compelled to express their "desire," but it remains to their readership whether their poetics will become more than simply a passing interest. We will continue our comparative reflections in the concluding chapter.

Conclusion

THIS PROJECT CULMINATES WITH a comparative consideration of the respective heroes of *The Brothers Karamazov* and *Thus Spoke Zarathustra* in more focused dialogue with the political theology of Henri de Lubac. In the preceding chapters it was necessary to outline the particular arguments of each author, suggesting points of comparison along the way. I began with de Lubac to build upon not only his own interpretation of Nietzsche and Dostoesvky, but to consider a larger theological framework by which to interpret their poetics.[1] However, to advance our thesis that the poetics of Nietzsche and Dostoevsky remain fruitful for theopolitical reflection, especially in critical dialogue with de Lubac, we must further examine the themes we have discussed in the previous chapters. In the introduction, I stated that the aim of this project was not only to consider the particular rationale for atheist humanism and its varying political embodiments in the context of Christendom, but also what Nietzsche, Dostoevsky, and de Lubac perceive as the path forward within the impending crisis of modernism, since, as de Lubac stated, "we are actors" in this drama. As we saw in chapters 1, 2, and 3, these authors are prophetically critical of the modernist conceptions of divine sovereignty, despite having at some points very different reasons for doing so. However, criticism of modernist thought, especially atheistic humanism, does not

---

1. In chapter 4, I provide a critique of de Lubac's concluding interpretation of Nietzsche's the eternal return.

entail the necessity of recovering some conception of an ideal past. When evaluating the merits of Western modern culture, we must not, argues de Lubac, retreat to a traditionalist mindset: "With others, an exacerbated romanticism develops an opposition in principle to any technical civilization and substitutes for the outdated idol of progress the 'the new idol of the curse of progress.'"[2] De Lubac is critical of those who "consider this will to transform the world, society and even humanity itself to be an even more monstrous collective revival of the crime of Prometheus."[3] As creatures formed in the *Imago Dei*, humanity is destined to imitate God in "his manner of dominating nature."[4] Scientific and technological progress are not inimical to the development of humanity created in the image of God. There is an intrinsic future-oriented thrust in de Lubac's thought, which is not simply a criticism of modernism and a withdrawal to some primitive ideal. What is at stake is the specific orientation of a spiritual trajectory, the theological "ideal" which draws the human desire for transcendence toward itself. Of course, for de Lubac, there are modern thinkers who have identified with Prometheus of whom he is critical, especially Nietzsche, who has "proudly proclaimed [himself] the spiritual heir of the rebel hero."[5] Nonetheless, the revolt against Prometheus, argues de Lubac, is not a revolt against God: "The rebellion against the gods is not, *ipso facto*, a rebellion against God. Our God is a jealous God: but his jealousy is quite different from that of the gods of fables. He does not envy his creatures their fire or any of the inventions that followed."[6] To clarify his point, de Lubac asserts that "time is given to humanity in order to perfect himself within the temporal order, and humanity is right to want to escape all kinds of cosmic or social servitudes with a view to a freer, more humane existence."[7] What is important is not the inhibition of the progress of humanity, but that it is conformable with the desire and will of the Creator. De Lubac will dare to suggest the paradox of a "Christian Prometheus." That is, the pagan Promethean desire to "dominate nature" must be redeemed and liberated with his use of the gift of "fire" in accordance with a proper relation to God. The desire of humanity to

---

2. De Lubac, *Drama of Atheist Humanism*, 411.
3. De Lubac, *Drama of Atheist Humanism*, 411.
4. De Lubac, *Drama of Atheist Humanism*, 414.
5. De Lubac, *Drama of Atheist Humanism*, 418.
6. De Lubac, *Drama of Atheist Humanism*, 419.
7. De Lubac, *Drama of Atheist Humanism*, 419.

transcend itself requires a transfiguration. The transfiguration of nature requires sacramental mediation. It is the sacramental reality that mediates the mystery of the divine, drawing humanity forward like a magnet, fulfilling its eternal destiny. We will delineate the results of the previous chapters under these themes: the desire for a higher unity, the sacrament of the eternal, and political embodiment. While they are interrelated, we will consider them each in turn.

The Desire for a Higher Unity

As I stated in the introduction, the fundamental crisis in Western Christendom and the rising development of atheistic humanism is a spiritual problem: "Of course, the pressure of the facts of all kinds, the development of technology, the necessities of the planned economy with the legitimate hopes that result from it, contribute to a part of the danger. But the profound cause is spiritual."[8] As de Lubac states in *Catholicism*, a spiritual desire for collective unity was created in the *Imago Dei*: "The unity of this human family as a whole is the subject, we have said, of the some of the deepest yearnings of our age."[9] As we see in *The Drama of Atheist Humanism* and *Catholicism*, Marxist socialism represents a modern illustration of an idolatry which yearns for universal unity. This idolatry "is not, we are well aware, the ideal cherished by those who dream of a stateless and classless society. They seek on the contrary, a future age when 'man shall be for man the supreme being.'"[10] According to de Lubac, what Marx envisioned was a "transfiguration of the here and now without the presence of a Beyond! An end of history in the midst of a time that continues to unfold!"[11] However, this radical divinization of the immanent and the human as the "end of history" is, suggests de Lubac, the "natural" reflex of the image of God which yearns for a transcendence. In the language of Nietzsche, Marxism is a "new festival" and new image, which fills the void of the death of the God and Christianity in the Western culture.

In chapters 2 and 3, I have demonstrated that Dostoevsky and Nietzsche suspect the underlying issue is also a spiritual problem, rooted

---

8. De Lubac, *Drama of Atheist Humanism*, 447.
9. De Lubac, *Catholicism*, 353.
10. De Lubac, *Drama of Atheist Humanism*, 359.
11. De Lubac, *Drama of Atheist Humanism*, 435.

in the question of the desire for a transcendent unification of humanity. However, in these chapters, I stressed that retribution and "resentment" was critical for Dostoevsky and Nietzsche. De Lubac is certainly aware of the resentment that underlies the modernist revolt against the Christian conception of the world: "A mysterious law, which one is tempted to believe inevitable, is once again verified before our eyes. Does not the search for a perceived good need to have been stimulated, not only by the observation of deficits or real needs, but also by the hidden or manifest action of some resentment?"[12] That is, for de Lubac, the modernist search for the image of the "new human," with the aim to transform nature itself, is born in resentment that desires to overcome the old values in order to create the new: "Does not the discovery of new values entail the depreciation of other, more fundamental values?"[13] While not despising, for example, technological advancement, de Lubac nonetheless states, "In one whole part of its active element, humanity no longer sees anything today but its effort toward earthly construction. The successes or the promises of technology have gone to its head. A kind of Dionysian intoxication has seized it."[14] In particular, for de Lubac, as I outlined in chapter 1, the spiritual crisis pertains to this scientific or materialist intoxication, an ontological rebellion against the Christian conception of humanity, and a noetic reduction.[15] This conception of the spiritual crisis is comparable to what we observed in the teachings of Zosima: modernism as the denial of the "higher half" of our being, which is the mysterious spiritual "other worlds" that have been sewn into the very fabric of our being. In other words, atheistic humanism has revolted against the image of God in which we are created.

Nonetheless, despite his insightful interpretations, I contend that de Lubac does not penetrate the narratives of *The Brothers Karamazov* and *Zarathustra* in *The Drama of Atheist Humanism* sufficiently. That is, going beyond de Lubac's reading, Zarathustra and Alyosha are dramatic responses to what both narratives perceive as the problem of retributive desire at work in Western culture and history. For example, in chapter 2, through the character of the father, Fyodor, we witnessed how shame plays a role in creating the deceptive illusions which deny the ontological

---

12. De Lubac, *Drama of Atheist Humanism*, 421.
13. De Lubac, *Drama of Atheist Humanism*, 421.
14. De Lubac, *Drama of Atheist Humanism*, 421.
15. De Lubac, *Drama of Atheist Humanism*, 422.

Conclusion

reality of humanity created in God's image. In Mitya, the spiritual problem is further described as a desire for beauty, a spiritual mystery of the heart whereby God and the devil engage in a battle for sovereignty. To be sure, in comparison with de Lubac, according to Dostoevsky, the modernist quest to transform the world is not itself an evil desire, but it endeavours to create it on a different ontological foundation; as Ivan states to Alyosha: "And those who do not believe in God, well, they will talk about socialism and anarchism, about transforming the whole of humankind according to a new order, but it's the same damned thing, the questions are the same, only from the other end."[16] The modernist socialist and the Christian share in common the desire to transform the world, to endeavour to work toward it transformation. As we see in the chapter "Rebellion," the Christian and socialist claim share a common "love of humanity" in solidarity with those who suffer from oppression. The desire of Ivan Karamazov, as de Lubac interprets Marx, is to root the moral foundation of a new humanity strictly on a "Euclidean" or materialist foundation. However, for Dostoevsky, the consequence of this materialism is a profound idolatry, the construction of new tower of Babel, which culminates in a radical tyranny. For instance, Ivan's retribution is a desire to revolt against the created freedom revealed in Christ, and, therefore, construct a unified society on demonic "images" of "miracle, mystery, and authority," as we see in the legend of the Grand Inquisitor. That is, Ivan constructs an alternative sacramental mediation, one that is rooted not in the spirit of Christ, but in the "spirit of non-being." The Christian desire for a higher eternal reconciliation through the mediation of Christ is an impossibility considering the suffering of the innocent, which no forgiveness can justify. Of course, in the chapter "The Devil," we do see that Ivan considers the possibility of creating a new humanity that goes beyond retribution. We see this in the "Geological Cataclysm," where the devil imagines a period when humanity, freed from God, can go beyond resentment: "Out of pride he will understand that he should not murmur against the momentariness of life, and he will love his brother then without any reward."[17] Within the novel, the fate of Ivan is left unanswered, and he falls into madness as a result of the internal conflict of his conscience; Alyosha is committed to tending to the spiritual and mental healing of his broken and tormented brother.

16. Dostoevsky, *Brothers Karamazov*, 234.
17. Dostoevsky, *Brothers Karamazov*, 649

Nietzsche, on the other hand, views Christianity and the modernist doctrines of socialist revolution as a revolt against the god of life itself, the Dionysian desire inherent in human existence to press forward in a state of "becoming." From the despair of Socrates at his death, to the abstract philosophy of Plato and ultimately to Christianity, Western culture has been possessed by a despairing and nihilistic desire for retribution against Dionysian existence. This nihilistic desire for revenge is dramatized in *Zarathustra* through the image of the great dragon, which has seduced moderns, seeking to unify humanity through false conceptions of the divine. This dragon represents the God of Christianity who has culturally ensnared moderns. The dragon thirsts for political as well as spiritual domination, as we saw in the section "The New Idol." For Nietzsche, both the Western church and the modern state are rivals for the allegiance and obedience of humanity, presuming to represent the highest transcendent aim of existence. Nietzsche's conception of the state is, therefore, comparable with the political vision of the Grand Inquisitor. As Nietzsche perceives it, the Western desire for unity justifies the sacrifice of human freedom and conscience. It uses violence and coercion to satisfy the desire for transcendence and a collective political unity. The state, whether Christian or atheistic, purports to be the highest aim of humanity and therefore, of human identity. However, for Nietzsche, the Christian and atheistic pretensions to sovereignty are idolatrous creations which falsely mediate Dionysian desire. This also means that both the agents of the church—priests and inquisitors—as well the modern state—the politicians and philosophers of the new idol—are in spiritual revolt against the intrinsic freedom of the body and its passions. The Grand Inquisitor, like the modernists in Zarathustra, are moral ascetics, who discipline desire through deception and violence. The body and its desires are, therefore, a reality that must be scorned, feared, and ultimately punished, if we are to live in societies of peace or at least with limited crime. The profound difference, of course, between Dostoevsky and de Lubac, on the one hand, and Nietzsche, on the other, pertains to our specific conception of transcendence in relation to the immanence of the body. We will further delineate this difference in the following section. However, at this point, I will state that for Nietzsche, the concept of transcendence remains firmly one that has derived from the natural itself rising into the consciousness of transcendent mystery. As bodily creators, our search for a collective identity and unity is essentially the creative labour of humanity itself, while for de Lubac and especially for Dostoevsky, bodily passional desire, the "Karamazovian force," is a created mystery that yearns for the beauty of the divine. Humanity will only "become" and be "transfigured" through the miracle of the higher mystery which descends to it through grace.

In response to the reality of retribution as it is embodied in Western culture and the varied institutions of the church and state, Zarathustra and Alyosha are poetic images that portray a form of justice and moral discernment that aims to move beyond retributive desire. In a theological sense, following what has been developed in this work, Zarathustra and Alyosha are meant to posit a new redemptive desire, engendering a healthier existence within culture. Furthermore, considering the theology of de Lubac, we can argue that, in a very real sense, it is as if the heroic figures of Zarathustra and Alyosha, as embodied within their dramatic narratives and interpreted considering the historical development of Western Christendom culture, disclose a kind of sacramental desire and intention. Or in the most minimalist sense, they symbolize or give witness to a transcendent sacramental reality that mediates the mystery of the divine in our immanent lives of existence, enabling the possibility of affirming life in the body, even in our suffering, and thus overcoming retributive desire. In this sense, Zarathustra and Alyosha are images that sacramentally mediate new desires that can engender new forms of moral discernment and thus, a new politic.

The Sacrament of the Eternal

What I discovered, however, about the theme of the embodiment of desire in these poetics works, is the importance of the question of the eternal, and how critical transcendence is for Zarathustra and Alyosha, which further substantiates the necessity of interpreting their narratives sacramentally. As I developed in chapter 1, de Lubac argues that "sacraments are the means of salvation" and "should be understood as instruments of unity."[18] That is, they are presented to us as a kind of bridge that moves people on a spiritual trajectory. It is not insignificant that Alyosha is portrayed as one who is "struggling out of the darkness into the light of love" or that Zarathustra views his teaching of the "overman" as a gift to assist humanity in a process of transformation. De Lubac, Nietzsche, and Dostoevsky are all attuned to a particular ontological notion of

18. De Lubac, *Catholicism*, 82.

"becoming." However, as de Lubac states, "'becoming,' by itself, has no meaning; it is another word for absurdity."[19] Therefore, "becoming" needs a "magnet to attract it."[20] It is in this context that de Lubac makes the case, contrary to Nietzsche, for the necessity of an "Absolute," which presupposes the movement of becoming. Therefore, it is necessary to consider their conceptions of the eternal and how the eternal is mediated. As stated above, "desire" is the power that propels us toward the higher. Yet how does this occur? According to de Lubac, signs and images are necessary to incarnate the transcendent, ushering desire forward in the process of becoming. As de Lubac argues, sacraments mediate the mystery of the sacred through the embodiment of the sign. Moreover, signs are not abstract entities, but are enfleshed, wrapped in dramatic enactments. Recalling de Lubac's distinction between myth and mystery proves useful here. While the language of symbol and sign bid us to consider the significance of myth, de Lubac asserts that Nietzsche made no distinction between myth and mystery, "whereas a selective use could be made of these words to signify two opposite types of sacredness."[21] Although connected, for de Lubac there is a wide gulf between these two words, myth rising up from nature and mystery descending from the heavens.[22] As I wrote in chapter 1, myth and mystery certainly can both engender a *mystique*, but these *mystiques* are

> as opposite in character as in origin: one is the Dionysian state, with its "heady, feverish, ambiguous" irrationality; the other is the chaste and sober rapture of the Spirit. If both shatter individuality, . . . their ways of doing so are very different, for the first only succeeds in merging the human being in the life of the cosmos—or in that of a society itself wholly of this earth—while

---

19. De Lubac, *Catholicism*, 354.
20. De Lubac, *Catholicism*, 354.
21. De Lubac, *Drama of Atheist Humanism*, 91.
22. We will quote de Lubac here again: "There is the sacredness of myth, which like a vapor rising from the earth, emanates from infrahuman regions; and there is the sacredness of mystery, which is like peace descending from the heavens. The one links us with Nature and attunes us to her rhythm but also enslaves us to her fatal powers; the other is the gift of the spirit that makes us free. One finds its embodiment in symbols that man molds as he pleases, and into which he projects his terrors and his desires; the symbols of the other are received from on high by man who, in contemplating them, discovers the secret of his nobility. In concrete terms, there is the pagan myth and the Christian mystery." De Lubac, *Drama of Atheist Humanism*, 91.

the second exalts the most personal element in each individual
in order to create a fellowship among all [people].²³

Mystery, of course, still makes use of myth, taking over "a part of it, filters it, purifies it—exorcises it, as it were. There is an authentic sacredness in the cosmos, for it is full of the 'vestiges' of divinity. There *is* a '*mystique* of the earth.'"²⁴ But, argues de Lubac, myth needs to be christianized: "When it aspires to reign alone, it is no longer even terrestrial; the mark of the Spirit of Evil is upon it."²⁵ This difference, suggests de Lubac, between myth and mystery, despite the overlapping thematic tendency, is the difference between the poetics of Nietzsche and Dostoevsky. Although they both write in the language of "myth," and even more so in the symbolic language of the apocalyptic, Nietzsche's apocalyptic is thoroughly envisioned as nature itself rising to create an immanent/transcendence, whereas Dostoevsky's poetics reflect the mediation of the transcendence as the divine descending upon and enveloping the immanent. As a result, Zarathustra and Alyosha represent drastically differing conceptions of the eternal. Zarathustra is a mythic figure who manifests a conception of the eternal that has its origins in the "earth," but rises up mystically in an eternally evolving transcendence. The dramatic narrative of Zarathustra, as much as his teachings regarding the Übermensch and the thought of the eternal return, is precisely the "sign" that will mediate the new desire for becoming the divine. This is achieved through the creative agency of Zarathustra who, using the raw materials, as it were, of our natural, pure, bodily desires, strives to become the eternal innocence of the "child." To be divine, to apprehend the transcendent, means essentially to be morally creative. Zarathustra is the dramatic embodiment of learning to affirm life as an eternal cycle of return, a mystery that defies human rationality as well as the Christian conception of the eternal. For Zarathustra, this means an eternity of becoming. It affirms embodied life itself as transcendent, reflected in the concept of the eternal return. That is, eternity reflects the cycles of nature itself and the endless process of the flow between life and death. This conception frees the self to affirm life as we have received it as an "accidental" gift and therefore overcome the despair that leads to resentment. This does not entail the celebration

23. De Lubac, *Drama of Atheist Humanism*, 91–92.
24. De Lubac, *Drama of Atheist Humanism*, 92.
25. De Lubac, *Drama of Atheist Humanism*, 92.

of suffering per se, but it reconsiders suffering as gift and catalyst for a further deepening into the eternal movement of becoming.

For Alyosha, on the other hand, we do not see him create or discover the eternal, but poetically with the narrative itself, we see the divine mystery of the eternal descend and envelop him. This, too, involves a process of resisting the spirit of retribution, but it is, as I read the narrative, primarily an act of grace, sacramentally mediated through suffering and death. Alyosha experiences redemption from retribution in a dramatic social environment, mediated through the early childhood memories of his interceding mother, through his relationship with the elder Zosima, in the sensitive response of Grushenka after the betrayal of Rakitin, and through the reading of the divine Word as Alyosha grieves the death of his spiritual father. In the climactic point, grace comes through a mystical vision of the eschatological Eucharist, the great apocalyptic wedding feast of Messiah. The divine is an eternal, personal, cosmic reality that enters and embodies Alyosha as he yields his body and spirit to the resurrected Christ. The bodily, emotional core of Alyosha is transfigured in this eternal moment. For Dostoevsky, this means that Christ as the divine, incarnational Spirit is not simply a moral ideal that stems from resentment, but an eternal agency that envelops and transfigures flesh, not eradicating the body and its desires, but transforming them, so that the "bodyspiritself" can be transformed through an eternal movement toward the divine, as well as toward a union with "humanity" in the context of the "whole" of creation.

Comparatively, therefore, Zarathustra represents an immanence rising up into transcendence through creative willing and desiring, while Alyosha represents the transcendence enveloping and transforming the self in the immanent through an internal posture of yielding and surrender. The critical difference, to be sure, is their respective conceptions of God. The God of Nietzsche is the God of the earth, of Dionysus, of creative chaos, which propels life-giving energies to strive forward in an eternal process of becoming, while the God of Alyosha is the personal God of self-sacrificial love, who suffered on behalf of "all and for all." This is in fundamental agreement with de Lubac's conception of the *mysterium crucis*, whereby "through Christ dying on the Cross, the humanity which he bore whole and entire in his own Person renounces itself and dies."[26] However, this mystery is deeper still: "He who bore all [humanity] in

---

26. De Lubac, *Catholicism*, 368.

himself was deserted by all. The universal [Human] died alone. This is the consummation of the *Kenosis* and the perfection of sacrifice."[27] It is this sacrifice of God in solitude which brings about the mediational possibility of the reunion of humanity: "This is the mystery of solitude and the mystery of severance, the only efficacious sign of gathering together and of unity: the sacred blade piercing indeed so deep as to separate soul from spirit, but only that universal life might enter."[28]

The divinity of Zarathustra is also sacrificial, giving of itself in the abundance of Dionysian life, and in overwhelming overflow that is morally creative, while the divinity experienced by Alyosha expresses itself in a sacrificial love, the giving of the divine self freely to the other sacramentally. Zarathustra, too, must achieve this through the solitude in the war against the dragon, his "last god." Still, with Zarathustra, the divine sacrifice of the self is essentially tragic, for there is no "afterworldly" existence or expectancy of bodily resurrection. There remains only the hope that the death of Zarathustra might occasion a "feast" for those that follow. For Dostoevsky and de Lubac, while there is certainly the acknowledgment of the tragic, there is also an underlying prophetic desire of the hope in resurrection. The humble, solitary One, was lifted up in resurrection. In agreement with what I have developed above, in Alyosha's experience, resurrection hope is a transcendent reality that envelopes and transfigures the body and the cosmos. It rejoices in the conjoining of heaven and earth, the transcendent and the immanent, the eternal and the mortal, to redeem all creation in the eternal self-giving love of Christ.

Political Embodiment

Finally, what kind of political ethic do their respective poetic visions suggest? What kind of community emerges within their respective conceptions of sacramental mediation? How is the desire for transcendent unity properly embodied? As I argued in chapter 1, de Lubac's theological aim is to recover the social implications of the Eucharist and the *corpus mysticum*. Despite having "no intention of drawing up for this century a plan of social reform inspired by Christianity," de Lubac believes that it is "in the intimate understanding of this mysterious *Catholica*, that is to be found, it seems to me, the fundamental explanation of the "social"

27. De Lubac, *Catholicism*, 368.
28. De Lubac, *Catholicism*, 368.

repercussions of Christianity in the temporal order, as well as a preventative against a "social temptation" which could cause corruption in faith itself if it were to yield to it."[29] For de Lubac, the Gospel of Christ is an apocalyptic mystery that reorients the church toward the eternal, while remaining firmly on earth and within the temporal. It thus creates a tension in society whereby the desire for transcendent unity and collective identity has been corrupted through false, idolatrous mediators. This tension can result in direct confrontation with the state because of the state's presumption of sovereignty. We saw, too, in the poetics of Dostoevsky and Nietzsche the rivalrous claims of the church and state for sovereignty. However, de Lubac's political theology endeavours to purify itself of the imperialistic interpretations of papal theory that were so important in the medieval period. The church represents a spiritual authority, not through imperialistic intent, but through its faithfulness to God through the sacraments. Social unity is achieved through free submission to God through the sacrament, which is mediated by the priesthood. As de Lubac argues in *Catholicism*, "That, then, is the first and foremost the social role of the Church; she brings us back to that communion which all her dogma teaches us and all her activity makes ready for us."[30] That is, for de Lubac, the social vision of the church is *to be the church* in its liturgy and worship through the sacraments, especially the Eucharist. This does not mean that the church cannot exert an influence in society: "The Church's proper mission is not to assume the general direction of social movements any more than intellectual ones, though she may exert on both, in many ways, an influence without compare."[31] For de Lubac, the Church is not a managerial body of temporal affairs, but does contribute, "in fact, much more than a program, and her authentic children contribute to the best of programs much more than an outward agreement or a mere technical competency. For according to a saying of St. Gregory the Great, which sums up all the traditional teaching contained in this book, *in sancta Ecclesia unusquisque et portat alterum et portatur ab altero*."[32] This is translated, "In Holy Church each bears the other and is borne by him." For de Lubac, this entails embodying the mystery of the

---

29. De Lubac, *Catholicism*, 16–17.

30. De Lubac, *Catholicism*, 362.

31. De Lubac, *Catholicism*, 362. An example of the impact that a "Social Catholicism" might entail is that of the Catholic Workers Movement, which was founded by Peter Maurin and Dorothy Day. Day, *Long Loneliness*.

32. De Lubac, *Catholicism*, 364.

Eucharist, the mystery of Christ in a personal intimacy within the community. It is the personalist enfleshment of the *mysterium crucis*, a people representing the eternal through a kenotic self-giving, sustained by the Presence of Christ through the sacraments. It is not an "implantation" of Christianity, which is translated into the temporal sphere. It is the self-offering of God through Christ, embodied in living persons as a united humanity. Incarnational living is "bearing the other" with the reciprocal "being borne by the other." That is, "charity has not to become inhuman in order to remain supernatural; like the supernatural itself it can only be understood as incarnate."[33]

In consideration of Zarathustra and Alyosha within their narrative environments, there is an interesting parallel with de Lubac's formulation of the church in the world. Both Zarathustra and Alyosha are characters that are not completely outside culture and its political institutions, but neither are they fully identified within them. Within their particular social worlds, they are viewed as oddities, even a bit eccentric, and in the case of Zarathustra, even as a threat to society. Alyosha, too, poses a challenge to those in the story, or at least a curiosity that disrupts normal social interaction. Nonetheless, it is Alyosha's very presence and character that seems to cause the greatest disturbance in the social environment. That is to say, Zarathustra and Alyosha are neither separated nor completely aligned with social worlds. Nor do they hold official positions of power, either in politics or society. While they engage with people in culture, they are not connected to particular institutions. They are not managerial technocrats. Certainly, Alyosha is connected to the monastery, but he has been commissioned by his elder to leave the monastery to re-enter the "world." However, this observation lends itself to the argument that as oddities in society, Zarathustra and Alyosha embody a social politic that also stands neither completely outside nor completely within culture. That is, as "mediators," they stand in a relational tension within society as both threat and promise.

For de Lubac, the political significance of the church and its message of the *mysterium crucis* creates a particular tension that becomes itself a new kind of crisis in culture. In the same way that the church causes a social and political disturbance, we see Zarathustra and Alyosha as social threats and disturbances. Zarathustra and Alyosha become objects of resentment, simultaneously desired and despised. I would argue that this

---

33. De Lubac, *Catholicism*, 365.

is the case because they challenge the presumptions of sovereignty with their narrative worlds, just as the gospel of Christ inherently calls into question the sovereignty of earthly rule. However, just as the church, in de Lubac's view, is inherently for the "world" and prophetically embodying the new creation of God's world that envelops and transfigures the "old world," so Zarathustra and Alyosha both embody the possibility of a new creation transforming and transfiguring the world. Zarathustra and Alyosha are poetic creations that are offered as a gift to the world.

For Zarathustra, there is an emphasis on an ethic of the heroic and the noble courage to live more "faithful to the earth." However, *Zarathustra* is a book for everyone and for no one. Certainly, it reflects Nietzsche's personal struggle and desire, which he poetically embodied in this strange figure. In many respects, this reflects Nietzsche, and this book is for him alone. However, the way of Zarathustra, the way of the Übermensch, is not a politically imposed teaching. Zarathustra is a public educator, bringing his message into the public sphere of the marketplace. Moreover, he goes into the marketplace, despite his failure, because he intends to bring a "gift" to humankind. He intends to become "human" again so that people might be raised up to his level of transcendent existence as one who creates new values. However, as I showed in chapter 4, after his rejection, he seeks out new companions. He recognizes that he will not be a "shepherd" of the herd, a populist leader, a political spokesperson, a revolutionary, or even a professional pundit, but an educator who goes about his work of living his teaching, while being open and available to those who seek him. He is the kind of political agent who engenders new values in the "stillest hour," a new kind of moral educator who will influence and shape political culture through his teaching and example that is freely given and freely received. This, at least, is what we see in the narrative. The kind of morality that Zarathustra advocates is a courage that strives for radical honesty with respect to the desires of the body, especially the will to power, to achieve what we described above—immanence rising up into transcendence. The paradox is that to become divine means to affirm our bodily enfleshed existence in all its pleasure and pain. Zarathustra espouses a courage to face our despair of suffering, to live a life that affirms the life we have lived and to will it for all eternity.

However, in the movement of becoming the Übermensch, Zarathustra's conception of morality does not give licence to moral licentiousness, depravity, or the freedom of violence, but rather, the intent of Nietzche's vision is to discipline and focus bodily desire and its energies to create a higher form of valuation, values that might occasion the possibility of a "grand politic" that unites peoples in the same, courageous, and honest way of living. As I argued in chapter 4, Nietzsche espouses a politic of friendship, a conversational community that does not seek to alleviate the suffering or even the despair that suffering creates, but a community that challenges sufferers to personally affirm embodied natural existence with all its pleasure and pain.[34] It is a community of value creators and makers of new "thinkable" divine myths which provide us the ability to mediate a more authentic embodiment of Dionysian desire. Nevertheless, Zarathustra's moral teaching also consists in the courage to challenge, rebuke, and even destroy the sick conceptions, values, and ideals, that are created out of resentment and thus falsely mediate and corrupt existence and life in the body. For Zarathustra, this explicitly means the perpetual commitment to "break the tablets." That is, Zarathustra spurs his followers to the ongoing commitment of conceptual warfare against the valuations and ideals of Western Christianity in both its theological and secular embodiments, the church and the state. It means engaging in a particular politics of "contention," a creative and courageous subversion with the aim of provoking the possibility of awakening Western culture from its moral slumber and lazy intellectualism so as to live faithfully aligned with Dionysian "realism." *Zarathustra* is, I argue, Nietzsche's poetic spur to imagine a new grand politic that intends to move Western culture beyond the church and the modern state in its various forms, such as social democracy and liberal progressivism, which are the secularization of the Christian ethic of neighbour-love.

In keeping with de Lubac, and contra Nietzsche, Dostoevsky's poetics "flesh out" further the meaning of eucharistic mediation. The poetics of Dostoevsky are deeply sacramental and reimagine a new kind of politic of the sacrament. While de Lubac, as a Roman Catholic theologian, seeks to recover the social implication of sacramental mediation beyond imperialistic intention, Dostoevsky's conception of sacramental realism and the possibility of a new community emerging out of atheistic humanism, stresses the personalist and monastic relational form in which divine sovereignty is manifest. For example, Alyosha signifies a movement from "darkness into the light of love." Like Zarathustra, he is not a teacher in the traditional sense, but is one who is drawn to the monastic path, especially the institution of elders, represented in the elder Zosima.

---

34. See also my comparative analysis between Nietzsche and Dostoesvky in pp. 292–95.

As we saw in chapter 5, Alyosha embodies the "heart of the whole," as one who overcomes the retributive desire of Ivan and incarnates the *kenotic*, humble self-giving love. His vocation, however, is attending relationally to the suffering of his brothers, as well as intervening among youth, entering their families, despite not always being received in the most pleasant manner. Alyosha does not devise a political theory as does Ivan, but he seeks to faithfully preserve what he has received from the elder Zosima, expressed in a relentless commitment to an active love in the immediate, personalist sphere of his social environment. Alyosha courageously, like Zosima, addresses the shame of our desires and the conflicted rivalry of the desires of our heart as imagined between "Madonna" and "Sodom." Alyosha embodies the ethic of active love, which humbly refuses the temptation to moral superiority, while remaining courageous in confronting the deceptions and lies that shame has created through retributive desire. In this way, the church as the "higher ideal" is actualized, not through extrinsic institutional mediation, but through social relational embodiment. Alyosha incarnates the social vision expressed by St. Gregory the Great, bearing the other and being borne by him. This does not eliminate the need for institution, but delimits it as a loveless abstraction, when not oriented toward the active practice of unifying persons in the authentic image of Christ. That is, the character of Alyosha reminds the church of what the sacrament is for and the kind of character the sacrament must engender for the sake of the world. However, it is the mystical experience of the resurrection, mediated through the Word, that seals the movement of Alyosha toward the "light of love," enabling him to assume the responsibility of being guilty for "all and everyone." De Lubac describes this process as "a turning around of the whole being, a mysterious passage through death, a revival and a recasting that are nothing other than the evangelical *metanoia*. No external 'revolution' will ever dispense with this inner revolution."[35] For de Lubac as for Dostoevsky, this phenomenon is none other than the embodiment of this statement of Jesus: "Whoever would save his life will lose it" (Mark 8:35). Interestingly, de Lubac's comments on the necessity of an "inner revolution" seem to be influenced by Dostoevsky: "If no one is to escape humanity for a solitary destiny, humanity as a whole must die to itself in each of its members in order to live, transfigured, in God. Such is the first and final word for Christian preaching. Such is the law imposed on humanity in

---

35. De Lubac, *Drama of Atheist Humanism*, 465.

each person—for each is responsible for all, the bearer of his share of the destiny of all."[36]

Although the Incarnation and resurrection mediated through the sacrament certainly precedes the possibility of moral action in the thought of Dostoevsky, in his poetics they are portrayed as being united. We see this in the apocalyptic vision whereby the elder Zosima encourages Alyosha to give his "onion." The divine Incarnate Word bears the fruits of the eternal through humble acts of active love toward the neighbour. Contra Nietzsche, this is not an expression of retribution or revenge against life, but the transfiguration of Dionysian desire through the regenerating power of the divine Spirit of kenotic love.[37] It pertains to the restoration of human "freedom." Neighbour-love, as reflected in Alyosha, is the non-coercive, non-imperial "conquering force" freely given in the desire to yield to "the other" in a relation of reciprocity and mutual service. This is ethic is reflected in the teaching of Zosima, the radical solidarity with the other as persons created in the image of God. The poetics of *The Brothers Karamazov* are ultimately the creative image that reflects the image of Christ, the "structure" upon which the new humanity is being constructed, which engenders the possibility of a politic of friendship. This politic of friendship, founded on Christ, is the ethical thrust of Dostoevsky's theopolitical vision of the "city of God." In Dostoevsky's politics, Alyosha embodies a radical personalism, attentive to the individual dignity of persons. However, this accentuates Alyosha's "realism" of faith, the commitment to the notion that in each person the seed of the divine image is implanted, expressed through the desire for the eternal, and fulfilled through the incarnational enfleshment of the resurrected, crucified Christ, mystically dwelling within the person and uniting personhood to humanity as a "whole." This politics of the "church" is a sacramental offering of love that necessitates personal appropriation freely of each person in light of the whole of humanity.

---

36. De Lubac, *Drama of Atheist Humanism*, 465.
37. Dostoevsky, *Brothers Karamazov*, 220.

Bibliography

Aiken, David W. "Nietzsche and His Zarathustra: A Western Poet's Transformation of an Eastern Priest and Prophet." *Zeitschrift für Religions und Geistesgeschichte* 55 (2003) 335–53.
Anderson, B. Roger. *Dostoevsky: Myths of Duality*. Gainesville, FL: University of Florida Press, 1986.
Augustine. *The City of God*. Edited and translated by R. W. Dyson. Cambridge: Cambridge University Press, 1998.
———. *The Trinity*. Edited by Edmund Hill. New York: New City, 2012.
Ausmus, Harry J. "Nietzsche and Eschatology." *Journal of Religion* 58 (1978) 347–64.
Bakhtin, Mikhail. *Problems in Dostoevsky's Poetics*. Edited and translated by Caryl Emerson. Minneapolis: University of Minnesota Press, 1984.
Balthasar, Hans Urs von. *The Theology of Henri de Lubac*. San Francisco: Ignatius, 1991.
Barr, L. David. *Tales of the End: A Narrative Commentary on the Book of Revelation*. Santa Rosa, CA: Poleridge, 1998.
Bartelson, Jens. *A Genealogy of Sovereignty*. Cambridge: Cambridge University Press, 1995.
Barth, Karl. *Church Dogmatics: Doctrine of Creation III.II*. Peabody, MA: Hendrickson, 2008.
———. *Church Dogmatics: Doctrine of Creation III.III*. Peabody, MA: Hendrickson, 2008.
———. *Church Dogmatics: Doctrine of Reconciliation IV.I*. Peabody, MA: Hendrickson, 2008.
———. *Community, State, and Church*. Eugene, OR: Wipf & Stock, 2004.
———. *The Epistle to the Romans*. Translated from the 6th edition by Edwyn C. Hoskyns. Oxford: Oxford University Press, 1922.
Belknap, Robert. *The Genesis of* The Brothers Karamazov: *The Aesthetics, Ideology, and Psychology of Making a Text*. Evanston, IL: Northwestern University Press, 1990.
———. *The Structure of* The Brothers Karamazov. The Hague: Mouton, 1967.

Berdyaev, Nicholas. *Dostoevsky*. Translated by Donald Attwater. New York: World, 1957.
Benson, Bruce Ellis. *Pious Nietzsche: Decadence and Dionysian Faith*. Bloomington: Indiana University Press, 2008.
Blake, William. *The Apocalyptic Vision*. Purchase, NY: Manhattanville College, 1974.
Bloomquist, L. Gregory, and Greg Carey. *Vision and Persuasion: Rhetorical Dimensions of Apocalyptic Discourse*. St. Louis, MO: Chalice, 1999.
Braaten, Karl E. *Christ and Counter-Christ: Apocalyptic Themes in Theology and Culture*. Philadelphia: Fortress, 1971.
Braun, Hermann. "Nietzsche im theologischen Diskurs." *Theologische Rundschau* 75 (2010) 45–68.
Brazier, P. H. *Barth and Dostoevsky: A Study on the Influence of the Russian Writer Fyodor Mikhailovich Dostoevsky on the Development of the Swiss Theologian Karl Barth, 1915–1922*. Eugene, OR: Wipf & Stock, 2008.
Camus, Albert. *The Rebel: An Essay on Man in Revolt*. Translated by Anthony Bower. New York: Vintage, 1984.
Caird, George B. *Principalities and Powers: A Study in Pauline Theology*. Oxford: Clarendon, 1956.
Collins, John. *The Oxford Handbook of Apocalyptic Literature*. New York: Oxford University Press, 2014.
Costa, Dennis. *Irenic Apocalypse: Some Uses of Apocalyptic in Dante, Petrarch, and Rabelais*. Saratoga, CA: Anma Libri, 1981.
David., Joshua B., and Douglas Harink, eds. *Apocalyptic and the Future of Theology: With and Beyond J. Louis Martyn*. Eugene, OR: Cascade, 2012.
Day, Dorothy. *The Long Loneliness*. New York: HarperOne, 1980.
De Alvarez, Helen Canniff. "The Augustinian Basis of Dostoevsky's *The Brothers Karamazov*." Unpublished dissertation, 1977.
Dellamora, Richard. *Apocalyptic Overtures: Sexual Politics and the Sense of an Ending*. New Brunswick, NJ: Rutgers University Press, 1994.
De Lange, Frederik. "Aristocratic Christendom: On Bonhoeffer and Nietzsche." In *Bonhoeffer and Continental Thought: Cruciform Philosophy*, edited by Brian Gregor and Jens Zimermann, 73–83. Indiana Series in the Philosophy of Religion. Bloomington, IN: Indiana University Press, 2009.
De Lubac, Henri. *Augustinianism and Modern Theology*. London: Chapman, 1969.
———. *Catholicism: Christ and the Common Destiny of Man*. Translated by Lancelot C. Sheppard and Sister Elizabeth Englund, OCD. San Francisco: Ignatius, 1988.
———. *Corpus Mysticum: The Eucharist and the Church in the Middle Ages*. Translated by Gemma Simmonds et al. Notre Dame, IN: University of Notre Dame Press, 2006.
———. *The Drama of Atheist Humanism*. Translated by Edith M. Riley et al. San Francisco: Ignatius, 1983.
———. *The Mystery of the Supernatural*. New York: Herder & Herder, 2018.
———. *The Splendor of the Church*. Translated by Michael Mason. San Francisco: Ignatius, 1999.
———. *Theological Fragments*. Translated by Rebecca Howell Balinski. San Francisco: Ignatius, 1984.
Dostoevsky, Fyodor. *The Adolescent*. Translated by Richard Pevear and Larissa Volokhonsky. New York: Vintage, 2004.

———. *The Brothers Karamazov*. Translated by Richard Pevear and Larissa Volokhonsky. New York: Vintage, 1990.

———. *Complete Letters*. Edited and translated by David Lowe. Vol. 5. Ann Arbor, MI: Ardis, 1991.

———. *Crime and Punishment*. Translated by Richard Pevear and Larissa Volokhonsky. New York: Vintage, 1993.

———. *Demons*. Translated by Richard Pevear and Larissa Volokhonsky. New York: Alfred A. Knopf, 1994.

———. *The House of the Dead*. Translated by David McDuff. New York: Penguin, 1985.

———. *The Idiot*. Translated by Richard Pevear and Larissa Volokhonsky. New York: Vintage, 2003.

———. *The Notebooks for* A Raw Youth [The Adolescent]. Edited by Edward Wasiolek. Translated by Victor Terras. Chicago: University of Chicago Press, 1969.

———. *The Notebooks for* Crime and Punishment. Edited and translated by Edward Wasiolek. Chicago: University of Chicago Press, 1967.

———. *The Notebooks for* The Brothers Karamazov. Edited and translated by Edward Wasiolek. Chicago: University of Chicago Press, 1971.

———. *The Notebooks for* The Idiot. Edited by Edward Wasiolek. Translated by Katherine Strelsky. Chicago: University of Chicago Press, 1967.

———. *The Notebooks for* The Possessed [Demons]. Edited by Edward Wasiolek. Translated by Victor Terras. Chicago: University of Chicago Press, 1968.

———. *Notes from Underground*. Translated by Richard Pevear and Larissa Volokhonsky. New York: Vintage, 1994.

———. *Selected Letters of Fyodor Dostoevsky*. Edited by Joseph Frank and David I. Goldstein. Translated by Andrew R. MacAndrew. London: Rutgers University Press, 1987.

———. *The Unpublished Dostoevsky: Diaries and Notebooks (1860–81)*. 3 vols. Edited by C. R. Proffer. Translated by T. S. Berczynski et al. Ann Arbor, MI: Ardis, 1973.

———. *Winter Notes on Summer Impressions*. Translated by R. L. Renfield. New York: Criterion, 1955.

———. *A Writer's Diary*. Translated by Kenneth Lantz. 2 vols. Evanston, IL: Northwestern University Press, 1994.

Eggemeier, Matthew T. "Christianity or Nihilism? The Apocalyptic Discourses of Johann Baptist Metz and Friedrich Nietzsche." *Horizons* 39 (2012) 7–26.

Emmerson, Richard Kenneth. *The Apocalyptic Imagination in Medieval Literature*. Philadelphia: University of Pennsylvania Press, 1992.

Fenn, Richard K. *Dreams of Glory: The sources of Apocalyptic Terror*. Aldershot, UK: Ashgate, 2006.

Fraser, Giles. *Redeeming Nietzsche: On the Piety of Unbelief*. London: Routledge, 2002.

Freeman, Timothy. "The Shimmering Shining: The Promise of Art in Heidegger and Nietzsche." *Comparative and Continental Philosophy* (2013) 49–66.

Frick, Peter, ed. *Paul in the Grip of the Philosophers: The Apostle and Contemporary Continental Philosophy*. Minneapolis, MN: Fortress, 2013.

Geffé, Claude, and Jean P. Joshua, eds. *Nietzsche and Christianity*. New York: Seabury, 1981.

Gemes, Ken, and John Richardson. *The Oxford Handbook on Nietzsche*. Oxford: Oxford University Press, 2013.

Girard, René. *Deceit, Desire and the Novel: Self and Other Literary Structure*. Translated by Yvonne Freccero. Baltimore, MD: Johns Hopkins University Press, 1965.

———. *I See Satan Fall Like Lightning*. Translated by James G. Williams. Maryknoll, NY: Orbis, 2001.

———. *Resurrection from the Underground: Feodor Dostoevsky*. Translated by James G. Williams. East Lansing: Michigan State University Press, 2012.

Gooding-Williams, Robert. *Zarathustra's Dionysian Modernism*. Stanford, CT: Stanford University Press, 2001.

Grabbe, Lester. *Knowing the End from the Beginning: The Prophetic, the Apocalyptic and Their Relationships*. London: T. & T. Clark International, 2003.

Hackel, Sergei. "The Religious Dimension: Vision or Evasion? Zosima's Discourse in *The Brothers Karamazov*." In *Fyodor Dostoevsky*, edited by Harold Bloom, 211–35. New York: Chelsea, 1989.

Happ, Winfried. *Nietzsches "Zarathustra" als moderne Tragödie*. Frankfurt am Main: P. Lang, 1984.

Harper, Ralph. *The Seventh Solitude; Man's Isolation in Kierkegaard, Dostoevsky, and Nietzsche*. Baltimore, MD: Johns Hopkins University Press, 1965.

Hauerwas, Stanley. *The Peaceable Kingdom: A Primer in Christian Ethics*. London: SCM, 1983.

Hauerwas, Stanley, and William H. William. *Resident Aliens*. Nashville, TN: Abingdon, 2014.

Hanson, Paul. *The Dawn of the Apocalyptic*. Philadelphia: Fortress, 1975.

Hays, Richard, and Stephan Alkier. *Revelation and the Politics of Apocalyptic Interpretation*. Waco, TX: Baylor University Press, 2012.

Heffernan, Theresa. *Post-Apocalyptic Culture: Modernism, Postmodernism, and the Twentieth-Century Novel*. Toronto: University of Toronto Press, 2008.

Heidegger, Martin. *Nietzsche*. 2 vols. Translated by David Farrell Krell. New York: HarperCollins, 1991.

Henrichs, Albert. "Loss of Self, Suffering, Violence: The Modern View of Dionysus from Nietzsche to Girard." *Harvard Classics in Classical Philology* 88 (1984) 205–40.

Higgins, Kathleen Marie. *Nietzsche's Zarathustra*. Lanham, MD: Lexington, 2010.

Hobbes, Thomas. *Leviathan*. London: Penguin, 1985.

Horsley, Richard. *Revolt of the Scribes: Resistance and Apocalyptic Origins*. Minneapolis, MN: Fortress, 2010.

Hovey, Craig. *Nietzsche and Theology*. London: T. & T. Clark, 2008.

Hubben, William. *Dostoevsky, Kierkegaard, Nietzsche, and Kafka; Four Prophets of Our Destiny*. New York: Collier, 1972.

Hübner, Hans. *Nietzsche und das Neue Testament*. Tübingen: Mohr Siebeck, 2000.

Isupov, Konstantin G. "Dostoevsky's Transcendental Esthetic." *Russian Studies in Philosophy* 50 (2011–12) 68–87.

Joós, Ernest. *Poetic Truth and Transvaluation in Nietzsche's Zarathustra: A Hermeneutic Study*. New York: P. Lang, 1987.

Kahn, Paul W. *Political Theology: Four Chapters on the Concept of Sovereignty*. New York: Columbia University Press, 2012.

Kantor, Vladimir K. "Confession and Theodicy in Dostoevsky's Oeuvre." *Russian Studies in Philosophy* 50 (2011–12) 10–23.

Kaufman, Whitley R. P. *Honor and Revenge: A Theory of Punishment*. Dordricht, Netherlands: Springer, 2013.

Kaufmann, Walter Arnold. *Existentialism from Dostoevsky to Sartre*. New York: New American Library, 1975.

———. *Nietzsche: Philosopher, Psychologist, Antichrist*. New York: Vintage, 1968.
Khomyakov, Aleksei Stepanovich. *The Orthodox Doctrine on the Church, an Essay*. Middletown, DE: ULAN, 2017.
Kierkegaard, Soren. *The Concept of Anxiety: A Simple Psychological Orienting Deliberation of the Dogmatic Issue of Hereditary Sin*. Translated by Reidar Thomte and Albert B. Anderson. Princeton, NJ: Princeton University Press, 1981.
———. *The Sickness unto Death: A Christian Psychological Exposition for Upbuilding and Awakening*. Edited and translated by Howard V. Hong and Edna H. Hong. Princeton, NJ: Princeton University Press, 1980.
Koch, Klaus. *Rediscovery of the Apocalyptic: A Polemical Work on a Neglected Area of Biblical Studies and Its Damaging Effects on Theology and Philosophy*. London: SCM, 1972.
Kroeker, P. Travis. "Educative Violence or Suffering Love? Radical Orthodoxy and the Radical Reformation." *Conrad Grebel Review* 23 (2005) 19–24.
———. *Messianic Political Theology and Diaspora Ethics: Essays in Exile*. Eugene, OR: Cascade, 2017.
———. "Whither Messianic Ethics? Paul as Postmodern Political Theorist." *Journal of the Society of Christian Ethics* 25 (2005) 37–58.
Kroeker, P. Travis, and Bruce K. Ward. *Remembering the End: Dostoevsky as Prophet to Modernity*. Boulder, Colorado: Westview, 2001.
Lampert, Lawrence. *Nietzsche's Teaching: An Interpretation of* Thus Spoke Zarathustra. New Haven: Yale University Press, 1986.
Leatherbarrow, W. J., ed. *The Cambridge Companion to Dostoevskii*. Cambridge: Cambridge University Press, 2002.
———. *The Devil's Vaudeville: The Demonic in Dostoevsky's Major Fiction*. Evanston, IL: Northwestern University Press, 2005.
———. *Fyodor Dostoyevsky:* The Brothers Karamazov. New York: Cambridge University Press, 1992.
Leigh, David. *Apocalyptic Patterns in Twentieth-Century Fiction*. Notre Dame, IN: University of Notre Dame Press, 2008.
Locke, John. *Two Treatises of Government*. Edited by Peter Laslett. Cambridge: Cambridge University Press, 2013.
Loeb, S. Paul. *The Death of Nietzsche's Zarathustra*. Cambridge: Cambridge University Press, 2011.
O'Leary, Stephen D., and Glen S. McGhee. *War in Heaven/Heaven on Earth: Theories of the Apocalyptic*. Oakville, CT: Equinox, 2005.
Oliver, Kelly, and Marilyn Pearsall. *Feminist Interpretations of Friedrich Nietzsche*. University Park, PA: Pennsylvania State University Press, 1998.
Martinson, Matthias. "Cultural Materiality and Spiritual Alienation: Blond, Nietzsche and Political Theological Materialism." *Political Theology* 14 (2013) 219–34.
Mihajlov, Mihajlo. *Nietzsche in Russia*. Princeton: Princeton University Press, 1997.
Milbank, John. *The Suspended Middle: Henri de Lubac and the Renewed Split in the Modern Catholic Theology*. 2nd ed. Grand Rapids, MI: Eerdmans, 2014.
Miller, C. A. "Nietzsche's 'Discovery' of Dostoevsky." *Nietzsche-Studien* 2 (1973) 202–57.
Miller, Robin Feuer. *The Brothers Karamazov: Worlds of the Novel*. New York: Twayne, 1992.
Moran, John P. "Dostoevsky on Christian Humility and Humiliation." *Cistercian Studies Quarterly* 48 (2013) 79–105.

Mühlhaus, Karl-Hermann. "The 'End of Religion': An Error of Bonhoeffer or a Challenge to Theology in the Postmodern Situation? Reflections on Bonhoeffer's Reception of Nietzsche." *Theology and Life* 30 (2007) 65–95.
Nietzsche, Friedrich. *The Anti-Christ*. Translated by R. J. Hollingdale. New York: Penguin, 1968.
———. *Beyond Good and Evil*. Translated by Walter Kaufmann. New York: Random House, 1966.
———. *Ecce Homo*. Translated by Walter Kaufmann. New York: Random House, 1989.
———. *The Gay Science*. Translated by Walter Kaufmann. New York: Vintage, 1974.
———. *On the Genealogy of Morals*. Translated by Walter Kaufman. New York: Random House, 1989.
———. *Thus Spoke Zarathustra*. Translated by Walter Kaufmann. New York: Random House, 1978.
———. *Twilight of the Idols*. Translated by R. J. Hollingdale. New York: Penguin, 1968.
———. *Untimely Meditations*. Translated by R. J. Hollingdale. Cambridge: Cambridge University Press, 1989.
———. *The Will to Power*. Translated by Walter Kaufmann and R. J. Hollingdale. New York: Random House, 1966.
Pattinson, George, and Diana Oenning Thompson. *Dostoevsky and the Christian Tradition*. Cambridge: Cambridge University Press, 2001.
Perlina, Nina. *Varieties of Poetic Utterance: Quotation in* The Brothers Karamazov. Lanham, MD: University Press of America, 1985.
Pipin, Tina. *Apocalyptic Bodies: The Biblical End of the World in Text and Image*. New York: Routledge, 1999.
Plato. "Symposium." *Great Dialogues of Plato*. Translated by W. H. D. Rouse. New York: Signet Classics, 2008.
Poettcker, Grant M. "Redeeming Wrath and Apocalyptic Violence: Girard and von Balthasar in Response to Nietzsche's Critique of Atonement Theology." PhD thesis, McMaster University, 2013. https://macsphere.mcmaster.ca/bitstream/11375/13431/1/fulltext.pdf.
Rosenshield, Gary. *Western Law, Russian Justice: Dostoevsky, the Jury Trial, and the Law*. Madison, WI: University of Wisconsin Press, 2005.
Reinhardt, David L. *Prayer as Memory: Toward the Comparative Study of Prayer as Apocalyptic Language and Thought*. Eugene, OR: Pickwick, 2012.
Rehmann, Paul. "Nietzsche, Paul, and the Subversion of Empire." *Union Seminary Quarterly Review* 59 (2005) 147–61.
Rosen, Stanley. *The Mask of Enlightenment: Nietzsche's Zarathustra*. Cambridge: Cambridge University Press, 2004.
Ross, David. *Flesh of Being: On Nietzsche's* Thus Spoke Zarathustra. Newcastle, UK: Cambridge Scholars Press, 2006.
Russel, D. S. *Apocalyptic, Ancient and Modern*. Philadelphia: Fortress, 1978.
———. *Prophecy and the Apocalyptic Dream: Protest and Promise*. Peabody, MA: Hendrickson, 1994.
Rust, Jennifer. "Political Theologies of the *Corpus Mysticum*: Schmitt, Kantorowiz, and de Lubac." In *Political Theology and Early Modernity*, edited by Graham Hammill and Julia Reinhard Lupton, 102–23. Chicago: University of Chicago Press, 2012.
Samolsky, Russel. *Apocalyptic Futures: Marked Bodies and the Violence of the Text in Kafka, Conrad, and Coetzee*. New York: Fordham University Press, 2011.
Scanlan, James P. *Dostoevsky: The Thinker*. Ithaca, NY: Cornell University Press, 2002.

Schmitt, Carl. *Political Theology: Four Chapters on the Concept of Sovereignty*. Translated by George Schwab. Chicago: University of Chicago Press, 2005.
Shestov, Lev. *Dostoevsky, Tolstoy, Nietzsche*. Athens, OH: Ohio University Press, 1963.
Soloviev, Vladimir. *The Heart of Reality: Essays on Beauty, Love, and Ethics*. Translated by Vladimir Wozniuk. Notre Dame: University of Notre Dame Press, 2003.
———. "Three Speeches in Memory of Dostoevks." In *The Heart of Reality: Essays on Beauty, Love, and Ethics*, by Vladimir Sergeyevich Solovyov, translated by Vladimir Wozniuk, 8–11. Notre Dame: University of Notre Dame Press, 2003.
Stoute, Martin. "Friedrich Nietzsche and Fyodor Dostoyevsky on Solitude." PhD thesis, McMaster University, 2000. https://macsphere.mcmaster.ca/bitstream/11375/13720/1/fulltext.pdf.
Taylor, Charles. *A Secular Age*. Cambridge: Harvard University Press, 2007.
Thompson, Diana Oenning. The Brothers Karamazov *and the Poetics of Memory*. Cambridge: Cambridge University Press, 1991.
Troncale, Joseph Charles. *Dostoevskij's Use of Scripture in* The Brothers Karamazov. Ann Arbor, MI: University Microfilms International, 1979.
Van Coillie, Geert. "Homer on Competition: Mimetic Rivalry, Sacrificial Violence and Autoimmunity in Nietzsche." *Bijdragen* 71 (2010) 115–31.
Ward, Bruce K. *Dostoyevsky's Critique of the West: The Quest for the Earthly Paradise*. Waterloo, ON: Wilfred Laurier University Press, 1986.
———. *Redeeming the Enlightenment: Christianity and the Liberal Values*. Grand Rapids, MI: Eerdmans, 2010.
Ware, Timothy. *The Orthodox Church: An Introduction to Eastern Christianity*. London: Penguin, 2015.
Webb, Stephen. "Save It for God: Confession and the Irrelevance of the Judicial System with Special Attention to Dostoevsky's *The Brothers Karamazov*." *Dialog* 52 (2013) 138–43.
Williams, Stephen N. "Dionysus against the Crucified. Part I: Nietzsche contra Christianity." *Tyndale Bulletin* 89 (1997) 219–43.
Wood, Robert E. "Monasticism, Eternity, and the Heart: Hegel, Nietzsche, and Dostoevsky." *Philosophy and Theology* 13 (2001) 193–211.
Yoder, John Howard. *The Politics of Jesus*. Grand Rapids, MI: Eerdmans, 1994.
Zakharov, Vladimir N. "What Is Two Times Two? or When the Obvious Is Anything But in Dostoevsky's Poetics." *Russian Studies in Philosophy* 50 (2011–12) 24–33.
Zweig, Stefan. *The Struggle with the Daemon: Hölderlin, Kleist, Nietzsche*. Translated by Eden Paul and Cedar Paul. London: Pushkin, 2012.

www.ingramcontent.com/pod-product-compliance
Lightning Source LLC
Chambersburg PA
CBHW071237230426
43668CB00011B/1475